George William Thomson Omond

The Arniston Memoirs

Three centuries of a Scottish house, 1571-1838

George William Thomson Omond

The Arniston Memoirs
Three centuries of a Scottish house, 1571-1838

ISBN/EAN: 9783337233624

Printed in Europe, USA, Canada, Australia, Japan

Cover: Foto ©ninafisch / pixelio.de

More available books at **www.hansebooks.com**

THE ARNISTON MEMOIRS
1571-1838

George Dundas of Dundas.

THE ARNISTON MEMOIRS

THREE CENTURIES

OF A SCOTTISH HOUSE

1571-1838

EDITED FROM THE FAMILY PAPERS

BY

GEORGE W. T. OMOND

ADVOCATE, AUTHOR OF "THE LORD
ADVOCATES OF SCOTLAND"

EDINBURGH: DAVID DOUGLAS
MDCCCLXXXVII

Walterus fil' copmanni om̄ib; p'ntib; h̄oib; suis, 7 oīnib; amicis suis tam futur' q̄ p̄sentib;, sal'. Sciant me dedisse 7 cōcessisse, 7 hac carta mea cōfirmasse Herue filio Huctredi dundaf p̄ servitio dn̄i m̄ichis illū 7 h̄edes suos, tenendū de me 7 h̄edib; meis in feudo 7 h̄editate, in ad'ī i ꝑagnisī in molendīnis, in p'tis in pasturis, cū oīnib; rect' divisis 7 ꝑtinentijs suis, Concedo v'ꝺq; ei uolo 7 p̄cipio, ut iste p̄dcus heluas istā t'ram habeat 7 teneat tam q'ete, 7 tā libe, 7 tā honorific̄, ut nullus miles de barone tenet l'bius, q'etius, 7 honorific̄ius, in tota t'ra regis Scocie. h'is testib;, Joh̄e filio orm̄, Walduo filio balderu. Rob'o s̄co michaele, Ind'a ꝺ habestanena, Wilto ꝺ copland, Wilto ꝺ hellebec, Adamo capn̄. Gerardo m̄atre, Joh̄e de ggm.

PREFACE.

MANY years ago, in the course of some building operations, the Charter-Room at Arniston was dismantled. Its contents, consisting of charters, rent-rolls, leases, accounts, and valuable family papers, were placed on the floor of an attic where, for a long time, they lay in confusion, uncared for, and in constant danger of destruction. About twenty years ago Dr. William Fraser, who was then beginning those researches which have thrown so much fresh light on the family history of Scotland, was requested by Mr. Dundas to give his help in examining the Arniston papers. Dr. Fraser arranged the charters, making a copious inventory of them, in which everything of local or family interest was described. He also deciphered the old estate, family, and colliery accounts down to the middle of the seventeenth century. The results of Dr. Fraser's labours suggested the idea of a family history to Mr. Dundas, who accordingly proceeded to arrange the letters and estate accounts, and compile a narrative from them to be left in the Charter-Room at Arniston in manuscript for the private use of the family.

There had been no intention of publication; but friends who had an opportunity of examining the materials thus collected by Mr. Dundas were of opinion that they were worthy of preservation in a more permanent form; and I was requested to undertake the task of weaving them into a continuous narrative and editing the volume of family history which is now published under the name of the *Arniston Memoirs*.

As originally planned, the work included a memoir of Henry Dundas (the celebrated Viscount Melville), who was a younger son of the first President Dundas. But it became apparent, as the work proceeded, that a complete account of his career, which, in some of its most interesting and important aspects, was that of a British Minister, could not be given without entering upon a variety of subjects inconsistent with the

Dundas Castle in the XVIIth Century

scope of the present volume. It has, therefore, been decided to omit the correspondence at Arniston between Henry Dundas and his brother and nephew. This correspondence, which extends over a large part of his public life, together with the voluminous collection of papers at Melville Castle, will form the groundwork of a separate work on the Life of Henry Dundas.

G. W. T. O.

May 1887.

Plaster Work Hall Arniston.

CONTENTS.

INTRODUCTORY CHAPTER.

	PAGE
Gospatric, the son of Maldred,	xxiii
The lands of Dundas,	xxiv
The Charter of Dundas,	xxiv
Helias, son of Huctred,	xxv
His origin unknown,	xxv
Early owners of Dundas,	xxv
Carmelite Monastery at Queensferry,	xxvi
Inchgarvie,	xxvii
George Dundas, founder of the Arniston family,	xxvii
The laird of Dundas persecuted in 1683,	xxviii
Sale of Dundas,	xxix
Different branches of the family,	xxx
The Arniston and Melville branches,	xxx
The Dundases of Beechwood,	xxxi
General Sir David Dundas,	xxxii
The Duddingston and Manor branches,	xxxiii
The Dundases of Virginia,	xxxiv
The Zetland family,	xxxiv

CHAPTER I.

THE PURCHASE OF ARNISTON.

Early history of Arniston,	1
Was part of the Temple lands in Lothian, and passed into the hands of the Hospitallers,	1
Purchased after the Reformation by George Dundas of Dundas,	2
Dame Katherine Oliphant,	2
Early description of Arniston,	3

CONTENTS.

CHAPTER II.

SIR JAMES DUNDAS, GOVERNOR OF BERWICK.

	PAGE
His birth and education,	5
His marriages,	5
Purchases of land by Sir James Dundas,	6
Arniston Burial-place at Borthwick Church,	6
Agricultural improvements,	8
The Home Farm at Arniston in 1628,	10
Servants' wages,	11
Death of Sir James Dundas,	12
His will and funeral,	12

CHAPTER III.

THE FIRST LORD ARNISTON.

Sir James Dundas, governor of Berwick, succeeded by his son James,	14
Dame Marie Home manages the estate,	14
Farming Customs,	15
Tenancy in Common,	15
Church affairs—The National Covenant,	16
The Covenant signed by Dundas of Arniston,	16
Marriage of James Dundas to Mistress Marion Boyd,	17
A case of Church Discipline,	18
Political State of Scotland in 1648,	21
Death of Dame Marie Home,	22

CHAPTER IV.

THE FIRST LORD ARNISTON—*continued*.

State of the Court of Session at the Restoration,	23
Sir James Dundas appointed a Judge,	24
The King decides that all Judges must sign a Declaration renouncing the Covenants,	25
Correspondence on the subject,	25

CONTENTS.   xi

	PAGE
Sir James Dalrymple's plan for meeting the difficulty,	26
Dundas is pressed to conform, but refuses,	29
Letter from Lauderdale,	30
Dundas resigns his Judgeship,	32
Correspondence with Sir James Dalrymple,	33
Dundas retires into private life,	38
His three marriages,	38
Marriage of his daughter to Lord Stair's second son,	39
Death of Sir James Dundas,	39
His funeral,	40

CHAPTER V.

THE SECOND LORD ARNISTON.

A blank in the records of Arniston,	41
Robert Dundas, son of Sir James Dundas, appointed a Judge,	41
Improvements at Arniston,	42
The Old House of Arniston,	42
Traquair's Bridge,	43
Esperston and Outerston,	43
The Arniston Ash,	46
Plantations,	49
Agricultural improvements,	50
The Jacobite Medal,	52
Proceedings against his eldest son, James Dundas,	53
Termination of the prosecution,	56
Death of Lord Arniston,	57

CHAPTER VI.

THE FIRST PRESIDENT DUNDAS.

Robert Dundas, second son of the second Lord Arniston, called to the bar,	58
His appearance,	58
His habits,	59
Marries Miss Watson of Muirhouse,	59

CONTENTS.

	PAGE
Appointed Solicitor-General,	59
Conduct of the Lord Advocate,	60
The Representative Peers,	61
Dundas appointed Lord Advocate,	64
Family Letters,	64
Quarrel with the Town-Council of Edinburgh,	65
Elected for Midlothian,	67
Attendance of Scottish Members in Parliament,	67
The Malt-Tax Riots,	68
Dundas dismissed from office,	69
Improvements on the estate of Arniston,	72
Landscape gardening,	76

CHAPTER VII.

THE FIRST PRESIDENT DUNDAS—*continued*.

Trial of Carnegie of Finhaven,	78
The opposition to Walpole,	78
The Independent Whigs,	79
Letters from Dundas to his son,	80
The Representative Peers Election,	82
Meetings of Opposition Peers,	83
Family troubles—Small-pox in 1733,	85
Death of Mrs. Dundas,	86
Dundas marries Miss Gordon of Invergordon,	87
Death of President Dalrymple,	89
Duncan Forbes appointed President,	90
Dundas accepts an ordinary Judgeship,	91
A visit to the Highlands in 1739,	92
The Goat-Whey Cure,	93
Resignation of Walpole,	96
Marquis of Tweeddale appointed Scottish Secretary,	96
Death of Duncan Forbes,	99
Intrigues for the President's Chair,	100
Dundas is appointed,	103
Private life of President Dundas,	107
Bills of Fare in 1748,	107
Death of President Dundas,	109
His merits as a Lawyer,	109

CHAPTER VIII.

THE SECOND PRESIDENT DUNDAS.

	PAGE
Robert Dundas, son of the first President Dundas.	111
Birth and Education,	111
On the Continent,	112
Correspondence with his cousin Lord Bargany,	112
Death of Lord Bargany,	113
Marriage of Robert Dundas to Henrietta Baillie,	114
Appointed Solicitor-General,	115
Fears of a Jacobite Rebellion,	117
The Scottish Administration,	118
Sir John Cope,	119
French Officers in Scotland,	121
Bad feeling among the Scottish Officials,	121
War against France,	123
Death of Lord Wilmington,	123
The Broad Bottom Administration,	124
Landing of Prince Charles,	126
Beginning of the Rebellion,	127
Letters from Mr. Mitchell,	128
Battle of Prestonpans,	131
Family Letters during the Rebellion,	132
Progress of the Rebellion,	134
Resignation of Lord Tweeddale,	136
And of Solicitor-General Dundas,	139
Ministerial Crisis of February 1746,	142
Close of the Rebellion,	143

CHAPTER IX.

THE SECOND PRESIDENT DUNDAS—*continued*.

State of old Lord Arniston's health,	144
He threatens to resign office,	144
Dundas requested to stand for Lanarkshire,	145
But declines,	145
Correspondence on the subject,	146
Mr. Stuart of Torrance elected,	148

CONTENTS.

	PAGE
State of Politics,	150
Dundas returned for Midlothian,	150
Illness of Mrs. Dundas,	151
Her death,	152
State of the Highlands,	153
Of the forfeited estates,	154
Cluny Macpherson,	155
Hume and the Advocates' Library,	157
The Tragedy of Douglas,	159
Second Marriage of Mr. Dundas,	161
Death of Lord President Craigie,	162
Dundas appointed President,	162
Letters from Lord Hardwicke,	163
The Militia Acts,	165
Autobiography of President Dundas,	166

CHAPTER X.

THE SECOND PRESIDENT DUNDAS—*continued.*

Death of George the Second,	169
Letters from Lord Hardwicke,	169
Resignation of the Duke of Newcastle,	171
His account of the Crisis,	172
The state of parties,	174
The "Scottish Manager" Question,	177
Death of Lord Milton,	179
The Douglas Cause,	180
Henry Dundas,	181
Midlothian Politics in 1770,	182
Henry Dundas elected for Midlothian,	184
Correspondence between Henry Dundas and the President,	185
The President's children,	186
Marriage of Miss Baillie,	187
And of her sisters,	187
Private Life and Improvements at Arniston,	189
Prices of Food,	191
Servants' Wages,	191
Sport,	192
Farming Customs,	193
Death of President Dundas,	197

CONTENTS.

	PAGE
His Funeral,	198
His Character,	199
Legal History 1748 to 1787,	201
Heritable Jurisdictions Act,	201
Abolition of Wardholding,	203
Montgomery Entail Act,	203
The Scottish Bench,	204
Lord Kames,	204
Francis Garden,	204
Lord Hailes and Lord Glenlee,	204
Lord Monboddo,	205
The Douglas Cause,	206
The Duntreath Case,	210

CHAPTER XI.

LORD CHIEF BARON DUNDAS.

Power of the Arniston family,	212
The Causes which led to it,	212
State of the Franchise,	213
Henry Dundas,	214
A Journey to England in 1772,	215
Robert Dundas, son of President Dundas, called to the Bar,	215
Appointed Solicitor-General,	216
His Practice,	216
Midlothian Election in 1784,	217
Marriage of Mr. Dundas,	220
Is appointed Lord Advocate,	221
Social Life in 1787,	221
Loch Ericht. An adventure in the Highlands,	223
Midlothian Election in 1790,	225
Agitation for Burgh Reform,	226
The Edinburgh Town-Council,	228
The "Friends of the People,"	229
The King's Birthday in 1792,	230
Riot in George Square,	231
Government Information,	233
Arrest of Thomas Muir,	235

	PAGE
Character of Lord Braxfield,	236
Trial of Muir,	236
Trial of Palmer,	237
The Lord Advocate challenged by Mr. Hamilton Rowan,	238
Arrest of Mr. Rowan,	239
Question in Parliament as to the legality of the proceedings at the State Trials,	240
Convention of the Friends of the People,	241
Arrest of Delegates,	242
Trials of Skirving, Margarot, Gerald, and Watt,	244
Contest for the Deanship of the Faculty of Advocates,	245
Defeat of Henry Erskine and election of Lord Advocate Dundas,	245
Midlothian Election of 1796,	246
Election Dinners last century,	247

CHAPTER XII.

LORD CHIEF BARON DUNDAS—*continued*.

Mutiny at the Nore,	249
Letter from Admiral Duncan,	250
Is created Viscount Duncan,	252
His death,	252
Mr. Dundas appointed Chief Baron,	253
A sea voyage in 1805,	254
Account of a journey from Arniston to England,	257
The Princess of Wales and Lady Hester Stanhope,	258
The impeachment of Lord Melville,	259
His acquittal,	260
The Cannings,	264
The Castlereagh-Canning duel,	265
Death of President Blair,	267
Death of Lord Melville,	269
Retrospect of his career,	269
The office of Lord President offered to Chief Baron Dundas,	277
But refused,	280
Death of Mr. Perceval,	281
Waterloo in 1816,	283
Tour on the Continent in 1817,	284
Journey through Holland,	285

CONTENTS.

	PAGE
Visit to Waterloo,	287
Review at Douchy,	289
Winter in Italy, 1818,	291
Chief Baron Dundas resigns.	292
His death,	292
Farming from 1787 to 1819,	294
Chief Baron Dundas's improvements at Arniston,	296
The Church of Borthwick,	299
Anecdote of 'Meg Dodds,'	299

CHAPTER XIII.
ROBERT DUNDAS OF ARNISTON.

Son of the Chief Baron,	301
His early days,	301
Field sports and game-preserving at the close of last century,	302
The Midlothian Coursing Club,	304
Journey through Greece and Turkey,	307
The Convent at Argis,	309
The Radical War,	311
Midlothian politics in 1820,	313
Marriage of Robert Dundas,	314
He is appointed Advocate Depute,	314
The Letters of Malachi Malagrowther,	315
The Town-Council of Edinburgh and the Representation of the City,	326
Politics of the Councillors,	328
Illness of Lord Liverpool,	329
Formation of the Canning Administration,	329
Resignation of Lord Melville and other Ministers,	330
Death of Mr. Canning, and Formation of the Goderich Ministry,	334
Formation of the Wellington Ministry,	335
Lord Melville appointed President of the Board of Control,	335
Correspondence on the subject,	335
Feeling against Sir George Clerk on account of his having taken office under Mr. Canning,	339
The Conservative party in Midlothian resolve not to oppose him,	342

Dissensions in the Cabinet,	343
Resignation of Mr. Huskisson,	345
Sir William Rae and the office of Lord Chief Baron,	349
The General Elections of 1830 and 1831,	350
Return of Mr. R. A. Dundas for Edinburgh,	350
Election Riot,	351
Passing of the Reform Bill, and preparations for the General Election of 1832,	352
The Edinburgh Election,	355
The Midlothian Election,	356
Victory of the Government, and fall of the Scottish Tory Party,	356

CHAPTER XIV.

ROBERT DUNDAS OF ARNISTON—*continued*.

CONCLUSION OF THE MEMOIRS.

Mr. Dundas retires to Arniston,	358
Improvements on the Estate,	359
Develops the working of coal,	359
Construction of Railways,	359
Scottish Agriculture in 1819 to 1839,	360
State of the Tory Party on the passing of the Reform Bill,	361
General Election of 1835,	362
The Peel Banquet,	363
Death of William IV., and General Election of 1837,	363
Mr. Dundas's closing years. Attendance at the General Assembly,	365
His Death,	366
Mrs. Dundas—The Durhams,	366
Mr. Nisbet-Hamilton,	367
Mr. Pitt Dundas,	367
The second and third Lords Melville,	367
Conclusion of the Memoirs,	368

ARNISTON MEMOIRS

Melville, and, secondly, to Lady Lucy, daughter of the second Earl of Chichester.

The uncle from whom Sir Robert Dundas of Beechwood inherited a considerable part of his fortune was David Dundas, third son of Mr. Robert Dundas, merchant in Edinburgh (a descendant of Sir James Dundas, first Lord Arniston), and Margaret, daughter of Robert Watson of Muirhouse. He was born in Edinburgh about the year 1735, and originally intended to study medicine. But his uncle, General David Watson, induced him to enter the army, and obtained for him a lieutenancy in the Engineers. General Watson was soon after this engaged in superintending a Government survey of the Highlands, and young Dundas accompanied him as one of his assistants in this important and difficult work. Between 1759 and 1762 he served in Germany and in the West Indies. Thereafter he held various appointments on the Irish establishment, and was, in 1781, promoted to the rank of Colonel. "Shortly after the peace of 1783, Frederick, King of Prussia, having ordered a grand review of the whole forces of his kingdom, the attention of military men throughout Europe was attracted by a scene so splendid. Amongst others, Colonel Dundas, having obtained leave of absence, repaired to the plains of Potsdam, and by observation and reflection on what he there saw, he laid the foundation of that perfect knowledge of military tactics which he afterwards published under the title of *Principles of Military Movements, chiefly applicable to Infantry*."[1] In 1790 Colonel Dundas attained the rank of Major-General, and his reputation in the service was finally established when, in June 1792, his system of tactics was adopted for the British army.

He was constantly on active service during the war against France. In 1804 he was installed as a Knight of the Bath; and, on the retirement of the Duke of York in 1809, he became Commander in Chief of the British Army, being the first Scotsman, it is said, who ever attained that high position. This

---

[1] *Biographical Dictionary of Eminent Scotsmen.*

The family of Dundas of Beechwood is descended from the family of Dundas of Dundas, through the Arniston branch, of which it is an offshoot. Sir Robert Dundas of Beechwood was the son of the Rev. Robert Dundas, minister of the parish of Humbie, who was a descendant of Sir James Dundas, one of the first of the Arniston family. He was born in 1761, and educated as a Writer to the Signet, and married Matilda, daughter of Baron Cockburn, and cousin-german, through her mother, of the second Lord Melville. Being their kinsman by descent, and their cousin by marriage, he became agent and factor for the Arniston and Melville families. After a few years' practice, his connection with the Arniston family obtained for him the offices of Deputy Keeper of the Sasines, one of the principal Clerks of Session, and Deputy to the Lord Privy Seal of Scotland. In short, it was said that his Dundas clients all held sinecure offices, and that he was "Depute" for them all. Partly by success in his profession and partly by inheritance from his uncle, General Sir David Dundas, Mr. Dundas acquired a considerable fortune. He purchased from his relative and client, the second Viscount Melville, the estate of Dunira, in Perthshire, with the house which the first Lord Melville had built upon it. In 1821 he was created a baronet; and at his death, which took place in 1835, he was succeeded by his son Sir David.

Sir David Dundas was born in 1803. He was educated at the University of Edinburgh, and called to the Bar, but never practised as an Advocate. On succeeding to Dunira, at his father's death, he settled there, and occupied himself with the discharge of the public duties of a country gentleman. Upon his estate his largest work was the building of the mansion-house. The former house at Dunira, built by the first Lord Melville, though large and commodious, stood upon a badly chosen site. From plans by Burn, the great Scottish architect of the day, Sir David built the present mansion, both site and house doing credit to the architect's skill. Sir David was twice married, first, to Catherine, daughter of John White Melville of Mount

Queensferry ; and under the vaulted roof of that old building, which has outlived so many changes in church and state since the day when, more than four hundred years ago, it was dedicated to the service of our Lady of Mount Carmel, the remains of the last Laird of Dundas were laid in March 1881.

CHURCH OF WHITEFRIARS, SOUTH QUEENSFERRY.

The ramifications of a family which, apart from the legendary and more remote period of its history, can be traced with certainty from the close of the twelfth century, are necessarily too numerous to mention. But it is possible, within the limit of a few pages, to give a brief account of some of the branches which have sprung from the parent stem.

The Arniston branch, descended from George, sixteenth laird of Dundas, forms the subject of these Memoirs.

Of the Melville branch, which has been rendered memorable chiefly through the great name of Henry Dundas, the first Viscount Melville, nothing need be said at present, except that it sprang from the house of Arniston towards the close of last century.

The laird of Dundas was brought before the Council and accused of allowing persons coming from a conventicle to pass through his lands. His defence was that he had not been at home at the time, and knew nothing about it for some days after. The Council, however, refused to admit this as a defence, and left it to the Lord Advocate to prove that, in point of fact, the people had passed through the lands of Dundas.[1] In commenting on these proceedings, Wodrow observes, "We shall hear just now, that in a parallel case this very day, they sustain the same defence in the Earl of Tweeddale, for it was now 'Show me the man, and I'll show the law.'"[2]

The history of the various lairds of Dundas during last century need not be detailed; and at last the time came when it was found necessary that the ancient estate should be sold. This was when the long life of the late Mr James Dundas was drawing to a close. He was born in 1793,—a posthumous child, his father having perished in the wreck of the Winterton Indiaman,—and, on coming of age, erected, at great cost, the modern Dundas Castle, a fine example of Tudor Gothic. He farmed, hunted, drove a four-in-hand from Dundas to Edinburgh, and was popular in the county, of which he was Vice-Lieutenant for many years. But his chief characteristic was a wonderful talent for mechanics, the pursuit of which led him into heavy expenses, beyond what his fortune was able to bear; for, clever and ingenious as Mr. Dundas was, his mechanical inventions usually ended in severe pecuniary losses. Such an expenditure, continued through the course of a long life, led to hopeless embarrassment, ending in the sale of the property which had been in his family for so many generations. The inexorable necessity which led to the loss of the estate was deeply regretted by all the neighbourhood. The sale of the greater part of Dundas took place in 1875. But the family reserved a portion adjoining the lands of Hopetoun, the island of Inchgarvie, and the Carmelite monastery in

---

[1] Register of the Privy Council, 17th July 1684.
[2] Wodrow, ed. 1830, vol. iv. p. 46.

descended the men of whose lives an account will be given in the following " Memoirs."

Sir Walter Dundas, the eldest son of George Dundas by his first marriage, had the honour of Knighthood conferred upon him by James vi. at the baptism of his son Prince Henry, "probably," it has been said, "for a pair of silk stockings lent by him to the modern Solomon." A fountain still remains at Dundas Castle which Sir Walter is said to have erected out of a sum of money which he had saved, and was about to use in the purchase of the barony of Barnbougle, when he found that it had fallen into the rapacious hands of the great Earl of Haddington.

We find the next owner of Dundas plunging into the troubled politics of the reign of Charles I., and deeply engaged on the Parliamentary side during that memorable conflict. He was made a Privy Councillor for life by the Covenanters in 1641, and acted on various Committees of the Estates, including that which was appointed for the trial of Montrose in 1641. In after years he seems to have been on terms of personal friendship with Cromwell, as several of the Protector's letters are dated from Dundas Castle. He survived the Restoration, and obtained a Charter for his lands, under the Great Seal, from Charles II.

Towards the close of the seventeenth century George, laird of Dundas, suffered from the rigorous laws against non-conformity. The Privy Council had passed an Act by which every heritor, on whose estate any conventicle should be held, was to be fined fifty pounds. It seems that, in the autumn of 1683, James Renwick and "other traitors" did "meet and convene at Brownrigge, in the laird of Dundas his land, and kept a numerous field-conventicle, where the said Mr. James took it upon himself to preach, and baptize ten or twelve children." Accordingly the Privy Council, on the 8th of November, fined the laird of Dundas fifty pounds.[1] Next year the same thing took place.

---

[1] Register of the Privy Council, Decreta, 8th Nov. 1683.

free labour and assistance given in delivering their Royal Persons furth of the Castle of Edinburgh, in which they were detained contrary to their Royal pleasure, by which their lives were in danger." He was also about to be created Earl of Forth; but the murder of the King in June 1488 prevented the fulfilment of the Royal promise. Dundas had faithfully adhered to the cause of James III.; and his estates were declared forfeited on the accession of James IV. When, however, a wiser policy prevailed in the councils of the young King, they were restored, with the exception of the barony of Bothkennar, instead of which Dundas received a grant of the rocky island of Inchgarvie, lying in the Firth of Forth, opposite the lands of Dundas. This Charter is dated the 14th of May 1491. By it the King gives "to our beloved familiar, our esquire, John Dundas of that ilk, and his heirs, all and whole the Island and Rock of Inchgardy." And the said John has power to build thereon "a castle or fortalice, to such height, length, and breadth as to the said John and his heirs shall seem most expedient, with iron bars, ramparts, portcullises, crenelles, and machicolations, and with all other fortifications and monitions as can be planned and devised for the security of the said castle." Of this castle Dundas and his heirs were, at the same time, declared to be the perpetual governors. The castle was built, and still remains in the possession of the family, although the island of Inchgarvie is now desecrated by the piers of an enormous structure[1] which, though it testifies to the progress of science, has done much to destroy the interesting associations of the past.

Passing over two generations, we come to George Dundas, who was served heir to his father, James Dundas, on the 11th of March 1554. He was the sixteenth laird of Dundas, and married, first, Margaret, daughter of David Boswell, of Balmuto, and secondly, Katherine, daughter of Laurence, third Lord Oliphant. The eldest son of the second marriage was James Dundas, in order to provide for whom the lands of Arniston in Midlothian were purchased, and from whom were

---

[1] The Forth Bridge.

have been a follower of Robert the Bruce. He built a monastery at South Queensferry for the Carmelite Friars, which is still the burial-place of the family, and perished at the battle of Dupplin in 1332.

James de Dundas, son of George, seems to have had a long dispute with the Abbot of Dunfermline about his right to some landing-place, or to some islands in the Forth, which he maintained so obstinately that the Abbot proceeded against him with the highest censures of the Church. But all differences were at last arranged, and Dundas was absolved from a sentence of excommunication in 1342. "By the dreaded power of excommunication the Lord Abbot of Dunfermline kept the mightiest of his lay neighbours in awe. The Lord of Dundas, whose massive stronghold frowns in sight of the Abbey Towers did once provoke a strife to his own bitter shame and humiliation. He laid claim to a certain landing-place at the south side of Queensferry, opposite his own castle, and molested the Abbot's boatmen. Abbot Alexander smote him with excommunication. But James of Dundas was proud and powerful, and obdurately resisted for some time. At length he quailed and bowed. Abbot Alexander and his Council proceeded to the disputed landing, and sat in public state on the rocks which served as the pier. James of Dundas on his knees humbly supplicated the Abbot to remove the excommunication, which the Abbot graciously did, when Dundas found security never more to repeat his offence."

The estates were forfeited to the Crown—a common fate in the fifteenth century—in 1449, but were restored to the family in the person of Sir Archibald Dundas, who enjoyed the favour of James II. and James III., and was frequently employed as an ambassador to the Court of England.

John Dundas, of Dundas, was served heir to his father, Archibald, on the 3d of October 1480. James III., with consent of his Queen, Margaret, conferred on him a grant of the lands and barony of Bothkennar, "on account of the faithful services done by him to them, and in special for his honorifice, ut nullus miles de barone tenet liberius et quietius et honorificentius in tota terra regis Scotie. His testibus: Johanne filio Orm, Waldeuo filio Baldewin, Roberto de Sancto Michaele, Helia de Hadestandena, Willelmo de Copland, Willelmo de Hellebet, Aldano Dapifero, Gerardo milite, Johanne de Gragin."[1]

If, as there seems little reason to doubt, the granter of this charter was Waldeve (Waltheof), Earl of Dunbar, the great-grandson of Gospatric, Earl of Northumberland, the date of the deed must be between 1166 and 1182, as Waldeve succeeded his father[2] in 1166, and died in 1182. There is no evidence to prove who Helias, son of Huctred, was; but, whatever his origin may have been, he founded the family of Dundas of that Ilk, as the estate remained in the possession of his descendants until 1875.

For a long time little is known regarding the successive owners of Dundas. Of one Hugh de Dundas we read, in Douglas's *Old Baronage of Scotland*, that he was "a man of singular merit and fortitude," and that "he joined the brave Sir William Wallace in defence of the liberties of Scotland, and embraced every opportunity of exerting his courage against the enemies of his country under that brave commander." His son George, the next Baron of Dundas, as became one whose father had fought with Wallace, is said to

---

[1] "Waldevus son of Cospatric, to all his good men and all his friends, present and to come: greeting. Know ye that I have given and granted and by this my charter confirmed to Helias son of Huctred, Dundas, for half a knight's service, to be held by him and his heirs of me and of my heirs in fee and heritage, in moors, in waters, in stanks, in mills, in meadows, in pastures, with all its right marches and pertinents. I grant, therefore, and will and charge that the aforesaid Helias have and hold that land so quietly and so freely and so honourably, as no knight holds of a baron more freely and quietly and honourably in all the land of the King of Scotland. Before these witnesses: John son, of Orm, Waldev son of Baldewin, Robert of Saint Michael, Helias of Hadestanden, William of Copland, William of Hellebet, Aldan the Steward, Gerard the knight, John of Gragin." A facsimile of this charter is among the National Manuscripts of Scotland, vol. i. No. xxxiii. The original is in the possession of the family of Dundas of Dundas.

[2] Gospatric of Dunbar, Earl of Lothian, and grandson of Gospatric, Earl of Northumberland.

banished Earl a grant of Dunbar and other valuable possessions in Lothian. "Lothian and the neighbouring lands, which, like Fife, soon became as English as Lothian, became," says the historian of the Norman Conquest, "the historical Scotland." To the north lay a savage region, almost as unknown, and inhabited by a people as untamed, as in the Roman days; while to the south was the border land, the debatable country, where the King's authority, weak even in the most settled part of his dominions, was practically ignored. In Lothian, therefore, was to be found whatever there was of stability in the institutions of the Scotland of those times.

It need hardly be said that even this favoured portion of Scotland was then for the most part little better than an uncultivated waste, covered with thick forest land or trackless heath, and abounding in game of every description. The chase was the favourite pastime of the people, when their energies were not employed in war; and thus it came to pass that the names of places were often taken from the kind of game which frequented them. In West Lothian, on the southern shore of the Firth of Forth, were the lands of Dundas, or The Hill of the Fallow Deer.

These lands either formed part of the possessions bestowed by Malcolm on Gospatric, or were acquired by his immediate descendants; for, in the twelfth century, "Waldevus filius Cospatricii" conveys them to one Helias, son of Huctred, by the following charter, which is one of the oldest titles to land in Scotland:—

"Waldeuus filius cospatricij omnibus probis hominibus suis et omnibus amicis suis tam futuris quam presentibus: salutem · Sciatis me dedisse et concessisse et hac carta mea confirmasse Helie filio Huctredi, Dundas, pro seruitio dimidij militis, illum et heredes suos tenendum de me et heredibus meis in feudo et hereditate, in moris, in aquis, in stagnis, in molendinis, in pratis, in pasturis, cum omnibus rectis diuisis et pertinencijs · Concedo itaque et uolo et precipio ut iste predictus Helias istam terram habeat et teneat tam quiete et tam libere et tam

INTRODUCTORY CHAPTER.

For some years after the coming of William the Conqueror, "Gospatric, the son of Maldred" appears from time to time upon the troubled stage of English history. When the Conqueror was holding court at Westminster, at Christmas 1067, Gospatric obtained, by the payment of a large sum of money, a gift of the Earldom of Northumberland, an honour to which he was well entitled to aspire, for royal blood ran in his veins, his mother being Algitha, the granddaughter of King Ethelred. But neither the possession of a rich earldom, nor the fear of William's vengeance, appear to have deterred him from taking part in, or at least encouraging, the sanguinary revolts by means of which the men of northern England attempted, for some time after the Conquest, to throw off the yoke of the Normans; and, at length, having been, in 1072, deprived of his Earldom, he was driven into exile, and went to Scotland.

On a former occasion, when his doings had compelled him to take refuge at the court of Malcolm, he had been accompanied by Edgar Atheling and his sister Margaret, and "all the best men of Northumberland."[1] And now Edgar Atheling, with his mother Agatha, and his sisters Margaret and Christina, were, says Mr. Freeman, "once more seeking a shelter at the court of Malcolm after the final ruin of their hopes in England." Gospatric, therefore, found himself among friends and kinsfolk. Malcolm and the Saxon Margaret, now his Queen, received him graciously, and bestowed upon the

---

[1] Hinde's *History of Northumberland*, p. 173.

appointment Sir David Dundas held for two years. His death took place in February 1820, when he was succeeded in his estates by his nephew, Sir Robert Dundas of Beechwood.

The Dundases of Duddingston and of Manor are also branches of the family of Dundas of that Ilk. That John Dundas who, in 1491, obtained a grant of the Island of Inchgarvie, had two grandsons, one of whom became the head of the family, and the other of whom was the progenitor of the Dundases of Duddingston and of Manor. Of the latter family, two at least have been distinguished in the profession of the law. Sir David Dundas, son of James Dundas, Clerk to the Signet, rose to eminence at the Bar of England during the opening years of the present reign, and was appointed Solicitor-General when Lord John Russell was forming his Ministry in 1846. Two years later he resigned office on account of ill-health, and, although for a short time he held the position of Judge Advocate General, his subsequent career was uneventful. Few of those, even of a generation far younger than his own, who have taken any interest in the public men of the Victorian era, can fail to have heard of the high qualities, and estimable character, for which Sir David Dundas was admired by those who knew him. He died in the spring of 1877, when a short but graphic account of his life was written by his friend the late Sir William Stirling-Maxwell, who did not long survive him.

His younger brother, George Dundas, had died eight years before. He was called to the Scottish Bar in 1826, and enjoyed a considerable practice. In 1845 he became Sheriff of Selkirkshire, and in 1868 a judge of the Court of Session, with the title of Lord Manor, an honour which he enjoyed for only one year, as his death took place on the 7th of October 1869. Like his brother, he was a man of culture and literary tastes, gentle, honourable, and high-minded.

About the middle of last century a member of the Manor branch of the Dundases went to America, and, remaining there after the Declaration of Independence, founded a family which acquired large estates in Virginia, which are still possessed by his descendants.[1]

Sir Lawrence Dundas, founder of the Zetland family, was descended from James, tenth laird of Dundas. He was the son of Thomas Dundas, a member of the Town-Council of Edinburgh, and is said to have begun life behind the counter. He entered the army, and rose to the rank of Commissary General. In this position, which he held from 1748 to 1759, he acquired an immense fortune; and, in 1762, he was made a baronet. At his death, in 1781, he was succeeded by his only son, Thomas, the offspring of his marriage to Margaret,

---

[1] An interesting law-suit arose out of this circumstance. In 1754 John Dundas of Manor, who had five sons, entailed the estate in favour of his eldest son Ralph, whom failing, in favour of his four other sons, Gilbert, William, James, and Thomas, successively. James went to Philadelphia in 1757, and married an American lady. He remained in America after the Declaration of Independence, and died in 1788. His son John, who was born in America, married a Miss Hepburn of Virginia, and had a son James. In 1828 Ralph Peter Dundas of Manor, who had succeeded as heir of entail on the death of his father, Ralph, eldest son of John Dundas, died without issue. Gilbert and William Dundas, the second and third sons of John Dundas, had already died without issue. James Dundas, in 1829, came from America to this country, and claimed the estate of Manor as nearest heir of entail. His claim was opposed by his cousin, Colonel Thomas Dundas, grandson of Thomas, fifth son of John Dundas, on the ground that he was not a British subject, and, therefore, debarred from succeeding on the ground of alienage. Both the Court of Session and the House of Lords decided in favour of Colonel Dundas, who accordingly succeeded as heir of entail. The following table will explain the descent of the parties to this case :—

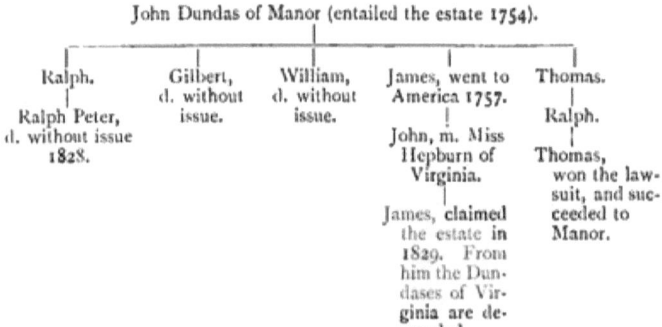

daughter of General Bruce of Kennet. Sir Lawrence represented Edinburgh in Parliament for some time, and also the Linlithgow burghs. His house in Edinburgh was the building now occupied by the Royal Bank in St. Andrew Square.

His son, Sir Thomas Dundas, was born in February 1741, and, in May 1764, married Lady Charlotte Wentworth, daughter of the third Earl Fitzwilliam. From 1768 till 1790 he was member for Stirlingshire. In 1794 he was created Baron Dundas of Aske in Yorkshire, and died on the 14th of June 1820.

His son Lawrence, who had sat in Parliament as Whig member for Richmond and the city of York till he succeeded to the peerage, was created Earl of Zetland on the coronation of Queen Victoria—an honour which he enjoyed for only a short time, his death having taken place in 1839. "The Earl of Zetland," says the *Gentleman's Magazine* for May 1839, "was one of the steadiest, most consistent, and disinterested advocates of civil and religious liberty England has known in later days. The closest intimacy subsisted between him and the late Duke of Kent; and last year Her Majesty presented the late Earl with a magnificent golden salver, as an acknowledgment of the kind services performed by him towards her father."

Thomas Dundas, second Earl of Zetland, was in his forty-fourth year when his father received the Earldom in 1838. He himself lived till May 1873, and, though a keen politician on the Liberal side, Grand Master of the Freemasons of England, and Lord Lieutenant of the North Riding of Yorkshire, perhaps during his long life he was best known as a spirited and honourable supporter of the Turf. "Only a fortnight before his death," says the *York Herald* of the 10th of May 1873, "he attended Catterick races, of which he was one of the stewards, when his carriage was the centre of a brilliant throng, the members of which little imagined that in two short weeks the genial old sportsman would be lying dead in Aske Hall." The "Aske spots" were immensely popular on every racecourse in Britain, particularly in Yorkshire; and it would be difficult to say how many descriptions have been written of the famous match run at York in 1851, when Voltigeur, who had won the Derby and the St. Leger for Lord Zetland in the previous year, was beaten at length by Lord Eglinton's Flying Dutchman, who had won these races in 1849.

It would be a mistake, however, to speak of Lord Zetland as a sporting peer and nothing else. His influence as a country gentleman, with the means of doing good in various ways, was very great. He was a sagacious man of business, and a generous landlord, and at his death was lamented, as was said at the time, by many "from the highest in the realm to the humblest menial who ever entered his service."

Such are some of the more important of the families which are descended from the ancient race of Dundas of Dundas. In the following pages the history of the Arniston branch will be described.

CHAPTER I.

THE PURCHASE OF ARNISTON.

The first purchase of land in Midlothian by the family of Dundas was made by George Dundas of Dundas, who bought the Mains of Arniston in 1571. He had been twice married, and had a family by both marriages. His eldest son by the first marriage was his heir and successor in the lands of Dundas, and it was with the object of providing an inheritance for the eldest son by the second marriage that Arniston was bought.

The early history of Arniston is quickly told. It was part of lands on the South Esk in Lothian, granted in the twelfth century to the Knights Templars by King David the First, whose munificence to the religious Orders of his time is so well known; and the estate on the South Esk was the first settlement of the Knights Templars in Scotland.

These lands were subsequently erected into the barony of Ballintrodo, which was the principal seat of the Templars until the suppression of the Order in 1309. At that time the Templars, stricken, in Scotland as in every other country of Christendom, by a sudden and awful doom, disappear from Scottish history; and their name, given to the parish of "Temple," is now the sole remaining link between that once mighty Order and the lands upon the South Esk of which for nearly two hundred years they were lords.

From the Knights Templars, Ballintrodo passed into the hands of the Hospitallers, or Knights of St. John.

At the Reformation, Sir James Sandilands, Preceptor of the Knights of St. John, obtained for himself from Queen Mary a grant of the estates belonging to his Order, by payment to the Crown of the sum of ten thousand crowns of the sun.

Shortly after obtaining this grant, Sir James Sandilands, who was likewise created Lord Torphichen, broke up the old Church barony of Ballintrodo, and sold its lands to a variety of purchasers, George Dundas of Dundas becoming possessor of Arniston. The contract of sale was between James, Lord of Torphichen, on the one part, and George Dundas of that Ilk, Dame Katherine Oliphant his spouse, and James Dundas his son, on the other part. It was executed at Dundas on the 24th of May 1571; and the price was 1000 merks paid directly to the vendor, and £3100 Scots paid to Michael Borthwick of Glengelt, who had advanced that sum upon the lands.

George Dundas, who thus acquired Arniston, was the sixteenth laird of Dundas. By his first marriage, to Margaret, daughter of David Boswell of Balmuto, he had two sons: Walter his heir, and George. By his second marriage, to Katherine, daughter of the third Lord Oliphant, he had two sons: James, who succeeded him in the estate of Arniston, and Robert, and one daughter, Elizabeth.

Previous to her marriage to George Dundas, Katherine Oliphant had been married to her cousin, Alexander Oliphant of Kelly. Tradition at Dundas Castle charges her with having damaged the family estate to obtain an inheritance for her son, while at Arniston her name has been handed down as that of a prudent dame, who had provided for her son from the savings of her pin-money.

Among other family relics there is still at Arniston a piece of tapestry, about seven feet long and three feet wide, in which the Oliphant arms, with the initials K. O., form the centre of the design, between two oval medallions, the upper one of which represents St. Paul pressing Timothy to take a glass of wine, and is encircled with the inscription, "Paul saying to Temothe tak a lytl vyn to comfort stomort;" and the lower one a gentleman bestowing a loaf upon a beggar, with the inscription, "The Lord commandes the to break ye breade, and gyf yt ye hongrie." The border of the design is enclosed within a series of Scriptural quotations in quaint letters. The piece is hand-worked tapestry of coloured wools worked into coarse linen, in rough tent stitches arranged to resemble fish-bone and other stitches.

There is also at Arniston a Venice glass, said to have been

Katherine Oliphant.
Wife of George Dundas of Dundas.

Katie Oliphant's wine-glass, to which the tradition is attached that its breakage would be followed by dire misfortune in the family.

The only information respecting the lands of Arniston as they were during the life of George Dundas is to be found in a bundle of papers in the General Register House at Edinburgh, recording the progress of a litigation between George Dundas, laird of Dundas, and his spouse, Dame Katherine Oliphant, and their son James, on the one part, and Nicol Elphinstone of the Shank, and, subsequent to his death, the tutors to his son John, on the other part, about a disputed boundary, and the extent to which the owner of Shank was entitled to graze his cattle on the muirland of Arniston. Appended to these papers is a plan of Arniston and Shank, and a verbal description of the boundaries as they then existed.

The appearance of the district at that time cannot be fully described from the plan, but a general idea may be formed of its leading features.

The manor-house of Arniston had not then been built; the Shank was a small manor-house, as was also Castleton, with its tower and chapel; but Arniston would seem, from the sketch of the buildings on the map, to have been little more than a farmhouse and offices. The river banks of both the Esk and Gore were covered with wood, as were likewise the banks of the Castleton burn. No trees are shown on the open country northwards from Arniston; but as none are shown around the yards and enclosures of the different farms, where they probably existed, the absence of isolated trees may be due to the hasty manner in which the map was drawn, describing only the boundaries which were likely to be required in the litigation with the owner of Shank. In the same way no roads or tracks are shown, with the exception of that from Edinburgh to Carrington, and thence by Castleton towards the Moorfoot Hills, although others are known to have then existed.

The litigation has an interest from its bearing upon the farming customs of the day. So long as the two properties had formed part of the same barony, no disputes had arisen about the exercise of the rights of pasturage and other servitudes—the tenants of Shank rendering their services to their Baron at hay-winning and harvest, and exercising in return the right of pasturing their cattle, jointly with those of the Arniston tenants, over the Arniston lands, except in wood, meadow, and corn land, and enjoying the other privileges of cutting fail and divot and winning peat within the Baron's lands. But the properties having passed into separate hands, disputes over the exercise of such vague and undefined rights at once arose. The Shank tenants complained that their ancient rights were curtailed, while the Arniston tenants were resolved upon tilling their land without molestation—a quarrel which, as will be seen further on, was terminated in the next generation by the owner of Arniston buying up the servitudes exercised by outside tenants over his estate.

Of the purchasers among whom the old Templar barony of Ballintrodo had been divided, George Dundas and his wife seem to have been the wealthiest and most active. They soon acquired other portions of the old barony, and reunited them to the estate which they were forming for their son. The ancient name of Ballintrodo also fell into disuse at this time, and that of Arniston took its place.

G. Dundas of y[e] ffe

Katharene Olyphant lady Dundas

CHAPTER II.

SIR JAMES DUNDAS, GOVERNOR OF BERWICK.

George Dundas of Dundas was succeeded in the estate of Arniston by his son James, who was Governor of Berwick, and received the honour of knighthood from James VI.

Sir James Dundas was born in 1570. He was educated at the University of St. Andrews, where he matriculated as a student of St. Leonard's College in 1585, and signed the Articles of Faith in 1586.

He married, first, Katherine, daughter of Douglas of Torthorwald, by whom he had two sons, James and George, who predeceased their father without lawful issue, and several daughters. In 1619 he married, secondly, Mary Home, youngest sister of Sir David Home of Wedderburn. The lands of Halkerstoun and Esperstoun, Wester Halkerstoun, called Cassiltoun, Rylawknowe, and Litill Johnsschott, three chalders meal, two chalders bere, and one chalder wheat from the Maynes of Arniston, and the teind-sheaves of the above lands, were assigned to the lady as jointure. Her own fortune was 10,000 merks. Power was reserved to the heir to win limestone within the jointure lands.

In 1617, Sir James's second daughter, Elizabeth, married Sir Patrick Murray of Langschaw, eldest son of Sir Gideon Murray of Elibank, Treasurer-Depute "to his maiestie of this realme." The young lady's jointure was fixed at 39 bolls oats, 13 bolls bere, good and sufficient stuff of the measure of the country, together with a good and sufficient ox, 12 long carriages and 36 short carriages,[1] and four dozen kain fowls, to be

---

[1] An obligation often laid upon the tenants to carry farm produce, etc., to market (or elsewhere, as the landlord might require) so many times in the year. What constituted a "long" or a "short carriage" varied according to circumstances.

laid within the place of Langschaw; also a liferent of the town and teinds of Langschaw. Sir James gave his daughter 12,000 merks as tocher. The witnesses to the marriage-contract were Sir John Murray of Phillophauch, and William Scott, younger of Harden.

Sir James Dundas continued the purchases of land commenced by his father and mother, and by the time of his death had acquired a considerable estate, stretching uninterruptedly from Whitehouse, in the parish of Newbattle, to the top of the Moorfoot Hills.

BORTHWICK CHURCH—ARNISTON BURIAL-PLACE.
(*After the Fire in* 1780.)

The papers relative to the purchase of a family burial-place in the kirk of Borthwick have been preserved at Arniston. They describe the ruinous state into which the parish church had been permitted to fall, and present a flagrant instance of the parsimonious neglect which, more than the hammer of the Reformers, or the fires of the English enemies, has stripped Scotland of so much that was valuable of its ecclesiastical architecture.

In the summer of 1606 the minister and elders of the parish of Borthwick complained to the Presbytery of Dalkeith of the state of the parish church. The choir and vestry were, they said, in a dilapidated state. The walls and roof were giving way; the wood-work was decaying; and, unless some remedy could be found, the building would soon become a ruin.

The Presbytery appointed Commissioners, who met at the church of Borthwick on the 4th of June, and held a conference with the minister and parishioners. The result of their deliberations was a refusal to rate or "stent" themselves for the repair of the church, and a resolution to offer the vestry, as a family burial-place, to any gentleman who would pay such a price as would enable them to repair the choir. Sir James Dundas of Arniston was "found meitest to quham thei sould mak offer of the same." After some hesitation he agreed to pay two hundred and fifty merks for the vestry, which thus became the family burial-place.

The sale of the vestry of Borthwick kirk to Sir James Dundas was afterwards ratified by Act of Parliament.[1] The church which had been suffered thus early after the Reformation to fall into so scandalous a state of disrepair was one of the small churches of the Norman period, with an oblong nave without aisles, a chancel, and semicircular apse.[2] The vestry and the south chapel were later additions, probably of the same date as the adjoining castle, built by Sir William Borthwick about 1430. What little is known of the sub-

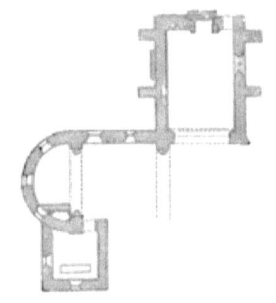

GROUND PLAN OF RUINS OF BORTHWICK CHURCH.

sequent history of the church between the sale of the vestry in 1606 and the destruction of the building by fire in 1780, can only be gathered from the appearance of the ruins as they lately existed. They showed that the arch between the chancel and the apse had been closed with masonry, the apse being left roofless, and that a gallery had been placed in the chancel, to make way for which the old Norman windows had been built up, and a square-headed door with window to match had been broken through the wall to give access to the gallery from an

---

[1] On 23d Oct. 1612; Act. Parl. Scot. vol. iv. p. 499.
[2] Characteristics of Old Church Architecture; Edinburgh, 1861.

outside stair. A fireplace for heating the church formed part of the alterations, with the certain result, which followed in 1780, of the church being burned down; thus bringing to a close the two centuries of neglect and carelessness which stripped Borthwick of its ancient parish church; and though destruction has overtaken most of our ancient Scottish churches, it is not often that so unblushing an avowal of parochial neglect has been preserved. Of late years the remaining fragments of the old church have been built into the walls of the recently erected parish church, with the object of their preservation.

Sir James Dundas was a zealous agriculturist, at a time when the poverty of the country and its backward condition raised obstacles to improvement greater than can now be conceived. Runrig and tenancy in common, vexatious servitudes, the absence of roads and facilities for carriage, the miserable condition of live stock, arising from the want of winter food, and the wretchedness of the accommodation for both man and beast, were but a few of the difficulties with which an improver in the sixteenth century had to contend.

Sir James, as the starting-point in his improvements, bought up the rights of pasturage and other servitudes exercised over his estate, thus securing his tenants against all molestation in the cultivation of their land. Upon the Arniston portion of his estate he was owner of the tithe or teind, as well as of the land, but upon some of his other purchases, where the teind belonged to the clergy, he secured his tenants against interference by obtaining for himself a lease of the teinds for the long period of "two lives and nineteen years,"—a great boon to his tenants, the laws for the collection of teind being most oppressive, no tenant being allowed to house his grain before the settlement of the teind had been made.

By the use of the coal and lime, found abundantly upon his estate, he brought into regular cultivation land hitherto cropped only at long intervals, and reclaimed muirlands which had till then lain waste. The valuation of the parish of Borthwick in 1626 shows the success attending Sir James's labours in improving his estate. The farm of Easter Halkerston, which had formerly paid 500 merks, had been brought by liming to pay 600; Wester Halkerston, which of old paid 40 merks, now paid 200 of rent, exclusive of tithe, the rise in

Sir James Dundas
Governor of Berwick

value being due to its coal and lime. Esperston was improved by the reclamation of waste land from the moor. The tithes of this farm, formerly reckoned at thirteen bolls victual, "are lyk to be moir worth because they are daylie fattit by making it inland."

On the home farm, the Mains of Arniston, the rise in rent was considerable. Before the farm was taken into the proprietor's own hands ("befoir it wes labourit in maynsing") it had paid ten score and eight bolls of victual, four score and ten bolls meal, forty bolls oats, fifty bolls bere, and twenty-eight bolls wheat, rent and tithe included.

There was no lime upon the farm; but it was brought by the proprietor from his other farms "with great labour and chairges, quhilk no fermer wes habill to underlie." After Sir James's death the Mains of Arniston was let to tenants, when the rent paid for crop 1630 was ninety-six bolls bere, twenty-six bolls wheat, and one hundred and sixty-two bolls oats; realising at the current prices of the year £2333, 5s. Scots.

These improvements, however, were not considered permanent. Lime was the sole meliorating agent; therefore "giff the coill [coal] of Cassiltoun fail, the lyming will be difficill," and the land would relapse into its former state. This and other considerations were urged by Sir James Dundas against his lands being valued for the commutation of teind at their improved rent. His protest also records the disastrous results arising from the abuse of lime, and the little faith entertained at that time in the permanence of agricultural improvements.[1]

It not unfrequently happened that small farms were feued with the right still attached of fail and divot, and of pasturing upon the barony muir and unenclosed land of the superior a number of cattle proportioned to the acreage of the feu. It is easy to conceive the extent to which these rights were "the occasioune of dyvers actionis, discordis, and trublis," betwixt the feuars and tenants of an estate, and the impossibility of improvement during their existence.

Within the lands of Arniston there were six feus or pendicles[2] possessing the right of exercising the above servitudes:

---

[1] See Reports made to H.M. Commissioners for Plantation of Kirks, 1627. Printed by the Maitland Club, 1855.

[2] Small holdings.

the Shank, Birkenside, Tailors Pendicle, the Burne, the Park of Halkerston, and Littlejohnsschott, or Castleton. Fortunately they all belonged to the same proprietor, and Sir James Dundas, by giving him eighty-one acres adjoining the Shank, his largest feu, obtained in return a renunciation of the servitudes over the estate, and the absolute possession of the other five feus. The contract of excambion is dated at Dundas, 1598, and is "betwix Sir James Dundas of Arnistoun, Knyt., with consent of Dame Katherine Douglas his spous, and of George Dundas of that Ilk his father, and Dame Katherine Oliphant his spous, on the one part, and John Elphinstone of Schank on the other."

The value of such servitudes to the tenants of small holdings is shown by the fall in the rent of the Shank from five chalders to four, on the loss of the supply of limestone from Arniston, it having no limestone nor "commoditie of moss" of its own.

Sir James Dundas farmed largely himself. He had in his own occupation the Mains and "Town" of Arniston, the farms of Newbyres Mains, and Whitehouse, and the hill farms of Howburn, Esperston Hill, and Blakehope, the latter being rented from the Earl of Lothian. The list of the stock at Arniston in 1628, given in the note, may be interesting as showing the character and value of a Midlothian laird's home farm at that time.[1]

	£ Scots.	s.	d.		£ Scots.	s.	d.
[1] 38 drawing oxen, at £24,	912	0	0	36 ewes, at Howburn, at 40s.,	72	0	0
12 horses, at £26, 13s. 4d.,	320	0	0	2 draught ewes, at 30s.,	3	0	0
7 cows, with their calves, at £16,	112	0	0	120 gimmers and dinmonts, at 48s.,	288	0	0
2 cows, without calves, at £13, 6s. 8d.,	26	13	4	46 hogs, at 30s.,	69	0	0
6 yeld cows, at £13, 6s. 8d.,	80	0	0	42 yeld sheep, at Esperston, at 50s.,	105	0	0
5 young nolt, one and two year old, at £8,	40	0	0	At Arniston—			
16 "cassin" oxen, at £13, 6s. 8d.,	213	6	8	183 threaves wheat, containing 68 bolls 3 pecks; price, with the fodder, £8 per boll,	545	10	0
87 ewes, at 40s., at Arniston,	174	0	0	3 bolls rye, with the fodder, at £6,	18	0	0
12 draught ewes, at 30s.,	18	0	0	852 threaves oats, containing 305 bolls 1			
4 tups, at 50s.,	10	0	0				
1 dinmont,	2	0	0				

About a dozen servants seem to have been employed in the home farm of Arniston. **Their** wages were calculated in victual. The largest amount paid to any one man **was sixteen bolls of oats, which, at £5** Scots **per** boll, came to **£80 Scots,** or £6, 13s. 4d. sterling, **for the year's** work. **Some received** £40 Scots, **or £3, 6s. 8d.** sterling. "James Jackson, smith and servant," **only** got £25 Scots; and the herd of Esperston was paid the **small** sum of £6, 5s. Scots.

Among **the** debts enumerated as owing by Sir James Dundas at his death **are** the wages to his domestic servants as follows:—

Mr. James Owsteane,[1] servand, for his yeiris fie, . .	100	merks.
To John Lorimer, servand, ...	100	,,
To James Nisbett, servand, ...	80	,,
To Mathow Boig, servand, ...	40	,,
To Thomas Crombie, servand, . . . £ Scots	20	
To Robert Browne, servand, ... ,,	20	
To Isobel Lowthiane, servand, ... ,,	30	
To Katharene Haig, servand, ... ,,	8	
To Katharene Hadden, **servand,** . . . ,,	8	
To Janet Drummond, **servand,** . . . ,,	5	
To George , coupar, . . . ,,	8	
To Alexander Galloway, **servand,** . . . ,,	5	
To John Hepburn, servand,[2]	100	merks.
To James Bruce, cuik, ... £ Scots	24	
To William Lowthiane, ... ,,	8	

	£ Scots.	s.	d.		£ Scots.	s.	d.
firlot; price, with the fodder, £5 per boll,	1526	5	0	69 threaves wheat, containing 20 bolls; with the fodder, £8 per boll,	160	0	0
357 threaves peas and beans, containing 40½ bolls 1 peck, with the fodder, at £6 per boll,	243	7	6	558 threaves oats, containing 171 bolls; worth, with the fodder, £5 per boll, . . .	855	0	0
499 threaves bere, containing 199 bolls 1 firlot; price per boll, with the fodder, £6, 13s. 4d., . . .	1028	6	8	3 threaves 1 stook rye, containing 1 boll 3 f. 2 pks., at £6 per boll, with the fodder, .	11	5	0
At Newbyres and White house—				100 threaves peas, containing 3 bolls 3 f., at £5 per boll, . . .	18	15	0
329 threaves beir, containing 65 bolls; with the fodder, £6, 13s. 4d. per boll, . . .	433	6	8	The pea-straw of the said 5 score threaves is estimated at . .	60	0	0

From **this list** it appears **that the** value of the stock was £7344, 15s. 10d. in Scots, or £612, **1s.** in sterling money.

[1] Tutor to the children.   [2] Steward and farm-overseer.

Sir James Dundas died in 1628. His will, executed at Arniston on the 28th of April 1627, commences with those quaint expressions of religious devotion which are often found in the testamentary writings of Scotsmen in the sixteenth or seventeenth centuries. The opening sentences are as follows:—

I, Sir James Dundas of Arnistoun, knycht, considdering with myself the many perrellis and daingeris quhairunto manes lyf is subject, and that thair is nothing more certane than death, and nothing more oncertane than the tyme and hour thairof, and thairfore I, being now of perfyt helth and judgement, have resolvit for ease of mynd, weill of my childrene, and sattling of my warldlie affairis, to sett doun my testament and latter will in manner following; revoking by thir presentis all utheris testamentis maid be me at any tyme befoir the dait of thir presentis. In the first I commit my saull to God quho gave me the same, and I belive assuredlie to be savit of his frie mercie by faith throw the pretious blude of his deir Sone Jesus Chryst, my onlie Lord and Saviour; and I ordane my bodie to be bureit in my bureall place at Borthuik kirk, thair to rest quhill the day of the generall resurrectioun, at quhat tyme I hoip assuredlie baith my saull and bodie sal be joynit agane to injoy and be partaker of that eternall glorie purchesit throw Jesus Chryst, his onlie death and passioun.[1]

In the Book of Household Accounts in the charter-room at Arniston, the expenses incurred at the funeral of Sir James Dundas are given in full detail. The accounts of the cloth and silk merchants for materials for the family mournings, and of the tailor by whom they were made up, are minutely rendered, each small charge, such as for thread, pins, buttons, etc., being made separately. The dresses both of the gentlemen and ladies, and of the men and women servants, were made by the tailor, who undertook every article of clothing, from the Laird's doublet and "breikis" to Margaret's gown and stomacher.

The apothecary's account for medicines supplied to Sir James during his illness contains some curious items, such as— Two ounces oil of scorpions, and 7 grains of Oriental bezoar, a costly drug, of which the price was £2, 6s. 8d. Scots.

---

[1] For a similar document see Tytler's Life of the Admirable Crichton, Appendix, p. 276.

The funeral, after the fashion of the day, was an elaborate affair. Messengers were sent with invitations to be present to friends in Fife, to Danglass, Traquair, Dundas, and Bancreiff.

The body was embalmed, as appears from the following items in the accounts:—

For odoriferous powders after the best manner, for the whole trunk of the body, etc., ...	£ Scots 13 6 8
For one ounce "centure candell," burnt the time of the evisceration, ...	1 4 0
Item, two jars ("piggis") to put the bowels in, . . .	0 12 0
To Dr. Arnot at time of the bowelling, ...	40 merks.
To David Pringle, chirurgeon, for doing same, . . .	20 merks.
To John Hamilton, apothecary, for his trouble, . .	30 merks.

The funeral procession was headed by trumpeters, heralds, pursuivants, and pages, carrying banners emblazoned with the family arms. The pall or dool-cloth was carried on a horse, and a horse-litter was provided for the widow and her daughters, the former wearing a veil, while the young ladies carried black fans. The bell of Borthwick kirk was tolled, and that there was a funeral service in the church is shown by the schoolmaster having led the singing.

The steward's accounts for the dinner which followed were on a similar scale; and, while the guests were feasted in memory of the deceased, the poor were not forgotten, a distribution of money having been made among them on the day of the funeral.

James Dundas of Arnistoune

CHAPTER III.

THE FIRST LORD ARNISTON.[1]

The next laird of Arniston was James, eldest son of Sir James Dundas, the Governor of Berwick, and Marie, daughter of George Home of Wedderburn.

At his father's death, in 1628, young James Dundas was only eight years of age. His guardians were Dundas of Dundas, Home of Blackaddar, and Sir Patrick Murray of Elibank; but the estate of Arniston seems to have been managed during his minority entirely by his mother.

Dame Marie was evidently a prudent housewife and a loving mother, who attended carefully to her son's interests. Some of the entries in her account-books may be mentioned, as giving an idea of the early life and surroundings of a boy in his position during the opening years of the seventeenth century. He was instructed by a tutor, who lived at Arniston and received a salary of one hundred merks a year. A pony was kept for him, and a man to look after it. In the accounts for the year 1633, there is a long list of clothes and other articles supplied to him, beginning with a saddle, £4, 10s. Scots; a pair of stirrups, 12s.; stirrup-leathers, 13s. 4d.; a bit, 6s. 8d.; a pair of girths, 10s.; and a pair of spurs, 12s. Among the clothes mention is made of a red satin doublet, lined with Spanish taffitie; while, for winter wear, he had a suit of English cloth.

In the year 1635 we find him fitted out with a red gown, with ribbons, buttons, and trimmings to match, and sent to St. Leonard's College, in the University of St. Andrews, where he is designated in the books as "Jacobus Dundas ab Arnistoune." In the following year his mother enters in her books the purchase of a Greek Grammar, Mercator's Geography (with her

---

[1] Senator of the College of Justice, with the title of Lord Arniston.

1st Lord Arniston

son's name printed on them in gold letters), and "ane case with a glass and combes to James."

In the meantime the estate was managed with prudence and thrift by Dame Marie. The crop on the Mains of Arniston had been sowed and reaped, for the year 1629, by the young laird's guardians, after which the farm was let to tenants. As was usual at that time, the farm was taken by several tenants in common. In this instance they were four in number. The rent was the third sheaf, or one-third of the produce, and the teind, both payable to the landlord in kind. Sometimes, however, instead of taking his rent in kind, the landlord sold his third sheaf and the teind to the tenants on the ground, taking the price realised as his rent. The straw of crop 1629, on the Mains of Arniston, was given by the landlord to the tenants, who tilled the land for the crop of 1630, and became bound to leave the same on their quitting the farm.

In 1631, half of the third sheaf forming the rent of the Mains of Arniston was sold to two of the tenants, on the ground; while the other half of the rent and the whole of the teind was taken in kind. The prices obtained for the produce of the crop of 1631 were as follows:—

Barley,	£5	10	0	Scots per boll.	
Wheat,	£9	0	0	,,	,,
Peas,	£4	0	0	,,	,,
Oats,	£4	0	0	,,	,,

In 1633 the crop of peas, both for third sheaf and teind, could not be collected, being "frost slane and all spilt."

It appears from the factors' books that, for many years after this, the rent continued to be the third sheaf, or one-third of the produce taken in kind. The landlord's sheaves were sometimes stacked in the tenant's yard, to be carted home at a convenient time. The teind still continued to be taken by the landlord separately from the third sheaf or rent. The factor's book for 1649 contains an account of various "third" or rent stacks, thrashed during the autumn of that year. A factor's post was, in those days, one of toilsome work. During harvest, every field had to be visited, and its crop measured for the settlement of "third" and "teind;" and after the harvest was over, and all disputes settled, there still remained the transport of the produce to the landlord's yard and barns.

The Arniston family, as strong Presbyterians, took a great interest in Church affairs; and, during her son's minority, Dame Marie frequently appeared before the Presbytery of Dalkeith, either personally or by a representative, to maintain his rights as a heritor in the parish of Temple. For instance, a visitation of the parish took place on the 22d of October 1635, "when wer present of the heretours the Lady Arnistoune for herselfe and her sonne." It was stated that "the Lady Arnistoun desyrit that sho might have a seat in the east end of the kirk befoir the seat under the loft,[1] and referred the quantitie and space therof to the minister and brethren then present, who designed the same place to her for a seat, provyding it hinder not the entrie to the back seats onder the loft, nor thair sight of the minister."[2]

But the Presbyteries were soon to be occupied with matters more serious than the settlement of disputes as to the pews of heritors in country churches. The mistaken policy of Charles I., in attempting to establish the Episcopal form of church-government in Scotland, was not long in producing its inevitable results. The whole country united in resisting him. The first copies of the National Covenant were signed in the spring of 1638; and before the close of the following year the power of the Covenanters had been consolidated.

The National Covenant is written in full at the beginning of the third volume of the records of the Presbytery of Dalkeith; and after the signatures of the ministers come those of the heritors. Lords Lothian, Dalhousie, and Ross sign first, and then follows the name of "James Dundas of Arnistoune." The date of his signature is 12th December 1639.

In July 1640, the young laird of Arniston was made an "elder" of the Church in the following circumstances. On the occasion of a Presbyterial "visitation" of the parish of Temple, the minister, the Reverend Robert Couper, stated that he earnestly desired the help of the civil magistrate "in matters of Kirk discipline." The lairds of Arniston and Temple nomi-

---

[1] Gallery.   [2] Records of the Presbytery of Dalkeith.

nated their bailies to assist the minister on their behalf. It then occurred to those present that Dundas, along with the laird of Temple and Thomas Meggit, laird of Cockpen, should be made elders, in order that they might have the right of sitting in the Kirk-Session with the minister. They were, accordingly, then and there appointed elders, and "gave their oath to be faithful." After this "the laird of Arniston" is frequently named as present at the meetings of Presbytery.

In the following year Dundas was married to Mistress Marion Boyd, daughter of Robert, Lord Boyd. The contract was signed at Edinburgh on the 12th of November 1641. On the part of the gentleman, the consenting parties were Sir David Home of Wedderburn; George Dundas of that Ilk; John Home of Blacader; James Dowglas of Stanypeth; and Dame Mary Home, Lady Arniston, his curators. On the part of the lady, Dame Christian Hamilton, Lady Boyd, her mother; John, Lord Lyndsay; Sir Patrick Hamiltoun of Prestoun; Sir John Sinclair of Stevinsone; Mr. John Sinclair, his son; and Alexander Moresone of Prestongrange, her curators. As jointure there was settled upon the bride the lands of Newbyres, Esperston, and an annualrent of 500 merks from the lands of Halkerston. On the narrative that the lands of Arniston were entailed upon heirs-male, it was provided that if there should only be daughters of the said marriage, the heir-male succeeding to the lands should pay to the said daughters the sums of money following: if but one daughter, 20,000 merks; if two, to the elder 15,000 merks, and to the younger 10,000 merks; and if there were more than two, to the eldest 12,000 merks, and to the rest 18,000 merks equally among them, on their attaining the age of fifteen years complete; and in the meantime he was bound to entertain, educate, and upbring the said daughters virtuously and honourably, according to their estates, until they should attain the said age. The bride's marriage portion was 17,000 merks.

This marriage took place while Charles I. was in Scotland, on that visit during which he made such immense concessions to the demands of the Covenanters in regard to various points in the constitution of the Scottish Government. The Parliament, which was sitting in Edinburgh in November 1641, encroached on the royal prerogative in a way which no monarch, least of all a monarch of the Stuart line, would have tolerated, had it not been evident that resistance to the popular demands was impossible. One of the most unpleasant tasks which was forced upon the King was to confer honours and offices on prominent supporters of the Covenant. The Earl of Argyll received a marquisate; Johnston of Warriston was knighted; Hope of Kerse was appointed Justice-General; and Balmerino became a Lord of Session. The newly married laird of Arniston shared in the good things which were going, as, four days after his marriage, the honour of knighthood was conferred upon him.

For some years after this Sir James Dundas appears to have lived quietly at Arniston, engaged in the management of his estate, and deeply interested in parochial business. In 1646 we find him taking a very active part in a case of church "discipline."

The Reverend Robert Couper, parish minister of Temple, was examined before the Presbytery of Dalkeith on a charge of tippling and swearing. Among other witnesses—"The Lard of Arnolstoun, being inquyret quhat he knew anent Mr. Robert Couper, his miscarriage, reported he hard of all the particulars quherof he wes accuset be the Synode, and moreover that on day going in to William Knox's to ask for Mr. Robert to speik with him, they first denying him, att lenth he fund him drinking with Master Pont and William Knox, whom, after he had called furth to speik with, he fund him so distemperet that he was forcet to leive him, for verifeing quherof he desyret to cause summond William Knox, buikseller, and Thomas Ker, his owne servant."

After several depositions by other witnesses regarding his playing at cards with the laird of Temple, and uttering "profane small oaths," Mr. Couper, "being poset[1] if he wes drinking in Simeon Wilson's house excessively, answered that cominge from the Newbyres,[2] quher he had been visiting the old Lady Arnolston, he met with the lard of Temple," who asked him to go in and "tak an drink."

As the process against Mr. Couper went on, he objected to

---

[1] Asked.

[2] The Tower of Newbyres was this time used as the jointure house of Arniston.

"Sir James Dundas sitting as one of the judges in the case—1st, in regard he wes cheiff accuser befor the Synode and Presbytery; 2d, he had never admonishet him in private of these faults; 3d, that he had alwayes bein his secreit enimie; 4th, that he had deterrit be violence his stipend from this long tyme; 5th, that he had at his owne table in Arnolston drunken to one of Mr. Robert his parochiners in thir termes, 'This to the drunken minister and elders of Temple.'"

The record of Presbytery goes on—"Mr. Robert being removet, the lard of Arnolston declaret vnto the bretherin that

NEWBYRES TOWER.

for the matter of his stepend he had offeret such satisfaction as wes thought sufficient be diverse of the bretherin, as also that he had regrated to sindrie of the bretherin Mr. Robert his miscarriage, and in particular to Mr. Patrik Sibbald quhen he wes at Newcastle, quhilk Mr. Patrik declaret to be so.

"The lard of Arnolston removet willingly desyret that he might know the mynd of the brethern whither they thought it expedient that he should sit as judge or no in Mr. Robert Couper's business. The most part of the brethern voycet this way, that they wish he would be pleaset not to sit as judge in that business. Quherwith he not being well pleaset, and desyring if he were removet the extract of the act of his removal, with the reasons of it, the brethern sent furth Mr. Oliver Colt and Mr. Robert Lichtoun[1] to deill with him, and to requeist that he would not sit as an judge in that business. Quhilk quhen he refuset, they desyret (he being callet in) that he would give his oath that in his cariage in this particular he wes frie of malice and splen, and had nothing befor his eyes bot the glory of God.

"After the quhilk oath given he sat as judge, bot upon this condition, that quhen his servants and tenents, who ar witness against Mr. Robert, shall depon he should remove himself, quhervnto he aggriet."

In the course of the depositions the laird of Temple stated that he and Mr. Robert Couper, while playing at cards, drank "four mutchkins of wine sack at the most," but that "Mr. Robert drank not immoderatly."

After a lengthy trial the charge of actual drunkenness was found not proven; but as the accused had been guilty of misdemeanours he was judged worthy of censure, which he was to receive upon his knees. But, on being called in for this purpose, he became so outrageous, and so insulted the Court, that they summarily suspended him from his ministerial functions.

In October following, Mr. Couper gave in a supplication confessing and regretting his "miscarriage," when, after due consideration, and testimony from several of the brethren, "and especially the lard of Arnolston," that he had behaved Christianly since his suspension, some difference of opinion arose as to whether they could relax him from the sentence of suspension without waiting to refer the matter to the Synod. The Presbytery, with the exception of Mr. Robert Lichtoun and Sir James Dundas of "Arnolston," voted for immediate relaxation, the two gentlemen named dissenting.

In the meantime great events had taken place. The Solemn League and Covenant, formed for the preservation of the reformed religion in the Church of Scotland, and the reformation of religion in the Churches of England and Ireland, had been adopted; and in support of this compact, in addition to

---

[1] Robert Leighton, afterwards Archbishop of Glasgow.

the National Covenant of 1638, the people of Scotland were, on the whole, united. But the "Engagement" for the relief of Charles produced immediate discord. Some Presbyterians, led by the Duke of Hamilton and the Earl of Lauderdale, supported it; but the majority, led by Argyll and Johnston of Warriston, regarded the concessions of the King as wholly inadequate, and bitterly opposed the idea of making terms with him, unless he submitted entirely on all questions of religion and church-government. Sir James Dundas was returned to Parliament as one of the members for Midlothian in 1648. But, though taking this prominent position in public life, he had apparently not signed the Solemn League and Covenant; and it was not until 1650 that he did so. In that year the Presbytery of Dalkeith questioned him on the subject, when he stated that he had certain scruples, "whereof he desired to be resolved." In the end he not only subscribed to the Solemn League and Covenant, but also declared that he regarded the Engagement as having been unlawful. This position, among the straitest sect of the Presbyterians, he afterwards, as will be seen, maintained in spite of the greatest temptations.

On the overthrow of the Royalist cause, and the triumph of Cromwell, the Government of Scotland was completely changed. The Executive in Scotland consisted of eight Commissioners, who sat in Council at Dalkeith. The Court of Session was abolished, and justice was administered by Commissioners appointed by the English Government. The Church was shorn of a great part of its power and influence. It was the boast of Clarendon that the civil government of Cromwell was more oppressive to the people of Scotland than the civil government of Charles, "whilst their adored idol, Presbytery, which had pulled off the crown from the head of the King, was trod under foot and laughed at; and their preachers, who had threatened their princes with their rude thunder of excommunication, disputed with, scoffed at, and controlled by artificers, and corrected by the strokes and blows of a corporal." Nevertheless, the English Commissioners displayed more tolerance than might have been expected; and the Presbytery of Dalkeith, with Cromwell's Council sitting in their midst, seem to have continued their ordinary routine of business—the disputed settlements, the cases of discipline, and the squabbles about the heritors' pews.

Sir James Dundas's mother, Dame Marie, survived the period of the Commonwealth, and lived to witness the Restoration. Her death took place in December 1661, when the following funeral letter, which has been preserved, and may be thought interesting as a relic of social customs in the seventeenth century, was sent out by her son :—

Sir,—It hath pleased God to take my mother out of the troubles of this lyf, to her eternal rest, and I intend the burial of her corps upon Thursday, the second of Jan. next, whereunto I shall desire the favour of yr. presence, and to that end that you wold be here at Arnestoune, the 2d day by ten of the clock in the forenoon, whereby you shall oblidge me to continue,—

Sir, Yr. affectionate friend,

Arnestoune, 27th Decr. 1661.   James Dundas.

Soon after his mother's death Sir James entered, for a short time, into that competition for office which, after the Restoration, engrossed the attention of so many public men in Scotland. The part which he took was highly honourable, and, as will be seen in the next chapter, formed a marked contrast to the conduct of too many of his fellow-countrymen.

CHAPTER IV.

THE FIRST LORD ARNISTON—*continued*.

The Commissioners who had administered justice in the Supreme Court of Scotland during the Commonwealth, ceased to act on the eve of the Restoration; and the Court of Session was soon re-established on its old footing. William, Earl of Glencairn, became Lord High Chancellor; and among his colleagues on the bench were several men, distinguished either for their legal knowledge or for the zeal with which it was expected they would promote the sinister projects of the new Government. The Lord President was Sir John Gilmour of Craigmillar, one of the ablest advocates who ever graced the bar of Scotland. Sir Archibald Primrose of Carrington, afterwards the author of the "Act Rescissory," obtained a seat on the bench. So did the famous Sir James Dalrymple of Stair, Sir Robert Murray of Craigie, the intimate friend of Lauderdale, and Sir George Mackenzie of Tarbet, afterwards Earl of Cromarty.

While the vacant judgeships were being filled up, Sir James Dundas applied to be made a Lord of Session, and his friend and cousin,[1] Sir Alexander Hume, undertook to bring the request under the King's notice. It was favourably received: "You shall know in short," writes Sir Alexander in the following spring, "that upon the first motion I made to the King in your behalf for the vacant place in the Session, I had a very good answer, but no positive grant, the King suspending his determination until he should have my Lord Middleton's advice in

---

[1] As Sir Alexander styles himself the nephew of the first Lord Arniston's mother, he must have been a grandson of George Home of Wedderburn, whose daughter Mary married Sir James Dundas of Arniston, Governor of Berwick.

it, which was rational enough in regard of the trust he had given him in his affairs of that kingdom." By the mediation of powerful friends, the Lords Crawford and Lauderdale, the Secretary was brought to concur in recommending Sir James Dundas to the King, as a "well qualified, loyal, and well affected person." Whereupon, continues Sir Alexander, "having this day spoken with the King, his Majesty hath told me he will give you the place." Sir Alexander's next letter, after mentioning the good offices of friends in London, introduces a new topic:—

  Sir Alexander Hume *to* Sir James Dundas.

           London, 17 *May* 1662.

 Now Cosen, I must (but under this caution that no man living know what I write you), acquaint you with one thing that hath been discoursed by some here, that when you have the King's grant of the place you may probably refuse to accept of it upon such terms as all that excerce any public office in that kingdom must submit to, which is to subscribe a Declaration that is expected to be enjoyned by the Parliament, wherein, amongst other things, it is believed the Covenant is to be renounced, wherein I hope so wise a man as you will make no scruple, for to pass by the evil consequences and sad calamities that have followed upon the Covenant, which may justly make all men out of love with it, I conceive that even those who approve of the contents of it would make no difficulty of submitting to the authority of Parliament in renouncing that instrument, which will in nowayes inferr a receding from any point of it, which they hold themselves in conscience bound to believe or practice; there being without question some points in it (such as maintayning the true religion, and defending the King's person, and divers others), which all men will confess ought to be inviolably observed, notwithstanding of the renunciation to be enjoyned which can signify no more but a disowning of that formall act as any tye upon them. This I trust will be your excuse in that matter, and that you will not by needless scruples disable yourself from doing God, your prince, and countrie such useful service as you may be capable of, in the employment you are called to.

 I presume you have heard the news of our Queen[1] being landed at Portsmouth. Next Monday the King goes to her, and will bring her to Hampton Court by this day se'night.

---
      [1] Queen Catherine.

A few days later, writing on the same subject, Sir Alexander adds :—

"The King hath been here (Hampton Court) some days with the Queen, who is a very lovely person, and the King extremely satisfyed with her."

Sir Alexander Hume to Sir James Dundas.

November 4, 1662.

I have received yours of the 17th, whereby you let me know you are in some hope the Declaration will not at this time be urged upon those of your order, and if it be so, it is very well, for then you will have time to consider what is fitter for you to doe. I am very confident some others whom you think to have scruples will overcome them, namely a person[1] of near relation to yourself, whom you mentioned in your last, he being, as I am informed by a discreet man that is intimate with him, resolved to take the Declaration, as I could heartily wish that you might, and hope you will if it be required of you.

On the 7th of August 1663, Parliament passed an Act ordaining that no person who had not subscribed a formal renunciation of the Covenant, should "exerce any publick trust or office within the kingdom after the elevent of November nextocum."

The following letters show the negotiations which passed between Sir James Dundas and Sir James Dalrymple, on the one hand, and those who acted for the King, on the other hand, with the view of finding some means of both satisfying the King and saving the consciences of those whom he appointed as judges :—

Sir James Dalrymple (of Stair) to Sir James Dundas.

Edr., *Sptr.* 12, 1663.

My Lord,—Since I saw you I have spoken at large with the Lord Commissioner and my Lord Secretar. I beleve they ar als desyrous to favour us as we can wish. That explanation I am fre to sign the Declaration with, non can say it should or in ther sense doeth comprehend mor. If after they sie the King, anything

---

[1] Sir James Dalrymple, afterwards Lord Stair.

may be done, it will be signifyed to us what you understand farther from tyme to tyme, pray you let me hear it from you by a line; the Widinsdayes weeklie post will carrie it, so that you need not want ocasione. Remember my service to that noble gentleman, your friend Sir Alex^r. Home, and to your good lady; so rests your Lordship's real friend and servant, JA. DALRYMPLE.

SIR JAMES DALRYMPLE *to* SIR JAMES DUNDAS.

EDR., *Sept.* 12, 63.

My Lord,—Since my last of this dayis date, upon the second thoughts of some of our eminent friends, it is desyred that we shuld goe up to London (though on pretence of other affairs), which they doe conclude as very little dubious, to atain our desyres. I durst on a sudden say nothing to it, bot I am to think upon it. It was the motione befor, bot ther is non of us can suplie for the other ther; seeing our only way is expected to be that we have given his Majestie satisfactione ther. I doe therfor lay it befor you that you may think upon it, and if you relish it, put yourself in readines and be ther with your friends. It is the greater incouragment for us that non of our great men, thogh discording in other things, may differ in this, that we be looked over in such a matter. If I had no mor difficulties then you, I wold doe it, bot my poor wiffe is near her ly in, that will so retard me as that tym cold hardlie suffice for me to goe, and returne in tyme. You will by the Air post comunicat your thoghts and purposes to, Your really affectionate friend, JA. DALRYMPLE.

SIR JAMES DALRYMPLE *to* SIR JAMES DUNDAS.

STAIR, *Septr.* 21, 1663.

My Lord,—Yours of the 16th instant I receaved. You have conjectured aright of thes tuo friends who wer thinking upon our concernments; I am fully of your mynd, that ther is nothing to be done till they goe up, and that then the easiest and securest way for us wer that our busines wer moved ther, and we both called (if need wer), thither to doe what wer necessar, onlie a man is a lyon in his owne caus, and will keepe it afoote till ther be some issue. I leave that to your prudent consideratione, bot trewlie I am not in any freedome to leave this place till I know what becomes of my wife, who besyde the hazard of chyld birth is very unweell and in great hazard otherwayes. I know you ar a kynder husband then to think that can be dispensed with, bot my opinione wold be that, without any noise of going till some tym after our great ones wer up, I might give a compt of publick affaires, yourself went up; you have not yet seen the King since he came home. And oftymes the (autumn) uses to be als good wether as any in the year. I sould be haartilie glad you wer presented whatever come of me, and I am suir you might be helpful to both, whatever you doe. Let the medium thought upon be als little known as possible, least thes who will be against it mor for the example of it then for our interest in it, prevent it. The termes I think safest and cleirest, I have inclosed ; let me hear your resolution, and remember me to your lady and all friends to whom you think fit to mention. Your really affectionat friend and servant,

JA. DALRYMPLE.

In this letter Sir James Dalrymple encloses, written on a slip of paper, the words which he proposed to add to the Declaration, and which he thought, as he expresses it, "safest and cleirest." The Declaration (to be taken by all persons in positions of public trust) was to the effect that it was unlawful for subjects to enter into Leagues and Covenants, and, in particular, that the National Covenant of 1638 and the Solemn League and Covenant were "unlawful oaths, and were taken by, and imposed upon the subjects of this kingdom, against the fundamental laws and liberties of the same." The words which Dalrymple proposed to add were, "I do declare against the actings above written in so far as they were against the law, and against the oaths and obligations aforesaid, as they are construed to import any obligations to act or endeavour against law."

In the following letter Sir Alexander Hume conveyed to Dundas the King's refusal to accept a qualified subscription to the Declaration :—

SIR ALEXANDER HUME to SIR JAMES DUNDAS.

WESTMINSTER, *this Tuesday 3d November /63.*

MY LORD,—Yesternight, late, I received yours of the 26th Octob., with an enclosed for the B. of Dumbl.[1] to wch if he hold his promise, you will receive an answer herewith. I had upon my journey much ill wather and bad way, yet, thanks be to God, I got safe hither on Wednesday last the 28th, without any ill

---

[1] Robert Leighton, Bishop of Dunblane (1661-70).

accident, whereof I should have given you notice sooner, but that I deferred untill I might withall let you know the arrivall of our great men, whom I expected every day, yet they came not till yester night about six o'clock. They went immediately to the king, who gave them a very gratious reception, and talked with them both together about an hour or thereby. Upon their withdrawing from the king, I waylaid upon them at my Lord Lauderdale's loging in the Court, but forebore at that time to say anything to them concerning you, untill I should understand from you upon what terms you left them, whereof your letter that I received afterward did inform me. So this morning early, I went to them both, and found Lauderdale newly comed out of bed, and Rothes afterwards still in bed. I spoke to them both very earnestly concerning your business, and Lauderdale told me of the signed paper you had sent with him, wherein both of them have promised at the very first opportunity to speak jointly with the king, this night if it be possible, but seem both of them to have small confidence of the success, the king having absolutely refused to accept my Lord Crawford's subscription with any manner of qualification, but punctually as the words lye. Upon this answer from them I went and found out the B. of Dumbl.,[1] and having given him your letter, spoke at great length with him of the thing, and found him as you described him, very much inclined to moderation, and against all rigid courses, but without any hope that the king can be moved to dispense in any sort with the acte made in that behalf. And for his speaking with the king in it, he declines it altogether, having seldom or never as he sayeth taken the freedom to speak with the king in any business, and rarely made any other address to him but to kiss his hands at coming or going. All that he thinks proper for him to doe is to speak with Rothes and Lauderdale, and endeavour all he can either by his advice for moderation in generall, or by recommending your person and my Lord Stair in particular, to dispose them to be earnest with the king for procuring an exemtion to you both from the acte. And to this purpose he sayeth he will make all the haste he can to see them, as soon as he can possibly absent himself for an hour's time from his brother, who is at present lying sick of a fever and flux in great extremity. In his discourse to me he said one thing, which to me seemed very rationall, that he thought the qualification you desired to insert (of disowning the particulars there mentioned, in so far as they were against

---

[1] Bishop Leighton.

law, and disclaiming all ordinances that may lead to the disturbances of the publick peace) is altogether superfluous, seeing the meaning of the declaration can be in effect no other, and no acting can thereby be understood to be disowned, but such as were against law, nor any ordinances disclaimed but such as are seditious. Which if you will take into serious consideration, together with what I have formerly urged when we were together, and consult your own judgement maturely in it, I do yet hope that you may overcome your scruples and subscribe the declaration simply as it stands, without addition of that postscript, though you may at the subscribing of it, by mouth declare the sense in which you think it is to be understood, which doubtless will be equivalent as if you should put it in writing. Yr. Lop's. most affectinat and humble servant, A. HUME.

Lord Arniston was not prepared to make the required renunciation, and did not take his seat on the bench after the 7th of November 1663. On the 18th of November, the renunciation was signed by all the judges present, twelve in number, which was reported to the King. His Majesty offered to allow time for subscribing the Declaration, but was determined that subscription should be enforced.

SIR ALEXANDER HUME to SIR JAMES DUNDAS.

LONDON, 8th Decemb. 1663.

MY LORD,—Having at this instant written another letter to you, by advice of Mr. William Sharpe, lest that should miscarry, or be slow of coming to your hands, I send this by the usual way, to let you know that having been this evening, as my custom is every post night, with my Lord Lauderdale, he told me he could now give me an account, but not such as he wished, of the business I came to inquire of, which was, that the king, notwithstanding all that could be sayd to persuade him, would upon no terms yield to accept of that explanation in writing which you desire to subjoyn to the declaration, as you will understand by a letter more at length that my lord hath writte to you himself, which he showed me. This answer I did expect, but I confess I am deceived in one point, for I did believe advantage would have been taken against all that failed at the day appointed, and their places disposed immediately without admitting of their subscription after that day. But it seems the king is so gratious as to leave place still for such as will yet comply with the law, and to that end is forthwith to send order to the Lord Chancellor to call for all the absent members of the house, and urge them to declare whether or no they will subscribe simply without any addition or explanation in writing, and such as shall then refuse immediately to declare their places voyd, and returne an account to his majesty. And it is withall a curtesy in my Lord Lauderdale to keep up the king's order for some days, and in the meantime to give my Lord Stair and yourself notice of it, that you may not be surprised at it. Now, I trust this grace of the king's and his lordship's civility will work that effect with you both for which it was intended, and that at last your eyes will be opened to see there can be no difference in reason or conscience, between writing and speaking the same words you desire to subjoine, which is the clear opinion of all I have spoke with about it; and amongst others of Sir Robert Morry, who was present this night when I spoke with my Lord Lauderdale. And for any explanation of that kind you shall desire to make by tongue, it will not be denyed. But for setting any such thing in writing, and so have the declaration subscribed in different wayes, the king looks upon it as making party against party, and believes it a thing of dangerous consequence, wherein I find all men here concur in his judgement. And whatever ground you may have to be scrupulous in the thing, yet I assure you, if you refuse to subscribe the declaration in the same way as the parliament, and councill, and all the Lords of Session, except yourselves, have done, it will be interpret by the king and by all impartiall men, as a factious inclination which is a scandal that worthy patriots and loyall subjects, as you two ar, I trust will avoyd to incurr. And this consideration above all that I formerly said, I hope will prevaile with you not to desert the station wherein God hath placed you, and wherein you may have occasion to doe God and your king and your Cuntrie, and your friends acceptable and usefull service.[1]

Earl of Lauderdale to Sir James Dundas.
Whitehall, 8th of Decr. 1663.

My Lord,—At my first arrivall, having found the king avers from such a declaration as y^r Lo. wold put in wryting, and knowing y^r absence secured you from being put to it, I delayed urging his maj^{ties} positive resolution untill I could doe it conveniently. And now within these 2 dayes I have his positive order to let you know that he cannot admitt of explanation, becaus that were posi-

---

[1] This letter is unsigned.

tively to state a partie of those who doe subscribe as the law requires & of those who subscribe with explanations. This his Maj^tie will on no termes admitt because of the example, and I am comanded to prepare an order to the Session to put all their members to a positive answer. But befor I sent it, I thought it my dewty to give you this warning that you might be not surprised. I doe not need I hope to profess my respects to you nor my desire to serve you. From that consideration, I who am elder must entreat you to consider well before you abandon your station; and this freedom I hope you will take well from, My Lord, y^r affectionate friend,
LAUDERDAILL.[1]

The following letter, which was Sir James's reply to Lord Lauderdale's letter of the 8th December 1663, is copied from the original, now in the possession of Richard Almack, Esq. of Melford, Suffolk:—

SIR JAMES DUNDAS *to the* EARL OF LAUDERDALE.

16th Dec. 63.

MY NOBLE LORD,—I received your Lordship's of the 8 dayes date yesterday in the afternoone, by which I understand that your Lordship hath been pleased not only to move the business you writ of once and againe to the king, but also to watch opportunities of doeing it to the best advantage. And as if al this wer to smal a testimonie of your respects for me, yow ar likewise pleased to give me ane express advertisement of the event that I should not be surprised by hearing it in a way which I cannot evite.

My Lord, soe verie great favor calleth for a greater acknowledgement than I am able to make, and not the lesse that the successe hath not been answerable to your Lordship's desires and endevours; soe I can verie frely say caveat successibus quisquis ab eventu. And not to misspend your Lordship's time (which all men know to be taken up with far greater things), I doe in a word return your Lordship most heartic thanks for this and all your favors; and if ever I shall be soe happie as to have an opportunitie to doe you service, I hope I shall not be capable of that unworthiness as to be found forgettful therof, who now subscribe myself most sincerely, y^r Lordship's most humble and obliged servant,
JAMES DUNDAS.

---

[1] Second Earl, and afterwards Duke of Lauderdale, Secretary of State and President of the Council.

On the 19th December 1663 the King wrote to the Privy Council, ordering them to "requyre the Senators of our College of Justice to appoint a short day, on which the absent Senators and other members may either subscribe or refuse, to the end wee may take care for supplying the places of such as shall on that account forsake their station."

The Lords accordingly, on the 5th January 1664, "did assigne ane certaine day for eache of the absent Lords, conforme to their severall distances to come in and give their positive answer either as to the subscrybing or refusing of the declaration aforsaid; viz., to the Lord Arneistoune, the eight of January instant, and to the Lords Staire and Bedlay, the nynteinth day therof, and to the Lord Tarbett, the second of February nixt."

In reply to the letter from the Chancellor, assigning the eighth day of January instant for subscribing or refusing the Declaration, Sir James wrote as follows:—

SIR JAMES DUNDAS *to the* LORD CHANCELLOR.

ARNISTOUN, 7*th Jan.* 1664.

MAY IT PLEASE YOUR LORDSHIP,—I did some weekes agoe send a demission of my place in the Session to the Court, which I hope befor this tyme is presented to the king's most sacred Majestie, whereby I am altogether incapacitat to give obedience to the Lords of Session their commands laid upon me as one of their number by their letter of the fift of this instant, signed by your Lordship in their name. This I hope will excuse me for not waiting upon their Lordships on Friday next according to their appointment, and shall entreat their Lordships may believe that, though I shall noe longer be able to serve them as a publick minister, yet I shall never omitt anything shall be in my power as a private man, whereby I may witness the deep sense I have of their Lordship's civilitie and kindnesse to me, while I had the honour to sitt amongst them, which can never be forgotten by—My Lord, y' lordships most humble servant,   JAMES DUNDAS.

On this letter being read, the Court pronounced the following sentence:—

"The Lords having considered the Act of Parliament, with his Majestie's letter, and the above written answer to the Lord's owne letter, they declare the said Sir James Dundas his place as ane of the Lords of Session vacant."

On the 15th January 1664, Lord Stair wrote from Ayr to the Lord Chancellor in much the same terms as Lord Arniston, and his place was in the same manner declared vacant.

Lord Bedlay was excused on the ground of ill-health, and his declaration of willingness to make the required renunciation. Lord Tarbett had already made the renunciation in his place in Parliament.

Sir James Dalrymple *to* Sir James Dundas.

STAIR, *Febr.* 15, 1664.

MY LORD,—Your last cam bot on of thes dayes to my hand. As to your desyre of my coming east in March to put some poynt to the difference betwixt my Lord Lothian and you, I will not have my horss to shoe when you have to doe, bot I think a little further, in the year when wether is fairer and the day longer, will be better. It is no small difficulty to draw me to Edinbrugh voyage. I much mor inclyne if your convenience so be to wait upon you at Lanrike, near my Lord Lea's, who is to be spared in travel als much as you can. We will be freer of diversion ther than at Ed^r. A night or two will serve in either case, my kyndnes and confidence made me so free with you in my last as not to conceale the observatione of others; if thereby you apprehend that I laid blaime on you, indeed it was far from my thought, bot it is my rejoyceing to have a sharer in my lot, whom I honor and love so much, thogh lyke motives moved us both without our premoving either the other. Remember my service to your ladie.—I sal ever continue your faithful friend and servant,

JA. DALRYMPLE.

Sir James Dalrymple *to* Sir James Dundas.

(From LONDON.)

MY LORD,—I beleive you will thinke it strange to hear of me from this place, it is even strange to myself, who had resolved retirement, bot being called hither by friends, upon finding of the kings kyndnes continowed with me and hopes of his favour to me, I obeyed, thogh I knew no particular (reason) that I did not come be you, bot keept Carleell way, wherbye I was als neir London as is Ed^r. I sal at meeting fully satisfie you in that, and that this is the first advertisement, you may be assured I shall not be forgetful of you, bot sal doe for you as you wer my brother, I cannot say what I can doe for myself or any other, bot I am suir I shall doe for you whatever I can. I am bot new come hither, and not yet in a rite postur to sie any bodie or doe anythinge, bot when I come to any ishue or expectatione, you sal be acquainted with it from your real friend and humble servant, JA. DALRYMPLE.

Send your letter to Daniel Dalrymple, at Mr. John Hay's chambers, or Master James Ross, at William Ros, Wryter to the Signet his chambers.

SIR ALEXANDER HUME *to* SIR JAMES DUNDAS.

WESTMINSTER, 18 *Apr.* 1664.

MY LORD,—I suppose that knowing of my Lord Stair's being here, you may expect to receive some account of his proceedings, which he was proposed himself to have given you by this post, but that he is invited this night to my Lord Lauderdale's countrie house at Highgate, some four miles out of town, from whence they are to returne on Monday next. Before his going out he was with me, and told me he had this morning a large conference with the king, being the first time he saw him, to whom he made an ingenous declaration of the motives that induced him to make scruple of the subscription required of all in publick trust, which he assured his mat^{ie} did not proceed from any want of loyalty. The particulars he had not time to tell me, only in general he sayd the king was very civile to him, and told him he would be very sory that he should desert his service. So at that time there was no conclusion made, but he is not without hope that the result may be such as he may keep his station, whereof he may be able after full communication with my Lord Lauderdale, to give you a particular account by the next post, that you may also resolve what is fitt for you to do. For seeing you both agree as well in sincere principles of loyalty as in scruples of conscience, it is reasonable to think your affaires may have the like event; wherein my Lord Stair and I will take the best care we can that your absence shall not prejudice you, and my Lord Lauderdale hath also promised his best offices. Perchance it may be necessary that you be at the pains of coming hither, for which at all adventures I would have you prepare yourself, though I shall rather wish you may avoyd the journey, unless it be absolutely necessary. I shall add no more at present, but, with my humble service to your lady, remaine ever, your most affectionat cosen and humble servant, A. HUME.

Although his seat on the bench had been declared vacant, Sir James Dalrymple when in London, during his interviews with the King, made the arrangement which is hinted at, rather than explained, in the following letters. He was to subscribe the Declaration as it stood, and the King was to allow him to salve his conscience by making a private verbal explanation of the sense in which he understood it.

Sir James Dalrymple *to* Sir James Dundas.

Whytehall, *Apryl* 19, 64.

My Lord,—Since my last I have bein with the king, and have fowned mor favour than I doe deserve, and mor desyr of my continwans in his Majesty's service then I could have expected, bot no possibilitie of obtaining an explanatione in wrytte, to be subjoyned to the declaratione. Something is spoken of in lieu therof, bot no effect as yet, nether may I at a distance mention it to you. It is necessar for yourself and me and others, it be so; and that nothing be spoken of, either endeavour or expectation, till I sie you, which if anything be done to satisfactione will be shortlie, bot I hope you will be out of dowbt of my dilligence for you. I assur you you have some very kynd friends heir who doe heartilie goe along with yr real friend,

Ja. Dalrymple.

Sir James Dalrymple *to* Sir James Dundas.

London, *May* 26, 1664.

My Lord,—I receaved two of yours together at Paris, and once since my returne, prior to both which Sir Alexr Home had. I must still forbear to be particular with you in what is past heir, and thogh you find difficulty to aprehend how it can be that we can sign without explanatione in wrytt, I sal say no more at distance, bot that ther is an equivalence in all respects of adjecting a declaratione or provisione to a wrytt, and getting the sam, under the hand of the wreater of the wrytt, that it is so accepted or so satisfactorie. I shall be full with you at meeting. I desyre you will be at Ed{r}. the 6th of June, for on the 7th or 8th I hope you shall see Yr real and affectionat friend,

Ja. Dalrymple.

Sir Alexander Hume to Sir James Dundas.

Westminster, 23 June 1664.

Just now I received yours of the 16th, and am very sorry you give me so little hope of that which you know I so much wish. I have already said as much upon this subject as I could, and have nothing now to adde, but that I cannot comprehend how you should be more difficult to receive satisfaction in your scruples than your friend (Dalrymple), who hath hitherto been of one mind with you. I doubt not but he hath fully acquainted you with his proceedings, and upon what grounds he hath been moved to comply, which I conceive was a conference he had with the king, who, being the party chiefly concerned, had power to declare in what sense he would allow the thing to be done. For God's sake consider seriously whether you might not in the same way be sett free, and if so, I could wish that you should of purpose make a journey hither to receive the same satisfaction, in the point that your friend did. In any case I think your journey would be usefull to let his mat[ie] know that your scruples do not proceed from any bad cause, but merely conscience.—My Lord, your most affectionat cosen and humble servant, A. HUME.

Although thus urged by Hume to follow Sir James Dalrymple's example, Dundas stood firm to his original position, and refused to sign the Declaration without a written qualification. This resolution was deeply regretted by Hume.

Sir Alexander Hume to Sir James Dundas.

Westminster, 9 Aug. 1664.

I have received yours of the 30 of July, whereby you have now cleared me more than I wished of your purpose, whereof I have often written, and with so much impatience expected your answer. I must withall confess to you I am farr disappointed of my hope in that matter, for having very justly heretofore from the former difference of your judgement and principles from your friends, collected that more might be expected from you than from him, I cannot comprehend upon what ground it can be that you now fall short of the length he comes, nor will I urge to know it, seeing it may not be without divulging your friend's secret, whereof it is not fitt for me to be inquisitive. But as to that which you say (that the paper being so much against your sense and his, you think it unreasonable that your signing of it should be publick and the salvo should be latent), give me leave to remind you of what you have often professed, that no consideration did hinder you to do it, but merely point of conscience; and if so, what need there should be to have the salvo publick is more than I can understand. But this or any thing else that I can say I doubt will be to little purpose, seeing that worthy person (Dalrymple) can neither with his persuasion nor his example prevail with you; therefore I shall forbear farther contending with your resolution; only as a last means, I shall intreat you to peruse two little books which I have sent you by our cosen (Home of) Wedderburne, and if they do not convince you I shall despair of it.

As for the king's inclination, touching the laws enacted by the parliament in order to conformity, I am not able farther to inform you, than I have often said, that I know he is not of a nature to use severity with any man in point of tender conscience; but how farr he may be disposed to grant any indulgence or dispensation from the obedience of those laws, is more than I know. Your friend (Dalrymple) may possibly know more than I, having, at his being here been intimately concerned with my Lord Lauderdale, who is best able to inform him. And now that I name that Lord, I must let you know that of late, having occasion to speak with him, he told me he was sorry to hear that you were not likely to comply, and wished me to use all possible means to persuade you to it, promising to keep the door open for you as long as he could. And indeed I see no great haste is made to fill any of the vacant places, nor doe I hear whom they mean to put in them. As for that person whom you wished to be your successor, there is no expectation for him though all these places were voyde, the resolution being unalterably taken to fill all with lawyers, according to the constant practice of this cuntrie (England), which is undoubtedly more fitt.

With hearty wishes of happy success both to your lady in a safe delivery,[1] and to your daughter[2] in her marriage, I remain ever, &c. &c. A. HUME.[3]

---

[1] Birth of his son Charles.

[2] Christian, married to Charles Erskine of Alva.

[3] This lengthy correspondence, on the positions taken by Sir James Dalrymple and Sir James Dundas in reference to the question of the Declaration, is somewhat tedious. But as the letters are of considerable historical value, it has been considered better to print them in full.

Neither the "two little books," whatever they may have been, nor the expression of Lord Lauderdale's desire to serve him, had any influence on Dundas, who steadfastly adhered to his resolution, and retired to private life.

Sir James Dundas was thrice married. His first wife was Marion, daughter of Robert, Lord Boyd. Of this marriage four children were born:—Robert, known, as a judge of the Court of Session, as the second Lord Arniston; Mary, wife of Sir J. Home of Blackadder, Christian, wife of Sir Charles Erskine of Alva; and Katherine, wife of the Hon. Sir J. Dalrymple of Borthwick. His second wife was Janet, daughter of Sir Adam Hepburn of Humbie, and widow of Sir John Cockburn of Ormiston. The children of this marriage were:— James, from whom the Dundases of Beechwood are descended; Alexander, and Charles. His second spouse died in 1665; and in the following year, Sir James married, thirdly, Helen, daughter of Sir James Skene, President of the Court of Session, and widow of Sir Charles Erskine of Alva.

The following letter is from Sir James's friend and cousin, Sir Alexander Hume, giving an account of his son Robert, afterwards the second Lord Arniston, then a youth returning from his travels; also condoling with Sir James on the death of his second wife :—

Sir Alexander Hume to Sir James Dundas.

HAMTON COURT, 4 *July* 1665.

My Lord,—I could not let this bearer[1] goe without a letter, though I have little subject left for one, having at length discoursed with him of everything that I could write; unlesse it be of the good opinion I have of him, which I could not express to himself without offending his modesty, for really it was much joy to me to finde him so well qualifyed, being (if my interest in him do not much deceive me) a discreet and knowing gentleman, without vice or vanity, and I am very confident he will give you cause to think his time and your money imployed in his travells well bestowed, and that his company will in a great measure lessen that affliction which it pleased God of late to lay upon you, by taking from you a deserving lady; which sad losse I had sooner condoled with you if I had known it, which I did not untill

---

[1] Robert Dundas.

I saw your sone goe in mourning for her; on which subject I can say nothing as to yourself, but that I know you are so good a Christian as to submit to the good pleasure of God; and as to myself I hope you do believe that whatsoever befalls you, I receive it with such a sense as becomes the friendship I owe you as, my Lord, your most affectionat cosen and humble servant,

A. HUME.

In the early part of the year 1679, Sir James's daughter Katherine was married to James Dalrymple, one of the principal clerks of the Court of Session, and second son of his friend Sir James Dalrymple, afterwards Lord Stair. The contract of marriage is dated the 2d of January 1679. On the part of the bridegroom the consenting parties are his father, Sir James Dalrymple, and his mother, Dame Margaret Ross. The bridegroom's mother, it is perhaps unnecessary to remind the reader, was the "Lady Ashton" of Sir Walter Scott's *Bride of Lammermoor*; and it is curious to notice that one of the witnesses to the contract is "David Dunbar, younger of Baldoon," who appears in that celebrated novel as "Bucklaw," the unlucky husband of Lucy Ashton.

Another of the witnesses is Sir George Mackenzie of Rosehaugh, who was, at this time, Lord Advocate, and deeply engaged in the persecutions, from which he earned his name of the "Bloody Mackenzie." His presence on this occasion shows that Sir James Dundas had not suffered from his refusal to renounce the Covenants, and was on terms of intimate friendship with the members of the ruling party in Scotland.

A period of greater trial was, however, at hand for the people of Scotland; and the time was now rapidly approaching when the passing of the Test Act was to drive Sir James Dalrymple into exile, and to furnish the pretext on which Argyll was sentenced to death. But Dundas was not destined to witness these events; for, not long after his daughter's marriage, he died at Arniston, in October 1679, leaving behind him the well-earned reputation of one who, at a time when principles were put to the severest test, had proved himself a resolute and conscientious man.

The heraldic painter's account for work done at the funeral of Sir James Dundas has been preserved. It consists of the customary items of a large coat-of-arms, etc., smaller shields for the decoration of the coffin, trumpets, and hearse. The ornaments of the coffin likewise included a headpiece and wreath to place on its head. The doors of the burial-place (yle, aisle) were blackened, and had emblematic tears painted on them. The cost of this funeral painter-work amounted to £98 Scots, a considerable sum for those days.

Sir James was succeeded in the estate of Arniston by his son Robert, who occupied a seat on the bench in days happier than those in which his father lived.

Da: Dunbar witnes

CHAPTER V.

THE SECOND LORD ARNISTON.

From the death of Sir James Dundas, in 1679, until the year 1688, there appears to be a blank in the records of the Arniston family. Moreover, there are no letters in the charter-room at Arniston for the period from 1667 till 1717. This want is, to some extent, supplied by a manuscript written by Robert Dundas (the great-grandson of the second Lord Arniston), who was Lord Chief Baron of Scotland at the beginning of the present century, and who found time to compose an interesting account of various matters connected with the family estate.

It appears that Robert Dundas, son of Sir James Dundas and Marion, daughter of Lord Boyd, was living abroad during the years which immediately preceded the Revolution. He returned to Scotland as a supporter of the Prince of Orange, and was chosen one of the members of Parliament for Mid-lothian in 1689, a position which he continued to hold until the passing of the Act of Union.

In Scotland the active pursuit of politics had always been thought compatible with the performance of judicial duties; and Dundas was appointed a judge of the Court of Session on the 1st of November 1689.

It was at this time that proprietors in Scotland began to improve their houses and grounds. Trees were being planted, to a considerable extent, round mansions and farm-"tounes," and enclosures were designed as well for ornament as for the protection of stock. Mansions were rebuilt or enlarged, gardens and pleasure-grounds were formed, and public roads were removed to a greater distance from the pleasure-grounds. Scotch lairds who had been residing abroad during the last years of the Stuart dynasty, returned home with minds improved by taste and cultivation, acquired on the Continent, and devoted themselves to the adornment of their houses and to the improvement of their estates.[1]

The following account of the changes made at Arniston is taken from the manuscript of the Chief Baron :—

NARRATIVE OF THE IMPROVEMENTS AT ARNISTON,

From the MS. by the Chief Baron Dundas.

"The old Manor-house of Arniston was situated exactly where the present house stands; the Oak-room and vaults beneath, being part of the old building. The vault beneath the east end of the Oak-room was the parlour or eating-room of my great-grandfather, Lord Arniston. The Oak-room was then divided into two apartments, one a dining-room used only on great days, and the other the principal bedroom for strangers of distinction visiting the family. The house was enclosed by a stone wall to the north. My great-grandfather, Lord Arniston, died in 1726, and his son before his death, either began to build the new house from a design by old Robert Adam, or at least took down part of the old chateau, with the view of preparing for it. I was told by my father, who was then about eleven or twelve years of age, that on pulling down the high wall, which enclosed the house to the north, they discovered that the sea was to be seen from the windows, and having notified this to the old man, he would not believe the fact till he was carried to the room for the purpose of satisfying his own eyes.

"The garden of the old house was immediately contiguous to it, on the south and east fronts of the present house, and in front of the present stables, stable-court, and cow-house; all beyond or without this was corn or the croft land of Arniston.

"The road from Edinburgh to the south was by Carrington, Arniston, Esperston, and thence through the Outerston Moss over the hill into Heriot Water, and by Dewar and Innerleithen

---

[1] Cosmo Innes, Highland Society Transactions, 1861.

2nd Lord Arniston.

to Traquair. Lord Traquair,[1] when Chancellor of Scotland, built, it is said, at his own expense, the bridge across the river at the foot of the bank below the meeting of the Temple and Carrington waters, which I am now (1811) pulling down.[2] By old people the bridge was always called Traquair's Bridge, his Lordship always riding through this road to Edinburgh. The path up the brae is still to be discerned. In some old

ANCIENT OAK-TREE WHICH IS SAID TO HAVE MARKED THE BOUNDARY BETWEEN THE ENCLOSURES AND CORN-LAND OF ARNISTON.

book, I have seen[3] Esperston marked as the first stage from Edinburgh, or the road to the south country. Outerston and Esperston were then large *Towns*, or hamlets, each containing a considerable number of inhabitants, most of whom kept pack-horses, on which they carried the lime burnt in great quantities on these lands, to all the neighbouring country.

---

[1] First Earl of Traquair; creation 1628.
[2] The piers of the bridge are still standing, 1886.
[3] Tradition still marks the site of the inn and blacksmith's forge at Esperston—about sixty yards to the south of the present farm-house.

"The public road then passed close by the old house of Arniston, and thence branched off to the eastwards towards Stobhill and Borthwick. Its direction from Traquair's Bridge was up the hollow path, through the south lawn, along the green walk from the Grotto, through the present greenhouse and dairy, and thence round the front of the present house into the Edinburgh approach, under the double row of ancient planes and ashes, at the end of which it took its direction to the east along the ridge of the north-east lawn, through Lawrence Law

THE HAMLET OF OUTERSTON.

Inhabited by persons making their living by farming, weaving, lime-burning, and carrying the lime on pack-horses through the surrounding country—Enlarged from Arniston Estate Map, 1758.

park, by an old ash-tree still standing, along Birkenside, where a farm-house stood, and thence eastwards near to Harvieston House, slanting diagonally through Harvieston south park, and downwards to Catcune Mill, and thence by the present footpath between Catcune and Haughead, up the water-side, under the row of plane-trees to Borthwick. This, before the formation of the turnpike road in 1753, was the only kirkroad, and my grandfather's and father's coach always went that way. I remember, when a child, the diagonal road through the south park of Harvieston ; and I have repeatedly ridden to church on my pony that way. I remember, to my great joy, getting leave on one occasion to ride (the first time I rode so far) with the old and respectable Earl of Kinnoull[1] and Lord Melville, then Mr. Henry Dundas, to Borthwick Kirk, while my father and the rest of the family went in the coach by

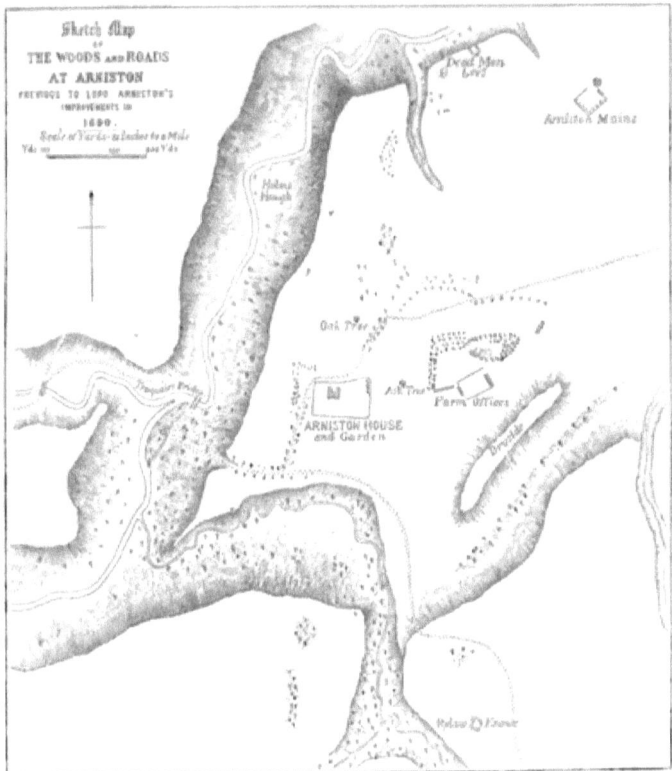

Torcraik. About this period it was shut up as a bridle road by common consent, and restricted to a footpath for the inhabitants of Arniston, Shank, and Harvieston going to church, and as such it is still used. It is necessary to state what trees existed around the old house of Arniston prior to Lord Arniston's return from Holland in 1688."

---

[1] Thomas, eighth Earl of Kinnoull.

The MS. then gives, in minute detail, the position, size, and age of a number of the trees on the grounds of Arniston; but these details would be of no interest to the reader. The narrative next goes on to describe

"The famous Ash-tree in the Orchard, of which it is right

THE ASH-TREE.

I should give some description. A drawing of this tree was made by my worthy friend, the present Earl of Morton, about the year 1792, when he did me the honour of passing a few days with me at Arniston. It then measured at its base, close to the ground, thirty feet in circumference. At the height of about six feet it divided into eight, or I think nine, different limbs, each of them large and lofty, and sufficient to have each attracted notice, if separate, as fine timber. Three or four persons could have stood without inconvenience in the centre where the limbs diverged. One storm of wind, in winter 1793, threw down four of the limbs, and it was then discovered what was long suspected, that the trunk was rotten and entirely gone, the bark and a plate of the external wood only being sound; the remainder entirely wasted and hollow. Another stormy day, in winter 1794, completed the destruction, and levelled all the remaining limbs to the ground. The timber of these was in general sound, and, even at the low prices then paid, brought at a sale £50. The age of this tree and its early history are unknown. It stood also in what was originally the croft or corn-field of Arniston. It cannot have been less than three hundred years old, not only from its size, and the circumstances of its appearance above detailed, but that my great-grandfather who, previous to the Revolution of 1688, passed his life abroad and returned with King William, had a bench placed in the centre of the trunk, where every day in summer he in his old age used to sit and amuse himself in reading, chiefly, as I was told by my father, Italian books, of which he was fond, and the *Pastor Fido*, which was a peculiar favourite. This was betwixt 1690 and 1725, and, as far as my father's observation carried him, no change but towards decay had occurred for eighty years afterwards. If I trace in imagination the springing of this seedling from the earth to some such accidental cause as Cowper has done in the beautiful lines on the ancient and decayed oak, and its date to the year 1450, the reign of the first James, I cannot believe myself much mistaken.

"My grandfather, the first Lord President Arniston, was naturally vain of this tree, and of showing it to his guests. When he was named President in 1747, the Magistrates and Council of Edinburgh came out to congratulate him on his appointment, and dined with him. Before dinner he walked them out in the garden to the Ash Tree. Deacon Milroy—I think that was the name—a house carpenter, after admiring and examining it with attention, told his Lordship there were at least . . . feet of timber in it, and that he would give him £ . . . for the tree. 'I would rather,' replied his Lordship, 'see you hung on its topmost branch.' A small piece of the trunk still remains (1811) as a memorial of the original. I caused my son Robert, on the 2d April 1809, to plant an oak-tree now growing there, produced from an acorn of the famous Greendale oak in Welbeck Park, Nottinghamshire, which my

BEECH AVENUE.

respected friend the Duke of Portland gave me in 1805, and which, with about twenty others, I sowed in the garden and transplanted to this and other situations to be hereafter mentioned.

"In 1690 the Earl of Tweeddale, who was a particular friend of Lord Arniston's, and with whom he agreed in politics, was employed in forming the plantations at Yester, and in planting the bushes which are now such noble trees, when Lord Arniston happened to pay him a visit. On returning home he gave Lord Arniston thirty beech plants and an elm, which were brought over behind the servant in the portmanteau, and planted along the side of the cow-park dyke, where, with the exception of a few now to be cut, they still remain, and are in general fine timber. My father thought they must have been cut over when planted, otherwise they could not have assumed the shapes they generally have done. These trees stand on the west side of the road and dyke fronting the garden.

"His Lordship also formed the bowling-green east of the present house, and planted the large spruce-fir still standing there, though now in a state of decay, and much altered in my remembrance. Another spruce of the same age, though not quite so large, stood opposite, and near to the middle door of the cow-house. I remember it perfectly. It was blown down about 1766. My brother and I had a small garden near to its root, where we amused ourselves when children. A row of hollies were also planted in the line of these two spruce-firs, and two *arbor vitæ* at the end of each row next to the house. One of these still stands.[1] The other *arbor vitæ* was blown up by the roots in 1766. Two large hollies also stood within the wall of the present stable-yard, near the cistern; these gradually decayed, and died away about 1780. Those in the bowling-green my mother did not like, and prevailed on my father to cut down, one excepted, sometime about 1760—at least I do not remember them; and for this the late Lord Kames has celebrated either her good or bad taste in his work entitled *Sketches of the History of Man*. The remaining holly stood till 1786, when, one frosty morning, some of the sheep fastened on it, and, before they were observed, had eaten off all the bark from the root upwards as far as they could reach. I had it plastered round, and as well secured as possible, but in vain—it died in the course of the year."

---

[1] This tree, one of the largest of its kind in this part of Scotland, was taken down in 1860, being quite decayed.

The first marked advance in the improvement of the Lowlands of Scotland may be said to date from the settlement of the country after the Revolution of 1688. A few years later, in 1695, an Act for the division of run-rig lands was passed—a most necessary measure; and in the same year an Act for the encouragement of the exportation of victual was also passed.

Statute labour, for the better repair of the roads, had been introduced a few years previously, in 1669, and in Midlothian, at all events, the traffic was carried on by wheeled carts. In the Arniston accounts the entries for payments to the wheelwright for cart-wheels are frequent, as are likewise payments for hired cartages of stone, lime, and other materials, but no allusion is ever made to pack-horse loads.

The wages of farm servants continued to be paid in grain; the shepherd, smith, wright, and even "the bedall," figuring in the factor's books for so many bolls of oats.

The land for the most part was tilled upon the in-field and out-field system, though an improved rotation of cropping was being introduced. On the better descriptions of in-field land the following course was adopted:—

1. Barley or wheat, dunged.
2. Oats.
3. Oats.
4. Pease.

The out-field was used as the common pasture for live stock of all sorts. The portion of it under tillage for the time being was enclosed within turf dykes, and dunged by having the sheep folded within the enclosures at night. The rotation on which the out-field was cropped was three or four crops of oats in succession, followed by from four to six years' rest.

Among the papers in the Arniston charter-room is the balance-sheet for crop 1699 of the lands of Howburn, a farm—at the foot of the Moorfoot Hills—of about 120 acres of arable land, and about 400 of hill pasture, river banks, and moss. A copy of this balance-sheet is given in the note on the following page, and is interesting as showing the style of farming and the prices realised on a Midlothian hill farm in 1699. Of the arable land only about 20 acres were *in-field*, or in regular cultivation, the remainder being broken up in small patches from time to time.[1]

Besides the improvements carried out by individual proprietors in Midlothian, the county obtained a Turnpike Act in

	£ Scots.	s.	d.
[1] Imprimis the rent formerly paid by the tenant was,	260	2	0
Item, the parson's teind was,	66	2	0
Item, the vicarage teind was,	13	2	0
Item, there will be used for 30 pints of tar yearly, at 4s.,	6	0	0
Item for 16 pounds of butter,	12	0	0
Item for interest of £1333 for stocking the farm,	80	0	0
Item for 7 bolls oats, at £4 per boll, 2 bolls pease at £6 as the herd's boll,	40	0	0
Item for 16 bolls of oats, 2 bolls pease, 1 boll bere, for a double hynd's boll,	82	0	0
Total (£ Scots),	£559	6	0

	£ Scots.	s.	d.
Imprimis for 25 stone of wool as the produce of 15 score of sheep, 12 fleeces to the stone, at £4 per stone,	100	0	0
Item, there may be 60 ewes casten every year, which being better than ordinary croaks, because not very old, for it will not be proper to keep them above three or four years upon the ground, 60 ewes at £2, 3s.,	135	0	0
Item for the milk of nine score ewes, at 6s.,	54	0	0
Item for five score of lambs, at £1 per head, the other four score being allowed in place of the 60 ewes to be sold as above,	100	0	0
Item for 20 neats' grass in the moss, at £2,	40	0	0
Item for hay, expenses paid,	60	0	0
Item for the produce of 20 bolls oats sown, counting the third corn price for the same, gives 40 bolls as product,	160	0	0
Item for 4 bolls bere sown, at the four corn, gives 12 bolls product,	72	0	0
Total (£ Scots),	£721	0	0

There must be necessarily 2 bolls pease sown yearly, but we can count nothing upon the profit, because of the uncertainty of the crop.

It is to be remembered that, by this account, the herd that keeps the twelve-score sheep upon the hill and the lady's ten-score sheep kept upon the farm is paid; which may compensate for what expense may be for the maintenance of the shearers in time of harvest. There is likewise no allowance here given for the upholding of plough and plough pertinents.

1714, and made a commencement of the magnificent system of roads by which the capital was brought into communication with every part of the kingdom.

In 1711 an incident took place which must have tried Lord Arniston's feelings, as a sound Whig and thorough-going supporter of the House of Hanover. His eldest son, James, was the leading spirit in a curious episode which caused considerable excitement in Scotland. In June 1711, the Duchess of Gordon,[1] wife of George, first Duke of Gordon, offered to the Faculty of Advocates, for preservation among a collection of coins in the possession of the Faculty, a Jacobite medal. The medal bore on one side Great Britain and Ireland, with a fleet of ships coming to them, and the motto "Reddite;" and on the other side the Pretender's head, with the motto "Cujus est." A dispute arose at a meeting of the Faculty as to whether this medal should be received or not. We have no means of knowing accurately what happened; but there can be little doubt that an acrimonious debate took place. *The Flying Post*, a London paper, published an account of the proceedings, according to which Mr. Robert Bennett, Dean of Faculty, presented the medal, and, in doing so, said, "Her Grace sends, as a present to you, the medal of King James VIII., whom we and the English call the Pretender. I hope thanks are to be returned for it." Objections were at once raised to receiving the medal, and it was proposed to return it, on the ground that to receive it would be to "throw dirt upon the face of the Government."[2]

But James Dundas made a very strong speech in favour of receiving the medal, and thanking the Duchess of Gordon for sending it. He ended his speech by saying, "But, Dean of Faculty, what needs further speech? None oppose receiving the medal, and returning thanks to her Grace, but a few pitiful scoundrel, vermin, and mushrooms, not worthy of our notice. Let us, therefore, proceed to name some of our number to return our hearty thanks to the Duchess of Gordon." The vote being taken, it was carried by a majority that the thanks of the Faculty should be given to the Duchess, and that Mr.

---

[1] The first Duchess of Gordon, Lady Elizabeth Howard, daughter of Henry, sixth Duke of Norfolk.

[2] *The Flying Post; or, The Postmaster*, $\frac{31 \text{ July}}{2 \text{ August}}$ 1711.

James Dundas and a Mr. Horn of Westhall should represent the Faculty on the occasion. According to *The Flying Post*, Dundas, in performing this duty, took occasion to say, " I hope, and am confident, so do my constituents, that your Grace shall have very soon an opportunity to compliment the Faculty with a second medal, struck upon the Restoration of the King and Royal Family, and the finishing Rebellion, Usurping, Tyranny, and Whiggery." The records of the Faculty are absolutely silent upon the subject; and there exist no means of knowing whether the statements of *The Flying Post* are well founded; but the Dean of Faculty threatened, in the columns of the *Edinburgh Gazette*, to prosecute the editor for publishing false news; and the Faculty, at a special meeting, rejected the medal, and passed a resolution declaring their loyalty to the Queen and the Protestant Succession.

The matter would soon have been forgotten had not James Dundas and his friends composed, and sent to the printer, a pamphlet in support of their conduct in receiving the medal. This found its way into the hands of the Government; and orders were given to prosecute Dundas on a charge of sedition.

The Government was not satisfied with the conduct of the Lord Advocate, Sir David Dalrymple. He was summarily dismissed from office; and Sir James Stewart of Goodtrees, who had previously held that high position, was reappointed in his place. It is in the hands of Dalrymple, just after his dismissal, that we last hear of the medal which had caused so much trouble. " I have this famous medal," he writes on the 26th of September 1711, "and shall be glad to receive directions to whom I am to give it up." [1]

There are no letters relating to the affair of the medal in the Arniston collection. The subject was probably an unpleasant one, which the family avoided as much as possible. There appears to have been great delay in bringing on the trial. In December Lord Ilay writes to the Secretary of State the following letter : [2]—

Decemb. 26, 1711.

My Lord,—I have taken the liberty to delay the returning an answer to your Lordship's letter of the 11th, till I should hear

---

[1] State Papers, Domestic (Scotland), 1711, Public Record Office.
[2] *Ibid.* Archibald Campbell, Earl of Ilay, and afterwards Duke of Argyll.

from Scotland of what had passed in that matter. When I inform your Lordship that I have the honour to be President of the Court before which Mr Dundass is to tryed,[1] I hope your Lordship will be sensible that her Majestie has commanded me only to observe in generall to your L{p} what occurs to me upon that subject. There is an appearance of Mr Dundass having acted against the Government in a very extraordinary manner. What the law may determine upon those facts I must leave to the Court. But admitting those facts criminal, as stated in the Indictment, I humbly conceive that it is impossible for her Majestie's servants here to give her any particular advice in the farther proceeding in that matter, unless the evidence her Majestie's Advocate has to prove the allegations, be distinctly lay'd before them. And I am of opinion that if the prosecution should happen to fail for want of proof, it might be of bad consequence, & encourage other dissaffected persons in a greater degree than if the Government had not taken any notice att all of that matter. I am informed that my Lord Advocate has lately made application for a delay of the tryal upon the account of his indisposition, & in order to get some papers he thinks necesary for the carrying it on. I will not enter into the reasonableness of the delay of a tryal, upon the indisposition of the Advocate, nor whether the papers he wanted might not have been found sooner. But I think myself obliged in duty to observe that unnecessary delays in tryalls cast a great damp upon them, & very often the speedy administration of justice has more effect towards deterring persons from crimes than the very punishment it self. These are, my Lord, my humble thoughts of this matter.—I am, my Lord, with all respect, your Lordship's most ob{t} & most humble servant, ILAY.

It was not till March 1712 that James Dundas was brought to the bar of the High Court of Justiciary, at Edinburgh, when the Lord Advocate produced an order, signed by Lord Dartmouth, directing him to prosecute. The following letter describes the stage which had been reached at that date : [2]—

SIR JAMES STEWART (LORD ADVOCATE) *to* SECRETARY OF STATE.

EDNR., 11*th March* 1712.

MAY IT PLEASE Y{R} LO{R},—I had the honour of a letter from you

---

[1] Lord Ilay had succeeded the Earl of Cromarty, in 1710, as Lord Justice-General of Scotland.
[2] State Papers, Domestic (Scotland), 1712, Public Record Office.

of the 27th Decemr last, wherin you aquainted me that what I had writ concerning the process raised against Mr Arnistoun for his contending to have a medal of the pretender received by the Faculty of our Advocats, and for his causing print a scandalous pamphlet called the *Advocats' Loyalty*, had been laid before the Queen, and that Her Majesty had been pleased upon the reasons I offered to order me to put off the tryal for some tyme, as I had proposed. In obedience to which letter I did put off that tryal fairly enough untill Arnistoun proved so obstinat as to take out a writ against me in the form of our Court requiring me to insist within sixty days, or otherways the process to fall. Wherupon, I being unwilling to give him the advantage of letting the process fall, did, by advice, chuse rather to insist and discuss the relevancy by an Interloqutor of Court, and then to adjourn the probation. And thus we have this day discussed the relevancy, and I herewith send to yr Lop both my information against Arnistoun, and Arnistoun's information in defence, with the Interloqutor ot Court past upon the Debate; and the Court as to the probation is adjourned to the 8th day of Aprile next, the longest time allowed by our Act of Parliament. But, my Lord, here is my strait, that my most matereal witnesses as to the pamphlet are George Lockhart of Carnwath, and Sir David Dalrymple, both Members of Parliament, against whom the Court could give no diligence. And thus my probation as to the pamphlet must fail, and even as to the medal it may be uncertain, because the lawyers whom I have cited as witnesses are now almost all gone to the country, it being vacation with us untill the moneth of June. It's true tho I should be necessitat to desert the process at the day appointed, yet the Act of Parliament allows me to recommence it upon forty days farder. But still I am unwilling to give Arnistoun that advantage, lest he and others should abuse it; and, therfore, I must humbly entreat yr Lop' for direction in this matter. For if I shall be obliged to insist in my proof at the day, I do truly fear it shall fail me, which would be a matter of too much insulting. And if I forbear at the day, yet the process will fall, which will also be of ill consequence, tho I may recommence it. And, therfore, I must farder adventure with all submission to offer my own opinion, which is that if at the day I shall find that my proofs and witnesses cannot be had for sufficient evidence, I would inclin to let the process rather fall than that the defendant should be dismissed. But for the honour and interest of the Government I would let it fall, with a protest that I may recommence it so soon as I may have my witnesses, specially these two Members of Parliament, that are indeed necessary witnesses.

My Lord, I have endeavoured to represent the casse as plainly as the termes of our law allow, and I hope y^r Lo^p will perceive my most sincere desire to aquit my selfe in this matter as I ought, and will therfore let me have the orders necessary. It is, indeed, some releif that this bussiness, I hope, which at first made so much noise, is now so far spent that Her Ma^{ts} Governm^t will be the less concerned, whatever be the issue.

My Lord, I wrote to y^r Lo^p on the first ins^t of poor Robert Fleeming's casse, under sentence of death for forgery, but several tymes reprived, and at present to the 21st of this moneth, that it might be considered, for he must die at the day if there be no remedy.—I am, my Lord, your Lop^s most humble and most faithfull servit^r.   JA. STEWART.

After this the proceedings collapsed; and this unfortunate episode was terminated by the abandonment of the prosecution.

Escaped from the dangers of a State trial, James Dundas married, in the following year, Mary, eldest daughter of Sir Alexander Hope of Kerse, but predeceased his father without issue. The common belief in Midlothian was that, to punish his disloyalty, James Dundas had been confined in a strong room at Arniston until his death!

The reader may recollect the Twelfth Chapter of *The Heart of Midlothian*, in which Davie Deans states his objections to the advocates whom Saddletrees proposes to retain for the defence of Effie: "'Weel, Arniston?—there's a clever chield for ye!' said Bartoline, triumphantly. 'Ay, to bring Popish medals in till their very library, from that schismatic woman in the north, the Duchess of Gordon.'" It is most unlikely however, that any such words would have been used by an Edinburgh citizen, in real life, for the "Arniston" of the time at which Deans is supposed to speak was Robert, James Dundas's brother, then just about to become a judge.

From this time until his death, in 1726, the life of Lord Arniston was uneventful. He had married, early in life, Margaret, daughter of Sir Robert Sinclair of Stevenson; and of this marriage James Dundas was the eldest son. After his death, the hopes of Lord Arniston were centred in his second son, Robert, who quickly rose to a high position at the bar. As his own health began to fail, the old judge had the satisfaction of seeing his son receiving promotion with extraordinary rapidity.

In 1717, only eight years after he was called to the bar, he became Solicitor-General, and in 1720 he was appointed Lord Advocate. In the following year he attained the high position of Dean of Faculty.

These successes doubtless cheered Lord Arniston; but in the latter years of his life he suffered severely from gout, which attacked him both in hands and feet. He was anxious to be relieved from the toils of office, and in March 28, 1721, writes to his son, the Lord Advocate:—

"I am now become very old, and the infirmities which age brings along with it will daily be coming upon me, which should make me more desirous of a quiet retreat, than to continue under the fatigue of a toilsome employment; neither is it, in my opinion, very advisable that a man should expose to public observation other failings which frequently, if not always, are more easily perceived by others than by the person himself."

In the autumn of the following year, he was so ill that, "although the accounts from Arniston do not threaten his immediate death," it was felt that, "considering his Lordship's age, 'tis not to be expected he shall recover to that state of firm health and strength as to attend the Session-house."[1]

This prediction came true; and his Lordship's health gradually failed until his death, which took place on the 25th of November 1726.

---

[1] Justice-Clerk Fletcher (Lord Milton), 18th Oct. 1722.

CHAPTER VI.

THE FIRST PRESIDENT DUNDAS.

Hitherto the heads of the Arniston family had been country gentlemen or lawyers rather than politicians; but in this chapter we enter upon a period, extending onwards until about the year 1830, during which there was always some member of the family occupying a high position in the service of the Crown. It is no exaggeration to say that during most of that period, the influence of the Dundases was supreme in Scotland, and that to describe, in full detail, the various transactions in which they took the leading part would be to write the history of Scotland during the greater part of the eighteenth century. The letters and other papers preserved in the charter-room of Arniston are of great historical interest, and give valuable information regarding the political movements of the times in which they were written. From these documents a large selection has been made, which, it is hoped, may not only throw light on an important epoch of Scottish history, but also serve to illustrate the private life and social customs of those days.

Robert Dundas, second son of the second Lord Arniston and Margaret, daughter of Sir Robert Sinclair of Stevenson, was born on the 9th of December 1685; and having, like other members of his family, been educated for the bar, he was admitted advocate on the 26th of July 1709. He rose rapidly to a high position. "His appearance," says Dr. Carlyle, "was against him, for he was ill-looking, with a large nose and small ferret eyes, round shoulders, a harsh croaking voice, and altogether unprepossessing; yet by the time he had uttered three sentences, he raised attention, and went on with a torrent of good sense and clear reasoning, that made one

1st President Dundas.

totally forget the first impression." Nor were his habits conducive to hard work or attention to business. According to a contemporary writer, "he was naturally averse to study and application, and (except when employed in the practice of his profession) consumed his time in convivial meetings, and the company of his friends and acquaintance." It is of him that Sir Walter Scott tells the well-known drinking story, in the notes to *Guy Mannering*; and there can be little doubt that, at a time when the convivial habits of the Scottish bar were notorious, Robert Dundas was celebrated as a *bon vivant*. Nevertheless, so great were his talents, and such was the influence of his family, that he was soon engaged in a large, and, for those days, lucrative practice. In the autumn of 1712 he espoused Elizabeth, eldest daughter of the deceased Robert Watson of Muirhouse. By the marriage-contract, which is dated 14th October 1712, Lord Arniston gave his son a portion of 15,000 merks; and the bride had a fortune of 18,000.

It need scarcely be said, in spite of the extraordinary conduct of James Dundas with regard to the Jacobite medal, that the house of Arniston stood firm to the Whig cause during the eventful year 1715; and two years later, on the dismissal of Sir James Stewart,[1] Dundas was appointed Solicitor-General. He had been only eight years at the bar when this important office was conferred upon him.

Duke of Roxburghe[2] to Mr. Dundas.

Whitehall, *June* 14, 1717.

Sir,—The King having been pleased to dismiss Sir James Stewart from his service as Solicitor in Scotland, I have, by his Majesty's order, prepared a warrant for your being Solicitor there in his stead, which was this day signed, and forwarded to Mr. Pringle. You will give me leave to wish you joy on this occasion, which I do with a great deal of pleasure, both on your own account, and your father's, for whom I must always have the greatest value.—I am, Sir, your most humble servant,

Roxburghe.

---

[1] Sir James Stewart was the son of Sir James Stewart of Goodtrees, Lord Advocate during the reigns of William III. and Queen Anne.

[2] Secretary of State for Scotland.

The unsettled state of the country, still throbbing with the dangerous passions which civil wars raise and leave behind them, placed a heavy burden on the shoulders of the law officers of the Crown; and the position of the Solicitor-General was, at this time, rendered more than usually difficult by the conduct of the Lord Advocate. Sir David Dalrymple, youngest son of the first Lord Stair, had been appointed Lord Advocate in 1709. He had been dismissed from office during the episode of the Jacobite medal, when the Government considered his conduct suspicious, but had been re-appointed in 1714. He served the Whigs with fidelity during the crisis of the rebellion; but as soon as civil proceedings took the place of military movements, his conduct began to displease the Government. He presented to the Secretaries of State a "Memorial concerning the prisoners on account of the late rebellion," which, in the opinion of Lord Townshend, meant that every rebel in Scotland was to escape. He declined to act in accordance with the wishes of the Duke of Roxburghe, the Secretary for Scotland. He opposed the passing of the Act by which the Treason Law of Scotland was assimilated to that of England. He did all in his power to obstruct the Commission of Oyer and Terminer, which was sent down to Scotland to try the rebel prisoners. The Forfeited Estates Bill he spoke of as "that damned bill of sale," and resisted by all the means in his power.

It requires great tact to occupy a subordinate place in a Government, under a chief who is distrusted by the prominent members of the administration; and although Solicitor-General Dundas had abundance of tact, he found his position so difficult that, in 1718, a year after his appointment, he applied for a seat on the bench, which had been rendered vacant by the death of Sir Gilbert Elliot of Minto. The Duke of Roxburghe replied that the vacant judgeship was to be given to Sir Walter Pringle of Newhall, but added, "I must say that I shall be very sorry, for my own sake, that you should wish to be settled upon that bench while I have the honour to be in this office, but at the same time hope you will not doubt of my good offices whenever a proper occasion happens, if you should then desire it; and am confident you need be afraid of no competition in that case."

These words were not mere flattery ; for the letters which passed between the Duke of Roxburghe and Dundas prove that, on most important questions, the opinion of Dundas was taken in preference to that of Lord Advocate Dalrymple.

In 1719 a proposal was before Parliament for abolishing the system of electing the sixteen representative peers ; and on this subject the following letter was written by the Duke of Roxburghe to Dundas :—

DUKE OF ROXBURGHE *to* SOLICITOR-GENERAL DUNDAS.

LONDON, *March* 14, 1718/19.

SIR,—I had yours of the 10th last night by a flying packet, and am sorry to find the proceedings of the House of Lords occasion such an outcry in Scotland. I never indeed doubted but the Jacobites there would at all times be against the taking away the election of the Peers, for I know that they have always reckoned the breaking the Union the likeliest way for them to encompass their designs, and, in one word, to set the Pretender upon the throne. It is likewise very certain that they have always looked upon the continuing the election of peers as the likeliest and surest means to bring about the breaking of the Union, both from the load that it is upon the Constitution and the opportunity it gives to the Peers to meet and consult together at an election ; for nobody, I believe, will deny that the scheme of the late rebellion in Scotland was laid at the last election there. So that it is very clear why the Jacobites should be fond of the election, though I am satisfyed, all that have sense among them must look upon it (taking it abstractly from Jacobitism) as a mean and dishonourable thing.

It is very true that when the Union was made, the election of the Peers was agreed to by both Parliaments. But it was never then imagined (let be mentioned) that no Peer of Scotland after the Union could be made an Hereditary Peer of Parliament ; but, however unjust that resolve may be, as I am sure I have always thought it, yet no one, I believe, thinks it will ever be taken off, so long as the election subsists. So that all that is now to be considered is our present disgraceful condition and how to mend it.

In the first place, there is not a subject of Great Britain, nay, the very meanest of the Kingdom, that is not capable of being made an Hereditary Peer of Parliament, except the Peers of

Scotland alone; and should any Peer of Scotland do the most signal and greatest service to the King and Kingdom, yet still he is incapable of receiving this honour, and for ever must remain so, while this election continues; and as for any advantage the Peers of Scotland have by the election, I know of none that the poorest among us would not be ashamed to own; and this I take to be our condition as it stands at present.

By the Bill that is now brought in, the Constitution is to be free from the dead weight of an election of Peers, and the Peers of Scotland (nay, Scotland itself) from the shame and ignoring of it, which last, in my poor opinion, is more than equivalent for the election itself.

But besides the being rid of the election, the Bill proposes that there should be five and twenty Peers of Scotland to sit Hereditarily in Parliament, the number of the Peers of England being at the same to be ascertained and fixed.

The Patents of the five and twenty Peers, who are to be named by the King, are to be restricted to the heirs-male. So that where those honours descend to the heirs-female, another Peer of Scotland is to be called up in the room of that female whose Scotch Peerage still continues, and will be capable of being called up to the House of Lords again, whenever there is a male in that family and a vacancy in the five and twenty. Now, considering the chance of families extinguishing, the chance of families merging in one another, and the chance of those titles descending to the females, I would gladly ask, whether the Peers of Scotland that happen not to be of the first nomination, are not in a more honourable and better condition from those chances, than they are at present, with the election, and at the same time the incapacity of being made Hereditary Peers of Parliament.

The commoners of Scotland are to be exactly in the same condition as the commoners of England, that is, capable of being called to the House of Lords in the room of English families that shall happen to extinguish, which, by a very just calculation, may be reckoned to be three or four in two years' time, which no wise man, I believe, will think too few, either for the Crown or for the commoners, unless one would wish to see the House of Commons made up of men, neither of worth nor consideration.

I must further add that, besides the three chances above mentioned, to the Peers of Scotland, if their eldest sons should be called up in the place of an English family extinct, it is impossible that it can be quarrelled if this passes, whereas if the election continues, it is not unlikely that the Earl of Kinnoull's patent may signify as little to him as the Duke of Dover's will to the Duke of Queensberry, though his father sat two years in the House as Duke of Dover; and this, I do assure you, has already been said very openly by some of as great consideration as any in the House of Lords.

I am sorry to have given you so much trouble, but the paragraph in yours on this subject made it impossible for me not to give you my poor reasons for the part I am, God willing, resolved to act in this great affair, which, if it passes, is entirely owing to the goodness of the King, and is what few of his predecessors would ever have agreed to; but as he has no design against the liberty of his people himself, so I am confident he wishes that none that may hereafter succeed to him should ever have it in their power to destroy it.

I shall only add one thing more, which is, that if this business is not done now, we are sure the Tories, whenever there happens to be a Tory administration, will not again risk its being to be done by the Whigs, and what the consequences of its being done by the Tories may be, I leave it to you to judge.—I am, Sir, your faithful humble servant,

ROXBURGHE.

No change was, however, made in the mode of electing the Scottish representative peers, and the system of sending down to Scotland a list of peers drawn up by the Government of the day, and known as the "King's List," continued for many years to come, causing endless dissatisfaction, and, on one occasion at least, raising a constitutional difficulty of the very gravest character.

In 1720, Mr. Dundas had been ill in London; and his father writes to him on the 10th of May :—

"I always thought the way of living there would be destructive to your health; therefore I heartily wish you would not come under any engagement to them (the Ministry) again upon any account whatever."

Respecting his proposed elevation to the office of Lord Advocate, which was now close at hand, his father writes :—

"There is talk of your being advanced to a post, however

lucrative, yet, I think, very little desirable in so disturbed a state of affairs. I wish heartily the King may be well and faithfully served. I am convinced all our safety, and particularly the security of the protestant religion, under God, depends upon his affairs being in a prosperous condition."

In May 1720, Sir David Dalrymple retired from the office of Lord Advocate, and became an Auditor of Exchequer. Dundas was at once appointed his successor. His father, Lord Arniston, however, continued for some time to dissuade him from a Parliamentary career, and to urge that the irregularities of London life might be prejudicial to his health.

Parliament met in the autumn of 1720, soon after the King's return from Hanover, towards the close of November; and early attendance having been urged by the Government, Mr. Dundas, though not yet a member of Parliament, went up about the beginning of December, accompanied by Mrs. Dundas. They seem to have had a bad journey. Her mother-in-law[1] writes to Mrs. Dundas :—

"I am very glad that you gott safe to y^r journy's end after such bad way and great watters. You have given great proof of y^r being an good wife in leaving such an great small family. I wish heartily my Son may have as much advantage as y^r family has disadvantage by the want of you. Lord preserve the poor young crettures from all evel."

The letter continues :—

" Robie[2] is hearty when I saw him, but I am very anxious to have this winter over his head, considering how bad he was last winter. I do not hear but the young ones is weell. I cannot get out to see them, my state of health is not now for going out. Arniston is not weell, he has the gout. . . . The concern about him did cast me in vapours. Tuesday and all yesterday I was sunke in my spirits. I realy do think that this winter will prove an seveir one for us both. . . . I am just going up to see littel Robine Dundas, he was by the docter's orders seeing an raice at Leith yesterday. He has a cold, but the docter is careful about him,

---

[1] Margaret, daughter of Sir Robert Sinclair of Stevenson, wife of second Lord Arniston.

[2] Mr. Dundas's eldest son, afterwards the second President Dundas.

and the docter hopes to get it off. Lordy[1] is to be sent out of town becaus of Robine's cough, but it is ordinary for all to take the cough on their coming to town. . . . This is all at present from her who is y^r afeetinet Mother-in-law,

MARGARET SINCLAIR.

Before his appointment as Lord Advocate, Mr. Dundas had been Assessor to the City of Edinburgh. In 1721, however, he found it necessary to resign this office, when the following correspondence, in which there is some plain speaking on both sides, passed between him and the city authorities:—

LORD ADVOCATE DUNDAS to BAILIE WIGHTMAN.

SIR,—I give you the trouble of this in absence of the Lord Provost, that you may be pleased to let the Town Council know, that I return my humble thanks for the mark of favour they were pleased to give me some few years ago, in electing me to be one of their assessors. But there are several reasons too obvious, I need not repeat them, why I judge it would be improper for me to carry this name any longer. This much I may be pardoned to notice that for some time after I was chosen assessor, I think until I had the honour to be called to the King's service, the Magistrates of Edinburgh did seem to put some confidence in me. But since that time they thought fit to carry quite in another way, for wh. I find no reason, if it be not one, that there must be some inconsistance between a faithfull discharge of my duty to the King, & being an assessor in the present management of the Magistrates of Edinburgh.—I am, Sir, y. most humble servant,

RO. DUNDAS.

EDINR., *July* 11, 1721.

BAILIE WIGHTMAN to LORD ADVOCATE DUNDAS.

MY LORD,—I communicated to the Council your Lop. letter to me of the 11 July, whereby you resigned the office of assessor. We forbore giving a return to it till we took my Lord Provost's & D. Gild's sentiments in so uncommon, yea, we believe, so unprecedented a matter. They having given their opinions, I am now

---

[1] Lord Bargany, son of the third Lord Bargany and Margaret, daughter of Lord Arniston.

authorized and directed to answer. The letter is written in so disrespectful terms, & injurious to us, & so little becoming the dignity and gravity of the office which His Majesty's great goodness has raised you to, that we wonder that a letter should have flowed from y^r pen so virulent, that if any other person had been the author of it, we should have called for y^r assistance in punishing them. When the Town Council made choice of you a few years ago to be one of their assessors, it was a mark of their favour, & a name, y^r Lo. thought then, both honourable and useful to you, and, therefore, ought not to be resigned in such a manner. But seeing now you have laid it aside, we take the opportunity to tell you we can so easily have the place supplied, that we are at no uneasiness at your quitting of it; but will make choice of one who, we doubt not, will be to y^r Lo's. approbation; a person who will give his advice to the Council when it is asked, and never attempt to disturb the Government of it; one who will faithfully discharge his duty to the King, & never presume to make use of His Majesty's name, to carry on his own private views, and support his ambition. The Magistrates and Town Council of Edinburgh have given such signal proofs of their affection to his Majesty since his happy accession to the throne, and did before the Union so zealously espouse the Protestant Succession when its opposers were under no disguise, that they are above the unjust reflections and impudent malice of their enemies. They have often, for their zeal for the interest of his Majesty now on the throne, and consequently for the good of their country, born with equal contempt the calumnies of the factions, and the injuries of the opposers of His Majesty's succession. We, the present Magistrates and Town Council, are resolved to continue stedfast in our duty to our King, and to our country, what ever advantage our conduct in that respect may yield to persons who may think of purchasing credit to themselves by destroying the reputation of their fellow-subjects. My Lord, we know the rules of good manners and duty so well, that so long as H. Majesty thinks fit to employ you in his service, we shall always take care to pay you that respect due to y^r office, and so long as we continue in our office we claim the same from you.—I am, signed in name & in presence of the Town Council, my Lord, y^r Lop's. most humble servant. To. WIGHTMAN.

EDINR., 2 *August* 1721.

With this interchange of compliments the correspondence

dropped. It was renewed on the part of the magistrates in the following way:—

EDINBR., 13 *Febry.* 172⅔.

MY DEAR LORD,—I think on Hansel Munday last we drowned all our quarrels, either political or personal, in a great quantity of very good liquor. I thenceforward forgot we ever had any. I'm sure I never will revive them, and will live with you on the foot we parted.

I that night told you I had nothing to ask for the town in which I did not believe you would join with us; of this nature is what I am now to mention.

The letter then reminds Mr. Dundas that £14,000, to be applied under the Treaty of Union for encouraging the manufacture of coarse wool in Scotland, had since the Union lain useless to the public, and proposes that it should be lent to the town of Edinburgh until required, at 2, 2½, or 3 per cent. interest, which would be "of considerable use to this poor place."

In the spring of 1722, Lord Advocate Dundas presented himself as a candidate for the representation of Midlothian. Lockhart of Carnwath declared that he himself could have defeated Dundas, but refrained from opposing him, because he had arranged, when the Commission under the Forfeited Estates Act was sitting, that, if the Lord Advocate saved the estates of certain Jacobites from forfeiture, he should be returned unopposed for Midlothian. In consequence of this curious bargain, which shows the free and easy manner in which elections could be managed at a time when the franchise was possessed by a mere handful of freeholders, the Lord Advocate was elected without opposition.

Considering the fatigue and trouble of the journey to London at that time, it is not surprising that the Scottish members were not over zealous in their attendance in the House of Commons, involving as it did a winter's ride of 400 or 500 miles. In perusing the official correspondence of those days, the reader constantly stumbles upon letters, almost pathetic in their tone, in which the Secretary of State implores the members from Scotland to come up and support him. In the Arniston collection there are many such letters. The Duke of Roxburghe, writing on the 5th of December 1723, says, "I am very sensible of your goodness in resolving to determine yourself as to your journey hither upon your friends' advice, and I must say your way of expressing it is by no means amiss. There is nothing in all my life I have more strictly taken care of than not to be rash in desiring my friends to come hither." In the following year, Sir Robert Walpole, writing at a time when the Lord Advocate's father, Lord Arniston, was supposed to be dying, says, "I cannot press your coming immediately to town, when you intimate it may be so improper for your private affairs. . . . I hope the generality of your members will be early here, and that we shall have your company as soon as you can without great inconvenience to yourself."

The year 1725 was rendered eventful in Scotland by the Malt Tax Riots. This tax had been extended to Scotland in 1713, in the face of a very strenuous opposition by the Scottish members; but payment had been evaded from time to time. In 1724, a motion was carried in Parliament that, instead of the Malt Tax, an additional duty of sixpence on every barrel of beer should be payable in Scotland; but this was opposed as furiously as the Malt Tax itself had been. It was finally determined that in Scotland a Malt Tax of threepence a bushel should be imposed; and the 23d of June was appointed as the day on which the duty was to be levied.

During the struggle against the Malt Tax, Dundas, though Lord Advocate, had joined the malcontent Scottish members, and at one of the meetings wrote, with his own hand, a resolution hostile to the Government measure. For this act of insubordination he was dismissed from office in May 1725.

The Duke of Roxburghe, the Secretary of State for Scotland at that time, had encouraged the opposition to the Malt Tax by means which, though less open and tangible than those employed by Dundas, were no less a source of embarrassment to Walpole. Nevertheless he still retained office, and was in correspondence with Dundas, who, at the end of May, informed him that his father, Lord Arniston, was anxious to resign his seat on the bench, and that he himself was ready to retire from the House of Commons, leave the bar, and succeed his father in the judgeship.

DUKE OF ROXBURGHE *to* MR. DUNDAS.

H. P.,[1] *June* 4, 1725.

. . . I had both yours of the 31st past this evening, and shall show one of them to the Chancellour of the Exchequer, as soon as I have an opportunity of seeing him, and shall make deliver your letter to him to-morrow. For since you yourself resolves to retire, it dos not become me at this time of day to endeavour to stop it. And all mankind, I believe, will think he acts very foolishly, if he does not, with joy, jump at your proposall, for few are so great but that they may be humbled, and the greater a man is the less dos he like to be opposed or tousled in Parliament. Your letter, I think, is as well as possible, both modest and manly ; but there are many that wish you well here, that, for their own sakes, will be sorry not to see you at London next session of Parliament.

As soon as I have seen Sir R. W.,[2] which, I suppose, will be at the Cockpit, you shall hear from me again ; but I have not called at his door these three months, nor yet at my Lord Townshend's, nay, not so much as to wish his Lord^p a good voyage. And yet I am not turned out, but am satisfied that they concluded that I would lay down, upon the changes that have just now been made in Scotland. But I have seen so many changes, and have outlived so many ministrys, that I am resolved not to give them that satisfaction this time, however uneasy and disagreeable the situation I am in may be to myself.

. . . I am extremely sorry that I cannot have the pleasure of reading your letters, that I received to-day, to the King, but yet I hope that a good use may be made of them. In the meantime I cannot help thinking that you have laid a load upon me in leaving it to me to destroy the letter inclosed or not, as I pleased, for though I can easily give up my own interest and resentment to your ease and satisfaction, yet many of our friends, I am sure, will be heartily vext at it, and blame me for it.

The hurry and uneasiness I was in when I wrote to you last made me forget to tell you that the only reason that was ever given to me for your being dismissed, was the part you had acted against Sir R. Walpole's scheme proposed in lieu of the Malt Tax, particularly your writing the proposall or resolution, at the meeting of the Scots members, with your own hand, but the easier the

---

[1] Henly Park.   [2] Walpole.

Malt Tax goes on, the more absurd will that scheme appear to have been. . . .—I am ever yours. Adieu.

In the meantime Dundas returned to the bar as an ordinary counsel, Duncan Forbes of Culloden having succeeded him as Lord Advocate.

DUKE OF ROXBURGHE *to* MR. DUNDAS.

WHITEHALL, *June* 10, 1725.

. . . I am very glad to know you are gone to the bar again, for I find that all your friends that understand that matter wish't you might do so.

I had yours of the 1st on Monday last, with y^r father's dimission inclosed, but have not spoke of it to any body, but the Marquiss of Tweeddale, who seems to doubt that it will be accepted of; concluding that my Ld Isla can never consent to it upon the account of his friends upon the bench. And I think he reasons well, but still I think I guess't right in what I said to you in my last. For in all probability Sir R. Walpole will consider himself in the first place; and as a token thereof, I must tell you what past between him and me yesterday upon the Lord Justice's meeting breaking up. I had disputed with myself a good while whether to mention your name to him or not, but perceiving that he did not seem inclined to speak to me, I at last went up to him, and told him that I had had a letter from you, wherein you very modestly represented that you were the first Advocate for Scotland that had been laid aside since the Revolution, that had been dismiss't the service without any gratification or compensation. But I said not a word of your father's dimission, nor, indeed, had I time if I had intended it, for he immediately told me, with a very cheerful countenance, that he had had a letter from you, and that he thought your proposal most just and reasonable. I said I was glad to find you was grown so old. Who? the father? said he; No, the son, said I, because he thinks of retiring so soon. Why, reply'd he again, I think what he proposeth is most reasonable, and I will be sure to write by the next post about it. I answered, I am sure I shall never be against it. And I perceived he had a great mind I should have said more, but I made my bow, and so left him to guess whether I was really for it or against it ; which, I believe, with all his penetration, he dos not yet know. And I must own to you that tho' your being upon the bench is most desirable, yet to me it is still a question whether you may not be more wanted in Parliament. However, that is over now, and I doubt not but that you will be upon the bench before the session riseth. . . But what I chiefly want to know is whom you think to set up in your shire in case you are upon the bench yourself; for, believe me, a mute will be of little use to us, nor do I know of any one that will be proper; but a lawyer of spirit and parts in my humble opinion wou'd do best.—I am ever yours.

Sir Robert Walpole to Mr. Dundas.

June 19, 1725.

Sir,—I ask your pardon for not sooner acknowledging ye favour of yours, which ye great hurry of business has been the only reason of, and must plead my excuse. The favour you have asked the King, I think so very reasonable, both in regard to y^{r}self & y^r father, that you shall have my best assistance to render it effectual. I am sorry there was a necessity for doing any thing that was disagreeable to you, and I shall, with a great deal more pleasure, take any opportunity to render you service, for I am, S^r, y^r most humble serv^t, R. Walpole.

Nothing came of the proposed changes. Lord Arniston retained his seat on the bench until his death in the following year, and his son continued to practise at the bar.

When the 23d of June came, the day appointed for the collection of the Malt Tax, there was a serious riot in Glasgow. The Provost and some of the magistrates were arraigned before the High Court of Justiciary, where they were defended by Dundas. They were admitted to bail; but no further steps were taken against them.

In Edinburgh the brewers, for the purpose of harassing the Government, combined to stop brewing until the duty on malt was abolished. Dundas was their chief adviser, and the advice he gave them was to set the law at defiance. The resistance to the Malt Tax continued till the Government took the strong step of advising the King to deprive the Duke of Roxburghe of the seals of office, and, at the same time, to abolish the Scottish Secretaryship. The moment this was done the opposition collapsed.

Mr. Dundas succeeded to the family estate on the death

of his father in 1726. He entered at once with characteristic energy upon the schemes of improvement projected during Lord Arniston's life. Though head of the bar, and leader of the Scottish Opposition in Parliament, he still found time for his country improvements at home, and, during the busiest period of his public life, built the modern house of Arniston, and laid out around it the long avenues stretching across what was then little better than open moor.

The Society of Improvers in Agriculture were at that time commencing their labours, pioneers in the march now so eagerly followed. They pointed out the necessity for relieving the land from the scourging routine of successive corn crops, and the advantages of a fallow as part of the rotation. They also showed the profit to be derived from draining, enclosing, summer fallowing, and from the culture of rape, turnip, cabbage, potatoes, and clover, as part of the rotation of the farm.

The manufacture of linen and wool still continued to be a large part of the work of a farm household, and shared the Society's attention with out-of-doors husbandry. Lord Stair, one of the most active of the improvers, established a manufacture of fine linen, made from flax raised upon his farm, and dressed at his Lordship's mill. Well-wishers to their country were urged to encourage Scottish manufactures by giving a preference to home-spun stuffs; and agriculture was to be encouraged by a similar preference being shown for ale and spirits made from Scottish barley.

Lord Belhaven, the supposed author of the *Countryman's Rudiments*, describing the condition of East Lothian, says, "Sown grass is, I know, a very great rarity among husbandmen, neither can they well have it as at present their farms are ordered." He recommended the "setting aside a piece of moist ground for pasture, and enclosing it with a dry-stone dyke made of the stones gathered off the land—the advantages would be the saving the wages of a horse herd; the horses may be left out at night in summer, and more labour will be got from the servants, whose time is now taken up with gathering thistles and other garbage for the horses to feed upon in the stables, and the great trampling and pulling up of your corn will be prevented." "As for your labouring oxen," he continues, "they require to be well fed in some moist pasture;

Dornden from the North.

though the grass be coarse it matters not, provided it be long, and enough of it to fill their bellies."

From want of winter food, sheep and cattle suffered severely during protracted storms, not recovering their condition till late in the succeeding summer. In one of his letters, written in the month of May from Castle Leod, President Dundas says, " After the starvation of the winter, I can get no cattle fit for the journey south."

It became about this time a stipulation in leases that tenants were to herd their cattle and sheep in winter as well as in summer, and to house them at night in place of allowing them to range over the country as formerly.

As may be supposed from the above, enclosures were few and far between, though from this time they began to be rapidly extended. The plan of the woods and pleasure grounds which were to be formed around the new mansion at Arniston included also a systematic design for the enclosure of the adjoining land. The home farm was to be sub-divided into rectangular fields of from twelve to sixteen acres each, separated by grass rides twenty feet wide, bordered on both sides by a margin of like width, planted with rows of trees; each field being thus surrounded by a belt of avenue sixty feet wide. This scheme was not carried out, and the enclosures were made with hedge and ditch in the ordinary way.

Plantations, as well for the supply of timber as for shelter, were being made throughout the country. The larch, introduced about the year 1725, was becoming one of the standard forest trees. A few were planted in the Wilderness, and as it is not often that the nurseryman's bill for what is now large timber has been preserved, the account is here subjoined:—

DUNDAS OF ARNISTON, *one of the Senators of the College of Justice.*

To Robert M'Lellan.

Feb. 6, 1738.

	£	s.	d.
To 2 large Larch trees, 4 and 5 feet high,	—	5	0
To 12 smaller Larch trees,	—	12	0

The sub-soil on which these trees have grown is a coarse gravel, at an altitude of 500 feet above the sea. One of them, at 3½ feet above the ground, has a girth of 11½ feet, and contains upwards of two hundred cubic feet of timber. The other is nearly as large.

The following account of improvements in the house and pleasure grounds at Arniston, begun at this time, is taken from the MS. of the Chief Baron Dundas:—

"Immediately after his father's death in 1724,[1] Mr. Dundas, then Dean of the Faculty of Advocates, commenced the extensive improvements he executed. The house he had already begun, and he completed the centre and the third part of the present house to the east, together with the two pavilions, the colonnades, and a small part of the stable next the cow-house, and the

---

[1] 1726.

blacksmith's shop, three years ago converted by me into a coach-house. He also took down the partition which had hitherto divided the oak-room into two rooms, and made the whole his

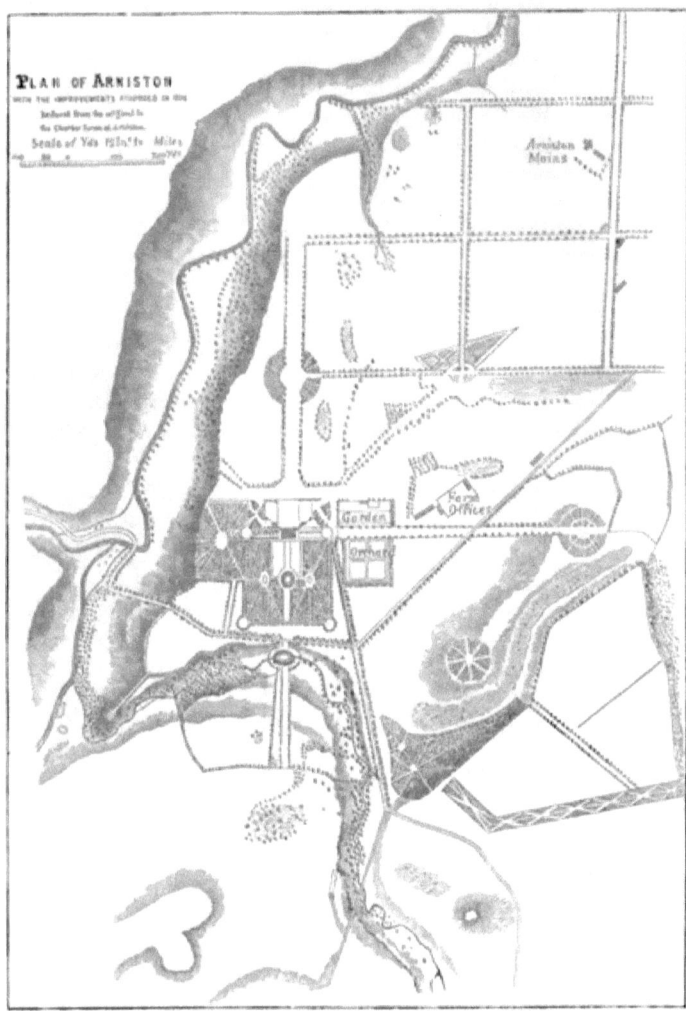

dining-room, and added to it the glass doors, where now the portico stands.

"Also at a very great expense he formed the cascade in the

Gardener's Park, which was let off when he and his guests sat down to dinner, and continued to run for about an hour. The aqueduct, which filled the reservoir pond at the top of the bank, was brought off by a dam immediately beneath the junction of the Deanhead and Castleton burns, the remains of which are visible in the wood to this day. I just recollect, and that is all, the taking down of this cascade, sometime, I think, about the 1764, when the present garden was made by my father. The steps and stages of the cascade, resembling that at Chatsworth, were of stone, and the appearance of the white water, tumbling down from one to the other, is still fresh in my recollection. The water fell into the pond which is now in the middle of the garden, and thence by a sluice into its natural channel near the Grotto."[1]

These works seem to have been proceeded with very slowly, part of the buildings remaining unfinished at the time of Mr. Dundas's death. The beautiful plaster-work in the hall and library is an instance of this.[2] It seems to have been the work of one man, Joseph Enzer, probably a German, who was engaged first for three years, and subsequently for a second period of the same duration, his employer binding himself to pay the said Joseph Enzer yearly the sums contained in the contract, and "entertaining him with bed and board in his said house, or any other place where he should employ him."

The out-of-doors work advanced more rapidly, and within a very few years woods and pleasure grounds round the new mansion had been completed.

The reduced copy of the plan of 1726 shows what was contemplated, and illustrates the Scottish landscape gardening of the day. In addition to the garden and orchard, the plan comprised what was called a wilderness or shrubbery, intersected in all directions by alleys bordered by yew hedges. Carlyle, in his Autobiography,[3] describes a similar garden at Drumore,

---

[1] The plan given on p. 45 shows the woods and grounds at Arniston in 1690. That on p. 75 shows the improvements proposed in 1726, and that on p. 77 shows what had been done by 1753, the date of Mr. Dundas's death. Naturally, during the period of nearly thirty years which elapsed between the commencement of Mr. Dundas's improvements and his death, various changes in the design for the remodelling of Arniston were made. The plan on p. 75, when compared with that on p. 77, will, however, give a general idea of what was proposed and what was carried out.

[2] See woodcut, page 110.   [3] Page 7.

in East Lothian, as "full of close walks, and labyrinths, and wildernesses, which, though it did not occupy above four or five acres, cost one at least two hours to perambulate." Towards the end of the century, wildernesses had had their day; the

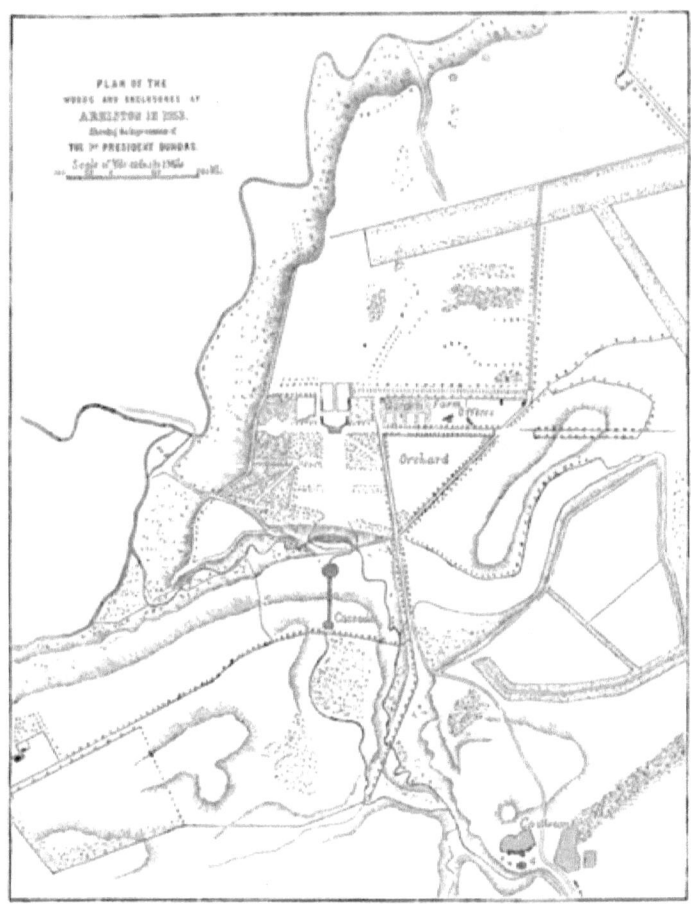

fashion changed, and people became weary of labyrinths with their endless paths and trim hedges. The wilderness at Arniston shared the fate of many others. Its hedges were grubbed up, except that here and there a yew bush or two were left, which, now grown into trees, serve to mark the lines of the original plan.

CHAPTER VII.

THE FIRST PRESIDENT DUNDAS—*continued*.

As a counsel at the bar, during the years which followed his dismissal from office, in 1725, Mr. Dundas achieved the very highest success; and his name is honourably associated, in the history of the Scottish bar, with the vindication of the rights of juries to return a general verdict on the guilt or innocence of the accused. From the time of Charles II., it had been customary in Scotland to restrict the jury to a verdict of *proven* or *not proven*, leaving it to the judges to determine the question of whether the facts, if found proven, were such as to infer the guilt of the accused. But in 1728, on the occasion of the trial of Carnegie of Finhaven, for the murder of the Earl of Strathmore, the eloquence of Dundas persuaded the jury to return a general verdict of not guilty, and the right of a jury to do so has never since been questioned in Scotland.[1]

Dundas no sooner found himself in opposition than the attractions of political life began to draw him steadily into the vortex of the Parliamentary struggle. There was soon no more eager or influential member among the representatives of Scotland. And, indeed, the times gave ample opportunity for a vigorous opposition. It was in 1733 that the star of Walpole began to sink. That year saw the introduction of those two financial measures of which it has been said, that the first was "certainly wrong, but carried by large majorities; the latter as certainly just and wise, but repelled by the overpowering force of public indignation." The first of these measures was a proposal to encroach upon the Sinking Fund, and apply half a million of money, which ought to have been

---

[1] A full report of this case will be found in the State Trials, vol. xvii. pp. 73-151.

applied to the reduction of debt, to the service of the current year. This measure, unsound in every way, was approved by Parliament and the country. The second measure was the Excise scheme, a measure which, based on sound principles and calculated to confer immense benefits on the country, had to be withdrawn in consequence of popular clamour and the opposition of the House of Commons.

Walpole did not re-introduce his Excise scheme; but he neither forgot nor forgave his opponents, public or private. One of the latter was Lord Chesterfield, who was a member of the Government, as Lord Steward of the Household, and who was dismissed from office two days after the withdrawal of the Excise scheme. Soon after this, the Duke of Montrose, the Earl of Stair, and the Earl of Marchmont, all holding offices in Scotland, were dismissed: other dismissals followed, with the inevitable result of strengthening the Opposition, whose influence was felt during the general election of 1734. The result of the election was a serious diminution in the strength of Walpole, who, however, had still a majority at his back amply sufficient to enable him to carry on the Government.

In Scotland, the opposition to Walpole was gaining strength. The dismissal of the Duke of Montrose and the Earls of Stair and Marchmont, had driven these noblemen into open opposition; and Lord Ilay, who since 1725 had managed the affairs of Scotland on behalf of the great Whig minister, now found himself confronted by the powerful opposition of an Independent Whig party. It is undoubted that the opposition to Walpole was, so far as most Scotsmen were concerned, directed not so much against the financial proposals of the minister, as against the power of his Scottish manager. Jealousy may, to some extent, have influenced the peers who led the opposition in Scotland; but they certainly persuaded themselves that the system under which Scotland was being governed was not fitted to serve the interests of the reigning family, and accordingly, in all their endeavours to subvert Lord Ilay, they were sustained by the belief that they were promoting the best interests of the country.

Mr. Dundas took an active part in leading the opposition of the Scottish representative peers and members of the House of Commons to the system of " corruption and oppression," by which, as they honestly believed, the government of Scotland was administered by the Earl of Ilay. He acted as adviser to the Scottish peers, and gave to their councils the aid of his Parliamentary experience and clear-headed talent for business. He seems to have anticipated ultimate disaster to the country as the result of the Government measures, and to have looked upon its prospects as gloomy in the extreme.[1]

Apart from his attachment to the Independent Whig party, and zeal for its cause, his opposition to the Earl of Ilay was stimulated by distrust in the loyalty of the Earl's agents.

Mr. Dundas *to his* Son (*afterwards* Second President Dundas) *at Utrecht, where he was Studying.*

MUREHOUSE, *Nov.* 3, 1733.

Son,—I was glad to know of your safe arrival at Utrecht, and hope you will take care not to make your journey as useless as most young people do. . . . I assure you the appearance of things abroad doth heartily alarm all of us who wish well to the present constitution, and have no places to take care of. God prevent our fears. Take care of your health and studies. Adieu.

Mr. Dundas *to his* Son *at Utrecht.*

Son,—I can give you very little account either of myself or of what is doing here. I have often told you that there is no such thing as writing news unless we have a mind that what we write should be read at the post-office. And, as for myself, the sum of the whole is, that I never was so harrassed with close attendance on our House of Commons to no other purpose than, far as we can, to prevent other folks doing mischief. Farewell.

Ro. Dundas.

LONDON, 21*st March* 1734.

LONDON, 2*d April* 1734.

Son,—. . . You know I never write any news for a very good reason. I must still leave you to make your judgment from what you hear, and, in general, not to believe one word but what you are well assured of. Our proceedings in Parliament will certainly

---

[1] Letter to his son, Feb. 6, 1735.

alarm every country either with joy or surprise; our last resolution surely shows more confidence, or more submission, than ever King William could obtain, or ever King Charles adventured to ask. . . . Farewell. Ro. Dundas.

Mr. Dundas to his Ward and Nephew, Lord Bargany, at Utrecht.

Edinburgh, July 6, 1734.

My Lord,—I am glad you are arrived safe at Utrecht, and hope you are in perfect health. As for divisions at the time of our Elections I had no share in them, tho' I had some of the trouble. However, our transactions make a good deal of noise, as you'll see by the public prints, and probably may make some more when the parliament sits down. Such a set of Peers I think we never had set up and forced through, in opposition to so many much greater men and the best families; acts of power too strong *et auri sacra fames.* As to the elections of our commoners, there are many more factious persons than even last parliament from the counties, and would have been more still if the returns had been fairly made, but such liberties were taken by the sheriffs and returning officers, and such barefaced things done, as power and a majority can alone screen and justify.

Mr. Dundas to his Son at Utrecht.

Feb. 6, 1735.

Son,—I have now been in London near a month, in a continual hurry, so as that resolved to write to you every post, I have slipped them from day to day. We go on much in the old way; there are a far greater number of opposers in the House of Commons than hath been seen at any time before; and, to be sure, the generality of the whole nation quite dissatisfied both with our M―――r and his measures, but, as they have a majority in the house, corruption and oppression in elections will probably increase it, and so we will be left to struggle for the sinking liberty of our country till God in his providence interpose to save us; and if he hath destined us for destruction, to be sure we must fall into it. For the other House, nothing can be expected from them; such a sixteen as we have. God pity them. . . .

"Such a sixteen as we have! God pity them!" The "sixteen" were the representative peers elected at Holyrood in the previous summer, during the general election. Those who are accustomed to witness the sleepy ceremony of electing the Scottish representative peers at the present time can hardly realise the passions which the same ceremony roused during last century. Before the dissolution it had been proposed, in the House of Lords, that the peers from Scotland should be chosen by ballot; but this proposal had been rejected. When the day of election, the 4th of June 1734, drew near, the King's list, a list of those peers whom the Ministry wished to be elected, was sent down in accordance with custom; but it was well known that trouble was brewing. A regiment of soldiers was stationed in the courtyard of Holyrood Palace, —for the purpose, the opponents of the Government said, of overawing the peers,—for the purpose, the supporters of Government said, of preventing confusion and rioting. When the voting took place the Government sixteen were chosen; and the peers separated, after a scene of angry recrimination, with their hearts inflamed with pride and jealousy.

This incident was of service to the Opposition. It has already been explained how Lord Chesterfield's dismissal from office, in consequence of his opposition to the Excise scheme, had been followed by the dismissal of the Scottish peers, Montrose, Stair, and Marchmont.[1] Chesterfield and Carteret, who, for some years, had been opposed to Walpole, even while holding offices in his Government, and who latterly had joined the Opposition openly, now approached Montrose, Stair, and Marchmont, and proposed that steps should be taken for the purpose of calling Ministers to account for what had taken place at the election of the Scottish peers.

Gradually the plans of the Opposition were laid. It would take many pages to describe the negotiations which took place; for letters on this subject are to be found in the public archives at the Record Office, among the Arniston letters, at Oxenfoord, among the correspondence of the second Earl of Stair, and in many other collections.

The chief advisers of the peers were Dundas and James Erskine of Grange, who had recently resigned his seat on the bench, on the passing of the Act which prevented Scottish

---

[1] *Supra*, p. 79.

judges being members of Parliament, and who now represented Clackmannanshire in the House of Commons. Parliament was to meet for business on the 14th of January 1735; and, two days before, on Sunday the 12th, a meeting was held at Lord Cobham's. Dundas had reached London two days previously.

MR. DUNDAS *to his* WIFE.[1]

LONDON, *Jan.* 11, 1735.

MY DEAREST DEAR ANNE,—Yesterday morning we got safe here, and considering what terrible roads we had, it is a wonder there was not one fall among us. We had fine weather all the way except Wednesday, which was one of the terriblest days ever was seen; and seems to have been much worse here than on the road, for it is amazing what mischief it hath done in this place; many houses blown down, innumerable chimneys, windows, and roofs; in short, vast destruction of all kinds, and a great many people killed; nothing hath been seen like it since the great hurricane in the year 1703.

Our parliament folks seem pretty well convened, and great talking of strong doings, but I believe our greatest battles will be about elections.

Make my compliments to my friends, and take care of my Dearest Life and Pleasure.

To the Lady Arniston, younger,
    At her house in Edinburgh.

At the meeting at Lord Cobham's there were present the Dukes of Hamilton, Queensberry, and Montrose, the Earls of Kincardine, Dundonald, Stair, and Marchmont, and Lord Elphinston; all of whom, with the exception of Lord Kincardine, represented the Scottish peers who had been rejected at the election. Lord Chesterfield and Lord Carteret were also there. Dundas and Erskine attended to advise the peers. A memorandum in the Marchmont collection describes what was done then, and at subsequent meetings.[2]

"Mr. Erskine read all the papers he had prepared upon the evidence. . . . After full reasoning upon the evidence, and when

---

[1] Anne, second wife of Mr. Dundas. She was daughter of Sir William Gordon of Invergordon, Bart. *Cf.* p. 87.
[2] Marchmont Papers, vol. ii. 57.

many objections had been made to it by Lord Carteret and Mr. Dundas, another meeting was appointed at Mr. Pulteney's. . . . Lord Polwarth was to lay the transactions in Scotland in general before the House, and to be seconded by Mr. Dundas and Mr. Erskine, and upon the being heard at the bar, Mr. Sandys was to move the impeachment (of the Earl of Ilay), and be supported by the rest.

"On Sunday, the 2d of February, there was a meeting at the Duke of Queensberry's. Present (most of the above), when the Lords reasoned long and fully upon the expediency of presenting their petition to the House of Lords, the Duke of Roxburgh and Marquis of Tweeddale reasoning against it. But, after long and full reasoning, and Mr. Dundas' delivering his opinion that it was absolutely necessary, for that the *Lords were betwixt the devil and the deep sea;* and Mr. Erskine being likewise of the same opinion, it seemed agreed to by all that the petition should be presented. . . .

"*Feb.* 8.—The Dukes Bolton, Hamilton, Queensberry, and Montrose, the Earls of Dundonald, Marchmont, and Stair, Viscount Cobham, Lords Gower and Bathurst, and Mr. Dundas, met at the Duke of Queensberry's and agreed to the draft of a petition, which is in the terms of the resolution offered in the House of Lords last session, and which, by the opinion of Mr. Dundas and those present, can be legally proved by the evidence ready to be adduced."

It was in the midst of these events that Dundas wrote to his son, "Such a sixteen as we have!"[1] The attack began by a petition, which was presented to the House of Lords by the Duke of Bedford, declaring that illegal methods had been used at the election of the peers. Inquiry was ordered, but the movement collapsed, probably because the Government was able to counteract the efforts of the Opposition to bring sufficient evidence to support the charge.

In the House of Commons, Dundas brought forward the subject of the peers' election in Committee of Supply, when a proposal was made to increase the army, by citing the use which had been made of the royal forces at Holyrood on the

---

[1] The sixteen representative peers chosen in 1734 were the Dukes of Athole and Buccleuch, the Marquis of Lothian, the Earls of Crawford, Sutherland, Morton, Loudoun, Findlater, Selkirk, Balcarres, Dunmore, Orkney, Portmore, Hopetoun, Ilay, and Lord Cathcart.

election day. But, rich as the Scottish opposition was in talent, for Dundas and Erskine of Grange were debaters of the first rank, it was impossible to make way against the majority which supported the Minister; and nothing came of that movement against Walpole.

Meantime there had been trouble at Arniston; and the following letters, relating to the losses in the family from small-pox, show in a striking manner the fearful mortality arising from that disease previous to Jenner's discovery of vaccination.

George, Lord Dalzell, and Lord Garlies' son, who are alluded to in these letters, were probably boys at the school of Dalkeith, which continued to be a well-known school down to the beginning of this century.

Mr. Dundas to his Son[1] at Utrecht.

Edinr., Nov. 13, 1733.

Son,—. . . Your brother George lies sick of the smallpox at Dalkeith, as does Lordie Dalzell. George is really bad enough, a vast load of them, and some bad symptoms, but we are not out of hopes. Poor James Stewart, Garlies' son, died of them there, on Sunday last. They are raging in all this country, and of a bad kind.

A week later, Mrs. Dundas[2] writes:—

Nov. 20, 1733.

My dear Rob.,—. . . It has pleased God to remove George by death upon Saturday last. This is no light dispensation, but we must submit to the will of God, who does everything wisely, both for his own glory and our good. I pray the Lord the loss of him may be made up in sparing and preserving both my dear Rob. and the rest. I hope you will be a comfort and blessing to your father, and so far as possible be observing of all his commands, and learn to become like him in all his qualifications.

You cannot copy after a better pattern, he has your good much at heart.—Yours, Eliz. Dundas.

---

[1] Robert, afterwards second President Dundas, then a student at the University of Utrecht.

[2] The first Mrs. Dundas, Elizabeth, daughter of Robert Watson of Muirhouse. Cf. p. 59.

MR. DUNDAS *to his* SON.

EDINR., *Dec.* 20, 1733.

SON,—I own I am in such confusion just now, that I can scarce write this letter, short as it will be. It hath pleased God to carry off your brother John, so that you are now left alone, and you have the more reason to take a proper care of yourself. I was to have gone out (to Arniston) this day, in order to have buried him to-morrow morning, but unluckily your mother, who is now six months gone with child, and hath kept her bed these several weeks, was taken so ill this morning about six o'clock, that I thought she would have expired in my arms before she got any help. Since I write this she is a little easier, and the physicians think she may yet escape even the losing of the child.—Farewell.

Ro. DUNDAS.

MR. DUNDAS *to his* SON.

Jan. 1, 1734.

SON,—The misfortunes of our family seem still to go on. Poor Susie is now in her grave, and Annie lies extremely ill with the smallpox. I came to town last evening, and have no expectation of seeing her again. Your mother hath been better and worse since I last wrote to you; these last four days she has been pretty easy, but certainly weaker . . . Her circumstances must be owned to be very ticklish. She knows nothing of Susie's death nor Annie's illness, and our design, if possible, is to conceal both their fates from her, till we see how it pleases God to dispose of herself.—Farewell.

Ro. DUNDAS.

MR. DUNDAS *to his* SON.

EDINR., *Jan.* 5, 1734.

SON,—I am glad to be able to tell you that your mother is no worse. . . . At the same time I have the misfortune to acquaint you that it hath pleased God to make another breach in our family. Yesternight Annie died, and I am just going out of town in order to bury her to-morrow.

Mrs. Dundas, however, died soon after this letter was written.

Mr. Dundas to his Son.

LONDON, *Feb.* 12, 1734.

SON,—I came to this place, Sunday was seven night, and have been as well since in my health as I could expect. I have heard from Scotland that the poor remains of our family are well. I had one from you Sunday last, the subject is too melancholy for me once to mention it; you have lost the best of mothers, and I an incomparable wife. I can write you nothing in way of news, all our letters being opened in the old way. Everybody must see the situation both we, and the country where you now are, are in with respect to public affairs. God send us a miraculous unforeseen deliverance. They say we are to have a short session of Parliament. I shall be glad of it; but I cannot entirely trust them; neither can they know. I lodge at Mr. Ross's. Take care of yourself, mind. I have no more, and farewell.

Ro. DUNDAS.

In the summer of 1734, Mr. Dundas married again, his second wife being Anne, daughter of Sir William Gordon of Invergordon. It appears from a memorandum on the flyleaf of a Bible which belonged to Mrs. Dundas, that the marriage took place on the 3d of June at Edinburgh.

Soon after this the following letters passed between members of the family :—

Lord Bargany to Robert Dundas[1] at Utrecht.

1734.

D. ROB.,—I had a letter from you lately, which came to my hand at Arniston, where I have been staying these eight days past.

The professor[2] of law and I have plyed the hunting close. The dogs run mighty well, but the stable is in very bad order, so that I suppose when your papa comes from London he will be so much out of humour that the dogs forthwith will be sent a packing. Indeed, before he went away, he seemed to be much cooled as to his keenness. Formerly he used to get out of bed to go a

---

[1] Robert, eldest son of Mr. Dundas, and afterwards second President Dundas.
[2] Laurence Dundas, Professor of Law in the University of Edinburgh, and founder of the Dundas Bursaries.

hunting by six or seven in the morning; and now, betwixt ten and eleven is reckoned a more proper hour.

Mr. Dundas *to his* Son *at Utrecht.*

ARNISTON, *Aug.* 11, 1735.

. . . I have this night got communicated to me by Sir William Cockburn an intrigue that it seems hath been carried on for some time betwixt Mr. Cockburn of Cockpen and my sister Martha, with my mother's concurrency, without paying me that small degree of civility ever to acquaint me of it. In short, I suppose it is to be a marriage, and so little to my taste for many reasons, that I could as soon see her drowned. You may judge what good blood this will make in our family, but there is no help for it.[1]

Mr. Dundas *to his* Wife.

LONDON, *Feb.* 17, 1736.

MY DEAREST LIFE,—Here I am, pretty well, yet still coughing, no more in love with the place than the first day I came to it. I have been at no publick place, but the House. I do not go to St. James's, and shall not be much in the play-house while this cold continues. There are few of my acquaintance here *en famille*, so that I have little to do of an evening but come home and read a book.

LONDON, *Feb.* 26, 1736.

I had the pleasure of yours from Dundas yesterday. I hope you are not the worse for that journey, but I am afraid it was too much hazarded in so bad weather and roads, and you will surely excuse my anxiety about what I value so much.

We are all like to be destroyed here by cold weather and hot elections. . . . My dearest, I desire you will tell John Dickson to take care the crows get not liberty to nestle on the trees at Arniston; this is their time of taking up their quarters, but I desire they may have none there. Let him get powder and lead, and shoot them, and get speelers of iron for the boys to climb up and pull down their nests. Tell him and the gardener likewise, that I desire the second row of Holly trees from the bowling green, on each side, may be taken out, and that the first row on

---

[1] The marriage took place; and in the following year a son was born, Archibald Cockburn, afterwards Sheriff of Midlothian, and the father of Lord Cockburn.

each side of the bowling green may be filled up with them, as far
east as the length of the opening of the walk that runs down the
barn croft, along which the Holly hedge runs on the top of the
sunk fence ; and that hedge where it is ill grown may also be cut
over. There are also some bad trees in the line next the bowling
green on the north side ; let the bad ones be changed, and better
ones of the second rows, which are to be taken up, put in their
places. There are likewise some gone back, on the south side of
the house, let them be supplied. I desired likewise, that the
little spot of ground in front of your windows, might be dressed
and planted with flowers. I have writ Woodhall[1] asking a supply
of flowers from him, if he can spare them, and probably he will
write to you about it. John Dickson may expect the clover seed
I was to send by a ship that sails on Saturday. I suppose by this
time he hath opened the view through the Fir park.

Sir Hew Dalrymple, President of the Court of Session,
died on the 1st of February 1737.[2] Twelve years had now
passed since Dundas had lost the office of Lord Advocate ; but,
during that time, he had gained so great a character for legal
ability, that it was natural he should aspire to the highest seat
on the bench. The Duke of Argyll and Lord Ilay, his brother,
had, however, so powerful voice in all Scottish appointments,
that without their support it was impossible to obtain so
important an office as that of Lord President. Indeed, at this
time, no Sheriff was appointed in Scotland except with the
approval of the Duke of Argyll. " The whole nomination "
(of Sheriffs), Andrew Mitchell[3] writes to Dundas, " seems to be
little more than a list of the sons, sons-in-law, and alliances of
those gentlemen whom the D. of A. has thought fit to place
upon the bench."

In the same letter Mr. Mitchell alludes to the Presidentship. " After what has happened," he says, " I confess I am
more doubtful than ever of the nomination of President, unless
what has been done shall be considered as a sort of compensation for what is to be done ; but of this I have little hopes,

---

[1] George Sinclair of Woodhall, afterwards a judge, with the title of Lord
Woodhall. He was third son of Sir John Sinclair of Stevenson.

[2] Sir Hew Dalrymple, third son of the first Lord Stair, had been President
since June 1698.

[3] Afterwards Sir Andrew Mitchell. He was ambassador at the Court of
Berlin during a great part of the reign of George II.

as the D. of A. grows every day more powerful, and of more consequence. He therefore must not be disobliged."

In the end the Government resolved to appoint the Lord Advocate, Duncan Forbes of Culloden, whose long and splendid public services, combined with great legal ability and high personal character, had certainly given him a very strong claim for the office. He was, moreover, a great friend of the Argylls.

There was, however, another vacancy on the bench at this time, caused by the death of Sir Walter Pringle of Newhall. Sir Walter had been made a judge in 1718, at the time when Mr. Dundas had requested Sir Robert Walpole to relieve him of the office of Solicitor-General, by giving him a seat on the bench ;[1] and Mr. Dundas had now to consider whether he should accept of the judgeship which, nineteen years before, he had unsuccessfully applied for. He wrote to Lord Ilay on the subject, and received an answer advising him to do so :—

Lord Ilay to Mr. Dundas.

. . . Some years ago I was not unwilling that you should have stood first oars (as we say here), which the other (Forbes) does now, so that all that remains is whether you should take the other (judgeship). Every office becomes greater or less in a great measure, according to the character and abilities of the person who enjoys it. The dignity of a judge shines strongly here in Cummings, and is lost in Page; Ld Anstruther added lustre to Lord Whitelaw, and so will Lord ———[2] to you. The preference, unavoidable at present, will appear manifestly to all the people of Scotland, not to arise from the comparison of the persons, but the situation of them, for the time being. . . . I am sensible of the great regard you have been pleased to show me, in desiring my opinion in this matter in which you are so nearly concerned, and when I presume to advise you to accept of it, I declare to you that I should think myself unworthy of your good opinion or friendship, and indeed of all mankind, if I did not do it with the utmost sincerity.—I am, Sir, your most obed^t & most humble servant,   ILAY.

14th May 1737.

---

[1] *Supra*, p. 60.   [2] Left blank in the original.

Mr. Dundas made up his mind to accept of the judgeship, and took his seat on the bench as Lord Arniston, on the 10th of June 1737.

Not long after his elevation to the bench, Lord Arniston met with an alarming accident, which he was of opinion might have proved fatal.

LORD ARNISTON *to his* SON ROBERT.

EDINBURGH, *July* 21, 1737.

SON,—I had one from you some days ago, since which I have not been able to write, by reason of a most unhappy accident that befell me. Thursday last, as I was going out to Arniston about mid-day in a single horse chaise, with Mr. Turnbull the minister along with me, in passing an empty hay cart betwixt Dalhousie[1] and Carrington, the cart horses, startled at the rattling of the chaise, ran away with the cart upon us, and the cartwheel, coming betwixt our wheel and the chaise, tumbled us, chaise, horse, and all topsie turvy, and dragged us a great way, chaise and all along the ground. I was pressed twofold below the chaise, by which my whole body, especially my breast, was most miserably bruised. What with repeated bleeding and cupping, I am now a good deal better, but still in considerable pain. I have reason to bless God that things are not worse; I had no prospect at the time that it was possible my life could have been saved, and nothing but Providence could have saved me from being crushed to powder. I hope there is nothing inwardly hurt, since I have had no fever, but my pulse quite calm, though my bones and muscles are in great pain. Mr. Turnbull was more lucky, the violence of the shock threw him some distance both from cart and chaise, so that he was little or no way hurt.

In the spring of 1739, Mr. Dundas, now Lord Arniston, and Mrs. Dundas, paid a visit to their relatives at Invergordon.

---

[1] The road from Edinburgh to Arniston still was by Dalhousie and Carrington, and across Traquair's Bridge, below the meeting of the waters.

The itinerary of the journey and their travelling expenses were as follows :—

			£	s.	d.
Thursday, April 19.—Arniston to Leith, and across the Ferry to Kinghorn :					
	Expenses at Leith,		1	15	10
	„ at Kinghorn,		1	8	8
Friday 20th,	Falkland,		0	8	1
„	Perth,		1	4	1
Saturday 21st,	Inver,		0	9	11
Sunday 22d,	Blair,		0	18	5
Monday 23d,	Dalnacardoch,		0	16	9
„	Dalwhinnie,		0	10	10
Tuesday 24th,	Ruthen,		0	17	11
„	Aviemore,		0	5	5
„	Corryburgh,		0	2	0
„	Dalinagarry,		0	13	11
Wednesday 25th,	Inverness,		1	2	2
	Kepock and Invergordon,		0	10	0

Simon, Lord Lovat, writes to express his regret that sickness had prevented him paying his respects to Lord Arniston since he came into that neighbourhood. He continues, in his customary strain of mock humility :—

. . . If your Lordship goes south by Inverness, the best road is within a quarter of a mile of this hut ; for I have made a very good coach road from this little house to Inverness, and if your Lordship would do me the honour and singular pleasure to come and lodge one night in this little hut, I can frankly assure your Lordship, that there were never, nor will be, any guests in it more welcome than my Lord and my Lady Arniston.

I beg your Lordship may believe that I am with the greatest truth, and the utmost esteem and respect, my good Lord, your Lordship's most obedient, most obliged and most humble servant,

LOVAT.

BEAUFORT, 26th May 1739.

A journey to Inverness was no easy matter in those days. General Wade had by this time completed the greater part of his system of roads throughout the Highlands ; but the main road between Perth and Inverness, which had existed for many years, was still of a very primitive description. Even the roads between Scotland and London were rough and dangerous, and a journey to the capital was a tedious and sometimes hazardous undertaking. We find Mr. Dundas writing from London to Mrs. Dundas, "Yesterday morning we got safe here, and, considering what terrible roads we had, it is a wonder there was not one fall among us." Again, he writes to his wife, who was near her confinement, "I beg of you to be very careful as to travelling, and consider whether it will be safer for you to go (to Dundas Castle) in a horse-chair, or in the coach. If you take the coach, see it go slow, and that the coachman take care of jolting."

In the early part of the eighteenth century, goat whey was in high repute as a corrective for the ills induced by a too liberal indulgence in punch and claret; and there were various places in Scotland where families used to go in summer, which were familiarly spoken of as "goat-whey quarters."

People used to speak colloquially of being at "the goat whey," just as now a-days they speak of being at the sea-side. Probably plain food, no claret or punch, and fresh country air were the real cures; but the universal belief was that the whey was what acted as a restorative. Between 1735 and 1746, Lord Arniston seems to have gone to the hills for this cure as regularly as a German goes to his brunnen. In the Arniston accounts there are entries of expenses in successive years at Struan in Perthshire, Rossdhu, Castle Leod, Luss, and other places, which were visited for the whey.

LORD ARNISTON *to his* WIFE.

CASTLE LEOD, *May* 9, 1740.

MY DEAREST LIFE,—I wrote to you yesterday by the foolish express that was sent to plague me. I hope your sister is not the worse of her journey, tho' she took a day less to it than she intended, tempted by the good day; this seems likewise a good one, so I hope to get some riding.

The whey is yet scarce, but enough for me. I cannot say it does quite so well with me as formerly; it gives me pretty smart colicks, but these I expect will leave me when I have used it several days longer.

All at Invergordon are well in health; we expect Sir William[1]

---

[1] Sir William Gordon of Invergordon, father of Mrs. Dundas and of the Countess of Cromartie.

here this day. Send me a parcel of twist tobacco here by next post. There is none tolerable to be got here.

There is strong thieving in this country by the Glengarry men, and some murders. This country is threatened with a famine, and I am afraid so are you at home. The cattle are likewise dying fast. I have inquired for cows to buy, but as yet can find none, nor do I believe there will be any fit to be driven for near two months; they have no fodder, neither straw nor hay, in all the country, and no grass come up.

ROSSDHU, *June* 3, 1741.

MY DEAREST LIFE,—I am here just in health as I left you, living quietly in the way you may guess, going on with my whey, which I do not find so strong, in my opinion, as at Castle Leod, riding and walking out, calling over in two days in my ride on Lady Castlehill,[1] reading my book, playing at backgammon with Lady Janet Boyle, fishing perches, but have not as yet had a day for chasing the otters, though the weather is tolerably good, but want of rain; but, I believe, liberty to be idle, and absence from the Session, is not the least agreeable part of the scene.

In 1742, Lord Arniston went to Rossdhu to drink the goat whey, Mrs. Dundas remaining at Arniston, where her son Henry[2] was born on the 28th of April 1742.

LORD ARNISTON *to* MRS. DUNDAS.

ROSSDHU, *April* 25, 1742.

MY DEAREST HEART,—I got here last night. I cannot say that I was quite well on the road. I was bad on Friday night at Glasgow; the journey did defeat me. This day I am somewhat tired, but have begun the whey.

Ap. 28.

I did not recover the fatigue of the journey for two or three days, and have not been on horseback since, nor had any other diversion than fishing perches on the Loch. There is not a soul here but he and she, so you may judge the rest, and not one of the neighbours at home.

---

[1] Martha, daughter and heiress of Sir John Lockhart of Castlehill, wife of George Sinclair of Woodhall.

[2] Henry Dundas, afterwards first Viscount Melville.

Lord Arniston in the following year went to Shien, near Amulrie, in Perthshire, for the goat whey, Mrs. Dundas remaining at Arniston for her approaching confinement.

LORD ARNISTON *to* MRS. DUNDAS.

SHIEN, *June* 15, 1743.

MY DEAREST PLEASURE,—We got to Stirling on Monday, and to this place yesternight, in good time, all safe, but were sadly put to it when we came, for our baggage got not up till one o'clock in the morning. So that we had neither knife, spoon, napkin, nor, worst of all, sheets, so that we had a prospect of sitting in our scabbards all night; till at last we were relieved. I kept the men all this day to rest the horses, which seemed pretty necessary. This place is rather worse than when we were here before; garden, house, and everything neglected in their absence; not so much as a cow here, but we are to have two or three sent over to us to-morrow.

SHIEN, *June* 17, 1743.

Lady Moncrieff hath been pleased to send her servant here with garden things to us, which are very welcome, we having nothing of that kind. The weather has been excessively cold, and we are but ill provided with firing. Fishing goes on, and Tom hath taken a little touch of shooting, but Currie and Vogrie's dogs seem good for nothing.

SHIEN, *June* 28, 1743.

I have about an hour ago your very acceptable letter, giving me an account of my being a grandfather, and that Henny[1] and her daughter[2] are both in a good way. You will congratulate her in my name in the most affectionate manner. I am heartily glad of her safe delivery, and now that she hath once rode the ford safely, I hope she won't be afraid to try it again in due time. Make also my compliments to my son. I give him joy, and hope for a continuance of all favourable circumstances.

SHIEN, *July* 16, 1743.

MY DEAREST KIND OBLIGING COMFORT,—We are here almost drowned, quite prisoners by a great flood; the water not passable, our horses and also the goats graze on the other side, so that we

---

[1] Henrietta Baillie, his eldest son's wife.
[2] Elizabeth, afterwards Lady Lockhart Ross of Balnagowan.

got no goat whey this morning, nor can get a horse over, unless we send by the bridge, which, backward and forward, would be a jaunt of six miles to get a horse here, and the half of that to get it back to the road. I think it is almost time for me to be looking homewards, so you may order the chariot to Crieff against this day seven night, that is Saturday the 23d. I suppose they will set out from Arniston on Friday, and may get either to Linlithgow or Falkirk that night, and thence to Crieff Saturday. The baggage horses may be either with them or a day later, as you think fit.[1]

In 1742, there was a complete change in the administration of Scottish affairs. Defeated by a majority of one on the Chippenham election petition, Walpole resigned all his offices, and retired to the House of Lords as Earl of Orford. Lord Wilmington was the new Prime Minister; and part of the policy of his Government was to revive the office of Secretary of State for Scotland, which was bestowed upon the Marquis of Tweeddale.

MARQUIS OF TWEEDDALE,[2] SECRETARY OF STATE FOR SCOTLAND,
to LORD ARNISTON.

MY LORD,—When you reflect upon the present situation of affairs here, how difficult it is for me, who have been unexpectedly in a particular manner distinguished by his Majesty, unassisted, without any proper advice, to determine what steps are proper to be taken upon my first entrance into so high and public a station, you will not be surprised at your receiving a letter desiring and intreating your presence in this place. Nor will you be at a loss to judge why I have wrote in the same strain to the President of the Session.[3] Half-an-hour's conversation could explain many things which it is impossible to do by letters. I know, and you will easily perceive, the difficulties surrounding me, yet I desire you may be persuaded that I never would have embarked myself had I not well known upon what footing I stood in the proper place, and that I have the satisfaction to be engaged with those in the Administration with whom I have long lived in friendship and connection, whose

---

[1] The journey from Crieff to Amulrie, a distance of about twelve miles, had to be performed on horseback.

[2] John, fourth Marquis of Tweeddale.

[3] Duncan Forbes of Culloden.

principles and views are the same with yours and mine. As to
our particular part, in so far as concerns the future government
of Scotland, a great deal depends upon the first steps taken by
which the outlines are shaped. I am diffident of my own opinion,
dare not venture to proceed till once I know your opinion, both
as to persons and measures. Your sentiments have always had, and
will always have, the greatest weight with me, and tho', from the
present situation of things, every thing that could be wished
cannot be at once effectuated, yet I dare venture to say more will
be than you probably imagine. Let me therefore intreat of you,
for the sake of your friends and country, grudge not to undertake
this journey. Nothing but want of health, which, I hope, is not
the case, can excuse you. Should the President of the Session
come up, and you stay behind, I may probably be more embar-
rassed. You can't be at a loss to know my meaning, yet, in all
events, let me have your sentiments freely, and without reserve,
both as to the measures and the proper persons to be employed
for the execution, since it is vain for me to have right and good
intentions unless I can find persons in whom I can confide,
proper to be employed in the service. Those may not be indeed
very easy to be found, but I sure the fittest will be recommended,
and occur to you. I am afraid you will neither be able to read
this, far less to understand it; it is wrote in a greatt hurry, but I
could not think of sending you a formal letter without assuring
you that I wish to enter into an entire confidance with you, & I
can say that there is no person alive has a greater value & honnour
for you than myself, and am sure it will be your own fault if
opportunities do not daily occur to convince you how much your
opinion and advice must have weight with me and others.

LONDON, *Feb. ye 23d,* 174½.

In the Cabinet the Duke of Argyll had a place, but he did
not long retain it. For many years he had engrossed the
whole patronage of Scotland, where Ministers had seldom taken
any steps without his advice or consent; and he now expected
that the Secretary of State was to be a new tool in his hands.
But Carteret, the most powerful member of the Government,
and Pulteney, whose influence was also great, let him know
plainly that there was to be a new system of managing Scotland.
Incensed at this, and at having failed to obtain a place for Sir
John Hinde Cotton, he resigned office, and joined the Opposition. "You would be surprised," writes Lord Tweeddale on

the 16th of March 1742, "at a noble Duke's resigning all his employments. Whatever may have been his reasons for it, most people, I think, seem to agree it was a rash and . . .[1] step. He now puts himself at the head of Tories, and the present question seems to be whether we ought to have a Whig or Tory administration."

The management of Scotland would have been, in any case, a great source of difficulty to the new Government, but the difficulty was much increased by the fact that they were opposed by the Duke of Argyll. It was suspected that the Duke had not only joined the open and constitutional Opposition, but was actually intriguing behind the scenes in favour of the Stuarts. Still it was impossible to make any sweeping changes in Scotland suddenly. The Duke's placemen could not be removed merely because they were his placemen; and the fabric of power which he had constructed during the ascendancy of Walpole would not fall to the ground merely because an Administration to which he was opposed had handed over to another the patronage which had been taken from him. It was among the English members that the strength of the Government lay; yet it would have been most impolitic to dissolve Parliament in the hope of unseating the Scottish members who supported the Opposition. "I know," Lord Tweeddale says in a letter to Lord Arniston, "it is his Majesty's intention to make as great an alteration in the persons employed in Scotland as the particular circumstances of this will allow of. We are in the beginning of Parliament. This is a Whig administration. A dissolution of the Parliament would ruin the Whig interest, since it is certain a new Parliament would be Tory. So there is no thought of that, which, as your Lordship observed, was a material question to be resolved, and must have great influence in determining how far it is proper to go."

The Government appear to have been anxious to obtain Lord Arniston's assistance in devising their measures for Scottish administration, and he was repeatedly invited to visit London for the purpose of helping Lord Tweeddale; but his health prevented him. In 1745, he passed the autumn in the north of England, suffering much from his old enemy the

---

[1] Illegible.

gout; and in the following year he was bent on retiring from public life, and retained his seat upon the bench only in deference to the wishes of his son, Robert, who had been appointed Solicitor-General in 1742, although he was then only in his thirtieth year.

Forbes of Culloden, President of the Court of Session, died on the 10th of December 1747. The appointment of a successor gave rise to considerable discussion, and "made more noise" in London than usually was the case with the disposal of a Scottish office. It was felt that the appointment would show "what set of men in Scotland were to be supported," whether Jacobites in disguise, or staunch adherents of the House of Hanover, and whether every consideration was to become secondary to the maintenance of the influence of the Duke of Argyll. The Independent Whigs believed that neither the King's authority nor their own property would be secure were the President's chair filled by one of his adherents. On the other hand, the Duke naturally was bent upon retaining his power as long as he could, and was quite alive to the importance of placing a faithful adherent at the head of the administration of justice in Scotland. There were four candidates for the vacant chair, William Grant of Prestongrange, who was Lord Advocate at the time of the President's death; Erskine of Tinwald, who was supported by the Duke of Argyll's influence; Craigie of Glendoick, who had been Lord Advocate during the Rebellion, but had lately resigned office; and Lord Arniston.

Even before the President's death, Lord Arniston had begun to take steps for the purpose of securing the place.

LORD ARNISTON *to the* LORD CHANCELLOR.[1]

Dec. 1747.

MY LORD,—I presume your Lordship hath heard before this time that the President of the Court of Session is in a very bad way, and in all human appearance cannot live many days. Though my own state of health makes it highly improbable that I can enjoy any office long, yet in point of honour I cannot tamely submit without remonstrance to see another put over me to that

---

[1] Lord Hardwicke.

Chair. I am older Lawyer than any of those who can be thought of; I was older in the Crown's service than any of them. I ran through both the Law offices at a time when, I believe, that service was as difficult as ever it was before or since; and when no Lawyers of any character at the Bar showed great zeal to set their faces to support the service of this Government. All I gained was envy and detraction, and instead of profit, a very great loss to myself and family, and a considerable sum never repaid by the Government, tho' laid out on the publick service.

I was vain enough to think my pretensions were full as strong as Mr. Forbes', at the time he was put over me, but court power and favour are not to be got the better of.

I do not pretend to compete with any man in point of personal abilities, but I hope it is not want of zeal for his Majesty's family and service that can make me deserve to have any new mark of indignity put upon me, and in these views I beg leave to submit the matter to your Lordships' consideration, and to hope that at least his Majesty may have the case plainly stated, which I do not know if I can expect from the great Duke of our country.—I remain, with the highest respect, etc.

LORD CHANCELLOR *to* LORD ARNISTON.

POWIS HOUSE, *Dec.* 17*th*, 1747.

MY LORD,—I will make no apology for not sooner acknowledging the honour of your Lordship's letter, besides assuring you that it by no means proceeded from want of respect, and that I thought, whilst I gave no attention to your request, it was better to suspend my answer till the event, which was not then certain, though very probable, should happen. Since I have been placed in my present station, I have made it a rule not to take upon me to recommend particular persons upon any vacancies amongst the Scotch judges, unless of such Barons of the Exchequer, as, by established usage, have been supplied with Englishmen. If, indeed, an affair of that nature becomes a consideration of the King's servants, I always think it my duty to give my opinion in such manner as appears to me to be most for his Majesty's service. I have, with great fidelity and exactness, laid the state of your case, as your Lordship have represented it, before his Majesty in his closet, with such other facts relative thereto, as have fallen within my knowledge and observation, and submitted it to his consideration. . . . I am extremely sorry for the loss of my old acquaintance, your late President, and heartily wish his Chair may be filled with a worthy successor, and am very sure that nobody would fill it with greater ability and sufficiency than yourself.—I am, with great respect, my Lord, your Lordship's most obedient & most humble servant, HARDWICKE.

(Probably) SIR CHARLES GILMOUR[1] *to* LORD ARNISTON.

Dec. 17, 1747.

MY LORD,—I received yesterday the hon^r of your Lops. of the 10th. I am informed the Chancellor got your letter, but what steps he has taken I know not, but a person told me this day, who dined where his son was yesterday, the conversation was about filling the President's chair; the young gentleman spoke very handsomely of you, and said he had often heard his father declare your great worth and abilities, and the assistance he had from you of late, without which he could not have carried through the laws that have passed.[2] . . . The filling the President's place makes more noise here than I had expected, and some people don't hesitate to say it will be a declaration what set of men in Scotland are to be supported, when they compare the behaviour of men in perilous times formerly.—I am ever yours.

Lord Arniston also wrote to the Duke of Argyll, soliciting his interest, and begging him not to forget that it was in consequence of the "persuasive motives your Grace gave me" that he had left the bar ten years before.[3] But the Duke of Argyll's influence was entirely given to his friend, Charles Erskine of Tinwald. Mr. Andrew Mitchell, a warm friend of Lord Arniston's, warned him that he had to contend against heavy odds. "The President's death has given great and real concern to me," he writes, "and I fear it will not be alleviated by the nomination of a successor."

For nine months no appointment was made. In his diary, published among the Marchmont Papers, Hugh, third Earl of Marchmont, narrates the course of the negotiations which took place before the vacancy was filled up, and the various expedients which were from time to time suggested by the rival interests. The choice of the Government lay between

---

[1] Sir Charles Gilmour of Craigmillar, M.P. for the county of Midlothian, and a Commissioner of the Board of Trade.

[2] An allusion to the Act abolishing Heritable Jurisdictions in Scotland.

[3] *Supra*, p. 90.

Erskine and Dundas, and the friends of both did all in their power to damage the reputation of their opponent.

It was believed that Lord Arniston would resign his seat on the bench, if he was not made Lord President. Marchmont, according to his own account, went to the Duke of Newcastle, and told him very plainly what he thought.

Dec. 3. I went to the Duke of Newcastle's and told him I was afraid of being officious, but thought it my duty to inform him of what I thought might affect the King's interest in Scotland. He said he should be glad of receiving any lights from me . . . I then said this conjunction was the more critical from the President's illness, and perhaps death. Ay, says he, who do you think the most proper man? I said . . . First, the man most unfit was T——;[1] he was a known Jacobite in 1715, and I have no faith in Scots Jacobites' conversions, and next he was a very dangerous man; and they might as well take the crown of Scotland off the King's head, and put it on the Duke of Argyle's, whose subject I could never be. I said, besides that, Lord Arniston would probably quit the bench; and I did not see how they could supply his place. He asked about him. I said he was very well, was the ablest man, one whom the whole kingdom pointed out for it; and as he had a great property, might quit on what would be thought an affront to him; and if he got it, as he was the most zealous friend to the King on the bench, so, I would be answerable he would belong to the ministers. . . . But as in this case (the appointment of Lord Advocate Craigie to the President's chair), Lord Arniston would probably quit, I did not see how they could supply his place; and that this would be the most fatal blow to the King's interest in Scotland.

Dec. 24. After dinner, Lord Chesterfield took me into his library, and told me, . . . they had had a meeting about the Presidentship of the Session, in which Mr. Pelham was for ——,[2] as the Duke of Argyle's man, which he owned, saying the Duke had assisted them, and was to be preferred to the squadron who were linked to Lord Granville, Sir John Gordon, and the Prince. But he added, he thought Arniston and his son were to be gained if possible, and therefore he would propose giving Grant now Ld Advocate the gown, and making young Dundas[3] Advocate. The

---

[1] Lord Tinwald. [2] Tinwald.
[3] Lord Arniston's son, afterwards second President Dundas.

Duke of Newcastle mentioned ———— and Arniston, but seemed to incline to Lord Elchies,[1] saying he thought they should name one who could make it apparent that the English Ministry had named him. . . . Then the Chancellor (Hardwicke) weighed what had been said in his Chancery scales of equity, and seemed to be of opinion they should name Arniston. But nothing was decided in this meeting.

Finally a compromise was effected, the English ministers, backed by the Independent Whigs, appointed Lord Arniston to be President; whilst the Duke of Argyll was conciliated by the appointment of his friend Erskine of Tinwald to the office of Lord Justice-Clerk, the vacancy being created by the retirement of another of his adherents, Fletcher, Lord Milton, who received the Signet for life, and the reversion of a place for his son.

DUKE OF NEWCASTLE *to* LORD ARNISTON.

NEWCASTLE HOUSE, *May* 12, 1748.

SIR,—I had the favour of your letter upon the subject of the place of President of the Session, which had then been long vacant. I did not trouble you with an answer till I would acquaint you with his Majesty's intentions relative to it. The knowledge I always had of your firm attachment to his Majesty's government, and of your distinguished ability in the law, made me wish to see you placed at the head of it, and I was extremely glad to promote the success of a scheme, which I hope will be equally to the satisfaction of those who are concerned in it, and have very just pretensions to his Majesty's favour. . . . If I have any merit with you upon this occasion, I must recommend to you in the strongest manner to promote the most perfect harmony and good correspondence between all his Majesty's servants in your part of the kingdom, which is so necessary for the true interest of it.—I am, etc., HOLLES NEWCASTLE.

MR. PELHAM *to* LORD ARNISTON.

May 12, 1748.

SIR,—You will hear from the Duke of Newcastle this night that the King has agreed to make you Lord President of the Sessions in the room of my old friend, Mr. Forbes. I can assure

---

[1] Patrick Grant of Elchies. He had been on the bench since 1732.

you, Sir, I have not been inattentive to the letter you honoured me with of December last, but as it is a maxim with me never wilfully to misguide any man, I chose not to return an answer to it till I could speak clearly, and show to you by facts, as well as words, the true regard his Majesty and his servants have for your ability in your profession, and for your zeal and attachment to the King's person and Government. I have always wished to see those distinguished who are true friends to both, but personal altercations and party divisions have too often prevented the execution of the best intentions for that end. I am sure you will not dislike my plain way of speaking and writing. I do not always suppose a man to be exactly what his friends partially represent him, much less do I give credit to the misrepresentation of an enemy; it is the uniform conduct of every man's publick behaviour that is the proper test of his principles and inclinations. With this view I am sure you would think no man deserves to have a friend who would give those up on slight insinuations, who have constantly acted faithfully to him, and, in his judgement, honestly to the publick. I therefore found in my own mind great difficulties how to determine my wishes upon the late event of the vacancy of the Chair in your Court, but as far as I was able to suggest anything that might unite the contending parties, and which ought to please both, I have not been wanting to lay before the King and his servants. The expedient has taken effect, and his Majesty, by the advice of all his ministers, has most readily agreed to it. You will therefore now give me leave in my turn to give some advice to you, as, I can assure you, I took very kindly by what you said in your letter to me. You will soon be at the head of the Court of Justice in Scotland. Your known abilities and private integrity will enable you to make a great figure there. Don't let politicks create you enemies, whom justice would make your friends. Unite cordially with those whom the King thinks proper to employ in the great stations of your country. You cannot want support here; don't let them want yours there. A great deal is to be done to bring the factious and disaffected in Scotland to a proper sense of their duty, which cannot be effectually brought about but by a thorough union amongst those who are true friends to the Government. If there are any persons encouraged who are publicly or secretly enemies to it, let us unite in rooting them out. Let the aim of honest men be to detect those that are not truly so, and wish that the number may be few, rather than artfully to whisper that there are as many, and detect none. These are my principles, and by these I desire to be tried. It is absurd for any man in a publick life to forget his old friends, but it is equally weak not to admit into his confidence those who are well intentioned to the Government he serves, and cordially disposed to reconcile former differences. I should not have taken up so much of your time in sending, perhaps, these useless lines, had I not thought your letter required it; and as I have faithfully kept yours a secret, I doubt not I may equally depend on your not showing this to any one. I have chosen to begin my correspondence with you in this frank and open manner, that you may see what I wish, and if you approve what I say, you may cultivate a further intercourse between us, which I shall be always glad to improve, upon the system and terms I have here represented. I most heartily wish you joy of the great mark of favour the King intends to show you, and am, with great respect, etc., H. PELHAM.

DUKE OF ARGYLL to LORD ARNISTON.

MY LORD,—I should not have been so rude as to delay for so long a time the answering your Lordship's letter, if it had been possible for me to have said any thing with precision. Such a vacancy as that was did naturally open a field for a variety of schemes. They were then very crude, and little more than hints that came from several of the King's servants, and which I was by no means at liberty to mention. It was only a very few days ago that anything was settled, and now I have the pleasure to wish you joy of matters being accommodated to your satisfaction. Your Lordship will now have the office which, you know, I many years ago thought you equal to, and which I wish you may live long to enjoy, being with great respect, my Lord, etc., etc., etc.,

LOND., *May* 13, 1748. ARGYLL.

ANDREW MITCHELL[1] to ROBERT DUNDAS, *younger*.

LONDON, *May* 14, 1748.

DEAR SIR,—I heartily give you joy of Lord Arniston's success. I confess such a President is worth any purchase, but some people turn every thing to their own advantage. Lord Tinwald[2] is to be Justice-Clerk, and the Justice[3] to have the Signet for life, with

---

[1] Afterwards Sir Andrew Mitchell.
[2] Charles Erskine of Tinwald, third son of Sir Charles Erskine of Alva, by Christian, daughter of Sir James Dundas of Arniston.
[3] Andrew Fletcher of Milton, son of Henry Fletcher of Saltoun.

a reversionary grant of Sir James Dalrymple's place for his son; sure the Government we live under is full of gratitude!

Mr. Pelham told me yesterday that he had wrote fully and freely to Lord Arniston. . . . I took the liberty to thank him in the name of the Whigs of Scotland for Lord A.'s promotion. . . . —I am affectly. yours,   A. M.

Lord Chancellor Hardwicke *to* Lord Arniston.

Powis House, *May* 24, 1748.

My Lord,—The great hurry I have been in by the close of the Session, and of the Term, which ended but yesterday, has hitherto prevented me from congratulating your Lordship on the signal mark of his Majesty's favour, which you have lately received by your advancement to the President's chair. Though my congratulations wait on your Lordship thus late, I beg leave to assure you they are as sincere as any you have received. Your Lordship has this satisfaction that you have had the concurrence of all his Majesty's servants in your promotion; and will, I am confident, look upon it as a proof that extraordinary merit in your profession, and strict impartiality in the administration of justice, attended with real affection and attachment to his Majesty and his Government (qualities in your Lordship, to which nobody can do more justice than I do) are allowed their due weight. As it will be difficult to add to that reputation which your Lordship has already so justly acquired, I need only wish you a long continuance of health and strength to sustain this laborious and important station, wherein I am sure it will be perfectly agreeable to all the well affected in Scotland to see you placed. As your Lordship had so meritorious a part in the model, newly established for the administration of justice in the room of the Heritable Jurisdictions, I need not press you to exert your endeavours to support and improve it. New schemes, however wise and well founded, have generally some difficulties attending the first execution of them, which require much judgement and a propitious disposition towards the measure, to remove. I much rely on your Lordship for both these, and that you will be particularly attentive to perfect this good work for the general benefit of the whole country. May I presume farther to recommend to your Lordship, what I doubt not your own inclination and right way of thinking will lead you to, I mean, to live in good correspondence with your now Lord Justice-Clerk.[1] My acquaintance with him arose in the same

---

[1] Erskine of Tinwald.

manner with that which I have the honour of with your Lordship, by having experienced you both in the same offices; and it will give me great pleasure to see my two friends co-operating together, and maintaining that harmony which, I am sure, will be of great utility to the dignity of the Court.—I am, etc., etc., etc.,

HARDWICKE.

Having thus obtained the object of his ambition, Lord Arniston passed the remainder of his life in tranquillity. In Edinburgh his house was in the aristocratic quarter known as Bishop's Land, a large tenement on the north side of the High Street, not far from where the North Bridge now joins that thoroughfare. But most of his time was spent at Arniston, where he was frequently visited by the members of his family and numerous friends. One of his sons, Robert, the offspring of his marriage to Miss Watson of Muirhouse, had already held the office of Solicitor-General, and was now Dean of the Faculty of Advocates. Henry, the future Viscount Melville, the son of his second marriage to Anne, daughter of Sir William Gordon of Invergordon, was, in 1748, a child of six.

From the Household Books kept at Arniston, we can gather some idea of the style of living at that time, and the following extracts may perhaps be thought interesting:—

BILLS OF FARE FOR A WEEK IN 1748.

Sunday, December 4, 1748.

DINNER.

Cockyleeky. Boiled beef and greens. Roast goose.
2 bottles claret. 2 white wine. 2 strong ale.

SUPPER.

Mutton steak stewed with turnips. Drawn eggs.
Rice and milk. My Lord's broth.
1 bottle claret. 1 white wine. 1 strong ale.

Monday, December 5.

DINNER.

Pea soup. Boiled turkey. Roast beef. Apple pie.
3 bottles claret. 2 white wine. 2 strong ale.

SUPPER.

Mutton steak. Drawn eggs and gravy. Potatoes.
My Lord's broth.
2 bottles claret. 1 white wine. 1 strong ale.

Tuesday, December 6.

DINNER.

Sheep's-head broth. Shoulder of mutton. Roast goose.
Smothered rabbits.
2 bottles claret. 2 white wine. 1 strong ale.

SUPPER.

Boiled hens, with oyster sauce. Cold goose. Cockel hags.
My Lord's broth.
1 bottle white wine. 1 bottle strong ale.

Wednesday, December 7.

DINNER.

Cockyleeky. Mince pie. Roast mutton.
1 bottle claret. 1 white wine. 1 strong ale.

SUPPER.

Scotch collops. Roast hens. Drawn eggs. Potatoes.
My Lord's broth.

Thursday, December 8.

DINNER.

Soup. Beef à la mode. Calf's head. 2 roast muirfowl.
Roast pig. Mince pie. Apples, with canels.

SUPPER.

Mutton steaks. Rice and milk. Drawn eggs. My Lord's broth.

Friday, December 9.

DINNER.

Hare soup. Roast beef. Fricasséed Rabbits. Boiled chickens.
Tongue. Boiled pudding. 2 roast ducks. Tarts.
3 roast muirfowls, with canels. Jellies. Jugged hare. Fritters.
12 bottles claret. 4 white wine. 4 strong ale.

SUPPER.

2 boiled hens, with oyster sauce. Jellies. Lemon puffs.
Mince pies.
3 bottles claret. 2 white wine. 1 strong ale.

Saturday, December 10.

DINNER.—Scotch collops.

SUPPER.

Fricasséed hen. Drawn eggs. Milk and rice. Broth.
1 bottle claret. 1 white wine. 1 strong ale.

In the years 1740 to 1749 the consumption of wine averaged £140 per annum; of spirits, £10. The wine was principally claret, with a little French white wine or Lisbon. Claret cost £22 per hogshead; Lisbon and white French wine, £16 per hogshead. From the quantity of sugar entered in the house books as "given out for punch," and the lemons in the housekeeper's books, rum punch was evidently a daily beverage.

Lord Arniston was President of the Court of Session until his death, which took place, on the 26th of August 1753, at the Mansion House of Abbeyhill, which stood close to what is now the line of the North British Railway, at the point where it is joined by the branch railway from Granton and Leith, to make way for which the old Mansion House was pulled down in 1872.

The first President Dundas died at the comparatively early age of sixty-seven. He had never been a robust man; and for nearly fifteen years before his death his letters contain frequent complaints of bad health. A hard worker and a hard liver, he had burned the candle at both ends; and, to some extent, the dissipated habits of his youth, never wholly abandoned, may have impaired his constitution. He faithfully fulfilled the duties of his office, and maintained a correspondence with Lord Hardwicke and Mr. Pelham; but it cannot be said that, as President of the Court, he was the equal either of his predecessor, Forbes of Culloden, or of his own son, the Second President Dundas. When he gained the President's chair his want of physical vigour rendered it impossible, in the opinion of his contemporaries, that he should do himself justice. "He was named," was the verdict of the *Scots Magazine* at the time of his death, "to be President of the Court of Session in his old age, when he was unable to exert the force of his genius in discharging the functions of it. Had he been raised to the office at an earlier period of his life, it can admit of no doubt that he would have equalled, if not surpassed, any who had presided in that Court; as no lawyer was ever more conspicuous on account of his singular merit and ability, or better qualified by his science in law, to perform the duties of the office."

Of his singular merits as a lawyer no better proof can be given than the testimony of Sir Hew Dalrymple. "I knew," he said, "the great lawyers of the last age—Mackenzie, Lockhart, and my own father, Stair; Dundas excels them all."

His career, both as a politician and a lawyer, had been a great success, and had laid the foundation of that extraordinary power over Scotland which was enjoyed by his family during the remainder of the century.

OLD CLOCK IN THE HALL AT ARNISTON.

CHAPTER VIII.

THE SECOND PRESIDENT DUNDAS.

ROBERT DUNDAS, son of the first Lord President Dundas, was born on the 18th of July 1713, and was, from an early period, destined for the profession of the law. "When he was at school and at college, he was," we are told by the *Scots Magazine*, "a very good scholar, owing to his quick apprehension and natural genius; but afterwards he was never known to read through a book, except, perhaps (and that but seldom), to look at parts out of curiosity, if he happened to know the author." He studied at first under the care of a private tutor, and was also for some time at school and at the University of Edinburgh. In 1733 he was sent to Holland, as his father and elder brother had been before him, to pursue his studies at the University of Utrecht. He remained abroad, at Utrecht and in France, till 1737, when he returned home.

The following extracts are taken from letters at Arniston relating to that period :—

From his FATHER.

EDINR., *Nov.* 13, 1733.

SON,—I have one from you by Saturday's post last. I don't wonder if letters miscarry when all are opened. I don't value what they open of mine. I have no occasion to write anything that I care who sees; and if I had I would not be fool enough to put any such thing in their way. . . . You begin a little smartly as to your draughts, and you could not do it at a worse time for me. Demands are so high in all quarters for other people's use more than my own. . . . As I have oft cautioned you to beware of gaming, I am not much afraid of your falling into it. But now I give you a new caution, not to enter too much into the taste of throwing too much money away on books; when that turns a disease, 'tis as bad as pictures. When I have more leisure I will write a little more fully on this subject, what I think you ought to do: I'll expect when you are settled to hear a fuller account of your economy, way of living, college, and these things.—Farewell, Ro. DUNDAS.

From his Cousin, LORD BARGANY.

MONTPELIER, *March* 23, 1734.

D. ROBIE,—I must own my fault in having so long neglected writing to you. No doubt Mr. Stevenson has writ to you our proposed jaunt, on which I am confident you will not baulk us. It is for us then to make the tour of Flanders during your summer vacance. I am so full of the thoughts of it, that every day seems to me a year, betwixt this and that time. You'll let us know by your next, your sentiments upon the affair. I have writ to Mr. Stevenson that we'll meet him at breakfast in your chamber on the first day of July.

I imagine you'll weary very much of Holland on account of the people's being of so villanous a temper. I assure you I begin to dislike France every day the more, because I see the whole aim of the people is self-interest. No such thing almost as sincere friendship even betwixt brothers. A man who will make you all the protestations and compliments, would, at the same time, see you hang'd for a sixpence. I now begin to believe that the proverb is true which says that the most agreeable part in going abroad is the returning home. . . . —Yours, BARGANY.

    Monsieur Robert Dundas,
        Gentilhome Ecossais
    Chez Monsieur Vion à Utrecht.

At this time the death of Augustus, king of Poland, had led to hostilities between the King of France and the Emperor Charles, each of whom supported a rival claimant to the vacant throne; and young Dundas proposed visiting the armies, then campaigning on the Rhine, in company with his cousin, Lord Bargany. His father writes in reply:—

EDINR., *June* 5, 1734.

SON,—I should easily excuse young people's curiosity in a thing of that kind if I looked upon it as a thing practicable, but if you consider upon it I believe you'll find it quite impossible. I have talked to some of our officers here, who are all of opinion that you will find it so. It's quite another thing for a private gentleman to go into an army of our own where he may have numerous friends among the officers, who will accommodate him with lodging in their tents, and with the use of horses to ride about and see what is to be seen, without which it's impossible to be in the army, and to go into an absolute stranger's army where you could not know one soul, nor not one of them take any notice of you. If you were to go such a road, you would not only be obliged to have equipages, servants, and horses of your own, which would amount to an expense, absolutely improper, either for my Lord (Bargany) or me. Besides this, which seems unanswerable, you don't seem to consider the present situation of the armies. The German army is at a vast distance, the French lying interjected betwixt them and you, so it would be both very difficult and very dangerous to attempt to get at the German army. When you consider these things I am persuaded you will see what you propose to be impracticable. I am afraid you are not in danger of losing an opportunity of seeing an army of our own before you come home, or of seeing another in a more convenient situation than you can see the Germans at present, and there is one other thing, I believe at present, it would not be well taken, if any of you went to any of the armies without express permission from the king. Ro. DUNDAS.

The proposed visit to the armies was, of course, given up—the two cousins making a tour of Flanders instead.

From LORD BARGANY.

SPA, *June* 9, 1734.

D. ROBIE,—I am greatly pleased with this wild romantic place, situated in a little valley, surrounded with hills covered with wood. I believe if I had anything of a poetical genius that this place would inspire me to write an ode on the beauties of the works of nature, which certainly human art can never equal. We have scarce any company here as yet, but in a few days there will be abundance. I would propose to you to come here and pass a week or ten days in the beginning of July. It's but three short days journey from you. . . .—Always yours, BARGANY.

Lord Bargany returned home soon after, and died in the following year, to the intense sorrow of his cousin, who, in one of his letters, declares that he is "heart broken" at the news.

Plate forming part of a Wedding Service made for Mr. and Mrs. Dundas, with the Arms of Dundas of Arniston and Baillie of Lamington in the centre, and figures of Hymen's altar, Cupid's bow, and other emblems on the margin.

In 1738 Dundas returned home, and passed advocate. He almost immediately obtained a considerable practice at the bar; but for the first five years of his professional life his fees only averaged £280 a year.

In October 1741 he married Henrietta, daughter of Sir James Carmichael of Bonnington, and Dame Margaret Baillie, his wife, heiress of the estates of Bonnington, Lamington, and Penston. Lord Arniston settled upon his son an allowance of £300 a year, from the lands of Newbyres, and upon Miss Baillie, as jointure, 1000 merks per annum out of the lands of Arniston and Newbyres. Miss Baillie settled a jointure of 4000 merks upon her husband, out of the lands of Lamington.

Among the papers at Arniston is a long Epithalamium composed in honour of this wedding. The unknown poet writes :—

> " Henrietta, Gracious, Affable, Modest, justly Kind,
> Whose face displays the Beauties of her noble Mind,
> Indulgent, smiling now in a comely wedding dress,
> May Heaven her Life with every Bounty still Bless."

He adds, "Let me know if this may be printed and published;" but the hint was not taken, as the lucubration, a most inferior production, exists only in the original manuscript.

In the following year, 1742, only five years after he was called to the bar, Dundas was appointed Solicitor-General in the Wilmington Ministry, which came into power on the fall of Walpole.

ANDREW MITCHELL *to* SOLICITOR-GENERAL DUNDAS.

WHITEHALL, *12th August* 1742.

MY DEAR SIR,—It is with the most sincere pleasure that I wish you joy of the honour His Majesty has been pleased to do you, in appointing you His Solicitor General for Scotland.

This mark of the Royal favour can not fail of being acceptable, as it hath been obtained in an honourable way, and without your asking or soliciting for it, and I cannot help considering it as an earnest of what His Majesty will afterwards do for you.

But what gives me most immediate joy is the satisfaction I shall have of being connected with you in business as we have long been in friendship : and as the ties are now double, I hope they will mutually support and fortify each other.

As you now are, there is hardly any thing left for me to wish you, only as I have been alarmed with the accounts of y^r health, I hope you will, for y^r country and y^r friends' sake, care to preserve it, and avert the danger which y^r ambition may prompt you to, of engaging in too much business.

I beg leave to offer my compliments to your Lady, and to my Lord Arnistoun, and hope you shall ever find me,—My dear Sir, yours most affectionately,   AND^W. MITCHELL.[1]

PRESIDENT FORBES to SOLICITOR-GENERAL DUNDAS.

DEAR SIR,—The last post brought me yours of the 25th of August, and with it a great deal of pleasure, as it expresses the very best sentiments that a young man entering upon office can entertain.

Insolence is so incident to Office that it is become proverbial, and a young man, of all others, ought to be the most on his guard against it. But then it has been ever observed, that it most commonly possesses low men, raised by some accident or jerk of fortune to employments above their merits, if not their hopes; it seldom lays hold of men whose abilities and rank in the world makes them equal to the office to which they are invited, and gives them reason to consider it as no elevation, tho' it be a preferment. I approve nevertheless mightily of the Resolutions you express. No man can be more securely guarded against an evil, which obscures, or rather, if I may be allowed the expression, which deforms every other good quality in the person whom it seizes. The apprehensions which made you deliberate on accepting the office, made, you may remember, no impression on me. I am glad you have dismissed them, and I entertain no doubt that the step you have taken will be to y^r own satisfaction, and to the satisfaction of y^r country. Nevertheless to make y^r mind easy I accept the first invitation you give me, and do promise you with the freedom of a friend to acquaint you with my sentiments on y^r conduct, whenever you think fit to ask after them, or, which I hope and believe will seldom be the case, when you do, or aim at, anything that may be blameable. You put, my dear Robin, too great a value on my friendship which may flow from selfishness, as it is the creature of y^r own making. The good opinion which you raised of y^{r}self in me begot it, and I hope it may serve, as long as you and I shall.

I am glad to hear that my brother Robin[2] has found great benefit from this summer's recess. I hope he has (during the fine weather which we have hitherto had) been improving it by exercise, and I would add, if it did not sound oddly from me, by abstinence.

---

[1] Mr. Mitchell was at this time Under-Secretary of State for Scotland.
[2] Lord Arniston, afterwards first President Dundas.

It is of great consequence that his health be properly established against our meeting in November. Pray give him this advice, with my compliments.—I am, my dear Robin, very truly, your most obedient and most humble servant,   Dun. Forbes.

CULLODEN, 4th Sept. 1742.

The Lord Advocate at this time was Robert Craigie of Glendoick, who had already been more than thirty years at the bar. Solicitor-General Dundas, on the other hand, was only twenty-nine years of age; but such was his natural force of mind that, in his official correspondence with the members of the Government in London, he never failed to hold his own, and he even sometimes spoke of his more experienced chief in a tone of kindly patronage. "I hope," he writes on one occasion, "a little more practice, not in the law but among men, will make him more cautious."[1]

Soon after his appointment as Solicitor-General, the first anniversary of his wedding-day arrived, when he received the following letter:—

From MRS. DUNDAS (HENRIETTA BAILLIE).

I have just now received your two letters, but my inclinations lead me in the first place to congratulate you upon the return of this day, as I find I have so large a share in the satisfaction it brings, and that's a happiness I hope shall ever increase, as long it pleases God to spare us together. I have signed the paper according to your direction, and think myself perfectly safe in following your advice, either with respect to business or anything else. . . .—Adieu my dearest. I am ever most affec^{ly} yours,

H. BAILLIE.

LAWERS, 18th Oct. (1742).

During the years 1743 and 1744 there was constant and ever increasing uneasiness in Scottish official circles. The fears of a new Jacobite attempt, which had never wholly ceased since the rising of 1715, were now increased by the dangers of a French war. The prevailing feeling with regard to the risk of a second rebellion was, indeed, one of incredulity, arising from an unwillingness to believe that the Highland clans would

---

[1] Letter to Mitchell, 23d Sept. 1742. Addl. MSS. British Museum, 6860.

again venture to take arms, and from an ignorant contempt of their powers. The real source of uneasiness was a lurking dread that the French might, in the event of war breaking out, attempt a landing on the shores of Scotland, where, among the followers of the Stuart dynasty, they might safely reckon upon a cordial welcome.

The Government of Scotland was, at this juncture, practically in the hands of a small group of men. The Marquis of Tweeddale was Secretary of State for Scotland. He had been appointed to this important office on the formation of the Wilmington Ministry in 1742; and his powers were ample, as ample, in Scotland, as those of the English Secretaries of State were in England. The patronage of all offices had, contrary to the wishes of the great Duke of Argyll, been bestowed upon him. The right of recommending to the Crown the persons who were to fill all legal stations, even the highest, was nominally vested in him; and all business connected with the administration of Scottish affairs was conducted in his office at Whitehall.

The Under Secretary of State for Scotland was Mr., afterwards Sir Andrew, Mitchell. Mr. Mitchell, who, for some time after this, was the constant correspondent of Dundas, was the son of the Reverend William Mitchell, minister of the High Church at Edinburgh. Originally destined for the bar, he is said to have abandoned that profession and taken to foreign travel, in order to drown the sorrow which he felt at the loss of his wife, whom he had early married. This course of life fitted him for the sphere in which he afterwards gained distinction; for, at the conclusion of his term of duty under Lord Tweeddale, he entered the diplomatic service, and was appointed Ambassador to Brussels. From Brussels he went to the Prussian Court; and at Berlin, having gained the character of a wit, he became a favourite with Frederick the Great. Several anecdotes have been told of his readiness in reply. On one occasion, during the Seven Years' War, the British Government failed to send a fleet, as they had promised, to operate in the Baltic against Russia and Sweden. Day after day Mitchell could only make excuses; until at length he found, one morning, that he was not invited, as usual, to the royal dinner table. "It is dinner-time, Mr.

Mitchell," said the officers of the household. "Ah, gentlemen," he replied, "no fleet, no dinner!" When Frederick heard this, he is said to have renewed his invitation. After the disastrous operations which led to the court-martial on Admiral Byng, the king said to Mitchell, "This is a bad business." "We hope, sir, with God's help, to do better," he replied. "With God's assistance?" said the king, "I did not know you had such an ally." "We rely much on him," replied the ambassador, "though he costs us less than our other allies!" These and many other well-known stories were told about him, and, though now forgotten, the Under Secretary for Scotland was a man of no little mark in his own day.

Lord Tweeddale and Mr. Mitchell were responsible for the Scottish Department in Whitehall. In Scotland the chief advisers of the Ministry were the Lord President, Forbes of Culloden, whose vast influence, great talents, and indefatigable energy had for many years been placed ungrudgingly at the service of his country; the Lord Justice-Clerk, Andrew Fletcher, Lord Milton, an intimate friend of the Duke of Argyll, and himself rivalling that statesman in his knowledge of Scotland and Scotsmen; Robert Craigie of Glendoick, a sound-headed and sensible man, whose career of industrious toil had raised him to the position of Lord Advocate; and lastly, Robert Dundas, the Solicitor-General, younger than his colleagues, but already displaying the administrative capacity for which his family was so distinguished. The ability and resources of this group of officials were about to be tried by the sudden and painful events of a civil war.

In February 1744 Sir John Cope was sent down to Scotland as Commander-in-Chief. Dundas was then in Edinburgh, and in constant correspondence with Whitehall (the Lord Advocate being absent in London); and the following letter throws some light on what was thought about Sir John Cope by men who knew him:—

Mr. MITCHELL to SOLICITOR-GENERAL DUNDAS.

WHITEHALL, 4 *Feb.* 1744.

SIR,—General Cope set out yesterday for Scotland. He was appointed Commander-in-Chief without much consultation. His

Majesty inclined to have conferred that command on Sir Robert Rich, but he declined it on account of his health, etc. Lord Mark Ker, and others, were very solicitous to have it. I am well assured that the D. of Argyll was not pleased with Sir J. Cope's being appointed, but notwithstanding of that, I make no doubt but he will be well received by the Lord and Lady J. C.[1] This gentleman[2] has been what the world call lucky in his profession. He has rose fast to considerable rank and preferment, without much service, and his success has been attended with the usual concomitants, envy and slander. But he certainly has both parts and address, to acquire the friendship of the great, and to make it useful to himself. As I have wrote you with great freedom, you will, I know, remember that what I have said is in confidence to you only, and I need not tell you how necessary it is that there be a perfect good understanding between you and the Commander-in-Chief. You will find him easy, well bred, and affable, and I fancy it will be an easy matter to gain his confidence. Some early civilities will make him yours, he being an absolute stranger in the country.—Yours, &c., And^{R.} Mitchell.

The fears of a French invasion increased among the members of the Government in London. It was the belief of Lord Tweeddale that "some desperate enterprise is resolved upon against this kingdom." In Scotland all seemed quiet; but Lord Tweeddale, on hearing this from Mr. Dundas, answered that he was not satisfied. "I am very glad to hear," he writes, "that there is not the least stir, as yet, in your parts, particularly in the Highlands; though I own I cannot help even suspecting so dead a calm at this time; and, therefore, I hope it will not make His Majesty's servants less upon their guard." Again Lord Tweeddale writes, upon the 25th of February 1744:—

LORD TWEEDDALE *to* SOLICITOR-GENERAL DUNDAS.

WHITEHALL, 25 *Feb.* 1744.

SIR,—I am glad to hear there has yet appeared no disturbances in Scotland; yet as I wrote to you in my last, I even suspect that dead calm. We know for certain that there are many French officers, Irish, and others, come over here, and are lurking about

---

[1] The Lord Justice-Clerk and Mrs. Fletcher, of Milton.
[2] Sir John Cope.

this town. I believe upon enquiry the same will be found so in Scotland. I have myself intelligence of two, whom I know to be there; the one Donald Stewart, brother of the same Stewart whom we were in search for last year, and who was formerly Quarter-Master in the Greys. The father of these Stewarts was once a farmer in the Knock of Kincardine, parish of Abernethy in Strathspey. The other is Alexander Bailey, called Capt. Bailey, but only a Lieutenant, as I am informed, in Clare's regiment in the French service. Both these officers are lately come from France, and are now supposed to be in the north of Scotland. I have, therefore, received His Majesty's commands to signify to you that it is his pleasure that warrants be issued for apprehending not only these two persons, but also all other officers at present in the service of France, who you happen to hear are in Scotland, since they can come here with no good design at this juncture. Supposing no invasion had been intended, their view, at least, must be enlistment for the service of that Crown. You will communicate this to Sir John Cope, and concert the manner of doing it with such of His Majesty's servants as you shall judge proper. Care must be taken, if any such persons should be seized, to secure all the letters and papers they may have about them, and those, if containing anything material, to be transmitted to me here, and the persons of such officers detained till further orders.—I am, etc.,

TWEEDDALE.

The letters which passed between Dundas and the Scottish Department disclose the fact, an unfortunate one for the public service, that he and the Lord Justice-Clerk were not on good terms. Lord Milton, as an intimate friend of the Duke of Argyll, may, very naturally, have been averse to admit to complete political confidence the son of that old leader of the Independent Whigs, who had, years before, opposed his patron with so much determination. He was inclined, Dundas complained to Lord Tweeddale, to consult Sir John Cope too much; and the Secretary of State had some difficulty in keeping the peace. "As to what you hint at," he writes, "in yours of the 28th, it is no more than I expected would happen. You know very well the Justice-Clerk is very assiduous in making his court to all strangers, and particularly to military men; but I think that should occasion no division at this juncture among you."

MR. MITCHELL *to* SOLICITOR-GENERAL DUNDAS.

WHITEHALL, *6th March* 1744.

SIR,—My Lord[1] had notice, by a letter from General Cope, that it was suspected the Marquis of Tullibardine was in Scotland. As his Lordship is not certain that this has been communicated to you as it was to the Justice Clerk, he desires me to tell you that, in case the General has failed in this particular, that it is his opinion you should show no mark of resentment on this occasion. The present state of the public affairs requires that such trifles should be overlooked, and that at least a seeming harmony should be preserved amongst His Majesty's servants. His Lordship is sensible that in your station some things may happen that will be disagreeable to you; but he depends upon your temper and prudence, and your zeal for His Majesty's service, that nothing of that kind will in the least influence your conduct at this juncture. I shall write to you by post this night.—I am, &c.,

ANDR. MITCHELL.

In subsequent letters the Marquis of Tweeddale and Mr. Mitchell continue to impress on the Solicitor General the necessity of preserving, "in appearance at least, a good correspondence between the Justice Clerk and you." Sir John Cope received express orders to consult both the Solicitor and his father, Lord Arniston, on the state of affairs; and "it is hoped," says Mr. Mitchell, "that Lord Arniston will not be shy in meeting and talking with them."

The position of public affairs was becoming more and more critical. "We are now," Mr. Mitchell writes on the 24th of March, "on the eve of a French war, and some of those who, these several years, have been bellowing for a war with France, now talk of nothing but the power of France, and the dangerous consequences of a war, a notable instance of how impossible it is to please a giddy and misinformed multitude."

In April Dundas began to feel the strain of continuous official work, and proposed leaving Edinburgh for a time. War had been formally declared at the end of March, and events in Scotland were more narrowly watched than ever. "I have," Lord Tweeddale writes on the 14th of April, "just now

---

[1] Lord Tweeddale.

seen a letter from you to Mr. Mitchell, wherein you signify your inclination of going to the country for some days. I cannot object to it, though I am sensible occurrences may happen in which I may wish to have your opinion as quick as the post will allow it; and, therefore, I desire you will take care that your letters be regularly transmitted."

Mrs. DUNDAS *to the* SOLICITOR-GENERAL.

I received yours with all the affection and gratitude imaginable, and it cannot but gratify my ambition to be secure of having the esteem and regard of a person whose judgement in nothing can ever be called in question, if it is not his partiality towards me. Your absence would have been more insupportable to me had I been in any other place than where I am.[1] Their manners here are, indeed, different from the generality of the world, and few are so well qualified to be friends; for they have all the accomplishments that are fit to constitute true friendship. I please myself with the thoughts of your agreeing perfectly with the country, and that your health is daily more confirmed. You are often made mention of here, and they beg, in a particular manner, to be remembered to you. My mama designs to write to you soon, and, in the meantime, begs you'll accept of her best wishes. —Believe me ever, my dear, most affectionately yours,

HEN. BAILLIE.

HOPT. HOUSE, *May* 21.

Meantime the war with France was in full progress; and the Arniston letters contain the accounts which reached Scotland of the varying phases of the contest, the successes of the English men-of-war and privateers, and the progress of the campaign on the Continent, mingled with directions for the arrest of suspected persons, instructions to watch the sea-ports closely, accounts of the debates in Parliament, warrants for the appointment of justices of the peace, with, now and then, stray items of court gossip,—while over all, coming nearer and nearer, hovers the shadow of the exiled family, the presage of impending civil war.

In July 1744 Lord Wilmington died, and Henry Pelham became prime minister. Carteret, whose motto, according to

---

[1] Mrs. Dundas was visiting at Hopetoun House.

Horace Walpole, was "give any man the crown on his side, and he can defy everything," was the royal favourite; and he and Mr. Pelham were estranged by mutual jealousy. The result was that, at the end of autumn, the country was plunged into a ministerial crisis. Carteret, now become, by the death of his mother, Earl Granville, had driven Mr. Pelham and his brother, the Duke of Newcastle, to inform the king that he must choose between their resignations and that of Lord Granville. Lord Granville resigned.

Mr. Mitchell *to* Solicitor-General Dundas.

Whitehall, 24*th Nov.* 1744.

Sir,—My Lord, who has not time to write, desires me to acquaint you that this morning the Earl of Granville resigned the seals, which His Majesty immediately gave to the Earl of Harrington. Next week there will be a new Commission for the Admiralty, but who will come in place of the Earl of Winchelsea, and what other changes will be made in that board, are not yet known, and perhaps not yet settled. How this will end I know not, but till the whole scheme is visible, those who wish well to a certain interest will, I hope, be very cautious of what they say or do.—I am, etc., And^R. Mitchell.

The administration which was now being formed was that which is known as the Broad Bottom Administration of 1744. "Great are the expectations of many," writes Mitchell, "and great will be their disappointment. Ld. G—lle, I am told, had very numerous levees there three days past;" and in another letter, on the 1st of December, "Nothing is yet done in the changes so much talked of, and indeed everybody, in their conversations, turn in and put out with so much freedom according to their affections and prejudices, that I can affirm nothing certain in these affairs." In a postscript to another letter he says, "I have heard that lately when a certain great man[1] brought a bundle of papers to be signed by ——,[2] that he said, 'Lay them down; I suppose these are warrants for your friends to come in and mine to go out,' etc. It is the general observation of those that attend the —— levee, that he speaks with

---

[1] Probably Mr. Pelham. [2] The King.

great affectation and temper to the late secretary, but hardly deigns to look at the reformers."

Mr. Mitchell to Solicitor-General Dundas.

WHITEHALL, 22 *Dec.* 1744.

DEAR SIR,—Inclosed I send you a list of such as have kissed hands this morning.[1] I believe the whole was not settled till late last night. What other changes will be made I cannot inform you, and with regard to your friend here,[2] some say the office will be suppressed, others that he will soon have a successor, and others that he will at least remain till the end of the session. Be this as it will, I hope you will continue to do the duty of your office, and you may be assured that so soon as anything is determined concerning your friends that you shall have timeous notice, that you may take the steps you shall judge most proper for your honour and satisfaction. . . . The bringing in of some of the Tories has given jealousy and discontent to many; and though I believe there will be no opposition immediately, yet a foundation is laid, from the discontent of the Whigs, and the disappointment of the Tories, which will one time or other break out with violence, for I believe the heads of the Tories will soon lose their influence with their party.—I am, &c., AND$^{R.}$ MITCHELL.

Mr. Mitchell remained at his post, so did Lord Advocate Craigie, and the Solicitor-General; and accordingly there was no change in the Scottish Department.

Mr. Mitchell to Solicitor-General Dundas.

WHITEHALL, 17 *Jan.* 1745.

DEAR SIR,—I had the pleasure of yours of the second, and I return you thanks for thinking of me during the Saturnalia, which you celebrated in the country. Happy should I have been to have shared in your mirth; but indeed this is no compliment, for I should be happy to be anywhere rather than here, so tiresome and so hateful is this evanescent state of being, in which I have not even the comfortable prospect of a sudden and honourable death. I will, however, follow the example of my betters, and stand by my

---

[1] Mr. Pelham's ministry of 1744 included Lord Hardwicke as Lord Chancellor, the Duke of Newcastle and Lord Harrington as Secretaries of State for England, the Marquis of Tweeddale as Secretary for Scotland, and Lord Chesterfield as Lord Lieutenant of Ireland.

[2] Lord Tweeddale.

standard till I am honourably dismissed, or meet with my fate. I have heard it rumoured that the office of ——— has been offered to the D. of Ar—ll, which he refused. Whether he had the option of naming a successor I do not know; but I am told he affects that both should be believed. Whatever be in this, I fancy we cannot subsist long, and I most sincerely wish that we may rather cease to be, than not be as we ought.—Dear Sir, I am most sincerely, yours affect*ly.* A. M.

Throughout the winter and spring of 1745 there were vague rumours of a Jacobite invasion. "There are," Lord Tweeddale writes to the Solicitor-General on the 2d of April, "several letters in town, mentioning a ridiculous story of a young man, who calls himself the Pretender's son, being in Scotland. By the description I have had of him, he appears to be the same person who was here about two years ago, and was actually taken up at the time of the invasion, and upon examination he appeared to be crazy; however, such stories and persons are not to be altogether neglected, and, therefore, you will enquire about him as prudently as you can." This story was, indeed, an idle tale. The young Pretender was still on the Continent. But towards the end of July other rumours reached Edinburgh and London, which were equally laughed at, but of which it would have been well for the Marquis of Tweeddale and Mr. Mitchell to have taken serious notice.

Prince Charles landed among the Western Islands on the 2d of August, or a few days before—the exact date is uncertain —and on the 2d of August Mr. Mitchell writes to Dundas: "I thought it needless to trouble you with any account of the intelligence about the young Chevalier, first, because I knew the Advocate would acquaint you with it, and then because I could hardly think seriously of that matter, the whole appeared to me so absurd that I was surprised to find the Lords of the Regency had ordered a proclamation; but they know best."

For many days the possibility of a serious attempt at invasion was denied.

MR. MITCHELL *to* SOLICITOR-GENERAL DUNDAS.

WHITEHALL, 17 *August* 1745.

DEAR SIR,—As you will be acquainted with the contents of the later expresses to Scotland, I shall say nothing of that matter, only I think the paragraph of the *London Gazette* fully strong for all the intelligence they yet have about this affair. It is surprising that this affair has made so much noise here, and occasioned a falling of the stocks. I wish I had money to purchase, notwithstanding the imminent danger.—I am, &c.,

AND^{R.} MITCHELL.

MR. MITCHELL *to* SOLICITOR-GENERAL DUNDAS.

WHITEHALL, 20 *August* 1745.

DEAR SIR,—As to the present affair, I have ever had doubts about the identity of the person said to be landed. The scheme appears so absurd and hitherto so ill supported that it seems to me more like a drunken frolic than a serious design. How anybody with you, where the truth may be easier known than it can be here, can be alarmed is to me astonishing, because there are troops more than enough for the purpose. I can imagine that from other views people may be glad first to magnify the danger, in order to raise their own merit, as physicians sometimes fright their patients only that they may cure them of something.—Yours,
A. M.

Even in Edinburgh it was the second week of August before it was known, that, beyond doubt, the young Pretender was in the Highlands. It was not till the 19th of August that Sir John Cope, promising to check the rebels easily, said good-bye to Lord Milton and Mr. Dundas, and started for the North. He was too late of starting, as all the world has known ever since. "I don't know what the devil possessed you all not to send Sir John north as soon as you at first intended," says Lord Deskford in a letter to Dundas. "Our country people are in great terror and consternation," writes Sir David Moncreiffe,[1] as the Highlanders were known to be approaching Perth. On the 9th of September, Mr. Hope of Craigiehall writes: "This morning I met one fresh from the north side, in whom there is no guile, but who, I know, is very well informed of what is given out at Perth by authority. Our conversation was much to the following effect: 'Well, what moves on your

---

[1] Sir D. Moncreiffe, Deputy King's Remembrancer, second son of Sir T. Moncreiffe of Rapness, and Margaret, daughter of David Smythe of Methven. He was afterwards a Baron of Exchequer.

side?' 'Nothing but what I suppose you have heard; they are now good 6000 strong, and gather strength every day.' 'Have they made any motion yet?' 'Oh no, they wait at Perth for Sir John Cope, if he'll come to them.' 'I hear he's at Aberdeen.' 'Yes, but there's a story that he dare not come forward, and intends to take shipping there.' 'Won't they go and meet him? It's not a great way from them.' 'No, they'll follow him south.' By this time I was almost struck blind by the strong blaze of Restoration in his face, and so we parted."

As it became known that Sir John Cope, instead of defeating the rebels, had never even given them battle, but had marched first to Inverness and then to Aberdeen, from whence he was to sail for the Forth, the "blaze of Restoration"—to use Mr. Hope's phrase—was seen on many faces. In Edinburgh all was uncertainty. The Whigs had ceased to despise the rebels, and were now seriously alarmed. The Jacobites were secretly exulting, and doing all they could to thwart the measures which, all too late, were being taken for the protection of the city. The Lord Advocate was on the spot, working night and day, and in constant consultation with Dundas. The citizens were clamouring for leave to take up arms, but were not allowed to do so by the Provost and Magistrates until the Lord Advocate and Solicitor-General had given a formal opinion that it was lawful.

MR. MITCHELL *to* SOLICITOR-GENERAL DUNDAS.

WHITEHALL, 12 *Septr.* 1745.

DEAR SIR,—I communicated yours of the 7th to my Lord Marquis. I wish you had been a little more explicit about the resolution of the Burgesses of Edinburgh, and how they came to have a dispute about a proposition in itself so clear. A particular narrative of this dispute, and of the arguments made use of, and by whom, might have been of very considerable service here at this juncture to show some people in their true colours, when stories are industriously and maliciously spread that I am ashamed so much as to mention to you for fear that you should imagine my keenness may have carried me too far.

It would surprise you was I to mention the little acts made use of to misrepresent everything that has been done, and to justify some great men's doing nothing. My Lord Justice-Clerk has wrote a most pathetick letter to the Marquis, setting forth the amazement and astonishment of his Majesty's faithful subjects, that no legal authority has yet been given for assembling and arming of them in defence of the Government. But his Lordship has skilfully avoided saying what authority was wanted, and my Lord has (by this express) desired he would point out what power he thinks at this time necessary for the support and protection of the well affected. I cannot help mentioning to you an opinion which I believe has been invented and published on purpose to justify the lethargy into which the Whig Clans seem to have fallen, and to excuse their not joining the King's troops, which is that by the law of Scotland it is high treason to arm without the King's special leave. I know no act that declares it so but that of 1661 for settling the King's prerogative with regard to troops, Militia, etc. But this Act declaratory of the prerogative, after a long usurpation, can never be extended to deprive the subject of the right of self defence, and in this country such principles are turned into open ridicule, as tending only to cover something that must not be avowed. Pray let me know your thoughts of this matter, and what you would think expedient to be done for the safety and protection of our country. It is impossible to persuade an Englishman that self-defence can be high treason.—Yrs., AND^R MITCHELL.

MR. MITCHELL *to* SOLICITOR-GENERAL DUNDAS.

WHITEHALL, 14 *Septr.* 1745.

DEAR SIR,—As I wrote to you by last pacquet, I have little to add, only I find, by the gross misrepresentation that is made of everything, how necessary it is to be informed minutely of what happens at Edinburgh, particularly if it had not been for the hint in your letter I might have so far been imposed upon by the boldness of the asserters, to have believed that the Crown Lawyers had averred that it was treason to defend the town unless the inhabitants had first an authority from the king. I wish, therefore, we had an accurate detail of the debate that happened in Council on that occasion, and who it was that suggested that ingenious scruple, and by whom it was supported, for the doctrine is so new and so extraordinary, that subjects have not the right of self-defence, that it has been matter of conversation in places where you could hardly think it would have reached. To be plain with you, a distinct account of this affair would be of very great service at this time.—Yrs.,   AND^R MITCHELL.

MR. MITCHELL to SOLICITOR-GENERAL DUNDAS.

WHITEHALL, 21 *Septr.* 1745.

DEAR SIR,—I had the favour of your's of the 18th from Dunbar, which I assure you has already been of very great service, and I hope you will soon send the second part when you have seen Baillie Hamilton. I wrote to him upon the first hearing of his stout and honest behaviour. I do not know whether he has yet received my letter, but a narrative from him of what passed in Council in the debate about arming the citizens would at this time be of use, and I fancy his own principles, and the usage he has met with, will make him not averse to give it. I imagine it is in his power to give an account of many circumstances previous to that debate that would give some light to the late dark and infamous transactions at Edinburgh. Had I leisure at present to write you but one half of the scandalous and malicious lies that have been invented, propagated, and believed, it would fully convince you how necessary it is at this time that friends here should be particularly and minutely informed of what happens in Scotland, for you know malice and slander, if they do not receive an early cheque, are at last not to be overcome.

I shall, in return, when I have a little more leisure, acquaint you with what turn is given to things here, and what arts are made use of to serve the most dirty purposes.

The part Lord Advocate and you have acted will be for your honour, when the particulars shall be known, as it has undoubtedly been for the service of the King and Country. I never thought to have lived to be almost ashamed to acknowledge my country. The late surrender of Edinburgh and the cruel reflections made upon the whole nation, must give every man pain who has the least sensibility, and the consequences of it will be severely felt afterwards. I hope this affair will be soon cleared up, and a particular narrative made out how and by whom it was conducted, that the innocent may not suffer in reputation with the guilty, and justice requires that the faults of a few should not be imputed to a whole nation. I am the more anxious that this should be done soon, because this dark transaction will be more easily traced while people's zeal is warm, and while their hearts are open with a sense of the injuries lately done them than afterwards, when I fear connections, and the specious, but false, humanity of screening the guilty by their silence will take place and disappoint national justice.—Yrs., And^r Mitchell.

The last of these letters was written on the 21st of September. On that day Sir John Cope had been completely defeated at the battle of Prestonpans; but this was not known in London until three days later. Dundas had left Edinburgh some time before, along with the Lord Advocate, and had, since the occupation of the city by the Pretender, been at Haddington, Dunbar, and Berwick. He accompanied Sir John Cope on his march from Dunbar to Prestonpans, and was by his side during the movements of the day before the battle. Late on the evening of the 20th, he and Craigie left the royal army preparing to bivouac for the night, with the rebels about a mile to the west, and rode off to spend the night at Huntington, the country seat of Mr. Thomas Hay, the Keeper of the Signet. Early next morning they heard the sound of guns, and soon learned that the force under Sir John Cope had been totally routed by the Highlanders. They then made the best of their way southwards to Berwick, stopping for a short time at Haddington, where Dundas assisted the Lord Advocate to write a hurried note to Lord Tweeddale with the news of Cope's defeat. This note reached Whitehall at midnight on the 24th of September.

Mr. Mitchell *to* Solicitor-General Dundas.

Whitehall, 24 *Sept.* 1745,
½ past midnight.

Dear Sir,—It was with unexpressible concern that I read this morning the accounts of the battle near Preston. God only knows what may be the consequences of it to our country. I shrink at the very thought of these scenes of blood and misery that must necessarily follow. I hope the Castle of Edinburgh will still be preserved. My Lord has wrote to the Advocate about it, who will shew you his letter. I hope the connexions you have in Edinburgh will enable you to do service on this occasion. Let no expense be spared, for it is of the utmost consequence to the nation.

Pray be very particular about what has happened. I never

before knew what it was to be so miserably anxious. A very minute detail of the facts and numbers is necessary, not for curiosity only, but for a justification of those you wish well to. . . . My heart bleeds for my friends who, besides these present hardships, must suffer the reputation of treachery, till the shameful surrender of Edinburgh be cleared up. I beg leave to offer my compliments to Lord Arniston. Pray let me know in your next where he is, and how he does.—I am ever most affectionately yours,
AND^W MITCHELL.

The following letter, which bears no date, was evidently written during the occupation of Edinburgh by the rebel army, and shows the alarm and uncertainty which existed among the relatives of those who remained true to the reigning family :—

LADY ARNISTON[1] *to her Stepson*, SOLICITOR-GENERAL DUNDAS.

(No date.)

MY DEAR ROBY,—I send this by express, both for security and haste, with one for your father which you'll be so good as to forward by the post, for I am afraid if the servant goes on all the way, he will not be back in time for to answer the end of sending him, which is to consult and get your advice what is proper for me to do. Since last Monday at eight o'clock we got two expresses from Edinburgh telling us that the town was to be destroyed by firing from the castle, unless a free communication was left for provisions to go up to them. The respite was only till twelve the next day, which occasioned a general consternation, sick people in bed, children with their nurses, men and women, all running out of town with carts full of goods, and of these we hear the Highlanders took a share. However, next day we were told the town had got a reprieve for six days till the return of an express from London, and by a proclamation, which you will see if the town is reduced, reprisals are to be made on all the abettors of the Government, which is a very general description. And as it is positively given out our houses are to be burnt, wherever protections have been given they are to be recalled. In short, we are to be ruined. If I could believe all this I would surely leave this place. But since the forfeitures of estates are to be given to defray the loss of what their friends may suffer, I can

---

[1] Anne Gordon, second wife of the first President Dundas.

hardly think they will destroy our houses or anything that may answer that purpose. However, I would be very glad to know if my husband and you would have me remove books and papers to any of our neighbours, where they could be safer than here—or if I shall run the hazard of their not carrying things to that extremity, and which is to depend upon the answer from London. I have no reason to expect ill from them personally, unless they change, for last night there was a protection sent out to me, dated yesterday. Since all this disturbance I was afraid to send it back for fear of exasperating them, but am resolved not to claim the benefit of it till I hear from you. I don't think it right to take a protection allegiance.—Farewell. God protect you and deliver us from these distresses. When Mr Dundas writes to me I beg you would forward it by express, in case it can be here time enough to serve for a direction for me.

Wednesday.—I would have wrote before, but knew not where to direct for either of you till last night.

―――― *to* SOLICITOR-GENERAL DUNDAS.

ARNISTON, *Oct.* 1, 1745.

DEAR ROBIE,—I came from your house [1] yesterday, where I left my Lady Carmichael a little frighted, but Mrs Baillie well and quite composed, really not more concern on her spirits than any rational man has, when his country is the scene of war, nor do I believe she will be easily cast down now that you are free from danger. ... Mrs Baillie delivered me your message, and I spoke to J. Fleming[2] to put the hounds all out to the tenants, for I thought they would be better there than in the kennel; and you may believe we will have very small joy in hunting when you are absent.

I sincerely wish you well, and that God may bless you and preserve you.—Yours, ADIEU.

No harm was done to Arniston by the rebels; and the Solicitor-General's wife seems to have remained safely at Ormiston Hall, his country residence at that time. "Mrs. Baillie," writes an anonymous correspondent, "is surprisingly easy and composed amidst the flying parties which have gone round about your house."

---

[1] During his father's lifetime Mr. Dundas lived frequently at Ormiston Hall, about twelve miles from Edinburgh.   [2] The factor.

ANDREW MITCHELL *to* SOLICITOR-GENERAL DUNDAS.

WHITEHALL, 28*th Septr.* 1745.

As my Lord Advocate will forthwith set out for London, my Lord Marquis leaves it entirely to you to determine whether you will remain in the north, or come here; but I cannot help on this occasion offering you my opinion, that you should continue for some time either at Berwick or Newcastle, in order to carry on the correspondence with Scotland, which at this time may be of the greatest service to the public, and I shall advise you from time to time of what is passing here.

Oct. 3*d.* 1745.

The Marquis of Tweedale requests Mr. D. to remain at Berwick or its neighbourhood, for the purpose of forwarding intelligence to Gov^t.

After this Dundas remained at Berwick till November. One Robert Mackintosh sends him a short journal, which may be given as a specimen of the shape in which information was frequently conveyed to the Government.

JOURNAL.

7th Nov.—From Berwick to Dunbar. 4 miles to East Dunbar, met a man passing off the way. Called on him, and he ran into a village, 'twixt the road and the sea, and was informed by another man that talked with him that he appeared to him to be a spy. Heard from a clergyman at Dunbar that advice had come from the Fife side to Admiral Byng of 3000 troops, mostly Irish, were embarked at Ostend, bound for the harbours of Montrose or Stonhyve.

8th Nov., Edin^r.—Arrived here and found all peaceable. But that last night Ro. Clark, vintner, and some others in liquor, walking the streets, insulted the City Guard, upon which a scuffle ensued, and Clark's leg was broke. It's given out here, from different hands, that last night 3000 Highlanders, viz., Frasers, &c., from the north, passed above Stirling to join the rebels (this fact is doubtful), and it's said that the 500 men that were reported as having deserted, are gone upon a secret expedition. A letter from a merchant in Lanark to his correspondent here mentions

that the Highlanders are passing there in numbers of ten to
fifteen in company, and enriching the country with arms of the
best kind, which they sell for what's next to nothing. It's
reported from good hands, that the Highland army, as they
marched from Edin^r., Dalkeith, &c., did not exceed 7000 in all,
and that they had thirteen piece of canon. That, upon search
made, more of the silver plate, &c., in Col. Gardner's house were
found in the house of one McLachlan in the Writer's Court.

DESPATCH (ANONYMOUS) to MR. DUNDAS.

EDINR., Sat., Nov. 9th.

. . . All accounts, from very different places in the country,
bear that the Highlanders are deserting in great numbers; sometimes 30 or 40 go off together. Several letters have been inter-
cepted from Lewis Gordon, brother to the Duke, directed to the
Duke of Perth, John Murray, &c. These letters are now in the
castle. I read two of the originals, the one directed to the said
Duke, the other to the said Murray. They are dated Huntly
Castle, October 28th, and bear that he finds the people in general
extremely averse to take up arms in support of the Prince, and
that force is absolutely necessary. This he says is entirely owing
to the vile Presbyterian Ministers, who instil into the people's
minds false and foolish notions, and speak disrespectfully of the
Prince and his abettors, but adds that he hopes to prevent their
future influence, as he has sent a written order to those of them
who are under his jurisdiction, requiring them not to preach in
their present strain, otherways they shall be forthwith punished
as the law directs. He speaks of his having formed a design to
take the President prisoner, but was disuaded from the attempt
by General Gordon, an old man who married Sir Thomas Mon-
crief's daughter, as a thing impracticable, in regard that 200 of
the Frasers, having attacked the President's house,[1] were repulsed
with considerable loss. He begs that General Gordon's name
may not be mentioned, as he does not choose to appear publicly.
The letter concludes with promises that he, Lewis Gordon, will
do all in his power to support the glorious cause, and an account
of the Lady Aberdeen's safe delivery of a son, who is now named
Charles. . . . This comes from the gentleman who parted with
you yesterday at Berwick, before you got out of bed."

[1] Culloden.

About the 12th of November Dundas returned to Edinburgh. The royal forces under General Handasyd were now approaching the city. On the 13th the General writes from Haddington: "Here I am, but much fatigued. Not being certain that the rebels were at Carlisle till Monday night at ten, it was twelve next day before I could leave Berwick. A worse march I never had. Pray make my quartering in the town easy for seven hundred horse, and fifteen hundred foot. I assure you we are so many. Almost dead with cold. Adieu."

Mr. Mitchell, though still in a state of great anxiety, finds time to say: "Pray desire any of your friends who have been in Edinburgh during the Highland Government, to write a detail of what passed, their reception, manner of living, and conversing, the P.'s intrigues, *bon mots*, and trifling incidents."

Very little trustworthy information regarding the movements of the rebel army reached either London or Edinburgh until it was known that, on the 4th of December, the young Pretender had entered Derby. The news reached London on the 6th, Black Friday, as it was called, and all was panic. "It is difficult to conceive," Mitchell writes to Dundas, "how few behaved like men." But on that very day the Highlanders were in full retreat to the north, and the invasion of England was at an end.

The year closed with brighter prospects than had lately seemed possible; but all danger was not over. "I am glad," Mr. Mitchell writes on the 31st of December, "that the city Edinburgh has had even a short reprieve from the fury of the rebels, for till the King's army has entered Scotland, I will not call it a deliverance."

In the meantime the Marquis of Tweeddale had made up his mind to resign the office of Secretary of State for Scotland. The jealousy between Lord Granville, the King's favourite, and Mr. Pelham, had not been diminished by the dangers of the Rebellion; in fact, they seem to have regarded the country's extremity as their opportunity for bringing matters to a crisis. Lord Tweeddale, as a member of the Granville faction, had for some time found his position becoming more and more uncomfortable, and he resolved to retire. In his letter to Dundas of the 31st December, Mr. Mitchell says: "My Lord Marquis has allowed me to communicate to you only that he intends to resign the seals on next Saturday. This I know you will not mention; and I am sure the news will neither surprise nor displease you. For my own part, and after what I have seen and suffered, the wonder is how he has had the patience to keep them so long." In a few days the resignation was publicly known.

ANDREW MITCHELL *to* SOLICITOR-GENERAL DUNDAS.

WHITEHALL, *2d Jan.* 1745-6.

DEAR SIR,—. . . The affair of my Lord's resigning is now publicly talked of, and he will deliver the seals next Saturday. I am sensible people will be divided in opinion about this step, but I think his Lordship would not do it without good reasons. Your own situation will make you sensible how disagreeable it is to act where there is not a perfect harmony, and a thorough trust in those you are concerned with, and the consequence of want of communication and confidence in a higher office is still attended with greater inconveniences and dangers. Whether the manner of giving up, and the time of it, be as friends would wish, I shall, when I am better instructed, inform you more particularly. In the meantime, give me leave to offer my opinion with regard to yourself, which is, that you should continue to act, as the public may suffer by your declining, and at this time an imputation of disaffection may be thrown out against you for not doing the duty of an officer, who, at this juncture, may be extremely necessary and useful to the King's service. I do not mean by this that you should continue in an office that cannot fail to be disagreeable to you, but only that you should not resign immediately, so as to to put it in the power of enemies to say that you have distressed them at a critical time. My reason for this is that, as your office does not depend on the Marquis, but on his Majesty directly, his giving up will not justify you. Besides, as you have taken great pains to enquire about the authors and abettors of this rebellion, your withdrawing at present may afford a pretence of letting people slip for want of evidence, and laying the blame, you know where. The friendship that has long, and I hope ever will, subsist between us, must be my apology for this freedom which I hope you will receive as I intend, being my own opinion only. I have not seen the Advocate since my Lord took his resolution; when I have talked with him, I shall write you what passes between us.

ANDREW MITCHELL *to* SOLICITOR-GENERAL DUNDAS.

WHITEHALL, 4 *Jan.* 1746.

DEAR SIR,—As I wrote fully by last post, I have now little to add. My Lord Marquis this day resigned the seals, and I hope his Lordship then took the opportunity of explaining to ———[1] his motives. I find this step has occasioned great variety of opinion; many disapprove of it as rash and ill timed. What may be in that you shall afterwards be informed.

When I wrote last you will believe, notwithstanding the length of my letter, that I was much hurried. I have since reflected on what I said, and I am confirmed in opinion that it will be highly improper for you to resign at least till affairs are settled, and those finished which you have begun. There is this material difference between you and our friend here that his office obliged him to move and give advice, and even right things from him were ill received, so that his country must suffer if he continued. But your case is different. Nothing can be required or expected of you but what is strictly legal and in the sphere of your employment. I may add as an additional argument that the Advocate, whom I saw this morning, is resolved to act till he shall be laid aside, and he promised to write to you by this post.—I am most sincerely yours,

A. M.

LORD ADVOCATE CRAIGIE *to* SOLICITOR-GENERAL DUNDAS.

LONDON, 4 *Jan.* 1746.

What determined the M.[2] to take this resolution is not proper for me to write, much less to give my opinion on the propriety or expediency of his taking it, especially at this critical juncture. His friends are of different opinions. But thus far I dare adventure to say that every reason of the Marquis's resignation at this time is against your or my copying his example . . . If his Majesty shall be advised to dismiss us either now or when the rebellion is over, possibly that may be best for us, and most desirable; but I cannot advise a desertion.

When the Solicitor-General's father, old Lord Arniston, heard of the resignation of Lord Tweeddale, he at once wrote to

---

[1] The King. [2] Lord Tweeddale.

his son expressing the opinion that nobody else should resign, "because resigning may shock the King, and we have always held it a medium in politics never to make war with the King whatever we do with his ministers." He adds, with a freedom of expression not usual in those days, when letters were liable to be opened at the post-office, "While you are in office it's your duty to correspond with some of the ministers, and 'tis my humble opinion you direct your letters to my Lord Harrington, not to *that brute the Duke of Newcastle.*"

But Dundas had made up his mind to resign, and told his father so. The old gentleman was indignant, and wrote his son a letter full of the most astute maxims.

LORD ARNISTON *to his Son,* THE SOLICITOR-GENERAL.

STOCKTON, *Jan.* 12, 1746.

SON,— . . . I hope you will think over the matter again before resigning, notwithstanding what ill usage or discouragement you may have met with. Some of many reasons I have against your resigning are: in the first place, since the Duke[1] is to all appearance coming to Scotland to command, and is, I hope, by this time set out on the road, your station and office must give you frequent opportunities of waiting upon him and forming an acquaintance; and whether you may not get the better of some other people, whose patron he does not much favour, is at least an equal chance, and the rather, considering the company that are to attend him, Duke of Montrose, Duke of Queensberry, and Earl of Rothes. Now, I don't think any advantage can attend your resignation just now, equal to what may arise from this opportunity and acquaintance. At least I should think this single incident sufficient reason for delaying your resignation two months. In the next place, I know the King's temper pretty well on this point. There is nothing he takes more amiss than resigning upon pretence, or reality, of disobligation or ill usage from his other servants. His way of thinking and speaking is that all his servants ought to have their eye to him, and that if one suffer wrong from another, he ought to find his own way of making his grievance known to him, and not to throw up, or, as he calls it, "refuse to serve him," because they are not pleased with one another; and, indeed, the doing so is a sort of injury to him, which he scarce ever forgets.

---

[1] Duke of Cumberland.

Now, I believe, it is a maxim amongst all good politicians, that however much they may be disobliged at one another, yea, tho' secretly they should be disobliged at the King himself, they are never to show it, if they don't resolve to incapacitate themselves from serving their King and country for that King's reign at least, which is a situation in which no man at your age should put himself.

In the third place, resigning at this time is plainly giving a great victory to those who may be your enemies. When a man is laid aside in the course of a change at Court, that is the effect of the King's pleasure and of the other side's influence there, which is thought nothing of, but ofttimes does a man honour, gains him more friends, and perhaps puts him in the way of making a better figure than before without the King's displeasure. But where people make a man so uneasy as to make him throw up from resentment, it is they that get the triumph. It is their deed and not the King's, for which they take the glory to themselves.

In the fourth place, whatever you may write or say with truth, as to your reasons of resigning, your taking this nick of time, immediately upon Tweedale's resigning, and also in the midst of so hot a rebellion, will give those who like to do it the strongest opportunity for misrepresenting you to the King, and to all the ministers, in as bad lights as they please. They can paint you as a bigotted party man, yea, as one disaffected; that you give up at this time, both to put matters into confusion, and to withdraw your service when the Government most wants it. They may go so far as to say, that at bottom it shows your inclination to another when you withdraw your hand from the plough in labouring time; and such prejudices will not be removed, however falsely impressed, by all your assurances to the contrary . . . Indeed, to conclude, I do not think resigning can be at all approved of in a time of such distress and danger. If they say they have no use for your service, and so throw you aside, why not? But I would not have you refuse to serve till the rebellion is at an end. When that is over then you may do what you will. It may then be a time to show resentments, and then time to shun what may come to be a disagreeable work. But now I don't think it a time at all to resign.— Farewell. Yours, Ro. Dundas.

In spite of his father's objections, Dundas resigned his office of Solicitor-General, giving as his reason the heavy nature of his duties; and his resignation was at once accepted. His real reason was the difficulty he found in holding his own against the Lord Justice-Clerk, who, it appears, did not treat him with sufficient confidence, and was, therefore, constantly putting him in a false position. Lord Arniston was much annoyed, and wrote his son a long and angry letter, in which he declared that "provocations from the L. J. C.[1] I never would have minded one figg . . . as I now know that neither his impudence nor his patron's high power could have been able to turn out one man, I mean either the Advocate or you. I must own, your so obstinate resolution, notwithstanding, has given and does give me very great vexation. . . . You have by this step established for ever the power of the very man that I believe you and I abominate."

LORD ADVOCATE CRAIGIE *to* MR. DUNDAS, LATE SOLICITOR-GENERAL.

LONDON, 16*th Jany.* 1746.

DEAR ROBIN,—I have yours of the 9th with the unpleasant account of your having resigned your office. It is too late for me to complain or to insinuate that the reasons of your conduct are insufficient. At the same time I cannot help wishing that in a matter so delicate you had waited until you could have had your father's opinion. I shall only add that I congratulate you on the quiet and ease you'll now enjoy. You'll have vacation till June, and I hope the disturbers of our quiet are got so far north as to leave you and your concerns free of any apprehensions of danger. I am still in the storm, and so is my little family, and God only knows how I shall ride it out, and when it will be over with me.

PRESIDENT FORBES *to* MR. DUNDAS, LATE SOLICITOR-GENERAL.

CULLODEN, 26*th Jan.* 1746.

MY DEAR ROBIN,—I have yours of the 16th, which gives me no small uneasiness. I can, without much auguring, see that your situation was difficult. But at a season such as this, a man must bear and rub them, those difficulties, as well as they can. I know how painful it is to bear the insolence of office; and I know you too well, to think that you would choose to submit to it, in a season of calm and tranquility. But there is somewhat in our present situation that makes me wish you had tugged a little longer at the oar, because the step you have taken may give your enemies an opportunity, not only to misrepresent you, but to lay

---

[1] Lord Justice-Clerk (Fletcher of Milton).

your act to the account of your friends. Arniston (for whose recovery I heartily rejoice) certainly advised right; and I sincerely wish for many reasons you had drudged on, till I might have had the good fortune to see you. There is, however, now no help for it, and I am convinced you will forgive me, for telling you my sentiments freely. . . .—I am, my dear Robin, affectionately yours,
DUNCAN FORBES.

LORD ADVOCATE CRAIGIE to DUNDAS.

LONDON, *Feb. 11th*, 1746.

DEAR SIR,— . . . I don't know if you have advice of the revolution in our Administration that happened yesterday, and is still going on to the surprise of most people. The Duke of Newcastle and Lord Harrington resigned the seals, upon what occasion I believe is not publicly known; and in the afternoon his Majesty sent for E. Granville, and gave him the seals. This morning Mr. Pelham resigned as Chancellor of the Exchequer, L. Gower as Privy seal, D. of Bedford as First Commissioner of the Admiralty, E. Pembroke as Groom of the Stole. The Chancellor resigns on Thursday, as to-morrow is the first day of the term. How many more resign is uncertain, or who are to be successors. E. Bath succeeds Mr. Pelham. They say D. of Argyll resigns; but whether he does or not, he has for once lost his power.—Yours,
ROB. CRAIGIE.

This letter alludes to an event which took place at the beginning of February 1746, and which is described by Lord Mahon as "a short but singular ministerial revolution."

"The Royal favour had been," says Lord Mahon, "for some time engrossed by Lord Granville (Carteret); the Pelham brothers found themselves treated with coldness and reserve, and apprehended that in carrying the supplies this winter they would only be paving the way for their own dismissal at the end of the session. To them the unquelled rebellion appeared, not as a motive of forbearance, but only as a favourable opportunity for pushing their pretensions. They determined, therefore, to bring the question to an issue, and to concentrate their demands on one point—an office for Pitt —to whom they were bound by their promises, and still more by their fears. The king, however, steadily refused his assent to this arrangement. . . . A resignation was now resolved upon by nearly all the ministers. In this affair the Pelhams prudently shrunk from the front ranks; the van therefore was led by Harrington, he being the first, on the 10th Feb., to give up the seals, and thus drawing on himself the King's especial and lasting resentment. He was followed on the same day by the Duke of Newcastle, on the next by Mr. Pelham. . . . His Majesty immediately sent the two seals of Secretaries of State to Lord Granville (who was indisposed) that he and Lord Bath might form an administration as they pleased. . . . After various offers and repeated refusals, this ministry of forty hours was dissolved, and Lord Bath announced its failure to the King. . . . His Majesty had no other choice than to reinstate his former servants, and admit whatever terms they now required. It was agreed to dismiss from place the remaining adherents of Bath and Granville, amongst others, the Marquis of Tweeddale, whose office as Secretary for Scotland was again abolished."

Craigie resigned before the end of February, and was succeeded, as Lord Advocate, by William Grant of Prestongrange. Dundas was succeeded, as Solicitor-General, by Patrick Haldane and Alexander Home, who held the office jointly. No new Secretary of State for Scotland was appointed in place of Lord Tweeddale. And thus, long before April came, with the final defeat of the Pretender at Culloden, a sweeping change had been made among the persons on whom had fallen the burden of maintaining the royal cause during the early days of the Rebellion.

CHAPTER IX.

THE SECOND PRESIDENT DUNDAS—*continued*.

AFTER the close of the Rebellion, Dundas attended assiduously to his practice at the bar, to which, as he no longer held office, he was able to devote his full attention.

Old Lord Arniston's health had been failing for some time. He suffered much from gout; but his intellect was still robust. The long letters which he wrote to his son, and particularly those in which he remonstrated with him for resigning the office of Solicitor-General, are full of acute reasoning, though couched in somewhat violent language.

During the Rebellion he was compelled, by an attack of gout, to leave Scotland for some time, and journeyed about, staying, among other places, at Stockton, Darlington, and Morpeth. When he returned home he was, evidently, suffering from low spirits, and his wife [1] found him very difficult to deal with. In one letter to her stepson, Mrs. Dundas describes how impossible she found it to induce the old gentleman to look into the state of his family affairs. When she pressed him on the subject he "shows the greatest signs of grief and perplexity, and wishes he were dead." At last he resolved to retire from the bench;[2] a resolution which nearly ended the brilliant career of his son, and which might, by destroying the influence of his family, have materially changed the course of Scottish political history. For Dundas declared that if his father left the bench he would leave the bar, and retire into private life. The following letter explains how he was induced to remain in office :--

---

[1] Anne Gordon, Lord Arniston's second wife.   [2] *Supra*, p. 99.

MRS. DUNDAS *to her* STEPSON.[1]

DEAR ROBY,—When I came home last night, as I found your father in a disposition to hear me, I entered on the subject you spoke to me of. I repeated all the arguments I could recollect against resigning, and concluded with assuring (him) that if he did throw off one gown, you would throw off the other; that the trifling gains you acquired were no inducement to you to slave in the manner you now do, but the hopes you had of being able, some time, to raise yourself into a station where you might be more useful in the world; that if he resigned all that was at an end. You was sure of being run down. He was impatient to let me finish what I had more to say, and, stretching out his hand,—"You need say no more. If my Roby thinks it would hurt him that I should resign, I will never do it. Let me bear affronts, contempt, &c. I never will be a hindrance to the views of a son I so much esteem as well as love." I thought it would be a pleasure to you to know this; and that makes me give you this early disturbance.—I am ever yours.

Thursday Morning.

P.S.—If you will send us Lord Lovat's trial, I should take great care of it and thank you, for your father grudges to buy one of them.

We have already seen how the death of Lord President Forbes, in December 1747, put an end to all Lord Arniston's ideas of leaving the bench, and how he not only secured for himself the vacant chair, but had the satisfaction of seeing Lord Justice-Clerk Fletcher—"that puppy," as he used to call him—thrust aside in the course of the intrigues which led to his own elevation.[2]

In 1750 Dundas was urged to offer himself for the vacancy in the representation of Lanarkshire, caused by the death of Sir J. Hamilton. His wife, Miss Baillie, was a Lanarkshire heiress, and it was thought that he would be a strong candidate in the Whig interest. He declined, however, as will be seen from the following letters, from unwillingness to enter Parliament at that particular time, and also from a feeling of doubt as to whether he would receive the support of the Government:—

---

[1] No date; probably in April or May 1747. [2] *Supra,* p. 103.

MR. DUNDAS *to the* HON. CHARLES HOPE WEIR.[1]

March 25, 1750.

DEAR CHARLES,—As the death of Sir James Hamilton is now beyond doubt, and as I am persuaded that you and I agree entirely in our sentiments of the politicks of that county, a letter from me on that subject needs no apology. My great and indeed only view is that we should if possible send a proper representative in his place to Parliament. It is some time since I disengaged myself from what I will be allowed to call these low schemes of politicks, which, to my grief, I have too much seen prevail in this country. But the great and fundamental scheme of Whig and Torie I will never divest myself of, since at all times I shall use my utmost endeavours to countenance the one and discourage the other. I therefore make no doubt you will concur with me in following it out. I had a message from one gentleman assuring your humble servant that if I had any view to Parliament he would endeavour to make the matter easy. But you know I have long preferred quietness to politicks, which makes me have no inclination that way. However, I gave for answer that I wished no hasty resolution to be taken until there was a general meeting of the county, when we might all consider of a proper person.

HON. CHARLES HOPE WEIR *to* LORD HOPETOUN.[2]

LONDON, *March* 20, 1750.

Within these few days we have lost our member for Clydesdale by the death of Sir James Hamilton. Mr Pelham sent for me yesterday morning to ask me about the situation of that county, and who might be a proper man to propose there. I told him (as it appeared to me) that if the person would think of it himself, the most proper man would be our friend Robin Dundas, and who I believe would be acceptable to all the friends of the Government in that shire; (and I really think in the present situation of the shire the friends of the Government, I mean the

---

[1] Hon. Charles Hope Weir, third son of the first Earl of Hopetoun by Lady Henrietta Johnstone, daughter of the first Marquis of Annandale. On the death of his uncle, the second Marquis of Annandale, Mr. Hope succeeded to the estate of Craigiehall, in West Lothian. He married the daughter and heiress of Sir W. Weir of Blackwood, in Lanarkshire. He was M.P. for West Lothian.

[2] John, second Earl of Hopetoun.

Whig interest, should and may make the member). Next to him I proposed John Lockhart of Castlehill. But I was still doubtful how far either of these gentlemen would be persuaded to come into Parliament, but that I was persuaded they would agree with me in supporting any man that should be proposed for the county upon a Whig interest, rather than let anybody come in on a contrary one. He said any friend to the Government would be acceptable to him, particularly a man of Mr Dundas's character, and wished we might all unite in support of the Whig interest, which surely is the natural one in the county. I promised to inform myself as soon as possible how matters stood, as if either our friend Robin or John Lockhart will think of it, to go down immediately and lend any poor help I could towards this scheme. I would have wrote to Mr Dundas himself, but as I don't know whether he may be in the east or west country, and that possibly you may before now know his opinion with relation to this affair, I thought it best to write to you, and beg you will let me know how matters stand. If necessary (I mean if you don't already know his sentiments) send him this letter. I don't offer advice nor opinion, but will heartily assist in the scheme if he has any such.

MR. DUNDAS *to the* HON. CHARLES HOPE WEIR.

March 26, 1750.

A few hours ago I had a letter from Lord Hopeton inclosing one which he had yesterday received from you concerning the election. . . . I wish the election may go to our minds. For my own part, if I were convinced that my going into Parliament could be of real service to the Whig interest, I should think it my duty to yield up my own private ease and tranquillity to serve a cause which I have ever warmly espoused. But I do not look upon myself as a man of so great consequence. I cannot at present vary my resolution of continuing in the private and retired sphere which I have acted in for some time past. You indeed mention in your letter that Mr Pelham would not be displeased with one of my character. As a friend to the Government I will not disown my being flattered by this expression, as it is my earnest desire that my attachment to the Government should be known and believed by every person in his Majesty's service. Since my name, therefore, has been brought upon the carpet, I trust that you, as my friend, will do me the justice of representing me as willing and desirous at all times of promoting his Majesty's interest, without regard to any mean or selfish views.

Mr. Dundas *to the* Hon. Charles Hope Weir.

Ormiston Hall, *Ap.* 10, 1750.

DR Cha.,—I was favoured last post with your letter of the 3^d. There was no occasion for any protestations either of your friendship or your sincerity in the sentiments you there express. I entertain not the least doubt of either. But friends daily differ in opinion, which is our case at present, as after the maturist deliberation I cannot see any sufficient reason to alter my sentiments of not offering my service to our county of Clydesdale. I never have indeed said that I am resolved at no time to go into Parliament, but at this time I am certainly resolved.

The Government interest was given to Patrick Stuart of Torrance, who was returned in the Whig interest in opposition to Hamilton of Aikenhead, who was put forward by the Hamiltons. Both Dundas and Mr. Hope Weir voted for Mr. Stuart. Those were the days of small constituencies; and at the election the numbers were:—

Stuart 17.
Hamilton 12.

Mr. Mitchell expresses in his letters the regret which he had felt on hearing that Dundas had declined to stand for Lanarkshire. Three years, however, passed before he made up his mind that the proper time had come for him to enter Parliament; and, when he did so, it was for his own county of Midlothian that he wished to stand.

Mr. R. B. Ramsay *to* Mr. Dundas.

By the misfortune of my horse's coming down with me in coming here from Kinghorn the 28th ult., I got a strain, which deprived me of the honour of waiting on you in paying the last duty to my Lord President's funeral, as I intended, whether I had been invited or not.[1]

You know so well that it is unnecessary to inform you how it

---

[1] The Lord President had died on the 26th of August. *Supra*, p. 109.

came about that I was elected to serve the county of Edinburgh in Parliament upon Sir Ch. Gilmour's death. As it was a thing, when proposed, that I had not entertained a thought of, so had I rested on my own opinion, without regard to those who intended me such an honour, I should have declined it. The most grateful return I could make those gentlemen who had importuned me, was to accept of their offer, and as the election happened in the middle of a Parliament, should I tire of this post of honour, which it was more than equal chance I should, I had only the half of a Parliament to attend. This was a lucky incident for me. I have not altered my sentiments, but am fully satisfied with the half Parliament, and you, I think, are the first person I should tell it to.

It was my sincere wish that you should have come in for the county at last general election. Whether from an aversion to the thing, or from a point of delicacy with regard to your friend (Sir C. Gilmour), I can't say, but you took an effectual method to prevent any solicitation on that score. I would fain hope you have now thought more favourably of this scheme, and will stand for the county next election. To remove all scruple with regard to me, I tell you again I am determined to the contrary. I will without compliment say farther, that tho' I were inclined to make another attempt, and were sure of success, yet I would cheerfully give it up, could I prevail upon Mr Dundas to take it up. You have the sincere good wishes of all happiness to you and yours of your most obedient humble servant,

Robt Balfour Ramsay.[1]

BALBIRNY, 14th Sep. 1753.

Dundas thought his time had now come, and was only waiting till the next dissolution of Parliament. He had little fear of opposition. Sir Alexander Dick writes from Prestonfield, on the 13th of October: "The letter you gave me for Lord Milton[2] I delivered him next day at Salton, and he expressed himself, as I took him, very hearty in your interest at next election, and said he knew of no sort of opposition you could possibly have, by which means I think our harmony is complete in this county."

---

[1] Mr. Ramsay of Whitehill and Balbirny, M.P. for Midlothian.

[2] Andrew Fletcher, who resigned the office of Lord Justice-Clerk in 1748, see *supra*, p. 103. He retained, however, his seat on the bench, as an ordinary Lord of Session.

The three years which had elapsed since Dundas declined the Lanarkshire invitation, had been uneventful. In England they were years of quiet, when nothing singular occurred in politics, except, perhaps, the appearance on the scene of Lord Bute as an aspirant for the honours of the State. In Scotland the policy of Mr. Pelham and Lord Hardwicke, and the feeling, now universal, that the Stuart cause was desperate, were slowly but surely bringing even the most lawless portions of the Highlands into order and the appearance, at all events, of loyalty. But the sudden death of Mr. Pelham, in March 1754, and the ministerial changes which followed, when his brother, the Duke of Newcastle, became Prime Minister, led to a dissolution of Parliament. The Midlothian election took place on the 25th of April 1754, and Dundas was returned unopposed in the Whig interest.

He had chosen exactly the right moment to enter Parliament. In July one of the judges, Patrick Grant of Elchies, died, and the Lord Advocate, William Grant of Prestongrange, succeeded him on the bench. The Duke of Newcastle, instead of appointing either of the Solicitors-General, Mr. Haldane and Mr. Home, to Grant's office, which would have been in accordance with the ordinary rule, gave the place to Dundas, who was accordingly appointed Lord Advocate on the 16th of August 1754. He was re-elected for Midlothian, having resigned his seat on taking office, on the 20th of December.

LORD TWEEDDALE *to* LORD ADVOCATE DUNDAS.

YESTER, *Aug.* 7, 1754.

I had great pleasure in hearing you were the person pitched on for the office of Lord Advocate, as I think it will be for the service of his Majesty and Government. The placing you in such a rank shows a just regard to your own merit, as well as a remembrance of your father's great services. I think you judge perfectly right for many reasons in making a trip to the Highlands. Whatever is in my power towards contributing to your executing this office with satisfaction to yourself, shall not be wanting in one who has always been with great truth and regard,—Yrs., etc. etc.,

TWEEDDALE.

P.S.—The Marchioness offers her compliments to you, as we both join in the same to Mrs. Baillie.

EARL OF MARCHMONT[1] *to the* LORD ADVOCATE.

REDBRAES, *Aug.* 20, 1754.

I received the favour of your letter by last post. I congratulate you most sincerely on the mark you have received of his Majesty's regard for you, and the justice done by it to your merit.

As I have always entertained the highest esteem for you, and the greatest desire to obtain your friendship, you cannot doubt my heart's exulting at every honour done to you, nor that upon every occasion I shall be glad to express my sentiments for you. I know your zeal for our happy establishment, and you will want no assistance but your own good sense to direct you in your conduct with the Ministers. Lady Marchmont presents her compliments and congratulations to Mrs. Baillie, to whom I desire to offer my respects. Be persuaded that I am with the greatest truth and esteem,—Etc. etc. etc., MARCHMONT.

Mrs. Dundas was not spared to see the remainder of her husband's career, as soon after his promotion to be Lord Advocate she sunk into bad health. In the spring of 1755 she was very ill, and he was summoned from London to see her.

MR. JOHN LOCKHART *to the* LORD ADVOCATE.

The good accounts I received by last post from Mr. Smith, of our valued friend Mrs. Baillie, gave a most sensible satisfaction to my wife and me, as some accounts we had got of her illness, a little before that, had given us inexpressible uneasiness. At the same time it was extremely agreeable to me when I reflected on the exquisite happiness you would have on your arrival at home, by finding her so much better than you could have reason to expect, from the accounts that were sent to you; and I assure your Lordship that I enjoyed a very considerable share of the pleasure that you would feel on that occasion. I most earnestly pray God for her speedy recovery, which is the greatest blessing that can happen in this life to you and your family; and I am certain it is most sincerely wished for by every person who hath the happiness of her acquaintance. The present scarcity of such characters in life make them of great value and importance. . . . I shall long, with great anxiety and impatience, to hear that Mrs. Baillie continues in a fair way of recovery, that you have suffered

---

[1] The fourth Earl of Marchmont.

nothing by your quick journey from London, and that Lady Carmichael and the rest of your family are in good health. All your friends here are well. They offer their most humble compliments to Lady Carmichael, Mrs. Baillie, and to you, and join in their most sincere wishes for long health and happiness to you and to all your family; and I am, with great respect and esteem, my dear Lord, your Lordship's most affectionate cousin and most humble faithful servant, Jn⁰ Lockhart.

CAMNETHAN, *Apr. 7th*, 1755.

In spite of all good wishes, and though from time to time there were hopes of her recovery, Mrs. Dundas grew worse. On the 10th of May Mr. Baird of Newby writes: "I most sincerely condole with you in your present distress, but hope all is not lost that is in danger. She has our constant prayers for her recovery." He then mentions some matters of business. But the answer is a hurried note, in the handwriting, apparently, of a clerk or secretary: "Lord Advocate desires me to acquaint you that he is in such distress about Mrs. Baillie, who is exceedingly low to-day, that he could not write you himself, nor can he at present think of any business." Three days afterwards she died, on the 13th of May 1755; and her husband was left to mourn the loss of one whom he describes as "one of the most sensible, amiable, and affectionate women that ever made a man happy."

In the following month, Charles Yorke,[1] in thanking Dundas for congratulations on his own approaching marriage, alludes to the death of Mrs. Dundas: "I thank your Lordship heartily for your kind and friendly congratulations. I will not say too much in answer to them, lest the contrast be too strong between the happiness which I have gained and that which you have lost. I feel greatly for your Lordship, upon the occasion; because though your mind is firm, and your reason well prepared, yet the best minds and the best understandings are always the most open to tender and generous affections. I beg you to continue a share of your friendship to me."

---

[1] Hon. Charles Yorke, second son of Lord Chancellor Hardwicke, and himself Lord Chancellor in 1770. He died on the 20th of January 1770, three days after his appointment, when about to be created Lord Morden.

When Dundas became Lord Advocate the country was in a very different state from that in which it had been when he last held office, and there was no longer any dread of a Jacobite rebellion. Nevertheless the Highlands were a source of considerable anxiety, and his attention, as first law-officer of the Crown, was constantly directed to the measures which were considered necessary for keeping the clansmen in order. A few extracts may be given from letters which show the state of things in the north at this time :—

Governor of Fort Augustus to the Lord Advocate.

Fort Augustus, 13 *Dec.* 1754.

My Lord,—I was much concerned at not seeing your Lordship before I left Edinburgh, to have received your Lordship's commands for the Highlands, and returned my grateful thanks for the many civilities received at Arniston House. . . . At present the country is pretty quiet, and no manner of theft among these wild Tartars ; and, with very little pains, I am confident that in a short time there will not be an outlaw left in this neighbourhood. Glengarry has behaved, among his clan, since his father's death, with the utmost arrogance, insolence, and pride. . . . He has declared that no peat out of his estate should come to this fort. As this garrison is to be supplied with coal next year, I have given out that I am heartily sorry that Glengarry, by his folly, will be the ruin of so many people, whose only subsistence and support are by the peat. The bait has taken, and the whole country complain loudly against him. His whole behaviour has greatly alienated the affections of his once dearly beloved followers. I shall take all opportunities of improving this happy spirit of rebellion against so great a chieftain, which may in time be productive of some public good."

From the Same.

Fort Augustus, 20 *March* 1755.

My Lord,—Although I had the honour of writing to your Lordship last post, I cannot omit acquainting your Lordship of a famous hunting match on Loch Laggan side by the Badenoch gentry, about a month ago, where many appeared in arms. Among them was M'Donel of Keppoch, M'Donel of Aberarder, Macpherson's son, of Strathmashie, and M'Donel of Tullacrombie, who

I hear has his Grace of Gordon's protection to carry arms. There were many more, but these were all I could get the names of. They killed ten deer, and sent two as a present to Lady Cluny.[1] The people of Badenoch are in great spirits on the prospect of a war, and say it will soon be an intestine one. I have people out, in several parts of the country, to find out if any strangers are come over, and what is doing among them. The two men who escaped being taken for perjury, about Lovat's second son, are now in Badenoch. I have sent one to try and fix them. I much doubt of success.

P.S.—Excuse the liberty I take in suggesting to your Lordship that, in case of a war, some notice should be taken of the many able Chelsea pensioners fit for service that live in this country, many of them Papists, and all disaffected.

On the 13th of August 1755, General Watson writes from Fort Augustus a long letter, in which he gives an account of a journey which he had just made through part of the Highlands. "Since I was last in Edinburgh," he says, "I have made the round of all the west coast of Argyllshire, and from Fort William came here. In this journey I had the pleasure of seeing a great change in all respects to the better, a foundation of both wealth and industry in many places; and the people sensible of their present happy situation. . . . I came through Appin and Ardshiels. The King's tenants[2] upon this last estate appear already visibly more happy than their neighbours, and the poor wretches everywhere cried out for schools and a kirk. Your Lordship will be amazed when I tell you the miserable Indians of this very country (who are in the parish of the island of Lismore) have not had access to any sort of worship for three years past. What a shame and disgrace! And yet they are called British subjects and Protestants. It gave me great pleasure to hear several instances amongst the common people, who, when they were like to be oppressed in the old way, actually refused, and threatened going to complain at Edinburgh, which threatening had the desired effect, and you'll easily believe I don't neglect the

---

[1] The wife of Macpherson of Cluny, whose husband was at this time an outlaw on account of the Rebellion of 1745.

[2] The forfeited estates were vested in the Crown, and their revenues devoted to improving the condition of the people.

doctrine of always encouraging the common people to mutiny against every ancient and usual piece of former oppression."

The stronghold of disaffection was in Badenoch. There, for nine years after the disastrous close of the Rebellion, Macpherson of Cluny had concealed himself from a large body of troops, who were stationed in the district for the express purpose of finding him. More than a hundred of his clansmen knew where he was; and a reward of £1000 was offered for information against him. Yet such was the fidelity of the Highlanders that nothing would induce them to guide the troops to that secure retreat which they had constructed for their chieftain among the precipices of Ben Alder. "When I came to Badenoch," General Watson says, in his letter to the Lord Advocate, "I found the Macphersons greatly alarmed at the unexpected visit of the troops. They had prepared a most plausible Highland story of Cluny's having left the country and gone to France, all which I knew to be a mere lie, so would not trouble your Lordship with a letter about the report. As they see the Government is in earnest, I must submit how far it would be proper to bestow some attention upon those who favour and countenance his staying in the country. I know it's what they expect and dread. If your Lordship approves of this measure, I shall send you one who will tell the names of his constant associates and harbourers. The fellow I mean is sorely disobliged, and, like a true Highlander, thirsts for revenge."

Cluny was never apprehended. He escaped to France in 1755 (perhaps he had already left Badenoch by the time General Watson reached it), and died, in the course of the following year, at Dunkirk.

Although the Arniston influence was not yet so powerful as it became during the last twenty-five years of the century, Lord Advocate Dundas was not much interfered with in dispensing the large patronage at his command. The power of Archibald, Duke of Argyll, was certainly great, and Andrew Fletcher, Lord Milton, the Duke's representative in Scotland, and the chief recipient of his confidence, was still as much suspected by Dundas as he had been in the days of old Lord Arniston. "I hinted to you," writes Sir David Moncrieffe to the Lord Advocate, who was then in London, "that a certain person was openly making up to Lord Milton, which proceeded from advice from Whitehall, and several others are following his example." He adds, in a postscript, "The President and his son-in-law dined on Friday at Brunstane;[1] and this day the visit was returned." In fact all Lord Milton's movements were narrowly watched, and Moncrieffe, whose duties as Deputy King's Remembrancer, kept him chiefly in Edinburgh, appears to have sent to Dundas when in London regular accounts of who called on his Lordship, who dined with him, and what new alliances he was supposed to be concocting. But, as a rule, Dundas had matters his own way, and enjoyed the full confidence of Lord Hardwicke, who represented the ministry in matters relating to legal patronage.

LORD HARDWICKE *to* LORD ADVOCATE DUNDAS.

POWIS HOUSE, *June 28th*, 1755.

. . . " He (first President Dundas) used to do me the honour to write his thoughts to me very freely on all vacancies that happened in the Court; and I thought it of great utility to the public service, for it often produced good, and generally prevented anything that might have been very wrong. I wish, as your Lordship does, that the present President[2] would do the same. Your notions of clanship, whether of the Highland or Lowland kind, are extremely right, and I shall endeavour to make the best use and application of them as occasions may arise. I hope the scheme[3] which I have opened to you is not tainted with anything of that nature. It is one of the worst infections that can creep into a Court of Justice. I have heard of something of that sort in the days of old Sir Hugh, but not since.

In 1752 Mr. David Hume succeeded Ruddiman as Keeper of the Advocates' Library. The proposal to appoint Hume was strenuously opposed. The candidate who was put up against him was Mr. Kenneth Mackenzie, at that time Professor of Civil

---

[1] Lord Milton's country house, about five miles from Edinburgh.
[2] Craigie of Glendoick.
[3] Two judges had died in June 1755 (Lords Murkle and Drummore), and the "scheme" was to appoint Andrew Macdowal of Bankton, and George Carre of Nisbet, to succeed them. This arrangement was carried out.

Law in the University of Edinburgh.¹ The contest excited great interest, not only among the members of the Bar, but among all classes in Scotland. "'Twas vulgarly given out," Hume writes, "that the contest was betwixt Deists and Christians; and when the news of my success came to the playhouse, the whisper ran that the Christians were defeated. Are you not surprised that we could keep our popularity, notwithstanding this imputation, which my friends could not deny to be well-founded? The whole body of cadies bought flambeaux, and made illuminations to mark their pleasure at my success; and next morning I had the drums and town music at my door, to express their joy, as they said, of my being made a great man. They could not imagine that so great a fray could be raised about so mere a trifle."²

Lord Advocate Dundas, at that time Dean of Faculty, had supported Mr. Mackenzie, a fact which was perfectly well known to Hume, and which doubtless gave additional point to an amusing letter which the historian wrote to Mr. Dundas, two years later, in the following circumstances. In June 1754, Mr. James Burnet,³ Mr. Thomas Miller,⁴ and Sir David Dalrymple,⁵ who were then curators of the library, found that three French books, *Les Contes de la Fontaine*, *L'Histoire Amoureuse des Gaules*, and *L'Écumoire*, had been recently purchased for the library. These books they forthwith ordered to be struck out off the catalogue of the library, and removed from the shelves as "indecent books, and unworthy of a place in a learned library." Against this absurd order, much more absurd than if the curators of to-day were to direct the removal of the works of Zola or Daudet, Hume remonstrated, and, at the beginning of the following winter session, he wrote as follows to the Lord Advocate:—

MR. HUME *to* LORD ADVOCATE DUNDAS.

20th Nov. 1754.

MY LORD,—Reflecting on the conversation which I had the honour to have with your Lordship yesterday, I remember that your Lordship asked whether I insisted that these three books

---

[1] Minutes of the Faculty of Advocates, 28th Jan. 1752.
[2] Hill Burton's *Life of Hume*, vol. i. p. 371.
[3] Lord Monboddo. [4] Lord Glenlee. [5] Lord Hailes.

must be in the library? I believe I answered that the books were indifferent to me, and that being once expelled I did not see how they could be restored except by being bought anew. This answer was the effect of precipitation and inadvertence. I take this opportunity of retracting it; that if your Lordship be so good as to interpose your authority in this affair, you may be informed of the grounds on which I conceive the matter to stand. The expelling these books I could conceive in no other light than as an insult on me, which nothing can repair but the re-instating them. Mr. Wedderburn and Mr. Millar, who certainly had no bad intentions, will not, I hope, regard my insisting on this point as any insult on them. And if any of the curators had bad intentions, which I hope they had not, there cannot in the world be a more rejoicing spectacle, nor one more agreeable to the generality of mankind, than to see insolence and malice thrown in the dirt. These qualities, which are always dirty, must in that case appear doubly so.

There is a particular kind of insolence which is more provoking as it is meaner than any other, 'tis the *Insolence of Office*, which our great poet mentions as sufficient to make those who are so unhappy as to suffer by it, seek even a voluntary death rather than submit to it. I presume it is chance, not design, which has exposed some of the curators to the reproach of this vice. But I am sure no quality will be more disagreeable to your Lordship, for if I may judge by the affable manner in which you received me, your late promotion will operate no such effect upon you.

As to the three books themselves, your Lordship has little leisure from more grave and important occupations to read them; but this I will venture to justify before any literary society in Europe, that if every book not superior in merit to *La Fontaine* be expelled the library, I shall engage to carry away all that remains in my pocket. I know not indeed if any will remain except our fifty pound Bible, which is too bulky for me to carry away. If all worse than *Bussi Rabutin*, or *Crebillon*, be expelled, I shall engage that a couple of porters will do the office. By the bye, *Bussi Rabutin* contains no bawdy at all, though if it did, I see not that it would be a whit the worse. For I know not a more agreeable subject both for books and conversation, if executed with decency and ingenuity. I can presume, without intending the least offence, that as the glass circulates at your Lordship's table, this topic of conversation will sometimes steal in, provided always there be no ministers present. And even some of these reverend gentlemen I have seen not to dislike the subject. I hope your

Lordship will excuse this freedom, and believe me to be, with great regard,—My Lord, your Lordship's most obedient and most humble servant,
DAVID HUME.

It is probable that Dundas approved of what the curators had done, and that Hume knew this when he wrote his letter. If so, the Lord Advocate's conduct, strangely narrow-minded in a man who had seen so much of the world, was quite consistent with the part he took in the squabbles which followed the production of the celebrated "Tragedy of Douglas."

It was in February 1755 that the Rev. John Home rode up to London with the manuscript of "Douglas" in his saddle-bags, soon to return and disappoint his friends by telling them that the great Mr. Garrick had pronounced it unfit for the stage. But in the following year it was brought out at the Edinburgh theatre, which was then managed by West Digges, the actor, the story of whose adventures would form a romantic chapter in the history of the stage in Scotland. Among those who strongly supported Home was Lord Milton, and this alone was sufficient to prejudice Dundas against both Home and his play. Either out of a spirit of opposition to Lord Milton, or for some other reason private to himself, the Lord Advocate incurred the lasting dislike of the Moderate party, in the Church of Scotland, by not only joining the ranks of those who attacked the Tragedy of Douglas and censured Home for writing it, but also by refusing to use his influence with the Presbytery of Dalkeith to induce them to withdraw their prosecution of Dr. Carlyle for his warm support of Home. "A word from him would have done," says Carlyle bitterly.

Home was compelled, in order to avoid deposition, to resign his living; and several clergymen, who had ventured to attend the theatre, were severely censured. But the common sense of the public triumphed.

"The play," says Dr. Carlyle, "had unbounded success for a great many nights in Edinburgh, and was attended by all the literati and most of the judges, who, except one or two, had not been in use to attend the theatre. The town in general was in an uproar of exultation that a Scotchman had written a tragedy of the first rate, and that its merit was first submitted to their judgment. There were a few opposers, however, among those who pretended to taste and literature, who endeavoured to cry down the performance in libellous pamphlets and ballads (for they durst not attempt to oppose it in the theatre itself), and were openly countenanced by Robert Dundas of Arniston, at that time Lord Advocate, and all his minions and expectants. The High-flying set were unanimous against it, as they thought it a sin for a clergyman to write any play, let it be ever so moral in its tendency."[1]

In 1756 Dundas was advised to marry a second time. The lady whom he proposed to espouse was Jean, third daughter of William Grant, Lord Prestongrange, his predecessor in the office of Lord Advocate.[2]

LORD HOPETOUN *to* LORD ADVOCATE DUNDAS.

(No date.)

DEAR ROBIN,—I have talked over your affair fully with my friend and well-wisher. We both agree in applauding the measure in general, not only as rational but even necessary in your situation, and I think it will be extremely lucky for your young family, especially the eldest, if they fall soon into such hands as we would wish for a meet help to you. A woman of prudence, good nature, temper, activity, economy, etc., etc. And for sake of the dear baby we would have her heart remarkably good, generous, and disinterested. Nothing less will please. But how far the person in view may come up to this character is what we are absolutely ignorant of, which we regret, because had we any access to know it nothing should be concealed from you in a point of such consequence, and where it is so difficult for you to come at the truth, even tho' your acquaintance had been longer and more intimate than it has been, or tho' she herself had been better known to the world. So that we can only add our best wishes that everything may be directed for the best. As to the family, relations, and connections, you are thoroughly acquainted with these particulars yourself, and can judge perfectly in them.

I expect the bearer will bring me a return from the Chief Baron, which you shall know, but at any rate Saturday shall be devoted to you in one shape or other.

I ever am most sincerely, My dear Lord,—Yours, etc.,

HOPETOUN.

---

[1] Autobiography, p. 311. [2] *Supra*, p. 150.

The marriage took place in September 1756, when Miss Grant brought her husband the small fortune of £2000. The first Mrs. Dundas had died shortly before Charles Yorke's marriage; and just three years after Mr. Dundas's second marriage he heard from Lord Hardwicke of the death of Mrs. Yorke.

LORD HARDWICKE *to the* LORD ADVOCATE.

GROSVENOR SQUARE, *July* 31, 1759.

MY LORD ADVOCATE,—I am much comforted by what your Lordship says that the country is so very quiet, particularly in the Highlands. . . . What you say of the Annexation Act is the highest commendation of it; for, if it terrifies the men of estates from going into rebellion, the lower people will not be easily drawn out in any numbers. This is an argument that always chiefly weighed with me, and which I much laboured in the debate in the House of Lords.

I think such a militia scheme as ours cannot take place in Scotland. But many schemes are going forward for raising regiments in several counties, and I wish you would be so good as to favour me with your opinion on that subject.

I have had an irreparable loss in my family by the death of your friend the Solicitor's[1] wife; had much illness in it, and been very ill myself. I thank God we are now much better, and I pray for your health.—I am, etc. etc. etc., HARDWICKE.

LORD HARDWICKE *to the* LORD ADVOCATE.

WIMPLE, *Sept.* 6, 1759.

I am extremely obliged to your Lordship for the kind and affectionate manner in which you take notice of the melancholy breach Providence has been pleased to make in my family. The loss is indeed never enough to be lamented, particularly by the poor Solicitor, who has been inconsolable. Nor can I blame him, for there never was woman formed with greater sweetness of temper or more amiable qualities. However, I hope his Christian philosophy and the necessary avocations of his business will in time work a cure. As to myself I had an ugly illness, partly occasioned by the effects of this heavy stroke, and partly by the

---

[1] Lord Hardwicke's son Charles, at that time Solicitor-General. He married Catherine, daughter and heiress of the Rev. Dr. W. Freeman of Hammels, Herts.

excessive heats of the season, but thank God I have had no relapse, and am now perfectly well. I hope your Lordship and all your family continue so, which I do most sincerely wish, and am, with great truth and esteem, etc. etc. etc.,

HARDWICKE.

Lord President Craigie died on the 10th of March 1760. Lord Advocate Dundas immediately proceeded to London to press upon Ministers his claim to the vacant chair. A negotiation had been set on foot for giving the President's chair to the Justice-Clerk, Erskine of Tinwald.[1] But Mr. Dundas's claim seems to have been at once admitted, for on the 18th of March he was able to acquaint Lord Prestongrange with "the material alteration in my situation of life," his Majesty having been pleased to declare his intention of appointing him successor to Mr. Craigie. Mr. Dundas was also successful in obtaining promotion for his friends Miller[2] and Montgomery[3] to the vacancies caused by his own elevation, the former becoming Lord Advocate, and the latter one of the joint Solicitors-General. Montgomery quaintly expressed his gratitude:—

"Gratitude I have always considered as a cardinal virtue; and if I am possessed of any good quality and know myself, I must be forgiven to say that I think I possess it in as strong a degree as any man living. I have a letter from London by this post, that so much fills my mind in that way that I cannot resist the impulse of writing your Lordship in this manner. The application will be easy."

LORD PRESTONGRANGE *to* LORD PRESIDENT DUNDAS.

PRESTONGRANGE, *March* 25, 1760.

MY DEAR LORD,—Your letter of the 15th I received here late on Saturday night. It contains a confirmation of the news your spouse had wrote to me the post before, and in my return to hers I have in effect answered this of yours, giving you my sincerest congratulations and best wishes on your new preferment. I am, however, obliged to you for informing me somewhat more fully of circumstances which I pretty well understand, tho' for historical

---

[1] Letter, Mr. Montgomery to the Lord Advocate.
[2] Thomas Miller of Glenlee, afterwards Lord President.
[3] James Montgomery of Stanhope, afterwards Chief Baron.

2nd President Dundas.

satisfaction there may yet be *éclaircissements* wanting, which in due time I may receive from you, when it shall please God that we meet. In the meantime it was agreeable to me to hear that regard and goodwill towards me are still declared by those from whom I expected that disposition. I say this is soothing whether there shall ever be occasion for its producing any benefit to me or not. As for yourself, distrust not your own abilities farther than to quicken your attention and diligence in discharging the duties of your new station. God has blest you with a ready apprehension and a good memory, which are valuable qualities for that office. Your eldest and youngest daughters are both well, and yesterday we heard at Edinburgh from Arniston that all the children were well there. It will be agreeable to us to hear from you when leisure permits. All here join in their compliments to you and your company, whom we constantly remember, and I am ever, my dear Lord, very affectionately yours, W. G.[1]

LORD HARDWICKE *to* LORD PRESIDENT DUNDAS.

GROSVENOR SQUARE, *June* 12, 1760.

MY DEAR LORD,—The great and inexpressible affliction I have been under ever since the receipt of your letter of the 31st of May, has prevented my paying my respects to your Lordship till now. Indeed, at this time, I am not very fit either for correspondence or company, but Providence requires that one should struggle with patient resignation under such tryals.

I am very glad that the rejecting of the Scotch Militia Bill is not disagreeable to many of the best friends of the Government. They judge very rightly, for I am thoroughly persuaded that the passing of it would have been advantageous only to its enemies. I know your Lordship has so much spirit, and so manly a way of thinking, as to despise the ill-placed abuse, which the

---

[1] Descendants of the three daughters of William Grant, Lord Prestongrange.

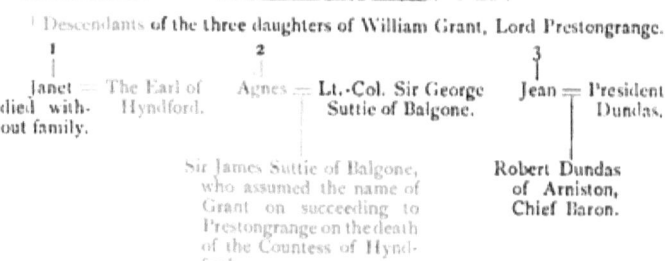

favourers of that scheme may throw out against you. You may safely wait for *the echo*. I am pleased you do not mention that it is likely to prejudice your interest in the county of Edinburgh. What I read in the printed papers you sent me are mere *bruta fulmina*.

It is my duty to acquaint your Lordship that the King is extremely pleased with the part you and I took in the bill to continue the laws relating to the tryal of treason comitted in the Highlands, and the disarming; as also with the success of it. I did not suffer that bill to pass through the House of Lords *sub silentio*, but made motion relating to it myself, in a full House.

As I trust your Lordship is by this time completely Lord President of the Session, permit me to repeat my congratulations on that subject. Nobody can possibly wish or augur better for your Lordship than I do, from the best evidence, experience, as well in respect of your own honour, the able and impartial administration of justice, and his Majesty's service. It may with truth be said of your family, *Non deficit alter aureus!*—I am, with the most cordial wishes for your health, and with the utmost truth and respect, My dear Lord, etc. etc. etc.,   HARDWICKE.

LORD HARDWICKE *to the* LORD PRESIDENT.

WIMPLE, IN CAMBRIDGESHIRE, *Aug.* 31, 1760.

MY DEAR LORD,—The kind letter, with which your Lordship honoured me on the 16th instant, was the longer in reaching my hands by reason of my residence at this place. I had heard of the misfortune which detained you from taking your seat in the Court of Session, and as I partake in every concern of yours, truly sympathised with you upon that unhappy occasion. My own wound is too fresh and too far from being yet healed not to make me feel very sensibly for those distresses of others.

I had a letter from your successor[1] in the Advocate's office, dated but two days before yours, wherein he says that for you which your Lordship's modesty would not permit you to say for yourself. I sincerely congratulate you on this happy entrance upon your high office, so much to the honour of your Lordship's abilities and temper, and I cannot help auguring from it all kinds of good success for his Majesty's service, the reputation of his justice, and the general utility of his people. Indeed, I never

---

[1] Miller of Glenlee.

entertained any doubt in my mind but that the event would be so, and rejoice to see it verified.

It gives me much satisfaction to hear that the clamour about Militia subsides. I always looked upon some of the compliments which were lately paid as efforts to keep alive the expiring embers, but notwithstanding them, I am persuaded it will not be long before they are extinguished, and shall look with pleasure upon the election for the county of Edinburgh passing without opposition as one proof of it.

The "clamour about Militia" mentioned by Lord Hardwicke was occasioned by the strenuous opposition of Dundas to the proposal to establish a Militia force in Scotland. The statute by which the Militia of England was organised, passed in 1757; but when it was proposed to have a similar body in Scotland, the Government hesitated, on the ground that too short a time had passed since the Rebellion, and that it would be unsafe as yet to arm large masses of the people. An influential party in Scotland were indignant at this; and the policy of Ministers was represented as an insult to the nation. The chief argument used by Dundas against the proposal was that the manufacturers of Scotland would be ruined by arming the population; but he was heartily abused for not advising the Government to have the same Militia law for all parts of Great Britain. A bill for the purpose of raising a Militia in Scotland was brought into Parliament in the spring of 1760; but it could not become law in consequence of the opposition of the Government. Dundas addressed the House of Commons against it (the rough notes which he used in making his speech are among the Arniston papers); and his opponents openly stated that "this speech was the price paid for his being made President immediately after." But for this accusation, it need hardly be said, there was no ground. The Militia Acts were extended to Scotland in 1793, in the days of his brother Henry Dundas.

Dundas had now reached the highest judicial position in Scotland, the duties of which he discharged, with the most distinguished ability, for the long period of twenty-seven years. At this point may be inserted an autobiographical account of his career, which the President wrote a few years before his death:—

"SKETCH OF MY SCHEMES OF MANAGEMENT FROM NOVEMBER 20TH, 1737, WHEN I RETURNED TO SCOTLAND FROM FRANCE.

"I got cash from my father £160, 10s., exhausted by arrears of board and wages due to my travelling servant, and expenses of entering advocate.[1] Discovered a claim on my Father most just, but would have vexed him greatly; I paid it without his knowledge, and thus began the world £300 in debt. Trusting to my resolution to be a man of business, I never demanded nor got a shilling more from my father. Lived with him, but never allowed money to be expended for myself, my servants, or my horses; when cash was necessary, e.g., for oats, I paid it. Indeed on my marriage in October, 1741,[2] I got a settlement, which at an average yielded £230 per annum.[3]

"I found affairs (on succeeding to Arniston at his father's death in 1753) much encumbered with a great load of debt, provisions to seven younger children, most of them young and still uneducated.

"I was advised to take the entailed estate, and not to intermeddle at all with the succession. I was greatly distressed betwixt duty to my own growing family, and abhorrence of a step which in some degree reflected on my father's memory.

"I was relieved by a few words from one of the most sensible, amiable, and affectionate women that ever made a man happy, who spoke nearly these very words: 'Take up his succession without hesitation, keep your father's estate, be kind to and educate your younger brothers and sisters, finish the house and policy about Arniston, it looks ill in its present situation; surely my estate and yours together will leave an opulent succession to our children; if necessary sell a part of mine, I will execute any deed you ever require.'

"Indeed, after this, my resolutions were easily taken, and I took up my father's total representation; but I mention the fact for the honour of Mrs. Baillie's memory.

---

[1] Entered advocate in 1738.
[2] President Dundas married, in 1741, Henrietta, daughter and heiress of Sir James Carmichael Baillie, of Lamington and Penston.
[3] The lands of Newbyres and Newbyres Mill, which were settled upon him by his father, as a provision on his marriage.

"But all these flattering hopes and pleasing prospects were totally blasted on the 13th May, 1755, by the unfortunate and unexpected death of one of the best of women. Then, indeed, I found myself in an awkward and ticklish situation. Possessed of my father's estate, partly entailed, and partly unentailed, a load of debt, paid or to pay for him, also seven of his younger children, and six of my own. I did deliberate with my own mind, and came to the resolution of executing a faculty personal to me, of selling a part of the entailed estate. To use all my interest—which was then something—with Lord Chancellor Hardwicke, the Duke of Newcastle, even the Duke of Argyle, and this to procure some assistance from his Majesty's generosity, and I was successful.[1]

"Thus have I explained my conduct with regard to money matters since my very first entry on the stage of life. On reviewing it I cannot blame the principles, but I frankly acknowledge I have perhaps misspent large sums of money. But as I have not hurt my paternal estate, surely a man may sport a little with his personal acquisitions, especially as any useless expense has chiefly been laid out to beautify and improve the estate which my son is to enjoy. Let it be also attended to that I supported a family and parliamentary interest, both here and in England. Had these been allowed to decay, Mr. Cockburn had never been Sheriff, nor Henry Dundas Member for the County, nor I President of the Court of Session.

"If my son follow business, things may answer with economy and good management. Idleness and dissipation produce certain ruin. When my manner of living, my attendance six sessions in Parliament, the education of so numerous a family, are all considered, it cannot surprise that I have never been able to diminish my debt. It is more just to wonder how I have hitherto gone forward in life. Let me then tell the principles which ensured what success in life I have enjoyed:—

"1st. Studying mankind to learn their tempers;
"2nd. Accommodating myself to various tempers;

---

[1] Alluding to a claim for repayment of money disbursed by his father in the service of Government after the rebellion of 1715. He received repayment to the amount of £4093.

"3rd. Preserving inflexible integrity;

"Lastly. For encouragement to my son in steady adherence to my profession, the profits of the Bar[1] have yielded £41,212.

"The character I gained created a degree of esteem in the young heart of Miss Baillie, which (though vile arts were used) never left her till it gained her total affection. This gained me the friendship of three worthy men, all inimical to my father—President Forbes, Lord Hyndford, and the Earl of Findlater; and in money it made me independent, set me out in a high sphere of life, and laid the foundation of all my future success."

---

[1] It must be remembered that these "profits of the Bar" represent the sum earned during a long and successful career of nearly fifty years, twenty-seven of which were passed in the President's Chair.

President Dundas entered Advocate in 1738. During the first five years of his professional life, his "Law Profits" averaged £280 a year. From 1743 to 1754, eleven years of what may be called the second stage of his professional career, when he held the office of Solicitor-General, and was chosen Dean of the Faculty, his "Law Profits" averaged £546. During the six years from 1754 to 1760 while Lord Advocate, and M.P. for the County of Edinburgh, at the head of his profession, and leader of the Scotch bar, his "Law Profits" averaged £1500 a year. His receipts as Advocate, during twenty-two years, were under £18,000. As President, his salary at first was £1200, subsequently £1500, and finally £1800 a year.

CHAPTER X.

THE SECOND PRESIDENT DUNDAS—*continued*.

King George the Second died on the 25th of October 1760; and in the world of politics men speculated on the changes which might soon be seen, the certain advancement of Lord Bute, the chances of the general election which was now necessary, and the distribution of honours with which the new reign might be expected to commence. The Lord President, though never allowing political concerns to interfere with his devotion to the duties of his office, jealously watched for any encroachment on the family influence (which now, indeed, was passing into the guardianship of hands abler even than his own), and continued, amidst all changes, his correspondence with official personages in London, by whom he was kept fully informed of everything that was passing in ministerial circles.

Lord Hardwicke *to* Lord President Dundas.

Grosvenor Square, *Nov.* 13, 1760.

My dear Lord,—The sudden, most melancholy, and afflicting event, which happened on the very day your Lordship's last letter was writ, so struck my mind and engrossed my thoughts, as well as brought on so busy and hurrying a scene, that I have been hindered from acknowledging it till now. I will only say we have lost a great and gracious master, whose memory I shall always revere, and to whom I shall ever acknowledge my many obligations with the utmost gratitude. I know your Lordship thinks in the same manner.

Our present sovereign sets out in the most amiable manner; engages all hearts by the sweetness of his temper, and every praiseworthy quality; and gives the most promising hopes of the happiest and best government. His Majesty has shown great grace and regard to the old servants of his grandfather; invited the Duke of Newcastle to continue in his service, who, notwithstanding his age, has accepted; which, as it was attended with the most pressing instances of all his friends, has met with a very general approbation. From hence your Lordship may safely conclude you have some friends about the Court.

LORD HARDWICKE to LORD PRESIDENT DUNDAS.

GROSVENOR SQUARE, *Dec.* 31, 1761.

Your letter of the 21st made me extremely happy by the persuasion it gave me of your Lordship's good health, and of your kind remembrance of your old friends. I am extremely obliged to you for the continuance of your goodness in the second volume of Ld Fountainhall's laborious lucubrations. Your Lordship's observation is extremely true that it does not furnish so many anecdotes as the former. That makes it fall short in indulging the curiosity of such readers as myself, who have look'd upon it historically. But it is much for the happiness of the country, and strongly marks the difference between the Government preceding the Revolution, and that subsequent to it; tho' I entirely agree with your Lordship in opinion, that the real and uniform liberty of Scotland commenced with the Union. Before that period, one reign might be better, and more regular and moderate than another. But the publick law of your country was under the greatest uncertainty, and subject to arbitrary decision and execution.

Your Lordship's friends here are in good health, particularly the Duke of Newcastle, and as much your friends as ever; not happy in being under the necessity of seeing a Spanish war added to a French one; but as it is plain that Spain had taken her part, and it was become unavoidable, it must be supported and repelled with spirit. *Ne cede malis, sed contra, audentior ito.*

LORD HARDWICKE to LORD PRESIDENT DUNDAS.

GROSVENOR SQUARE, *March* 16, 1762.

I am extremely obliged to your Lordship for your kind present and kinder letter, which gave me much pleasure. The latter made me hope that you were got free from the gout, and had recovered your health and spirits. This was very agreeably confirmed to me by Mr Moncrieff when he was so good as to deliver me the book of decisions of the English judges during the usurpation by your Lordship's order. I will confess to you that I am a little angry with the editor for publishing a work of that kind so drily and nakedly, without the names of those judges, or any historical anecdotes accompanying it. This was the more material, as it is chiefly a matter of curiosity, since I doubt much whether your Lordship and your brethren will suffer the decisions to be quoted upon you as authorities. There is very little to be found about this constitution in the histories of those times. . . . In Whitelocke's Memorials I find two short notes, page 508, of their first appointment to sit at the usual place; and page 509, that they met and heard a sermon, and that *Mr. Smith*, one of them, made a speech to the company on the occasion of their meeting. This is the only name I can find; and 'tis remarkable that it is the same with your first English Chief Baron after the Union. If your Lordship could, without trouble, procure me any historical anecdotes concerning these *Kinless Rascals* I should esteem it a favour.

As a Scotch militia has been stirring in Scotland, so it has to a certain degree here, and a meeting of the Scotch members has been held upon the subject. As to myself I have made up my mind upon that point; *omnia praecepi et mecum animo ante peregi.* But I had the comfort to be informed yesterday that it is likely to be entirely laid aside, at least for this session. I am sure it would be destruction to Scotland, and, as a friend to that country, am entirely against it. Those who shall prevent its being brought in will act the wisest part, not only for this administration but for Scotland itself.

I am much penetrated with the friendship of what your Lordship is pleased to say about my son Charles.[1] I must own it gives me no small satisfaction to see him placed in so high a station in his profession, which I filled for so many years. It is a natural vanity in an old man and a father.

I showed your letter to the Duke of Newcastle, who is much obliged for your kind remembrance and regard to him. You have made us very idle in the House of Lords by letting us have no Scotch appeals.

It was not long before the ascendency of Lord Bute led to trouble. The old Duke of Newcastle loved office with an abiding love; but even he could not consent to be Prime Minister in name, when he found himself deprived of all voice in questions of either policy or patronage. He, therefore, resigned on the

---

[1] Charles Yorke, appointed Attorney General in 1762.

plea that he could not remain in office unless the war subsidy to Prussia was continued. His real reasons are given in the following long letter to the Lord President:—

DUKE OF NEWCASTLE *to* LORD PRESIDENT DUNDAS.

CLAREMONT, *June* 5*th*, 1763.

MY DEAR LORD,—The return of our most worthy friend, Sir Alex^r Gilmour, to Scotland, furnishes me with an opportunity of renewing to your Lordship, by a safe conveyance, the sincere assurances of the continuance of my affection (if you will allow me to make use of that expression) and most unalterable regard and respect for you. Permit me to add the great satisfaction which the universal credit and reputation, which, by confession of everybody, your Lordship has established, not only in your own Court, but thro'out the kingdom, has given me, who have always known and have been glad to do justice to your Lordship's merit, your ability and zeal, in the cause of your country, and in the support of the Protestant succession in his Majesty's Royal Family. No absence or distance can make me alter my opinion upon your Lordship's subject, and I am equally persuaded that if you had been here you would have approved of every step which the Duke of Devonshire, my Lord Hardwicke, and myself, have taken in public affairs.

When the nation (and indeed all Europe) had the misfortune to lose my late dear Master, under whom it had been happy for so many years, I despaired of being of any further service, in employment to the king, my country, and my friends. I concluded (as has happened) that new men must produce new measures and new favorites. However, his Majesty was pleased to desire that I should continue in my employment, and most graciously promised me his countenance and support. Lord Bute *seem'd* also to wish that I should continue. But that which determined me to make the trial was the gracious, the very earnest exhortation of his Royal Highness, the Duke of Cumberland, the strong importunities of my friends, the Duke of Bedford, the Duke of Devonshire, the Marquess of Rockingham, and, in short, all those who had the greatest regard for the late king's memory, and for the support of the Government, upon the same principles that it had been carried on ever since the happy accession of his Majesty's Royal Family to the Crown.

I did apprehend that things would end as they have done.

But, however, I submitted to my friends, who put the whole upon the necessity of making a trial, and not deserting the Whigs and that cause, till I should see that I could not be of any service, which they now own that I have sufficiently seen.

When I found that I had not the least credit even in my own office, and that my own Board were to act against me, and measures, relating to the supplies to be ask'd in Parliament, were in direct opposition to my opinion, countenanced and supported by my Lord Bute and his successor, Mr George Grenville; and when the Duke of Devonshire, my Lord Hardwicke, and myself (who constantly agreed), found that we had not the least weight in Council, and that no attention was given to our opinions there, I then thought that it could be no longer expected that I should make such a contemptible figure in business, when I could not be of the least service to the King, the public, or my friends. I therefore, with the approbation of my friends, resigned my office in the Treasury.

Some time after the violence began, and all possible marks of disgrace, contempt, and resentment were shew'd to those who had acted all their lives with the most distinguished zeal for this Royal Family, and, as was my unfortunate case, even to all persons who were supposed to be my friends, whether they were put in by me, or by Sir Robert Walpole, or my brother, of which there are some very strong instances.

All sorts of reports are spread, and imputations thrown out without the least foundation, against those who are supposed not to approve the present measures or men, and particularly, endeavours have been used to make all your countrymen believe that we are enemies to Scotland and to everybody there.

It is very unfortunate for the public that the conduct of the administration has been such as might bring any point in dispute which related to either part of the United Kingdom. All true friends to their country are friends to both. And I am sure your Lordship knows us too well to have any the least thought or suspicion that we old friends here can have any intention of that kind.

It has indeed grieved and mortified us, both as to England and *Scotland*, to see that the favors are generally bestowed upon those families in both parts of the kingdom who have not (till now) ever distinguished themselves for their zeal for this Royal Family. And I can never imagine that our zealous friends in Scotland, no more than in England, can ever think the disapprobation of such distinctions and such preferences ought to be blamed in us.

My good friend, Sir Alex^r Gilmour, who acts upon the same principles, and in concert with the same persons, as your Lordship and his father did, and he himself has done ever since you so kindly gave him your powerful assistance in his election, is very much threaten'd by those with whom he and the rest of his friends have differ'd; and particularly that he shall not be chose again for the county of Edinburgh. I thank God, in all appearance, new elections are very remote, but I have ventured to assure him of the continuance of your Lordship's goodness and powerful support of him; and if I could ever merit any attention from your Lordship, I should hope you would continue your good opinion of Sir Alex^r Gilmour, who indeed deserves it. Sir Alexander is greatly esteemed by all who know him, and particularly by the Duke of Grafton, Lord Granby, my Lord Hardwicke, my nephew, my Lord Cornwallis, and myself.

A desire to give your Lordship some sketch of our situation here, and particularly of myself, has brought this trouble upon you. You must see the confidence I repose in you, and I must insist upon it, as an old friend and humble servant, that you do not suffer one word of this letter to be known to anybody but my Lord Kinnoull and yourself; and that your Lordship would let me have the satisfaction to know that you have burnt it.

My own hand is scarce to be read by anybody but those who are constantly used to it. I have therefore taken the liberty to make use of my chaplain's hand, whom I entrust with all my secret correspondence. I beg you would make my compliments to my old friend, your father-in-law, and to all those who may have the goodness to preserve some regard for one who has been a very sincere friend and humble servant and well-wisher to all your Lordship's friends, and to those who acted upon your principles.—
I am, My dear Lord, with the sincerest respect and affection, your Lordship's most obedient and humble servant,

HOLLES NEWCASTLE.

LORD HARDWICKE *to* LORD PRESIDENT DUNDAS.

GROSVENOR SQUARE, *June* 12, 1763.

Having a convenient opportunity by our worthy friend, Sir Alex^r Gilmour, I presume to renew a correspondence which has been long intermitted. The opinion which prevails of the infidelity of your post, has been the chief occasion of it on my part; how far it may have been any ingredient on yours I am not a competent judge. But if one cannot write to a friend with that freedom which is requisite to let him into the writer's way of thinking on the subject in question, I am sure it cannot inform, and may possibly mislead.

The scene is prodigiously changed since your Lordship saw us; indeed, it has changed several times. The actors who have gone off and come on you know, and in general the motives are no secret. I think none of the persons whom you honoured with your friendship here have been left upon the stage some time. As to myself, no great part could be taken from me, because I had none. But that seat which I had been permitted to retain in the King's Council I was excluded from just before the last session of Parliament. When I said *the motives of these alterations are no secret*, I meant the object of them must appear to everybody to have been the elevation and support of *one man's power*. A conduct too, in my apprehension, not necessary to that end, if it be considered from the time of our friend, the Duke of Newcastle, being forced out to this day. For a *forcing out* it undoubtedly was, and it was afterwards followed by a cruel and unheard of persecution of all his friends and dependants, especially in the inferior employments, altho' they had given no offence. Surely nothing was ever more unnecessary or unwise than to break that administration before a peace was made, which, I am convinced, might have been much better made, and more to the public satisfaction, had that administration been kept entire. And the consequence has been, according to present appearances (how real and sincere I will not pretend to answer for), the pulling down of *that power* which it was meant to build up.

Your Lordship has undoubtedly heard of me as an opposer. It is true that, in conjunction with several of your Lordship's and my old friends, I have opposed certain particular measures. When I have done so it has been according to my judgement and conscience, with the greatest duty to the king, and a sincere zeal for his service, and that of the publick; and I am not ashamed of it. That great scene, the Parliament, is over, but we are now got into a strange flame about an object, in himself of no great consequence, Mr. Wilkes; and it has spread far and wide. I trust your Lordship will not believe that I have made myself a partizan in that cause. How far the particular paper for which he is prosecuted is a seditious libel, is by the Crown submitted to the Law, and there it ought to be determined. I daresay your Lordship will not suspect me of countenancing any indecent treatment of the king, whom I honour and revere, and for whom my duty and affection are invariable, and that you will as little suspect me of approving any abuses and calumnies upon Scotland as a nation—a practice which I have always, in concurrence with my friends, disapproved and condemned.

I have had the happiness to be acquainted with too many persons of worth and honour in Scotland, to give an ear to such injurious reflexions. And I hope I may appeal to my zealous endeavours, both in and out of employment, for extending the liberty, and promoting the welfare of that country, as well as for improving the Union in general, as proofs that I am utterly incapable of giving countenance to anything that may tend to postpone and disappoint that great national end. I don't say this from an apprehension that I stand in need of a justification to your Lordship. It would be doing injustice to our friendship to suppose it. But I have heard that attempts have been made to represent or insinuate me and my friends as enemies to Scotland, and was willing to enable you positively to contradict them. I do not mean that your Lordship should do this officiously, or by avowing that you have it by any direct correspondence with me, but only to warrant your doing it with certainty, whensoever you shall see occasion.

I hope your Lordship enjoys perfect health. I need wish you no more, for I hear with the greatest pleasure how successfully and honourably you go on in discharging the functions of your high office, with an encrease of applause in the public and of your own fame. On this head I can only say, *Fac ut facis ;* and for the rest, be assur'd that I continue to be, as you have always known me,—My dear Lord, your Lordship's most faithful and most obedient humble servant,   HARDWICKE.

May I presume to beg that when you see my Lord Hopetoun, you will be so good as to present my most respectful compliments to his Lordship, and not to forget my old friend, Lord Prestongrange.

June 27th.—My letter was writ at the time of the first date, but has lain by, by reason of Sir Alex^{rs} very rightly staying here to attend his Majesty in his post at the review of the Guards.

A curious episode in the history of Scottish Administration happened in 1765. In that year, when the Regency Bill was under consideration, the omission from its clauses of the name of the Princess Dowager of Wales led to the dismissal of Grenville. He was succeeded, as Prime Minister, by the

Marquis of Rockingham, who, at the request of the Duke of Cumberland, formed a Ministry. In that Ministry the Duke of Newcastle was Lord Privy Seal. To him was apparently intrusted the duty of arranging the manner in which the business of Scotland was to be carried on, for, on the 15th of October, the Lord President received from his friend Lord Hopetoun a letter in which was enclosed a piece of paper, on which were these words: "Copy of a paragraph of a letter from the D. of N. to Ld. H., Oct. 10, 1765. I wish for my own private information that I could know my old friend the President's thoughts, and your Lop.'s, into whose hands the affairs of Scotland should be put. My present thoughts are, and I believe of all my friends here, that in some shape or other my Ld. President must have the correspondence and the conduct of them."

In his letter to the President, enclosing this paragraph from the Duke, Lord Hopetoun said that he understood it "as a way of asking whether you would undertake what is proposed, to avoid making any more propositions that may be declined." He advised the President to write to the Duke, and at the same time declined to give his own opinion on what he described as "too delicate a point to give advice upon." The rough draft of the President's letter to the Duke of Newcastle is among the Arniston papers, so full of erasures and marginal additions as to be almost illegible. It seems to have been corrected and recorrected with the greatest care. In the end it was a decided expression of opinion that it would be improper for him to assume the functions of a Scottish Minister. "I confess," he says, "that I have long entertained an opinion that the management of the public affairs in Scotland is improper for any Judge, if not entirely incompetent with his character. We are, or ought to be, sequestered, in a great degree, from the world for six months,[1] and deprived of a free interchange and communication with our friends."

He was requested to go to London and consult Ministers, but declined; and with the following letters the correspondence on the subject ended:—

---

[1] During the sittings of the Court of Session.

LORD GEORGE BEAUCLERK[1] *to the* LORD PRESIDENT.

UPPER BROOK STREET, 18 *Oct.* 1765.

MY LORD,—We arrived here on Sunday last. I can't say it was so pleasant a journey as I expected, as I was obliged to leave two of my horses sick at Newark, and the other four at Stilton, but got here the remainder of the road post. . . . This morning I went to pay my respects to the Marquis of Rockingham, who had a private levée. . . . I took the liberty to say it would be necessary to have somebody in Scotland to correspond with. He agreed in that point very readily, and said he had some knowledge of your Lordship. I assure you I was very happy in having an opportunity of acquainting his Lordship that I had a particular knowledge and regard for your Lordship. He then asked me if your business could permit you to come up now, as he would be very glad to have some conversation with you, which would answer much better than by letter, in which to be sure he was right, but at the same time I said I was afraid it was not possible now, as the Sessions were to meet the 12th of next month. I told his Lordship there would be an intermission of the Court at Xmas for three weeks or a month, and was not certain whether that might not suit you, etc. etc. etc., G. BEAUCLERK.

THE LORD PRESIDENT *to* LORD GEORGE BEAUCLERK.

ARNISTON, *Nov.* 9, 1765.

MY LORD,—My having been from home, and indeed the desire of coolly considering some part of the contents of your Lordship's letter is the cause of my not sooner acknowledging your goodness and friendship expressed in it. But I little expected that I was to answer it with a heart full of real grief and anguish by the accounts we received of the death of his Royal Highness the Duke.[2] Your Lordship knows better than any other person now living my sentiments in publick affairs, and also the regard and esteem as a private man I bore for that valuable personage. Nobody can, better than your Lordship, form an idea of my private concern and of my publick fears. The first must be combated in my own mind, but I wish to God the last may be disappointed, and that I may find myself wrong in my present notions. So great a publick loss scarce leaves any place for mourning the losses of private

---

[1] General Lord George Beauclerk, sixth son of the first Duke of St. Albans.
[2] The Duke of Cumberland.

families, but I assure you that (as on every other thing relating to your Lordship and Lady Beauclerk) I take part in the death of so near a relation.

I cannot refrain from returning your Lordship most sincere and unfeigned thanks for the friendship you have shown me in the conversation you mention with a noble Lord. It was extremely right to say that coming to London at this time was impossible, but it is equally impracticable at Xmas for only three short weeks' vacation, when I must employ a good deal of the time in preparing the causes to be determined in the two following months. But, indeed, another objection occurs. My going to London at that unusual season would make a great noise, and make me considered either as a Scots Minister, or as a person seeking it and disappointed. The impropriety of the last is apparent. As to the first, I am nowise proper for it, nor would my character permit me to act or correspond on many affairs very material for his Majesty's servants in England to direct. I need only mention elections, etc. At the same time I will freely unbosom myself to your Lordship, who knows my real regard for the constitutional principles, and for many of the particular persons who now act under his Majesty. I am not so self-denied as not to believe I might be of some use in this country in pointing out whom they might trust and whom they ought not, and perhaps in some matters I could serve them by the private interest and connections I have formed. Your Lordship well knows that nobody can maintain a proper interest without being able at times to recommend, and you also know how abundantly the smallest connection of *certain people*[1] in this country have been rewarded.—I am, etc., R. DUNDAS.

In December 1766 Lord Milton died, in his seventy-fifth year, having survived his old patron, the Duke of Argyll, but maintaining to the end his interest in the intrigues and political changes of the time. He had retained his seat on the bench after resigning the Justice-Clerk's chair in 1748;[2] and there was, therefore, now a vacancy among the judges. The member of the bar chosen to take his place was James Burnett of Monboddo, afterwards well known as the learned but eccentric Lord Monboddo, whose theory that the human race was originally "gifted with tails" was the subject of so many jokes

---

[1] Adherents of the Argyll interest.
[2] *Supra*, p. 103.

in the Parliament House. Burnett was one of the counsel for Mr. Douglas in the famous Douglas cause, which had now, for five years, been agitating all classes in Scotland to an extraordinary extent. The following letter which President Dundas received, on the subject of the proposed appointment, shows how bitter were the passions excited by this great lawsuit:—

DUKE OF QUEENSBERRY *to the* LORD PRESIDENT.

MY LORD,—As I had reason to believe that your Lordship approves of Mr. Burnett's coming on the bench when the expected vacancy shall happen, and finding no difficulty here when I first proposed him, I thought it would be giving your Lordship unnecessary trouble to desire you to express your sentiments in a letter. But a very extraordinary occurrence has lately happened which makes it very desireable.

The Duchess of Hamilton has taken it into her head within these few days to exclaim against Mr. Burnett's being to be made a judge, because he was a zealous Advocate against her cause (as she calls it). That is a strange reason to give, and if admitted as an objection, would imply a very injurious reflection. She has, however, seriously and warmly applied by letter and otherwise to the Ministers of State to endeavour to prevent Mr. Burnett's appointment by the most unjustifiable means. My conduct has shown that I have a very different way of thinking, never doubting that justice will be strictly attended to by men of probity on the bench, howsoever they may have been engaged as counsel. . . . The Ministry in general look upon her Grace's objection in its true light, as being very absurd and founded in malice, except one man among them, who has been influenced by her. For my part, I have declared to them all that if it were possible that her Grace's opinion should prevail against mine, I would no longer hold the office I have; but at the same time I have appealed to your Lordship's opinion. . . .—I am, etc., QUEENSBERRY.

Both the late and present Chancellor treat the objection as it deserves. I have not informed Mr. Burnett of this malicious attack upon him, which I hope will be soon put an end to, and therefore I have not wrote to him at present.

Burnett was appointed; and it is said that a habit (one of his well-known peculiarities) of preferring to sit among the clerks at the table, rather than among the other judges, began from the day on which he had to deliver his opinion on the Douglas cause, when he declared that, having been a counsel in the case, he felt a delicacy in giving his judgment from the bench! Lord Cockburn, however, says that "some offence had made him resolve never to sit on the same bench with President Dundas; and he kept this vow so steadily that he always sat at the clerks' table even after Dundas was gone."

It was on the 7th of July 1767 that the Court met to give judgment. The question, it is perhaps necessary to explain, was whether Archibald Steuart was or was not the son of Sir John Steuart of Grandtully and Lady Jane Douglas, sister of the Duke of Douglas. If he succeeded in establishing that he was, he was entitled to claim the estates of the last Duke of Douglas, who had died in 1761. The guardians of the Duke of Hamilton, then a minor, opposed him, maintaining that he was the son of poor parents, a Frenchman and his wife, from whom Lady Jane and her husband had fraudulently obtained him. The date of his birth was said to be July 1748. Both Sir John Steuart and Lady Jane were now dead.

The case, simple as the actual issue was, presented formidable difficulties from the complicated nature of the evidence. The judges were equally divided; and Lord President Dundas gave his casting vote against the claimant.

Public feeling was entirely in favour of the other view of the case; and the President's vote was most unpopular in Edinburgh. The result was that when, in February 1769, the House of Lords reversed the decision of the Court of Session, the city was in an uproar of joy. The President's house was attacked on the evening of the 2d of March. The windows were destroyed; an attempt was made to break in the door; and the family were much alarmed. On the following morning he was insulted on his way to Court; and the mob threatened to pull him out of his chair. But the presence of a few troops of dragoons soon put an end to the disturbances.[1]

In the meantime, the President's brother, Henry Dundas, was rising high in the profession of the law. He had been appointed Solicitor-General in 1766, at the early age of twenty-

[1] Lord Justice-Clerk Miller to Lord Rochford, 3d March 1769, State Papers, Scotland. There are no letters on this subject in the Arniston Collection.

four, and when he had only been three years at the bar; and it was already seen that his career would equal, if not surpass, that of any member of his family. The great Lord Mansfield, who met him in London, writes to the President: "Your brother will certainly go as far as his career can carry him; and his short visit has been of use to him. There is great difference between being personally known, and by name only, let it sound ever so high." He had not yet entered Parliament, but was resolved to represent Midlothian, as his brother had done before him. The Arniston influence was not at this time absolutely supreme in the county, and occasionally difficulties arose, as the following letters show:—

Mr. John Dalrymple to Lord President Dundas.

My Lord,—A thing with which my father, Sir William, surprised me lately makes me trouble your Lordship with these lines. He says your Lordship complained to him that I do not use to salute you when I pass you on the street, nor to pay you proper respects in the Court. This is supposing me so perfect a fool, that I cannot let it stick without assuring your Lordship that anything of that kind is altogether accidental and undesigned on my part.

I would the less have indulged such childishness, that Davy Dalrymple[1] last winter repeated to me a conversation which passed betwixt you, Lord Coalston, and Auchinleck on my account, in which I thought myself obliged to you. I did at that time think of expressing my sense of it. But visits in that way look so like flattery and design, and particularly in one so little apt to stoop as I am, that I did not do it, the more so that I thought you could not fail to see that I must have a just sense of it.

A good many years ago I offered to your Lordship to declare to all that I held this county from you, and to restore it to your family at the end of seven years. When this was rejected, I took up with other friends, yet even then the first public visit I paid was to you, when I had the honour to repeat the same offer. If this showed a disinclination to connect with your Lordship, I know not what that word means.

Your Lordship will permit me to mention to you that though I know a way by which above twenty votes can be created in this

---

[1] Either Lord Hailes or Lord Westhall.

county in an hour, and know a man who would be very glad of such a secret, yet I have kept it to myself, so little idea have I of doing things from wantoness that are disagreeable to you.

I have the honour to be, with very great respect, my Lord, your very obedient humble servant,

JOHN DALRYMPLE.[1]

EDINBURGH, *Monday*, 18*th Jan.* 1766.

HENRY DUNDAS *to his Brother* THE LORD PRESIDENT.

EDINBURGH, 27*th Sept.* 1770.

MY DEAR LORD,—I was obliged to come to town last night, for some days, upon some business which I have not got finished before, and did not chuse longer to delay. Soon after coming John Davidson called upon me, as a common friend betwixt Sir Alexander Gilmour[2] and me, with a message from Sir Alexander, to this purpose, that he was not at liberty to explain the ground of it, but that it was not impossible there might be a re-election in this county before long; that having heard from different quarters that I was making great impressions upon the county of Midlothian, he wished to know from the first authority upon what footing he might consider himself in that respect. My answer immediately was that I could not speak with absolute precision upon the subject of a re-election speedily to happen without having other things understood betwixt us with regard to future contingencies, and desired Mr Davidson and him to call upon me this forenoon, which they just now did.

The general purport of the conversation was this: that I wished to be in Parliament next general election, and had no desire for it sooner, that every consideration led me to cast my eyes upon the county of Midlothian, that I had a most sincere affection for him, and a very great aversion to divide old connexions in the county; on the *contrary*, as well for my own sake personally as for the sake of others in my family, who might hereafter have the same views as I have, I wished if possible to keep it whole and entire. In short, that if we could both be in Parliament, so much the better, but if that could not be the case, I hoped he would not attempt to divide the county. He readily agreed that I asked no more than he thought reasonable. He then added that I might be convinced from what he now said that he had no desire to set up a separate interest in this county,

---

[1] Afterwards Sir John Dalrymple, father of the eighth and ninth Earls of Stair.   [2] M.P. for Midlothian.

and therefore hoped that the particular passion I might have to represent this county would not induce me to insist upon that preference, if the consequence thereof should be a total exclusion of him from Parliament, while at the same time events might occur whereby we might be enabled to sit in Parliament together. My answer was that if two seats should cast up I still must insist upon his yielding up this county and betake himself to the other, except it could be supposed that an event should happen of any set of electors being determined not to accept of him but willing to accept of me.

In that case I fairly owned that my desire not to divide the county, old connexions and my regard for him, who did not appear desirous to set up any independent interest, would incline me to leave the representation of the county with him rather than that he should be put in a situation (I mean out of Parliament) which I knew, as his affairs were circumstanced, would be highly inconvenient for him.

Our conversation to the above purport ended with me telling him that what I said was what occurred to myself upon this subject, and that, although from any conversation I ever had with you upon the subject, I had no reason to think that you had inclination towards him anyways more unfavourable than I had, yet it was highly necessary that the matter should be understood in your presence and under your approbation, after which our final resolutions, if cordial, should never go farther.

I have sent this by express to let you know this interview, which, tho' unexpected, I am glad it has happened.

I suppose the unexpected early meetings of Parliament has brought it sooner on.

Sir Alexander, Mr Davidson, and the Edmonstone people, I mean Wauchope and his wife, dine at Melville to-morrow, as it is the only day I will be there for a fortnight, and I wished this matter fully adjusted. I have sent this so soon, in the hopes you will be able to-morrow to dine at Melville, where we may, in presence of Mr Davidson, have some minutes conversations with Sir Alexander before dinner.—Yours sincerely,   HENRY DUNDAS.

Ultimately Henry Dundas succeeded in securing his election, and was returned as member for the county at the general election of 1774. At the age of thirty-three, on the 24th of May 1775, he was appointed Lord Advocate in the Government of Lord North.

LORD MANSFIELD *to the* LORD PRESIDENT.

BLOOMSBURY, 3*d May* 1775.

MY DEAR LORD,—As your brother has much more than answered the expectations I gave, that notwithstanding it came at so early a period of his life, he would do credit to his first promotion, and honour to those who espoused him, I cannot help congratulating your Lordship upon the fortuitous concourse of circumstances which has opened the way to his second advancement, and wish you joy of it, and of the certain success which can't fail to attend him in the career he has still to run. I have recommended his successor, which I would not have done, tho' he has a call of connexion upon me, if I had not believed him qualified to fill the office with some reputation. I feel myself pledged for the figure he shall make.

I can think of no way so effectual to assert his endeavours, as to beg your friendship, countenance, and protection to him. If you find he has merit, lend a kind hand to lift it up and show it to the world. I flatter myself you cannot have a stronger motive than that of doing a very sensible pleasure to your most aff. ob. humble servant, MANSFIELD.

A voluminous correspondence passed between Henry Dundas and the President from this time until 1783. Besides the remarks upon the progress of political events during these stirring years, the correspondence frequently turned upon the change which was about to alter the future course of Henry Dundas's life. Though still holding only the subordinate office of Lord Advocate, his ability for business, and his skill in debate, had placed him in the front rank of the supporters of Government. Of his position in Parliament he was fully aware, and the charm of its combined power and independence was among the reasons which delayed his acceptance of offices which were pressed upon him. Moreover, he was devotedly attached to the Scottish bar, proud of his position as its leader, and most unwilling to quit it entirely. Son of one President, and brother of another, he saw before him the succession to the President's Chair, to which he could look forward at the close of his parliamentary career. And even after his resolution to resign the office of Lord Advocate had been taken, he expresses in a letter to his brother, in October 1782, his desire to retain the post of Dean of the Faculty of Advocates, as a badge to indicate that his connection with the Scottish bar was not to be totally dissolved.

While his brother was thus displaying his ability to maintain the credit of the family, the President's children were growing up, and going out into the world. By his first marriage, to Miss Baillie of Lamington, he had four daughters, and by his second marriage, to Miss Jean Grant, Lord Prestongrange's daughter, he had four sons and two daughters. His eldest son, Robert, was only a lad of seventeen when his uncle Henry became Lord Advocate; but, as we shall afterwards see, he was himself destined to fill that responsible office, and to end his days upon the bench.

The first of the President's daughters to marry was Miss Elizabeth Baillie or Dundas, and the choice which she made was not at all in accordance with her father's wishes.

LORD LYTTELTON *to* PRESIDENT DUNDAS.

TUNBRIDGE WELLS, *Aug.* 15, 1761.

MY LORD,—I have been so fortunate as to meet with Miss Bailey at this place, and as I find she is to pass the year in England, I cannot help begging to have the honour of her company at my house in Worcestershire in the month of October, when my daughter, and I believe my sister, will be there to attend her. It would give me the greatest pleasure to show her, by my best attentions at Hagley, the grateful sense I have of the many favours I received from your Lordship in Scotland. I see with all the joy of a most sincere friend that time, and your care and cultivation, have brought to perfection all that her amiable infancy promised when I was at Arniston. To have an opportunity of conversing with her will be a great advantage to my daughter. I may venture to say that the goodness of my girl's heart and the innocence of her manners make her a safe companion, and in Miss Bailey she will see what my fondest wishes would have her to be. You will therefore lay me under a great obligation, if you will permit Miss Bailey and Mrs. Whitney to pass some time with us. I hope you will excuse me if I add that Miss Bailey is in every respect so amiable that I will not venture my son's being at Hagley at the same time, if a passion he might perhaps entertain for a young lady of such uncommon merit would certainly meet with your disapprobation.

I beg my most respectful compliments to Mrs. Dundas, and have the honour to be, with the sincerest respect and attachment,—My Lord, your Lordship's most obliged and most obedient servant,
LYTTELTON.

Please to direct to me at my house in Curzon Street, near Berkeley Square, London.

The writer of the foregoing letter was Sir George Lyttelton, who had been created Lord Lyttelton in 1757. His daughter of whom he speaks was Lucy, who married in 1767 the Viscount Valentia, subsequently created Earl of Mountnorris. Lord Lyttelton died in 1773.

"Miss Baillie" was President Dundas's eldest daughter Elizabeth, who on the death of her brother William succeeded to her mother's estates of Lamington and Penston. At the time Lord Lyttelton's letter was written, the young heiress had been sent for a year to England under charge of Mrs. Whitney for the completion of her education. A little later Miss Baillie met Captain John Lockhart, and with the connivance of Mrs. Whitney engaged herself to Captain Lockhart without her father's knowledge or approval of the match. The President was excessively angry at the conduct of his daughter and of Mrs. Whitney; but he seems later to have forgiven her want of respect, and to have been on affectionate terms with her husband. Captain Lockhart ultimately succeeded to his family honours, and became Admiral Sir John Lockhart Ross, having assumed the latter name on succeeding his uncle, General Ross of Balnagowan.[1]

Another of the President's daughters, Anne, was married to George Buchan of Kelloe, in April 1773; and in June of the same year, a third, Margaret Dundas, was married to

---

[1] The immediate descendants of Sir John Lockhart Ross and Miss Dundas or Baillie were:—1st. Sir Charles. He married first Matilda Theresa, daughter of Count Lockhart of Carnwath, by whom he had a daughter Matilda, who married in 1812 Captain, afterwards Admiral, Sir Thomas Cochrane. Their son, Alexander Baillie Cochrane, succeeded to his mother's estates, and in 1880 was created Baron Lamington. Before marriage she had inherited the estate of Old Liston, and had assumed the name of Wishart. Sir Charles married secondly Lady Mary, daughter of second Duke of Leinster, by whom he had a son, Sir Charles, who inherited Balnagowan. 2d. Captain James Ross. He married Catherine Farquharson, heiress of Invercauld, by whom he had a son, James Ross Farquharson of Invercauld.

General John Scott of Balcomie. Miss Peggy, as she was called, did not fly in her father's face as her sister Elizabeth had done, as appears from the letters written at the time the marriage was being arranged.

The correspondence commences by Miss Peggy, in terms savouring strongly of the complete letter-writer, informing her father of General Scott's offer of marriage. "The love and affection," she begins, "you have always had towards all your children merits the return of filial duty from inclination as well as principal" (*sic*).

General Scott commences by expressing his happiness at receiving the lady's consent, and "the flattering circumstance of her being confident that it will receive your Lordship's entire approbation." However, "as he is anxious to avoid any unnecessary delay," he plunges at once *in medias res*, and enters into his views on marriage settlements. He thinks a jointure of £1000 a year suitable, half to be forfeited in the event of remarriage. But "as the jewels he has already foolishly bought" are too valuable to come under the head of paraphernalia he will, at his death, bequeath to his widow £2000 in their stead. As to children, the General considers it to be highly improper that they should be made in any shape independent of their parents, and he reminds the President that his Lordship some years ago found the bad effects of an heiress being independent of her father. In a subsequent letter to his bride, the General most handsomely insists that her fortune shall be divided between her two unmarried sisters, as an addition to theirs.

The President replied to General Scott assuring him that "his sentiments as to independency of children coincided strongly with his own. He had seen it to be a source of vexation and disappointment to parents (*this* you will say I once felt), and of ruin and destruction to the children themselves."[1]

General Scott concludes the correspondence by insisting, through Henry Dundas, upon providing the trousseau for his bride. For, he says, "it is ridiculous that anybody should clothe another man's wife." "In short," continues Henry Dundas, "he means to be superb in everything, and let him be indulged."

---

[1] The children of this marriage were three daughters—1. Henrietta, m. the fourth Duke of Portland. 2. Lucy, m. the ninth Earl of Moray. 3. Margaret, m. the Rt. Hon. George Canning.

These letters were written in March. "I suspect," says Henry Dundas, "the Scotch whim of not marrying in May will put off the affair till June." And so it was. In the marriage-contract, signed at Arniston on the 9th of June 1778, General Scott renounces the "tocher" intended for Miss Dundas, and requests that it may be applied to increasing the portions of her sisters Henrietta and Anne.

Henrietta Dundas accepted the hand of Captain Adam Duncan,[1] R.N., in 1777, and, by doing so, dismissed another suitor, whose letters (which, even at this distance of time, it would be cruel to publish) show that he suffered the most bitter disappointment.

Lastly, Miss Grizzel Dundas was married, in September 1778, to Adam Colt of Auldhame.

The family, thus gradually diminishing in number, lived in Edinburgh during winter, and at Arniston in summer.

The President's Edinburgh house was considered in those days as almost out of town. It was built by himself on a site which lately was known as Adam Square, a block of buildings, as those who know Edinburgh may recollect, which stood at the corner of the South Bridge, close to the University Buildings. Adam Square was pulled down in 1871; and the President's old house had then been occupied for some time as a shop and warehouse. The drawing-room was a handsome room with a panelled ceiling; and the chimney-piece belonging to it is now in the dining-room at Arniston.

The President made considerable additions to the estate of Arniston. In 1753 he purchased the Barony of Shank, for £3000, from the descendants of Sir George Mackenzie of Rosehaugh (the "Bloody Mackenzie"); and other purchases of lands were made between that time and 1777.

Various changes, too, were made in the grounds. A new garden was formed, with a pond, which was stocked with trout from Duddingston Loch. Hothouses were built, and other modern luxuries introduced.

The improvements made upon the mansion-house and pleasure grounds at Arniston by the second President Dundas are described by Chief Baron Dundas in the MS. narrative from which quotations have already been made:—

---

[1] Afterwards created Viscount Duncan, on gaining the battle of Camperdown.

"The first President Dundas died in 1753, leaving the house unfinished. As already related he pulled down the old chateau, with the exception of the oak room and the vaults beneath, round three sides of which the modern house is built. His son, the second President, built the addition to the west of the old house, consisting of the present dining-room and drawing-room, and the rooms above. He also completed the different offices which had been left unfinished at his father's death. Some time about 1764[1] he removed the kitchen garden from east of the stables to its present site, and at the same time took down the cascade which his father had built in the Fountainhead Park. His plantations in the immediate neighbourhood of the house were—

"1st. The wood called Thomson's Braes, which now contains very thriving timber. It was planted in the year 1755; it has been regularly thinned from time to time by him and me. I cut down three years ago (1803) an ash which stood too near to the large chestnut in the haugh under the rock, which sold for two guineas.

"2d. About the year 1756 my father planted up the small park called at that time the Rawmuir, west of the Hunter's Park, which now forms part of the high wood, and the lower division of which is thriving timber. At the upper end, next the Castleton march, an old earthen mound and ditch still remaining, there was a long belt of Scots fir planted by my grandfather which ran from the top of the Diamond eastward as far as the Witches Knowe. I remember these trees when I was a boy; my father cut them all down about the year 1768.

"3d. In 1760, by William Cranston's[2] information, my father planted the Diamond, part of which now forms the South Lawn, and is included by me in it (1812). I was at the expense in 1813-14 of digging, fallowing, and trenching all this field, and of grubbing up all the useless and bad trees, and sowing it off with grass seeds. In winter 1810, when the old road to Carrington was stopped, I extended the shrubbery round to the gardener's house, and planted the clump immediately to the east of the house.

---

[1] In 1763 there is in the factor's book an entry of a payment for lime for building the new garden wall.

[2] Forester at Arniston.

"4th. In 1776, when my mother formed the walk down to the Shank, my father planted up the wet bank immediately under the Deadmanlees; also the small haugh under the Hut above the Red rock opposite to Carrington. The oaks there are in a thriving state. All, or a greater part of the larches were cut down in 1809-10, and used in Outerston[1] farm-house.

"5th. The belt from the Auchenshadow Beech Knowe eastwards to the turnpike road at Pirnhall, or Lumsden's Gate,[2] was originally formed by my father in 1775, at the same time that he planted the belt at the Baker's Avenue."

This attention to the beauty of woods and parks was now spreading among the great landowners of Scotland. The formality and stiffness with which they laid out their grounds was in keeping with that punctilious attention to small matters of etiquette which characterised their social intercourse, with the artificial nature of a great deal of their daily life, the powder, the patches, and the enormous head-pieces. But such defects were soon removed by the exuberance of nature; and the progress of time has rapidly changed the straight, formal avenues, and prim rows of trees, into scenes of natural beauty.

From the household books of the President's family, some idea may be gathered of the style of living, and cost of food, in Scotland from the middle of last century until about the year 1780. Hens cost sixpence, and chickens threepence each. Grouse and partridges sold for sixpence a bird. Ducks cost a shilling, and turkeys about three shillings. Eggs averaged about threepence a dozen. Mutton was the kind of butcher meat of which most was consumed; while rabbits, plovers, snipe, and woodcock were frequent articles of diet. The price of beef was from threepence to threepence halfpenny the pound. Nuts, oranges, pomegranates, and grapes were procured from Covent Garden, the grapes costing one shilling a pound.

The wages paid to servants are duly recorded. There was a man cook, at £8 a year, and an under-cook who received £3. The butler had £20 a year, and Mrs. Dundas's maid £3, 10s.

There is little about sporting matters among the private

---

[1] This larch timber lasted until 1875, when the house had to be almost entirely renewed, owing to decay.
[2] The Lodge of this old gate was taken down in 1875.

letters of this period; but occasionally hounds and "hunting," by which probably coursing is meant, are spoken of. Game preserving was not strict at that time; and it is amusing to find the Lord President receiving, at the end of August 1782, a note with what would now be considered a very cool request: "The officers of the Royal Dragoons quartered at Dalkeith present their compliments to the Lord President; ask permission to shoot on his Lordship's grounds in that neighbourhood." Lord Arniston appears to have been a little staggered at the prospect of giving the officers of a cavalry regiment *carte blanche* to do what they pleased among his fields. His answer is an admirable specimen of combined courtesy and caution. He gives them leave, however.

"The President," he says, "was favoured with a card from the officers of the Royal Dragoons at Dalkeith. Could have wished to have known particularly the gentlemen who ask permission to shoot, etc. etc. The President has a very great regard for Colonel Goldsworthy, and some others of the reg^t. of his personal acquaintance, and is very desirous of obliging them, or any other officers of that regiment. Shall, therefore, make them welcome to hunt for partridges on his grounds of Stobhill and Kirkhill, which are those adjacent to them—persuaded himself that these liberties will not be abused. Indeed, he must fairly explain himself that he understands this liberty is to be confined to the gentlemen themselves shooting for their amusement, and that they will not permit any other person whatever to hunt. The fields in question are reckoned among the very best for hounds in this country; and as the Pres^s. good friend, Sir Arch. Hope (indeed his own son), often sport there (if the Pres. himself seldom or never courses a hare); and therefore is confident if the officers will, in no shape, destroy any hares, he knows they are welcome to the share the sport of hounds hunting."[1]

The improvement of the country in agriculture, interrupted for a few years by the Rebellion of 1745, was carried on with renewed vigour during the latter half of the eighteenth century. The factor's books at Arniston during that period show a continuous expenditure upon building, planting, and

---

[1] If the President's composition seems faulty, it must be recollected that only a rough draft of his letter has been preserved.

enclosing. A marked improvement on the farm buildings is observable, consequent upon the increased growth of green crops and roots for winter feeding, and of the greater attention paid to the condition of the live stock upon a farm. In Midlothian, where building materials were abundant, and easy of access, the walls of a farm steading were solidly built with stone and lime, though the roof still continued to be covered with "divots." These farm-steadings were, of course, very different from the buildings which are now seen in a lowland farm in Scotland. The farm buildings on Arniston seem usually to have consisted of a small hamlet, or cluster of cottages standing at a short distance from each other; whose inhabitants, in addition to their ordinary work of farming and home spinning, carried on the trade of lime-burners, and carriers of lime throughout the neighbouring country.

The increasing wealth of the country also began to be shown by the greater number of tenants with capital sufficient to stock a good-sized farm, before whom the joint tenants, holding a farm in common, began to disappear. The consolidation of small holdings into large farms was also going on rapidly—in Midlothian at all events. Among other changes the tithe or teind, as a separate payment by the tenant, was being given up, and was included in the rent, as was also the case with a variety of old servitudes. Payments to country tradesmen, such as joiners, blacksmiths, and others, were, however, still made to a considerable extent in kind, as also were farm servants' wages.

Home spinning being still part of the business of the farm, the cottars were obliged to sow a stipulated quantity of flax seed in their gardens for the supply of the family.

The farm implements continued to be rough and strong, such as could be made and repaired at home—the ploughs large and heavy, and drawn by four horses—the plough harness of plaited hemp, as shown by the frequent entry in the factor's books of "hemp for the ploughmen."

In tillage, the land was still laid off in high crooked ridges, with intervening spaces of unploughed land.

The turnips, which were grown by enterprising farmers, were sown broadcast, though the use of drills was recommended as possessing the advantages of a bare fallow.

It was also becoming generally known that sown rye grass and clover could feed three times as much stock as the growth of natural grasses.

The drainage of wet spots of land was being extensively carried on. The drains were cut in the wet spots to the heads of the springs, and were filled with small stones, brushwood, or straw to within a foot of the surface. The main drains were conduits formed with large stones. In England, where the practice of draining wet pieces of land was more general than in Scotland, the drains were made 32 inches deep, 20 inches wide at top, and 4 inches wide at bottom. When filled with small stones the cost was about 7d. per rod. It was found that by an outlay of £3 or £4 per acre on draining and manuring, the rent of land might be raised from 10s. to 20s. per acre.

The following were the terms of an Arniston lease in 1760; and similar terms were probably usual at that time in Scotland. The farm was that of Newbyres, and the principal conditions of the lease were as follows:—

Duration, nineteen years. Rent, £98 and six hens. Tenant to keep and maintain two hounds for the use of the landlord.

Thirled to Newbyres Mill; tenant to assist in keeping the mill dam and lade in repair, also to allow the tenant of the mill to cut whins on Newbyres for the use of the kilns.

To carry, from Leith or elsewhere, timber for cradling the coalpits, for the stairs in them, or for the lodges; also to bring to Stobhill the furniture of any coalier that may be engaged for the coal work.

Tenant to have the exclusive privilege of brewing and retailing ale within the barony of Newbyres.

Among the Arniston collections is a paper showing the rotation of crops proposed by the Second Lord President for his home farm, of which a copy is given as illustrative of the agriculture of the day.

ROTATION OF CROPS, 1769-1778.

	BIRKENSIDE.		BOGEND FARM.					ARNISTON MAINS.					HOME PARK.	
	West.	East.	Field 1.	Field 2.	Field 3.	Field 4.	Field 5.	Field 1.	Field 2.	Field 3.	Field 4.	Field 5.	Field 1.	Field 2.
1769.	Faugh and Turnip.	Oats and Pease.	Oats.	Oats.	Pasture.	Pasture.	Pasture.	Barley, Oats, and Clover.	Clover.	Clover.	Clover.	Pease.		
1770.	Wheat, Oats, Barley.	Faugh.	Oats.	Oats.	Oats.	Oats.	Oats.	Clover.	Faugh and Turnip.	Clover.	Oats.	Oats.		
1771.	Oats.	Oats.	Faugh. Turnip.	Faugh. Turnip.	Oats.	Pease.	Oats.	Wheat.	Barley.	Faugh. Turnip.	Clover.	Clover.		
1772.	Grass.	Grass.	Oats.	Oats.	Faugh.	Oats.	Pease.	Clover.	Clover.	Barley.	Faugh. Turnip.	Oats.		
1773.			Pease.	Pease.	Oats.	Faugh.	Oats.	Clover.	Wheat.	Clover.	Barley.	Faugh. Turnip.		
1774.			Oats.	Oats.	Pease.	Oats.	Faugh.	Faugh. Turnip.	Clover.	Wheat.	Clover.	Barley.		
1775.			Faugh.	Oats.	Oats.	Pease.	Oats.	Barley.	Faugh and Turnip.	Clover.	Wheat.	Clover.	Oats.	Oats.
1776.			Oats.	Faugh.	Oats.	Oats.	Pease.	Clover.	Barley.	Faugh and Turnip.	Clover.	Wheat.	Oats.	Pease.
1777.			Pease.	Oats.	Faugh.	Oats.	Oats.	Wheat.	Clover.	Barley.	Faugh. Turnip.	Clover.	Oats.	Oats.
1778.			Oats.	Pease.	Oats.	Faugh.	Oats.	Clover.	Wheat.	Clover.	Barley.	Turnip. Faugh.		

HOUSE OF PRESIDENT DUNDAS IN ADAM SQUARE.

DEATH OF PRESIDENT DUNDAS.

In the full possession of all his faculties, and in the enjoyment of fair health, with the exception of a weakness in his eyesight which prevented him reading with ease, the Lord President lived, sometimes in Edinburgh, and sometimes at Arniston, until 1787. On the 13th of December of that year, he died in his house in Adam Square, in the seventy-fifth year of his age. "His last illness," says Lord Woodhouselee, "which, though of short continuance, was violent in its nature, he bore with the greatest magnanimity."

On hearing of the death of the head of the Court, Henry Erskine, then Dean of Faculty, wrote to Robert Dundas, the late President's eldest son, who had now been Solicitor-General for three years:—

MR. ERSKINE *to* SOLICITOR-GENERAL DUNDAS.

EDINBURGH, 14 *Dec.* 1787.

MY DEAR SIR,—I condole with you from the bottom of my heart on the unfortunate event which has deprived you of a worthy and affectionate parent, and the country of a most able, upright, and active Chief Judge.

I need scarcely inform you that the Faculty of Advocates, who feel in a peculiar manner the weight of this misfortune, have resolved, on their part, to do everything on this melancholy occasion that can show the high respect they entertain for his Lordship's memory, and the regret they feel for his death.

They have desired me to express these their sentiments to yourself in person, and to know from you, what particular mode of showing their feelings on the approaching funeral will be most agreeable to the family, and best suited to the manner in which that ceremony is proposed to be conducted.

I would not immediately press on your present distress, but will have the pleasure of waiting on you the moment I learn that it will be agreeable.

I beg you to be assured that my feelings as an individual keep pace with my conduct in my official capacity, as at the head of the Faculty, because in addition to my full sense of the merits of the deceased, I recollect with grateful satisfaction the many marks I have received of his Lordship's regard and affection towards myself in circumstances not less honourable to him than flattering to me.—I am, with real regard, my dear Sir, your most ob. faithful servant, HENRY ERSKINE.

The President was honoured by a public funeral. Fifty years before the Bar of Scotland had met to consider whether they should attend the funeral of a judge, and it was resolved not to do so lest the profession should be brought, by establishing such a precedent, "under the dishonourable necessity of paying extraordinary outward compliments in future times where equal merit may not call for the same inward respect." But on the death of Lord President Dundas, such was the veneration felt for this great judge that an exception was made to the established rule, and the Bar attended, with the Dean of Faculty at their head. The *Scots Magazine* thus describes the scene :—

"On Dec. 18th his Lordship's remains were interred at the family burial-place of Borthwick. At ten o'clock before noon, the funeral procession began from the Parliament Close in the following order :—

Town-Officers, two and two ; their halberts covered with crape.
Mace-bearer and Sword-bearer of the city ; the mace
and sword covered with crape.
Lord Provost, Magistrates and Council in their robes ;
three and three.
Mace-bearer of the University ; his mace covered with crape.
Principal and Professors of the University in their gowns ;
three and three.
Four Mace-bearers of the Lords of Session ; two and two,
their maces covered with crape.
Lords of Session in their robes ; two and two.
Principal Clerks of Session, and Clerk of Teind Court
in their gowns ; two and two.
Bar-keeper to the Dean and Faculty of Advocates in his gown ;
his baton covered with crape.
Dean and Faculty of Advocates in their gowns ;
three and three.
Macer to the Court of Exchequer ; his mace covered with crape.
Barons of Exchequer, in their gowns and bands ; the Chief Baron
supported by the Lord Advocate and Baron Norton, followed
by the principal Officers and the Attornies belonging
to the Court, in their gowns ; three and three.
Officer of his Majesty's Signet, in his gown ; his mace covered
with crape.

Depute-Keeper, Commissioners, and Clerks to the Signet, in their gowns; three and three.
Preses of the Agents, and his brethren; three and three.
First Clerks of Advocates; three and three.

"The procession proceeded down the Fishmarket Close, up the Horse Wynd, and along by the front of the College, to the Lord President's house in Adam Square, where it went round the Square till the corpse was brought out. Immediately after this the mutes, etc., proceeded forward to Nicolson Street, where the hearse waited. At this time the Principal and Professors of the University reversed their manner of walking, the junior Professors going first, and the Principal of the College last. The Lord Provost, Magistrates, and Council observed the same etiquette, so that the Lord Provost came to walk immediately before the corpse, preceded by the sword and mace bearers. The rest of the procession was conducted in the same order in which it set out, by which means the Lords of Session fell to take place immediately after the corpse. The friends of the deceased, etc., walked after the Advocates' first Clerks. In this order the whole procession moved on to Nicolson Street, where the corpse was put into the hearse, and conveyed to the place of interment, attended by the relations and friends of the family in mourning coaches, and by several of the nobility, Lords of Session, etc., in their own carriages. The great bell tolled during the procession, which was escorted by the military from the castle and the city-guard; and while the body was conveying from Adam Square to Nicolson Street, the band of music belonging to the military played the 'Dead March in Saul.'"

Lord President Dundas had risen to eminence by a combination of family influence and personal talent. He was never a laborious student, or an eloquent speaker. "While he continued at the bar," says a contemporary, "he did not allow business to interrupt his pleasures. Though he could have got as much employment in his profession as any of his contemporaries, yet he refused to be engaged in a great many causes, and confined himself to those of the greatest importance, which completely answered his views of acquiring such a character and reputation in business, as entitled him to be preferred to the first offices in the law department. As his speaking cost him little trouble, and he endeavoured to avoid the writing of papers, which required more application and pains than he inclined to bestow, he easily accomplished his intention without submitting to much drudgery. When he did undertake to write, he executed well in point of good sense and argument, though he might be liable to criticism in what regarded the composition or style of his papers, to which he never paid any attention."

His father, the first President Dundas, bore the impress of the seventeenth century, though he had no share in its transactions. He would have held his own among the statesmen of the last days of the Stuarts. He had that peculiar suppleness of intellect, and those strong resentments, which were developed in the politicians of a time of great constitutional struggles, when adherence to a party meant a great deal more than the acquisition of power or personal distinction. The public character of the second President was moulded by the times in which he lived. He lived at a period of transition, when, as the student of history will observe, the old traditions of unblushing intrigue and unscrupulous rivalries were passing away, and giving place to the new methods of modern political life.

The second President was probably the greatest judge who ever presided in the Court of Session; certainly as the head of the Supreme Court he was regarded by his compeers as without a rival. He cleared the rolls of court of a vast accumulation of arrears. He paid the most minute attention to the duties of his office. "For many years," it has been said, "after he was promoted to be President, I have heard it observed by those who attended the House, that he seldom or never was mistaken in any fact or circumstance relating to any cause." His regard for the honour of the Bench was such that he gained for it fresh dignity in the eyes of the nation. To the Bar he was courtesy itself, hearing counsel to the end, and teaching his colleagues to control the impatience which able and experienced men feel in listening to the argument of a raw or dull-witted pleader.

The office which he held was always one of great dignity and influence; but during the eighteenth century the President

of the Court of Session occupied a position of peculiar power. Though the Act of Union had removed the Parliament to London, Edinburgh was still a capital. Scottish society clustered in the closes and lofty tenements of the picturesque street which runs from the Castle to Holyrood; and in Edinburgh, and among that society, the Bar and the Bench exercised an extraordinary influence. The President was, therefore, a great personage in those days; to be courted by suitors, who had inherited the belief that private interviews with the judge were likely to be useful in a lawsuit; and the object of constant attention from all kinds of office-seekers, from the peer who wanted a place about the Court in London down to the aspirant for the poorest clerkship in the Outer House. For at that time the Lord President was not only a judge, but also one of the regular advisers of Government in matters both of policy and patronage. It appeared so natural, to statesmen in London, that the head of the Scottish Courts should take an active part in politics that the Duke of Newcastle, as we have seen, wished President Dundas to be the recognised "Scottish Manager" under the Rockingham Ministry of 1765. Dundas declined this position, from a due appreciation of the proper character of a judicial office; but, in private, like other Presidents of the eighteenth century, he continued his correspondence with the leading statesmen of his day, and had a voice in those important questions of policy which arose, from time to time, with regard to the affairs of Scotland. In this difficult position, combining the functions of the politician and the judge, Dundas succeeded in securing the confidence and admiration of the country.

The first President Dundas occupied the chair of the Court of Session from 1748 to 1753. The second President Dundas occupied it from 1760 to 1787. Thus the father and son, except for six years, presided continuously over the Supreme Court of Scotland for the long term of nearly forty years.

The legal history of this period commences with the passing of the Act by which the Heritable Jurisdictions were abolished. These jurisdictions, which enabled their possessors to administer whatever they chose to regard as law and justice in complete independence of the King's judges, were spread like a network over the whole country; and the British Government, convinced by the events of 1745 that the question of Scotland must be settled once for all, resolved to abolish them without delay. The measure for effecting this reform was drawn by Lord Chancellor Hardwicke, with the assistance of the judges of the Court of Session. It abolished all the heritable jurisdictions of justiciary, and restored the criminal jurisdiction of the country to the King's Courts. The sheriffships, which had been handed down from father to son, for generations, in many families, were taken away; and the right of appointment was once more vested in the Crown.

Although compensation was to be given to the possessors of heritable jurisdictions, a strenuous resistance was made to the bill. No money could, in the opinion of many a Scottish nobleman and laird, be a sufficient compensation for the loss of dignity which was implied in the loss of the cherished "power of pit and gallows." It was denounced as a violation of the rights of property, as a breach of the Treaty of Union, as a dangerous interference with the proper relations which ought to exist between landlord and tenant, and as only the prelude to a system under which no man could be sure that his possessions were safe. One argument, used in the House of Commons, reads almost like a prophecy. Some future minister, it was said, may declare that it is necessary for the public good to compel every man in the kingdom to part with his property in land for a reasonable price.

Nevertheless, the bill ultimately passed both Houses of Parliament; and this important measure of law reform, which has conferred inestimable blessings upon Scotland, found a place in the statute-book.

The sum paid as compensation to the owners of heritable jurisdictions was considerable, although far less than they had demanded. The total sum claimed was more than half a million. The sum actually paid, in April 1748, was about £150,000.

This was the commencement of the present system of Sheriff Courts. A member of the bar was appointed as Sheriff to each county of Scotland; and it need hardly be said that the filling up of so many offices at one time was a source of great delight in the Parliament House, and of equally great trouble to the dispensers of so much patronage.

The session during which the heritable jurisdictions were abolished put an end also to the system of land tenure known as wardholding, under which lands were held on condition of military service rendered to the **feudal** superior. This fatal blow at the clan system met with little opposition, and, coupled with the Acts for disarming the Highlanders, put it out of the power of the chieftains to force their unwilling vassals into another rebellion.

These were great and salutary changes in the law. But the period from 1748 to 1787 was singularly destitute of legislation for Scotland. Indeed the only other statute which need be mentioned is the Montgomery Entail Act of 1770. Since the original Entail Act of 1685, the custom of putting lands under the fetters of a strict entail had gradually taken deep root. In 1764 the Faculty of Advocates, impressed by the evils of the law of entail, had condemned the system by a large majority;[1] and in 1770, Lord Advocate Montgomery succeeded in carrying through Parliament a bill "to encourage the improvement of lands, tenements, and hereditaments, in Scotland, held under settlements of strict entail."

By the Montgomery Act the heir of entail obtained power to grant leases, under certain conditions, for thirty-one years, or for fourteen years and an existing lifetime, or for two existing lifetimes. He was also enabled to grant leases for the erection of houses or villages for any number of years up to ninety-nine, and was encouraged to improve his estate, by means of enclosing, planting, draining, and building farm-houses, by a provision that he should have a claim against the succeeding heirs of entail for three-fourths of any money laid out in this way.

The benefits which followed the Montgomery Act were not so great as had been expected; but it paved the way for that abolition of the law of entail which has since almost completely taken place.

The fact that Parliament was not employed in the development of the law of Scotland at this time threw a great responsibility on the Court of Session; and it is to the decisions of the judges over whom the two Dundases presided that the

---

[1] Minutes of Faculty, 4th August 1764.

student of legal history, during this period, must chiefly devote himself.

A very superficial account of the men who occupied the Scottish bench, during a great portion of the eighteenth century, is sufficient to prove that they were distinguished, in many cases, not only by a profound acquaintance with the science of jurisprudence, but also by great literary attainments. One of the most loveable of these old judges is Lord Kames, whose career may be studied in the fascinating pages of Lord Woodhouselee. His youthful imagination was fired by the spectacle of Lord President Dalrymple at his daughter's tea-table, enjoying the pleasures of domestic happiness towards the close of a long and busy life; and he determined to join the bar. He combined, throughout his own life, a deep knowledge of the law with an unceasing devotion to philosophy, literature, and classic learning. "As a judge," says Lord Woodhouselee, "his opinions and decrees were dictated by an acute understanding, an ardent feeling of justice, and a perfect acquaintance with the jurisprudence of his country, which, notwithstanding the variety of pursuits in which his comprehensive mind had alternately found exercise, had always been his principal study, and the favourite object of his researches. . . . The state of the bench, during the greater part of the time in which he occupied a seat in the Court of Session, was favourable to the exertion of superior abilities. It was no ordinary mental energy that could distinguish itself in the daily comparison with such men as Pringle of Alemore, Ferguson of Pitfour, Sir Thomas Miller of Glenlee, Lockhart of Covington, Macqueen of Braxfield, and the younger President Dundas."

Another of the Judges of this period was Francis Garden of Gardenstoune, whose acquirements in the languages of Rome and Greece were equalled by a fluency in that of France, which astonished the spectators, when, in the great Douglas cause, he opposed Wedderburn before the Parliament of Paris.

Sir David Dalrymple of Hailes was on the bench from 1766 to 1792, and found time not only to discharge his official duties, but to enrich the literature of his country with the results of much laborious study in the field of historical inquiry.

Sir Thomas Miller of Glenlee had, according to Baron Hume, "a fondness for the Greek and Latin classics, which, even in the busiest periods of his life, he found opportunities to indulge." He was Lord Justice-Clerk for nearly twenty-two years, from 1766 to 1788, when he succeeded Dundas as President of the Court; and throughout that long period he was regarded as one of the ablest lawyers on the bench.

Of Lord Monboddo it is hardly necessary to say anything. His " Attic Banquets," when " the master of the feast crowned his wine, like Anacreon, with a garland of roses," his quaint theories regarding the origin of man, his eccentric habits, and his constant flow of humour, are household words among Scottish lawyers at the present day.

These judges, and others among their colleagues, were profound lawyers, and, at the same time, men of very high attainments in general literature. They all flourished while the two Dundases were at the head of the Court.

The Court of Session during this period consisted of the Lord President and fourteen ordinary judges. Of the fourteen ordinary judges, one sat each week in the great hall of the Parliament House, which was then known as the "Outer House," and heard causes argued before him, while the rest of the judges were sitting, as one Court, in the "Inner House." The Court rose at midday, as a rule; and in the afternoons, two of the judges sat, by turns, to hear witnesses in those cases in which evidence of disputed facts was required. "This Court," says Lord Bankton, " is justly admired for its contrivance, in order to despatch of business, and at the same time, with great solemnity and deliberation." If there was great solemnity, there was also great deliberation; for many years sometimes passed before the litigant reached the point at which his case came to be argued before the whole Court, "*in presentia Dominorum.*" "Ye must stand primed," says Alan Fairford's father, " for a hearing *in presentia Dominorum*, upon Tuesday next." " I, sir?" I replied in astonishment, "I have not opened my mouth in the Outer House yet." " Never mind the Outer House, man," said my father, " we will have you into the Sanctuary at once—ever shoes, ever boots." " But, sir, I should really spoil any cause thrust upon me so hastily." " Ye cannot spoil it, Alan," said my father, rubbing his hands with much complacency, "that is the very cream of the whole business, man—it is just, as I said before, a subject upon which all the *tyrones* have been trying their whittles for fifteen years; and as there have been about ten or a dozen agents concerned, and each took his own way, the case is come to that pass, that Stair or Arniston could not mend it; and I do not think even you, Alan, can do it much harm—ye may get credit by it, but ye can lose none."

The greatest Scottish law-suit of the eighteenth century was the case of *Hamilton* v. *Douglas*, best known as the Douglas Cause, to which allusion has already been made.[1] Lady Jane Douglas, sister to Archibald, Duke of Douglas, was, on the 4th of August 1746, privately married to Colonel Steuart, afterwards Sir John Steuart of Grandtully. She was then in her forty-ninth year. Soon after the marriage, Lady Jane and her husband, accompanied by her confidential attendant, Miss Helen Hewit, and two maids, went abroad. They lived at the Hague, Utrecht, and Aix-la-Chapelle till May 1748. At Aix-la-Chapelle the fact of the marriage was disclosed to some of Lady Jane's friends; and about the same time it was rumoured that Lady Jane was soon to be confined. On the 21st of May they left Aix-la-Chapelle for Rheims. Here the two maids were left, and Lady Jane, then supposed to be within a week of her delivery, her husband, and Helen Hewit, started for Paris, which they reached on the 4th of July. Here, it was said, Lady Jane gave birth to male twins, in the house of a Madame Le Brun. In the end of the year 1749, Sir John and Lady Jane returned to England with the two boys, one of whom died, while the other lived to be the defender in the famous Douglas Cause.

In July 1761 the Duke of Douglas died, and three competitors appeared as claimants of his estate. The Duke of Hamilton, as heir-male of the family of Douglas, claimed the whole landed estate, except what the Duke of Douglas had himself purchased. The Earl of Selkirk claimed the estates of Angus and Dudhope, as heir of provision under certain deeds of settlement executed by James, Marquis of Douglas, father of the late Duke. Archibald Steuart or Douglas, the survivor of the twins said to have been born in Paris, claimed the whole landed estate, as heir general and of

---

[1] *Supra*, p. 181.

line, grounding his claim upon certain deeds of settlement executed by James, Marquis of Douglas, and upon a settlement made by the late Duke of Douglas a few days before his death, by which he revoked a settlement in favour of the family of Hamilton, and executed an entail of his estates in favour of the supposed son of Sir John Steuart and Lady Jane. In September, the third claimant, Mr. Steuart, was served heir to the late Duke, according to the ordinary forms of the law of Scotland. The service was unopposed. But before long rumours, which had been current for several years, to the effect that the story of the birth at Paris was an invention, led the tutors of the Duke of Hamilton, who was a minor, to cause an inquiry to be made into the circumstances. The result was that they came to the conclusion that the claimant was not the son of Lady Jane, but of a certain Nicolas Mignon and Marie Guerin, his wife, from whom he had been obtained for fraudulent purposes. An action to reduce the service was at once instituted by the Duke of Hamilton; and thus the sole question in the great Douglas cause came to be, Was or was not Archibald Steuart the son of Sir John and Lady Jane?

Lady Jane had died in November 1753, pouring forth, in her dying moments, blessings upon the youth whom she declared to be her son.[1] Sir John died in June 1764, having, on his deathbed, declared that the story of the claimant's birth was true.

The case speedily resumed gigantic dimensions, and for a long time engrossed the attention, not only of lawyers, but of general society to an extraordinary extent. There were proceedings in France at which counsel from Scotland, Francis Garden, Burnet of Monboddo, Dalrymple of Hailes, and Rae, afterwards Lord Eskgrove, attended and gained great distinction. The evidence was intricate, and in many instances contradictory. But at length the Court of Session met, on the 7th of July 1767, to give its final judgment.

Lord President Dundas spoke first. "My Lords," he began, "in delivering my opinion on this great and important cause, it was my resolution to have spoken last, and not until I had heard the opinions severally given by your Lordships,

---

[1] Case for the Appellant, p. 46.

This was my resolution so long as we sat fourteen in number, and so long as there was a certainty, that the question could not fall to be determined by my casting vote. But, as we now sit fifteen in number, and that there is a possibility that my casting vote may be called for, I judge it my duty to speak first, to state my opinion and the grounds of it, not doubting but that, if it is erroneous, some of your Lordships who are to speak after me will correct me."

Having stated the point at issue, in succinct terms, he at once revealed his own opinion to be that the story of the birth at Paris was untrue. "I observe, in the first place, that the defender's story is improbable.

"That a lady of Lady Jane's age, so near to the period of her delivery, and in her first child, should leave Aix-la-Chapelle, travel to Liége, thence to Sedan, from thence to Rheims, and from Rheims to Paris, without absolute necessity, is to me extremely improbable. That, in this journey, they should linger eight days at Sedan, and near four weeks at Rheims, when her resolution was to go on to Paris, and her delivery fast approaching, is still more so; and that she should drop her maids at Rheims, at the time when she stood most in need of them, and when they could have been carried to Paris at the expense of a few livres, is not to be believed.

"It is to me equally improbable, that Lady Jane should have concealed her being with child so carefully, as it is said she did. Was not her being with child the accomplishment and crown of all her wishes, the very end and motive which had led her to give her hand to Colonel Steuart? Why then conceal it?"

Having examined the evidence in detail, and given his reasons for regarding the account of the defender's birth as inconsistent and suspicious, he concluded by referring to the solemn declarations which Sir John and Lady Jane had made at the end of their lives. "The deathbed declarations in this cause do not move me. When crimes are committed, the committers rarely choose to confess, if by concealing they can escape that infamy which otherwise would pursue them. Lady Jane could not but see, that, when the Rubicon was past, there was no retreating. Had she been tempted to have divulged a secret so important, the consequences would have been, infamy on her own memory, and capital punishment on her associates. That in Sir John's judicial declaration many things are false, cannot be denied. Between an oath and a declaration there is little difference; and yet Sir John, upon his deathbed, does not confess them; and tho' he makes a deathbed declaration, takes no notice of any of them."

As soon as the President had ended, the other judges proceeded to give their opinions. Six days were occupied by their speeches, from Tuesday the 7th of July to Tuesday the 14th;[1] and when Lord Monboddo, who spoke last, had finished a long examination of the evidence by declaring "that the tale told by the pursuers is the most improbable that was ever told in any Court of Justice," it was found that, excluding the Lord President, seven judges had voted on each side.

His Lordship then said, "As this is a cause of civil property, I think myself bound to give judgment according to my own opinion; and therefore I am for sustaining the reasons of reduction."[2] As a matter of course, the case was instantly taken on appeal to the House of Lords. In addition to members of the Scottish bar, some of the most celebrated English advocates were retained, among whom were Thurlow, Wedderburn, and Charles Yorke. "Mr. Charles Yorke," says Horace Walpole, "was the least admired. The Duchess of Douglas thought she had retained him; but, hearing he was gone over to the other side, sent for him, and questioned him home. He could not deny that he had engaged himself for the House of Hamilton. 'Then, sir,' said she, 'in the next world where will you be, for we have all had you?'"

Lord Campbell, in his *Lives of the Chancellors*, is not exaggerating in the least when he says that in Scotland the Douglas Cause had almost led to a civil war between the supporters of the opposite sides, and that in England even it had excited more interest than any question of private right had ever done before. "The appeal," he says, "was heard in the session of

---

[1] The Court did not sit on Monday the 13th.

[2] The Court divided as follows:—For the pursuer, Lord President, Lord Justice-Clerk (Sir Thomas Miller), and Lords Alemore, Kennet, Barjarg, Elliock, Stonefield, and Hailes; for the defender, Lords Strichen, Kames, Pitfour, Gardenstoun, Auchinleck, Coalston, and Monboddo.

1769, and drew vast crowds to the bar of the House of Lords to listen to the weighty and eloquent argumentation of Thurlow, Wedderburn, and the other most eminent advocates of the age. It was conjectured that the law Lords were for the appellant, but the great body of the peers had attended the hearing of the appeal, and were to take part in the decision; there had been much canvassing for the 'Douglases' and the 'Hamiltons,' and a great degree of suspense existed down to the very morning of the judgment."

When judgment came to be given, the proceedings were opened by two lay peers, the Duke of Newcastle and Lord Sandwich, the latter of whom seems to have delivered an oration which would have been more in place among the cloisters of Medmenham Abbey.[1]

They were followed by Lord Chancellor Camden. "We have one short question before us," he said—"Is the appellant the son of the late Lady Jane Douglas, or not? I am of opinion that he is; and moreover that a more ample and positive proof of the child's being the son of a mother never appeared in a court of justice, or before any assize whatever." Lord Mansfield took the same view, and the judgment of the Court of Session was reversed without a division. The joy which this decision gave in Scotland has already been described.[2]

The Douglas Cause was a romance. But, during this period, the Court was constantly engaged in pronouncing decisions by which an intricate system of land rights was developed, and the law of entail rendered as strict as possible. The Duntreath case is an instance of the favour with which the Court regarded even a defective entail.[3] This decision the House of Lords, under the advice of Lord Mansfield, reversed, much to the annoyance of the judges of the Court of Session. But, although during the whole of last century our judges were laboriously building up that structure of the feudal law, which the legislature has during a great part of this century been as laboriously demolishing, nevertheless no one could, in those

---

[1] *Lives of the Chancellors*, vol. v. p. 289.
[2] *Supra*, p. 181.
[3] Edmonstone v. Edmonstone, 15th April 1771. M. 4409, 2 Paton, 225.

days, hold his own upon the Scottish bench without being not only well read in the law of Scotland, but also a proficient scholar in the lore of the civilians and canonists, whose writings were daily quoted by a school of pleaders who had studied in the famous universities of the Continent, and who were, most of them, as good classic scholars as they were lawyers.

OAK ROOM ARNISTON.

"I am always happy in finding myself in the old Oak Room at Arniston, where I have drank many a merry bottle, and in the fields where I have seen many a hare killed."

SIR WALTER SCOTT'S *Diary*, January 1828.

CHAPTER XI.

LORD CHIEF BARON DUNDAS.

For almost a hundred years before the death of the second President Dundas there had never been a time when some member of the house of Arniston was not either a judge, or Solicitor-General, or Lord Advocate, or President of the Supreme Court of Scotland, with the exception of from 1726 to 1737; and during that short period, Robert Dundas (afterwards the first President) had been the leader of the Independent Whigs, who were in opposition to Sir Robert Walpole. During four generations the Dundases had exhibited, to their country, the spectacle of a family in which each succeeding heir was the rival of his father in capacity for affairs and in the power of achieving a high position in the service of the state. This fact alone explains, in some degree, the extraordinary influence which they had now acquired. But other circumstances combined to secure their ascendency. Not only had the official life of this remarkable family extended over nearly a century, but the marriages of the Dundases, and the private friendships which they formed, all tended to advance their political influence. By marriage they were related to families, in every part of Scotland, whose widespread connections it would be tedious to describe, but who possessed, in their counties, an amount of personal and political influence, which, in the altered circumstances of our own times, it is difficult to realise. The narrow limits within which the franchise was confined, and the constitutional maxim of those days—that land alone was entitled to representation—put immense power into the hands of a few families in each county; and the Dundases, not only connected by kinship with many of those families, but also possessing the means of bestowing places or pensions on them, were able to secure, very frequently, a voice in deciding who should be the county member.

The small number of electors made it easy, as a rule, to manage the elections. It is probable that, about the time of the second Lord President's death, there were not more than 2600 county votes in Scotland, if indeed there were so many. In Midlothian there were not a hundred electors. In Cromarty there were only six. All over the country the constituencies were small select bodies, consisting of the freeholders, who alone had the right of voting. Nor were the county electors merely few in number. A majority were "paper barons" (or faggot voters as they would now be called), whose qualifications had been created in order to confer a vote, which they were bound in honour to give in favour of the candidate who was supported by the landowner from whom they obtained it. The county constituencies were, in fact, entirely in the hands of a few families; and, therefore, the powerful house of Arniston, with its social and official influence in almost every county, was able to secure an unprecedented sway over the political destinies of Scotland.

In the burghs, too, the Dundases had now great influence. There the state of matters was, if possible, more anomalous than in the counties. For the burgh members were chosen by the town-councillors; and the town-councillors having been chosen by themselves, there was nothing in the shape of popular representation. In Edinburgh, for instance, the self-elected Town-Council, numbering thirty-three persons, chose the member; and thus in a city where the Supreme Court of Scotland sat, which was famous for its school of medicine, and which had been the home of Principal Robertson and David Hume, neither lawyer, physician, nor historian had the franchise. Large towns like Paisley or Greenock did not return a member to Parliament; and even Glasgow, rapidly rising to be a power in the commercial world, only shared a member with the insignificant burghs of Renfrew, Rutherglen, and Dumbarton. At a time when county families lived chiefly on their estates, and usually passed at least a part of the winter in the county town, they had many opportunities of acquiring influence with the town-councillors; and, accordingly, the same means which were used to manage the counties could be applied to the burghs. And, apart from such local influences, the distinguished position of the Dundases, as the dispensers of patronage, naturally made the average town-councillor willing to support the Government, in the hope that his allegiance might be rewarded by some snug place in the Customs or the Post Office.

And now, when the long career of the second President had closed, the vast social and parliamentary interest of the family was left under the management of his brother Henry, to whose success in the House of Commons allusion has already been made.[1] He had been Solicitor-General and Lord Advocate in the government of Lord North. Lord North was succeeded by Rockingham, under whom Dundas retained his office. Rockingham was succeeded by Shelburne; but the only effect which the change had on Dundas was that the Prime Minister, in order to secure his support, gave him, in addition to the office of Lord Advocate, the Treasurership of the Navy, and the whole patronage of Scotland. On the formation of the Coalition government he lost his offices; but when, in December 1783, Mr. Pitt became Prime Minister, Dundas became Treasurer of the Navy, and was the premier's right-hand man during the long struggle between the Ministry and the Commons. After the dissolution and general election of 1784, which secured the triumph of Mr. Pitt, and placed him in power for the next seventeen years, Dundas reached the pinnacle of his greatness, and occupied the position which Lord Cockburn describes in such graphic terms. "Henry Dundas," he says, "was the Pharos of Scotland. Who steered upon him was safe; who disregarded his light was wrecked. It was to his nod that every man owed what he had got, and looked for what he wished."

Though not the head of the Arniston family, Henry Dundas was the guiding spirit, by whose councils the family interest was maintained as of old. In the estate of Arniston the second President was succeeded by his eldest son, Robert, who was born on the 6th of June 1758.

A journal in the collection at Arniston, kept by young

---

[1] *Supra*, p. 185.

Robert Dundas, describes his first visit to England, when a boy in 1772, with his father and mother. They left Arniston on the 9th of May, and reached Buxton on the 23d. The route taken was by East Lothian, Berwick, and Newcastle. Thence they went by Durham to Nottingham; and from Nottingham by Derby to Buxton. Besides the carriage, they had saddle horses with them; and the President and his son varied the monotony of the long drive by riding, whenever a pleasant part of the country was being traversed. The sights which would attract the attention of a Scottish boy on his first visit from home, the cathedrals and great churches, and the bridges over the Tyne and Trent, are described, and also a gibbet near Newcastle, on which the body of a malefactor was hanging in chains. At Nottingham he saw an English stage-coach for the first time. "When we came back to the Inn (The Blackamoor's Head) we saw the stage-coach for London come in. It was a great hulk of a thing, with a large cover behind. They immediately set off again: in about an hour after the coach from London came, which was to stay all night till two in the morning."

He was called to the bar in 1779; and as the son of the Lord President, and the nephew of Henry Dundas, everything was in his favour. When on a visit to London he pleased his granduncle, Mr. Thomas Dundas, son of the second Lord Arniston, and Sheriff of Galloway, who had supposed that young Dundas would be wholly engrossed with the amusements of the town, by writing him a letter in which he described the great figure which his uncle Henry was making in the House of Commons. The old gentleman, in return, gave him some very good advice.

MR. THOMAS DUNDAS *to his Grand Nephew* ROBERT DUNDAS, YOUNGER OF ARNISTON.

KEITH, *April* 10, 1781.

MY DEAR ROBIE,—What you write me concerning the Advocate,[1] is most agreeable, for you know, no man can wish him better than I do, and indeed his parts are surprising and his openness and courage most delightful; he is plagueing Charles Fox and

---

[1] Henry Dundas.

the faction, but, what you are not aware of, he will plague you more after this. You will very probably succeed him and represent Mid-Lothian, and the higher the pyramid he raises, the more strength it will take to support it. It will rob you of many nights' rest, and cost you immensity of labour not to degenerate from the fame of your predecessor. In London, at present, your nights may be devoted as you please, perhaps to Mammon, but the day to serve God and your country. Your language must be purified, a most difficult task, for it generally sticks, like original sin. Your knowledge, by ardent study and the conversation of mankind, must be improved, and graces of speaking learned from the best masters, your orators in Parliament, and then, like the Advocate, you will be esteemed and courted by high and low. . . .—I am always, etc. etc. etc., Tho^S· Dundas.

He had not long to wait; for in January 1784, soon after Mr. Pitt's government took the place of the Coalition, he received a letter from Lord Sidney, who was then Under-Secretary of State, informing him that he was appointed Solicitor-General. He was only twenty-five years of age. This was rapid promotion; but it seemed natural. His father had been Solicitor-General at twenty-nine, and his uncle Henry at twenty-four. Lord Cockburn attributes the success of young Dundas entirely to family influence, and forms a very low estimate of his capacity.[1] He certainly had not the talent of his kinsmen, who had held office before him; and, without family interest, he might not have risen as he did. But though his abilities were moderate, it must be remembered that Lord Cockburn bore no goodwill to his cousin Robert Dundas. Cockburn's separation from the political party among whom he had been brought up, at a time when party spirit ran high, could not fail to carry with it a tinge of bitterness towards former friends. And it was no secret that it was towards Robert Dundas that this feeling was chiefly directed.

His statement that Dundas, when at the bar with all the advantages of his position, all the favour of agents, and all the partiality of courts, never commanded any independent private practice, is by no means correct. In the first year of his prac-

---

[1] *Memorials of His Time*, p. 156.

tice, including £93 in complimentary retainers from his father's friends the Dukes of Buccleuch and Gordon, the Earls of Kinnoull, Findlater, and others, young Dundas's fees amounted to £220. In the second year of his practice they amounted to £319; in the third to £364; and in the fourth to £503; which would be considered a good start in business, even with the higher scale of fees of the present day.

In the fifth year of his practice Dundas was appointed Solicitor-General, and his practice at the Scottish bar was interrupted by his entering Parliament, but while holding the office of Solicitor-General his fees averaged £1443, including only £368 of official salary. In 1790 he was appointed Lord Advocate, and in the two succeeding years his fees averaged £2707, including a salary which averaged £1333.[1]

It was to the influence of his uncle Henry that Robert Dundas owed his appointment as Solicitor-General. The Coalition Ministry was dismissed on the 18th of December 1783, and Mr. Pitt became Prime Minister. Mr. Henry Dundas took the office of Treasurer of the Navy for himself, and at the same time took care to secure that of Solicitor-General for Scotland for his nephew.

Mr. Henry Dundas's seat for Midlothian becoming vacant by his acceptance of office, a new election was necessary; and the following account of what took place, taken from the *Caledonian Mercury*, shows how easily things were managed in a county constituency consisting of less than a hundred freeholders :—

"The election of a representative for the county of Midlothian was held in the Parliament House to-day—a vacancy having been created by the appointment of Mr. Henry Dundas to the office of Treasurer of the Navy. Sir Alexander Dick was elected Preses, and the roll of freeholders having been called, the meeting unanimously re-elected Mr. Dundas.

"Mr. Robert Dundas then addressed the meeting, and in the necessary absence of his uncle on public business, thanked

---

[1] Lord Cockburn's mother was Miss Janet Rannie, younger daughter of Captain Rannie of Melville. Her sister was married to Henry Dundas. His father was a nephew of the first President Dundas. *Supra*, p. 88.

them for the honour they had done his relation in electing him for the eighth time their representative. He apologised to them for the active part he had taken in canvassing the county for his absent relative. He had been informed that a formidable opposition was intended, and after observing meetings of freeholders called by public advertisement with the view of naming a different candidate, he felt himself called upon to watch over his interests, and solicit the continuance of the support of the county. The numerous and respectable appearance of the day convinced him that his hon. friend still possessed the confidence, the friendship, and the support of an independent county, and whilst he continued to hold his seat by so honourable a tenure he was sure that all opposition to him would prove fruitless. After the election was over, the freeholders were entertained at dinner in the Assembly Hall."

Besides political reasons the opposition to which the young Solicitor alluded arose from a jealousy on the part of a few of the freeholders of the representation of the county becoming a *Peerage*, as it was termed, in one family, and the freeholders being thereby reduced to insignificance. Mr. Henry Dundas, however, secure in his long experience of the county, was not in the least alarmed. "I have heard," he says, in a letter to his daughter Elizabeth, "from different quarters the accounts of my late opposition in the county. From what I can learn, it has been matter of much speculation in your part of the world. Here, it was laughed at, and I should have joined in the laugh if that sensation had not given way to another of a more pleasing nature, I mean my nephew Robert. Every letter I have received upon the subject is full of his praises. I therefore must rejoice at the opportunity that has been afforded him of making himself known and in fighting my cause. I trust he has laid the foundation of acquaintance and connexion that will one day be of material benefit to himself."

In the spring, just before the dissolution of Parliament, Mr. Dundas came down from London, and attended a dinner given by the Town Council of Edinburgh to the city member, Mr. James Hunter Blair. Young Robert Dundas was there; and among others present was James Boswell, who had not long before celebrated the fall of the Coalition Ministry by publishing a "Letter to the People of Scotland," of which Dr. Johnson had been pleased to express approval. "Many excellent constitutional toasts were given by the Lord Provost. Mr. Boswell sang a ballad of his own composition on the *Midlothian Address*, the last verse of which (alluding to Mr. Solicitor-General's very interesting appearance at his honourable uncle's late election) was as follows:—

> Young Robert again, with his modest fine fire,
> Will draw praise from all present, and tears from his sire.
> Huzza then, brave boys! send it off by express,
> And let Melville present the Midlothian Address." [1]

The young Solicitor-General had, in the meantime, fallen in love with his cousin Miss Elizabeth Dundas. In a boyish letter written to her soon after he came to the Bar he laments the fact that neither he nor she was tall. "Heaven," he says, "seems to have been rather niggard in its bounties to you and I, whilst it has been no less lavish on some of the younger branches of the family. Not only has it cruelly curtailed our statures among the sons and daughters of man, but it has mortified us by giving to William and Ann in the same proportions that it hath taken from us." This recalls Lord Cockburn's description of him as "a little, alert, handsome, gentleman-like man, with a countenance and air beaming with sprightliness and gaiety, and dignified by considerable fire; altogether inexpressibly pleasing," and also the complaint which Mr. Ferguson of Pitfour, the member for Aberdeenshire, is said to have made, during a division in the House of Commons, when Dundas came to be Lord Advocate,—"The Lord Advocate should always be a tall man. We Scotch members always vote with him, and we need, therefore, to be able to see him. I can see Pitt and Addington, but I can't see this new Lord Advocate."

The William alluded to was his younger brother, a very handsome man, who retained his good looks to an advanced age. Ann was his cousin Elizabeth's sister, who also deserved

---

[1] The allusion is to an address in favour of the Ministry which had recently been adopted at a county meeting in Midlothian.

the praise for personal appearance bestowed upon her. She married, in February 1786, Mr. Henry Drummond, banker, of Charing Cross, and was the mother of Henry Drummond, M.P. of Albury.

On the back of young Dundas's letter to his cousin there is a brief note—written long years after—"The oldest letter the Chief Baron ever wrote me, when I lived at Millhead in 1782 or 3." His addresses had been favourably received; and Henry Dundas, too, had formed a very high opinion of his nephew, for he had already requested his brother, the President, to show him all his letters. "When," he says, "I write you confidential letters, show them all to your son Robert; for I have that good opinion of his understanding and perfect discretion, I have no thoughts of ever being upon reserve with him in anything." But it was not until three years after his appointment as Solicitor-General that matters were finally arranged. Then, nothing having occurred to interfere with the affair, the elder members of the family were consulted on the subject in the spring of 1787, when the lady's father wrote to the Lord President, expressing his approval, and making arrangements for a suitable provision for the young couple.

HENRY DUNDAS *to his Brother, the* SECOND PRESIDENT DUNDAS.

WIMBLEDON, *Saturday, 17th March* 1787.

MY DEAR LORD,—The Solicitor and Elizabeth having explained themselves to each other, I do not think anything you or I have to do in the business need take much time, or give us any trouble. He mentioned to me in a conversation he desired with me yesterday an intention of desiring James Newbigging to come up, and to bring up papers with him, in order to show me particularly how his situation and prospects stood. There is not the smallest necessity for any such step. He has shown me enough to make me understand that he has large landed property under large incumbrances. But they are not such as in any respect to create any idea of anxiety. On the contrary, it is clear to me that, with your attention, joined to his own industry, and a rational economy, he has within his powers the certainty of establishing his family on a most respectable footing. And he shall act very much indeed contrary to my opinion if, for the sake of having a little larger

income a few years sooner, he shall ever part with one ridge of his landed property. The size of the house and policy of Arniston ought to have a corresponding estate, and they ought to be knit together by an indissoluble entail. For we must not always take it for granted that the proprietors of Arniston are to be men of business and of virtue; and it would be hard if one profligate fool should have it in his power to dissolve what has been the collection of ages. These being my general sentiments with regard to the Solicitor's situation and prospects, in which I truly believe I am not less interested than you, a marriage-contract between your son and my daughter must be a very simple business. . . . I suspect I have put your eyes to the trial to read this letter, and shall, therefore, relieve you with only further saying that if our two young friends do not make each other happy, I shall despair of ever seeing it again.—Yours faithfully,

HENRY DUNDAS.

The marriage took place in the following month, April 1787, and proved a very happy one in all respects.

In September 1789, Ilay Campbell, who had been Lord Advocate since the fall of the Coalition Ministry, was appointed Lord President on the death of Sir Thomas Miller of Glenlee; and Robert Dundas became Lord Advocate in his thirty-second year.

No better picture of the social life of this time has ever been drawn than that given by Lord Cockburn in a passage in his *Memorials*, which, though well known, will bear repetition. His father, then Convener of Midlothian, had gone to a meeting of road trustees, and taken some of his family with him. "It was a bright, beautiful August day," says Lord Cockburn; "we returned to the inn of Middleton, on our way home, about seven in the evening; and there we saw another scene. People sometimes say that there is no probability in Scott's making the party in Waverley retire from the Castle to the Howf; but these people were not with me at the inn at Middleton, about forty years ago. The Duke of Buccleuch was living at Dalkeith; Henry Dundas at Melville; Robert Dundas, the Lord Advocate, at Arniston; Hepburn of Clerkington at Middleton; and several of the rest of the aristocracy of Midlothian within a few miles; all with their families, and luxurious houses; yet had they, to the number of twelve or sixteen, congregated in this wretched ale-house for a day of freedom and jollity. We found them, roaring and singing and laughing, in a low-roofed room scarcely large enough to hold them, with wooden chairs and a sanded floor. When their own lacqueys, who were carrying on high life in the kitchen, did not choose to attend, the masters were served by two women. There was plenty of wine, particularly claret, in rapid circulation on the table; but my eye was chiefly attracted by a huge bowl of hot whisky punch, the steam of which was almost dropping from the roof, while the odour was enough to perfume the whole parish. We were called in, and made to partake, and were very kindly used, particularly by my uncle Harry Dundas. How they did joke and laugh! with songs, and toasts, and disputations, and no want of practical fun. I don't remember anything they said, and probably did not understand it. But the noise, and the heat, and the uproarious mirth—I think I hear and feel them yet. My father was in the chair; and he having gone out for a little, one of us boys was voted into his place, and the boy's health was drank, with all the honours, as 'the young Convener. Hurra! hurra! may he be a better man than his father! hurra! hurra!' I need not mention that they were all in a state of elevation; though there was nothing like absolute intoxication, so far as I could judge."

At this time, and for some years after, Lord Advocate Dundas used to spend a part of the summer on the shores of Loch Ericht, while Mrs. Dundas lived with her father at Dunira, his estate near Comrie in Perthshire.

Loch Ericht is a romantic Highland lake, lying on the northern confines of Perthshire, among the wilds of Badenoch, and surrounded on all sides by a bare and desolate region. On its western side is Ben Alder, a magnificent mountain, among whose gloomy recesses Macpherson of Cluny had found a safe hiding-place, in which he defied the Government forces, who were searching for him, for nine years after Culloden. About five miles to the south of Loch Ericht, and separated from it by rough moorlands, is Loch Rannoch, at the western end of which (that nearest Loch Ericht) is Rannoch Barracks, a place which was built as quarters for the soldiers who occupied that district after the rebellion of 1745.

The following letter describes an adventure which some of the Dundas party had among these hills in August 1789. It appears that the Lord Advocate's younger brother, Francis Dundas,[1] along with Mr. Henry Dundas's son Robert, resolved to walk from Killin, at the west end of Loch Tay, to Loch Ericht; and any one who has traversed the trackless waste known as the Moor of Rannoch, over a part of which their route lay, is aware that it was a long and difficult walk.

LORD ADVOCATE *to* MRS. DUNDAS.

LOCH ERICHT SIDE, *Thursday, 27th Aug.* 1789.

You made me very happy, my dearest Elizabeth, by receiving your letter from Francis, who arrived here about six o'clock this morning. What you are doing, how you are, and all the little minutiæ going on at Dunira, are to me the most pleasing intelligence of any you can possibly communicate. To return, my sweet wife, the same pleasure which I believe my letters give to her, she may now look for a full narrative of the proceedings at Loch Ericht, and I must warn her they are a little extraordinary.

I had just got to bed last night about eleven, when a knock at the window from the outside made me jump up, surprised not a little, as everybody in the house were quiet. Guess my amazement when I heard Robert's voice, who immediately after entered; and guess my still greater astonishment when he told me the Governor and he had walked that day from Killin, upwards of forty miles, through inaccessible hills; and that he left Francis in the moor about three miles off, unable to proceed a step further. This intelligence made the whole family turn out, the ladies excepted. By this time it was half-past eleven, pitch dark, blowing and raining a tempest. A couple of Highlanders and a pony were immediately dispatched in quest of Francis, whose situation, I can assure you, alarmed me more than I can express. Your brother was immediately taken care of in every way; and as soon as he got to bed, with some warm chops and Madeira to comfort him, he fell asleep as sound as a top. The account he gave me of Francis was, that he had forced him on with directions to send people for him; but was totally unable to drag a leg after him, and was sitting on a stone at the loch side.

---

[1] Second son of the second President Dundas.

That they had got to Rannoch Barracks early in the afternoon, and expecting the boat to meet them, at the end of the Loch[1] (twelve miles from hence), they had agreed to walk the five miles of moor betwixt the two lakes, which after their dinner they thought themselves able for. For these three days it has blown a perfect hurricane from the west, which rendered it absolutely impossible to row the boat down to meet them; and I accordingly yesterday morning dispatched a courier to Rannoch with a note to Francis, telling them why the boat could not meet them. But unfortunately the fellow missed them by the way. About two miles from hence there is the only shealing on the loch; which Robert, in stumbling through the moor, fell in with, and sent the Highlander back to Francis with whisky and some oat cakes, whilst he himself proceeded on here with a boy he got at the shealing. I sat up till one o'clock, when one of the Highlanders returned with intelligence that the Colonel was asleep in the shealing, and that his neighbour and the pony were waiting there till he should awake. I then went to bed, so far satisfied; and at six this morning his honour arrived, such a figure as you never saw. He had slept on the moor, with the rain pelting on him, till the Highlander came from the shealing, and assisted him to it, when, after eating some cheese, and drinking half a bottle of whisky, he had slept on the man's bed till daybreak. Their baggage and servants were left some miles behind on the moor, where they were forced to stand all night, there being no road, and the night so dark that they could not pick their way.

Unfortunately part of this letter has been torn off, and accordingly the story ends abruptly; but neither of the travellers suffered. Francis Dundas, who was at that time Colonel of the Scots Brigade (afterwards the 94th Regiment), lived to be a General in the army; and Robert Dundas succeeded his father, in 1811, as the second Viscount Melville.

Nothing can better illustrate the complete change which had taken place in the Highlands, since the rebellion, than the fact that the district in which Mr. Dundas was now living in perfect safety had been, when his father was Lord Advocate, not fifty years before, one of the most dangerous and disaffected parts of the country. Every mile of the heather over which his brother and cousin stumbled on that August evening in

---

[1] Loch Ericht.

1789 was, in August 1749 and for several years after, guarded by outposts of armed clansmen, who allowed no one to approach the fastnesses of Ben Alder. A change too has taken place since 1789. The Highland Railway runs within a few miles of Loch Ericht; and though the Moor of Rannoch is as desolate as ever, Rannoch Barracks is now a comfortable shooting lodge.

At the general election of 1790, Mr. Henry Dundas was returned as member for Edinburgh, having given up his seat for Midlothian in order to make way for his nephew, who was elected for the county on the 26th of June. The *Edinburgh Advertiser* thus describes what took place:—

"On Saturday there was a very full meeting of the freeholders of the county of Edinburgh in the Parliament House, the Right Hon. Henry Dundas, Treasurer of the Navy, in the chair. Mr. Dundas addressed the meeting in a nervous speech, returning his warmest acknowledgments for the honour they had so often and for so long a period conferred upon him, having been no less than seven times unanimously elected their representative. Mr. Dundas then quitted the chair, which Lord Hailes[1] was called to fill. The election proceeded, when the Right Hon. Robert Dundas of Arniston, Lord Advocate, was unanimously chosen.

"The Lord Advocate expressed his gratitude for the honour done him in choosing him to fill the high station which his ancestors had filled for two centuries in the Scottish and British parliaments. The Parliament House was crowded. A number of ladies were in the galleries, among whom were the Duchess of Gordon and daughter. The gentlemen afterwards dined in the new Assembly Room."[2]

The Lord Advocate entered Parliament as a devoted follower of Mr. Pitt, but without any great confidence in his own abilities. He modestly and eagerly accepted the advice which Mr. Pitt, though young in years, was so well qualified to give to a new member. "I am going down," he writes to his wife on the 23d of March 1791, "at half-past four, to attend the

---

[1] Sir David Dalrymple of Hailes. He had been on the bench of the Court of Session since 1766.

[2] The Assembly Rooms in George Street, Edinburgh, which were opened about the year 1785.

Committee on the Corn Bill, which I suppose will last all this evening. I wrote you in very bad spirits and in worse humour with myself for having risen on Friday last to give my opinion about that business. It seems, however, that I was mistaken, as Pitt was much pleased, and said what I had stated was in point of matter and manner more to the purpose than anything he had heard on the subject. In short, he thinks I shall do him good; and in proof of it, I was admitted, by his own desire, to the previous meeting at his house yesterday, of 8 or 10 of his friends, to consider what was to be stated in answer to the expected attack on the bill for appropriating the unclaimed dividends. He says he never wants me to make a set speech, but wishes me to make myself previously master of the business to come on, and not to rise and speak on it, unless I feel inclined, and anything occurs which I think myself able to answer. If I do ultimately turn out of use to him in any way, I shall be abundantly satisfied."

For some years after this Lord Advocate Dundas occupied a peculiarly trying position, during which things were done in Scotland which all parties are now united in condemning. Two movements were in progress which he was bound, as a faithful adherent of Mr. Pitt, in the unfortunate position which that illustrious statesman was led to adopt during the last ten years of the century, to oppose both as a politician and as first law officer of the Crown in Scotland. These movements were the agitation for Burgh Reform, and the agitation for Parliamentary Reform.

The grievances which were complained of in the Scottish burghs were such as can hardly be realised in our own day. It is only necessary to mention a few of them. In the first place, the town-councils were self-elected; and, accordingly, year after year the same persons managed or mismanaged the affairs of the burghs, the burgesses having no power of discarding from their service even the most unworthy or incompetent of the councillors. To such an extent was this absurd system carried that there were instances of men continuing to act as town-councillors for periods of from twenty to fifty years without interruption. Sometimes one family would secure the power of managing a burgh, and hand it down from father to son. At other times the management fell into the hands of a council, many of whose members were non-resident and totally ignorant of the burgh business.

These self-elected councillors refused, in many cases, to allow the burgesses access to the books of council, and insisted on spending the public money without any supervision or control by the tax-payers.

There were many instances in which the public property had been alienated without the consent, or even against the wishes, of the inhabitants. At Inverness, for example, this was a great grievance. "The revenues of this burgh, dilapidated away within the last century by the different leading magistrates, in favours of themselves and their adherents, for trifling feu-duties not exceeding £20 per annum, now yield above £3000 sterling. The revenue of the town is at present [1] £500 sterling a year or thereby; a great part of which is expended in entertainments and pensions to the friends and adherents of the leader."[2] At Dundee the same thing had taken place. "Had the town retained the property of their lands, the revenue would have been very great. But these, except an inconsiderable part (which have been feued on very disadvantageous terms), were distributed among the friends of the men who formerly composed the town-councils, many of them without the shadow of a remuneration, and others for such avowed causes as bore no proportion to the value of the property given away."[3]

Taxes, too, were imposed without the authority of Parliament. In Glasgow potatoes were taxed on the ground, it was said, that they had partly superseded the use of meal, on which a tax had been established by usage![4]

It followed, as a matter of course, that jobbery of every kind was rampant. Building contracts were given, not to the lowest offerer, or to the best contractor, but to those who were relations or friends of the town-councillors; and work was often ordered, not because the town needed it, but simply in

---

[1] 1787.
[2] *A Memoir concerning the Origin and Progress of the Reform proposed in the Internal Government of the Royal Burghs of Scotland.* By Archibald Fletcher, Esq., Advocate. Part iii. p. 56.
[3] *Ibid.* [4] *Ibid.* p. 115.

order to enrich those whom the irresponsible town-council wished to favour.

Lastly, this system of self-election, with its natural accompaniments of jobbery and peculation, was guarded by what was known as the Beautiful Order, a farce devised for the purpose of securing that, on those occasions when the election of a new councillor could not be avoided, any new member of corporation should stand by all that was done within the secret conclave of the council chamber. The new councillor was elected on the express condition that he would solemnly promise always to abide by the vote of a majority of his brother councillors.[1]

In 1788 a conference of burgh delegates was held, by which an agitation for reform was originated; and four years later, after an immense quantity of evidence had been collected, an attempt was made to induce the Government to deal with the question. Mr. Henry Dundas was approached upon the subject. "But Mr. Dundas," says Fletcher, "in perfect consistency with the manly openness of his character, told us at once that he would not support, but oppose the object of the Burgh Reform." It would, indeed, have been difficult for Mr. Dundas to have assisted a movement, one of the first results of which would have been to irritate, and probably estrange the town-council of Edinburgh, which returned him, or any member of his family whom he chose to nominate, to the House of Commons. Lord Cockburn describes the Edinburgh council chamber, which seems to have been well suited for its occupants, as "a low-roofed room, very dark and very dirty." "Within this Pandemonium," he says, "sat the town-council, omnipotent, corrupt, impenetrable. Nothing was beyond its grasp; no variety of opinion disturbed its unanimity, for the pleasure of Dundas was the sole rule for every one of them. Reporters, the fruit of free discussion, did not exist; and though they had existed, would not have dared to disclose the proceedings. Silent, powerful, submissive, mysterious, and irresponsible, they might have been sitting in Venice." With such an institution at his doors, it was not likely that Mr. Dundas would take a leading part in promoting a reform of the corporations of which it was merely a specimen.

---

[1] Fletcher on Burgh Reform, Part iii. p. 32.

Mr. Henry Erskine, however, and the Whigs in Scotland, were active in agitating for some measure of burgh reform; and they were supported by Mr. Sheridan and the Opposition in the House of Commons. They continued their efforts for some time; and in 1792 the Government yielded to a certain extent. Lord Advocate Dundas brought in a bill to regulate the mode of accounting for the common good and revenues of the royal burghs of Scotland. But the system of self-election, from which the reformers declared all their grievances sprung "as rivulets from a fountain," was left untouched; and the bill, after the second reading had been passed, was abandoned.

But the question of burgh reform was forgotten for a time, in the midst of the fierce passions which were aroused by the larger and more exciting topics to which the attention of the country, now brought face to face with a demand for a change in the system of parliamentary representation, was for some years to be directed.

In Scotland the horrors of the French Revolution had rent society in twain. Mr. Burke's *Reflections on the French Revolution*, which appeared in 1790, but faintly echoed the fear of change, the burning indignation against those who ventured even to hint at reform, and the intense distrust of the masses which was felt by many at this time. The publication, in the following year, of the *Vindiciæ Gallicæ* only added fuel to the flame; and events soon took place, in which Lord Advocate Dundas was a leading actor, of a most painful and harrowing description.

It was to the proceedings of the "Society of Friends of the People" that the attention of Government was chiefly directed. This association was formed in England during the spring of 1792. At first it consisted of about one hundred members, most of whom were persons of some position in the country. One of the original members was Thomas Erskine, afterwards Lord Chancellor Erskine. Sir James Mackintosh acted as secretary. Lord Lauderdale, Lord John Russell, Mr. Grey, afterwards Earl Grey, Mr. Fox, Mr. Sheridan, and Mr. Whitbread, were also members.[1] Their object was strictly constitutional, and was defined as "obtaining a Parliamentary Reform."

---

[1] The first general meeting of the Friends of the People was held in the Freemasons' Tavern, London, on the 26th of April 1792.

But a society whose leaders have in view a legitimate end, which they purpose to attain by legitimate means, cannot always control the action of all its adherents. The whole history of reform shows that, as a rule, side by side with legal and constitutional agitation, there is found an illegal movement, conducted by men who rely upon acts of violence or intimidation. In the seventeenth century the memorable resistance to the Scottish administration of Charles the Second and James the Second was stained by the murder of Sharpe and other outrages. At the commencement of the present century the Cato Street conspirators purposed, by wholesale assassination, to advance the cause for which the Whig members were contending within the Houses of Parliament. And, in like manner, there was, in 1792, a dangerous spirit of violence, if not of actual disloyalty, among many of the working classes. In the meantime, however, nothing worse took place than ordinary rioting in Edinburgh, Dundee, and some other places in Scotland.

The King's birthday was the 4th of June. During the day all was quiet in Edinburgh; and for some time in the evening nothing of importance happened. Bonfires were lighted, and fireworks displayed by the street boys, as usual. But, in the course of the evening, some dragoon officers, who chanced to be walking along the High Street, attracted the attention of the mob. Stones were thrown at them, and they ran for shelter to the Riding School, where some of their men were stationed. The dragoons turned out and patrolled the streets, where the mob attacked them with stones and squibs. The 53d Regiment, which was then quartered in the Castle, marched into the city; and the crowd, turning its attention from the soldiery, was allowed, unmolested, to burn the sentry boxes which stood at the Tron Church; after which it dispersed. No attacks were made on private houses that night.

As may be supposed, the Arniston family, one of whose members was Home Secretary,[1] and another Lord Advocate, was peculiarly obnoxious to the mob; and the following newspaper account, which is probably accurate in most of its

---

[1] Henry Dundas had become Home Secretary in 1791.

details, describes an attack which was made upon them on the following night:—

"On Tuesday, June 5th, it was expected that the riots in this city were at an end, and the dragoons who had been brought to town on Monday were on Tuesday forenoon sent away to their respective quarters. In the evening, however, a number of people assembled in George Square, and proceeded to break the windows of the houses of Mrs. Dundas, Dowager of Arniston, and the Lord Advocate. The Sheriff earnestly intreated the mob to retire, but in vain. He then sent for the 53d regiment from the Castle. When they came they were insulted with stones. The Sheriff informed the mob that if they did not disperse, the soldiers would fire upon them. They then apparently dispersed, and the soldiers were ordered away, except an officer and twenty men, who were left to guard the houses that had been attacked. About an hour afterwards, the mob again assembled, when the Sheriff and the small party of soldiers endeavoured in vain to disperse them. The mob continued to insult them, and to break the windows of a house in the square. The Sheriff, after ineffectual efforts to disperse them, gave orders to a few of the soldiers to fire, but the mob finding none of their number wounded became more bold and abusive. The Sheriff then gave orders to fire a second time, when six or seven persons were wounded, two of them very dangerously.

"At a meeting of the authorities, held next day, it was observed that many false reports had been propagated to inflame the minds of the people, particularly one that Mr. Secretary Dundas was bringing a bill into Parliament to raise the price of meal."

On the following evening, the 6th of June, the mob again assembled, and attacked the Lord Provost's house, which was in St. Andrew Square. All the windows were broken; but the riot lasted only a short time. Two signal guns were fired from the Castle, on which the soldiers turned out, and the rioters at once dispersed.

Alarmed by the excited state of public feeling, some of the landed proprietors in Scotland appointed delegates to hold a conference in Edinburgh " to consider the present state of the election laws for the return of members to Parliament." The meeting was held in the Assembly Rooms on the 2d of July. Sir James Montgomery of Stanhope was in the chair. "A motion in favour of a reform in these laws was moved by Sir Thomas Dundas, and seconded by Lord Advocate Dundas, and agreed to

HOUSE OF LORD ADVOCATE DUNDAS, ATTACKED ON 5TH JUNE 1792.

unanimously."[1] A committee was appointed to consider the subject; but in the end the movement led to no practical result.

The plan of operations which the Friends of the People intended to follow, was to organise, all over the country, a number of affiliated societies for reform (one in every parish, if possible), which were to send delegates to a general conven-

[1] *Edinburgh Advertiser*, 3d July 1792.

tion. The first meeting of the Scottish branch of the Society was held in Glasgow at the end of October. Colonel Dalrymple of Fordel was elected President; and two resolutions, one in favour of Parliamentary Reform, and the other in favour of a shorter duration of Parliaments, were passed. This meeting was followed by a "Convention" of delegates, which assembled in Edinburgh on the 11th of December, and continued to sit for some time.

These proceedings caused great uneasiness among the Ministerialists; and the letters which Lord Advocate Dundas wrote to his uncle in January 1793 constantly refer to the subject. "Two factious papers printed here, the *Caledonian Chronicle* and the *Edinburgh Gazette*," were sent regularly to the Home Office. "I hope," he writes on the 3d of January, "not without some anxiety, that an Edinburgh jury will do equal justice on our seditious gentry that a Middlesex one has done with you." From this time onwards the reports of spies in the employment of the Government came in from day to day. "I have wrote you twice as to the main point, a little cash to reward our spies and emissaries."[1]

One of these spies was a man named Robert Watt. On the 13th of January the Lord Advocate writes to his uncle Henry, "Watt was with me last night. He was in Perth about a week ago. James Wylie, merchant there, whom I know to be the most intemperate revolutioner in Scotland, is, he informs me, engaged in a foreign correspondence with France. He suggested, and that very earnestly, the propriety of opening his letters at the post-office. Any coming from abroad, addressed to Mr. Wylie, merchant in Perth, may be attended to in London, if you think that measure proper. All letters from Perth, which, of course, have the Perth mark on them, addressed to France, can be easily stopped here, or forwarded to London to be examined, if it is judged expedient to take that step. But without hearing from you, or receiving your directions, I shall take no steps in the business."[2]

---

[1] Lord Advocate Dundas to Nepean, 4th Jan. 1793. State Papers, Domestic, Scotland, Public Record Office. Mr., afterwards Sir Evan, Nepean was Under Secretary for the Home Department at this time.

[2] Lord Advocate Dundas to the Home Secretary, 13th Jan. 1793. Public Record Office.

Later in the month Dundas was able to inform his uncle that everything was still quiet; but he thought that the spirit of discontent was only smothered for a time, not extinguished. "The great object," he says, "is to satisfy the country that, within the British dominions, none of these fellows is safe."

The following letter, one of many on the same subject among the Scottish papers in the Record Office, is a specimen of the reports which were sent from Scotland to the Home Office:—

MR. KENNETH MACKENZIE *to* MR. PULTENEY.[1]

EDINR., 3*d Jany.* 1793.

SIR,—The account you require of my journey from the North I trust will, upon the whole, prove satisfactory, as I can with truth inform you that I found the towns of Inverness, Nairn, Forres, Elgin, Banff, Aberdeen, Cupar in Angus, and Perth all increasing in wealth and industrious pursuits, and the principal inhabitants well affected to the measures of Government, with some few exceptions at Perth and Dundee, where some turbulent people are still endeavouring to disturb and mislead the populace, and with too much success. At a new inn near Gordon Castle I was informed that a party had come to the Duke's village at Fochabers and erected a tree of liberty at His Grace's gate: that the Duke had offered a ten guineas' reward to discover the people concerned without success. At Lawrence Kirk in Angus a refractory innkeeper, not the principal one in that place, had summon'd sixty members of a club to be held there in the course of this week, for the purposes of establishing a plan of reform, etc. etc. At Perth I learned from a considerable manufacturer of that town, that the principal inhabitants were well affected to Government, but that riots and frequent meetings still prevailed among the lower order of the people there, whose proceedings were supported and greatly promoted by some leading people, preachers and others from Dundee, to such an alarming degree, that Lord Kinnoul judged it necessary on Sunday the 23d ulto. to frame certain resolutions in support of those proposed by the gentlemen of the county of Perth, and in support of the measures of government: that his Lordship went to his parish church with the

---

[1] Enclosure in a letter of Mr. Wm. Pulteney's to Mr. Secretary Dundas of 4th Jan. 1793.

view of signing these resolutions in presence of the congregation, which he did, and got his parson, factor, and gardner to sign them by way of encouragement to the rest of the parishioners, who were all charged by an orator from Dundee to decline signing any such aristocratic resolutions as subversive of their grand object of reform, and accordingly there appeared only three or four signatures to his Lordship's resolutions. These turbulent spirits at Dundee are well known, and have acknowledged themselves the authors of several inflammatory hand-bills in circulation in and about Perth, where I understood several respectable inhabitants had assembled, and sent a report of these proceedings to the Lord Advocate for advice. Permit me to acknowledge my obligations for your unremitting attention to me during my progress on the Ullapool road, and to hope that the supply now wanted for the further prosecution of that work will very soon be obtained.—And I have the honour to be, most respectfully, Sir, your most obed^t and obliged hb^{le} servant,

KENTH MACKENZIE.

William Pulteney, Esq.

In the meantime an important arrest had been made. Walking the floor of the Parliament House at this time was a young advocate whose fair hair, blue eyes, open countenance, and pleasing manners, did not seem to point him out as a dangerous conspirator. Yet Thomas Muir, younger of Huntershill, had been a marked man for some time. He was a member of the Society of the Friends of the People, and a delegate to the Convention. In the deliberations of that assemblage he had taken a prominent part. Although a Scotsman, he had been enrolled as a member of the Society of United Irishmen. He had been heard to recommend the study of Paine's works, and was suspected of being in correspondence with the Republican leaders in France. On the 2d of January he was arrested, liberated on bail, and indicted for trial in the following month on a charge of sedition. He did not appear on the appointed day, but was afterwards apprehended and brought to the bar of the High Court of Justiciary on the 30th of August 1793.

Lord Advocate Dundas appeared for the prosecution. Muir defended himself. This was probably a mistake. But the most eloquent counsel at the Scottish bar could not have obtained an acquittal that day, for the trial took place before Lord Braxfield and a packed jury.

Robert Macqueen, best known as Justice-Clerk Braxfield, succeeded, at the trial of Muir, and at the other state trials of that time, in destroying all confidence in the fairness of any trial before the High Court of Justiciary in Scotland. In the picture of Lord Braxfield, by Raeburn, we see a face whose features display a combination of hateful qualities; a cruel sensual mouth; hard eyes, which twinkle with shrewdness and low cunning; an obstinate chin; and a wide, well-shaped forehead, whose outlines clearly show that he had not the excuse of stupidity for his conduct on the bench. Indeed the only excuse which can be found for his conduct is one which was put forward at the time, that he was at heart cowardly, and really believed that Muir and his associates were endangering his life. " Are we quietly to allow the Friends of the People to cut all our throats?" he is said to have asked on one occasion.

Lord Advocate Dundas was a man of a singularly amiable disposition; and it has never been denied that he conducted the celebrated prosecution of Muir with moderation, and the utmost courtesy. His language in addressing the jury was certainly harsh and injudicious, cruel even, it may be termed, as applied to a professional brother. But his general management of the case was, apart from the merits of the question at issue, perfectly fair. It was the conduct of Lord Braxfield which shocked all beholders, and roused the indignation of the country. In the first place he deliberately packed the jury. By the law of Scotland at that time the judge named the jurors. Lord Braxfield, in spite of Muir's objections, put into the jury-box fifteen men, all of whom were members of a political association, called the Friends of the Constitution, which had refused to receive Muir as a member. Having packed the jury, the Justice-Clerk, throughout the whole trial, bullied the witnesses for the defence, repelled all objections taken by the prisoner to the witnesses for the prosecution (although some of these were certainly well founded), and behaved to the prisoner in the most brutal and insolent manner. The result, as is well known, was a conviction, on which sentence of transportation for fourteen years was at once passed.[1]

---

[1] The trial of Muir is reported at full length in vol. xxiii. of the *State Trials*.

Next month another of the Friends of the People, the Reverend Thomas Fyshe Palmer, was tried at Perth, and sentenced to seven years' transportation.

Muir was detained for some time in Edinburgh; but the Lord Advocate was very anxious that he should be removed to London as soon as possible.

LORD ADVOCATE *to* MR. SECRETARY DUNDAS.

EDINR., 28*th Octr.* 1793.

MY DEAR SIR,—I am extremely sorry to find from a letter of Mr. Chapman's this morning that the intelligence we had these two days flattered ourselves with receiving this day a confirmation of, is unfounded.

The bad consequences of Muir's remaining in prison here, become every day more apparent. And although it is still my opinion that, if possible, no distinction should be made between him and any other convict, yet rather than allow him to remain longer here, I consider his removal to London, as early as convenient, to be essential for the peace and quiet of this city. There is a convention of the friends of the people to be held here to-morrow. And tho' no respectable persons have as yet appeared amongst them, I am sorry to say that the exertions of the ringleaders for these six weeks past have been too successful. Almost all the clubs of last year have been revived, have been attended by very considerable numbers, and are proceeding in the same regular and systematic plan which last year was so fortunately subdued. Ld Lauderdale visited Muir on Saturday, and was long with him. The purpose of the visit, it is reported, was to enquire if he meant to apply for any mitigation of his punishment, and to assure him that his case was to be brought before both Houses of Parliament. The countenance thus shown him has given already to the clubs additional spirits: and the bad news from the Continent will not contribute to lower them. I leave these things to your consideration; and trust, if you concur with me in opinion, that the measure I have suggested will soon be complied with.

Francis, I understand, mentioned to you a correspondence opened with me by a Mr. Hamilton Rowan, secretary of the Society of United Irishmen. I have since received a second letter from that gentleman. Private information from one of the clubs here, and a letter received this morning from a gentleman in Dublin to

Col. Pringle, leave me little room to doubt that, as Lord Fitzgibbon has been some days ago called upon by one Mr. Butler, I shall probably to-morrow or next day be visited by Mr. Rowan, or receive through a third hand a similar message.—Yours faithfully, R. DUNDAS.[1]

Archibald Hamilton Rowan of Killileagh, to whom allusion is made in the foregoing letter, was one of the most truculent members of the Society of United Irishmen, and an associate of Napper Tandy and Wolfe Tone. During the preceding summer he had become a hero among the revolutionary party in Ireland from his open defiance of the Government, and had now come to Edinburgh for the purpose of challenging the Lord Advocate, who, during the proceedings against Mr. Muir, had spoken of the Irish leaders as "wretches who had fled from punishment."

Mr. Henry Dundas, who was aware of what was going on, wrote to the Solicitor-General, with a broad hint that steps should be taken to prevent a duel.

MR. SECRETARY DUNDAS *to* SOLICITOR GENERAL BLAIR.

LONDON, 2d *Novr.* 1793.

DEAR SOLICITOR,—You will easily perceive the reason why this letter is addresst to you rather than to the Advocate. I have heard, what of course you are acquainted with, the correspondence which has been passing between him and an Irish gentleman, Mr. Rowan Hamilton. I have thought very maturely upon the subject, and am well aware of its delicacy. I know that the habits of the world and a man's own feelings do not admit of his doing what in theory may be thought best. It is certainly an absurdity on the face of it that publick men acting in the course of their duty should be supposed amenable as individuals to every man who thought proper to be offended, and it would in the present case be still more intolerable when it would appear to be a part of that lawless confederacy which strikes at all order, law, and legitimate authority. I have not thought it right to say a word on the subject to the Advocate himself, but as you will, of course, know everything that occurs on the subject, you will act in such a manner, as, without bringing any imputation on the Advocate's honour, to take care that the authority of the law is not

---

[1] State Papers, Domestic, Scotland, 1793.

trampled upon. The Advocate is a man of spirit, and no circumstances will ever deter him from going forward directly and manfully in the execution of his duty. But if this system is to be permitted to go on, you may depend upon it neither judges nor juries will do their duty; at least on many of them it will have that pernicious effect.—Yours very sincerely,   HENRY DUNDAS.[1]

On reaching Edinburgh, Mr. Rowan and the Hon. Simon Butler, who had come to act as second at the intended duel, went to Dumbreck's Hotel, in St. Andrew Square; and Mr. Butler at once proceeded with a hostile message to George Square. He saw the Lord Advocate, who said that he did not consider himself bound to give any explanation of what he had said in his official capacity, but that he would answer Mr. Rowan without delay. The answer took the form of a warrant for the arrest of Mr. Rowan and his second. They were apprehended and taken before the Sheriff of Midlothian. Colonel Macleod, M.P., however, went bail for them, and they were liberated. Some of the Friends of the People entertained them at dinner in Hunter's Tavern, in the Royal Exchange, after which they left Scotland and went home.

Muir and Palmer were sent up to London on board a revenue cutter, in irons, and among a number of felons who had been convicted of various crimes. Their case had roused great interest. "There is a devil of a stir here about Muir and Palmer," Mr. Nepean writes to the Lord Advocate. Indeed, so strong was the feeling among the Whig members that it was fully expected that a question would be raised in Parliament as to the legality of the sentence which had been passed upon them.

MR. SECRETARY DUNDAS *to the* LORD ADVOCATE.

(*Private.*)   WIMBLEDON, 16*th Novr.* 1793.

DEAR ADVOCATE,—I had a visit from Lord Lauderdale, Mr. Grey, and Mr. Sheridan, on the subject of Mr. Palmer and Mr. Muir. I desired to be furnished with any communication they had to make *in writing*, and I would then decide what I would do upon it. They sent it after two days' delay, and in so far as it

---

[1] Copy of a letter from Mr Secretary Dundas to Robert Blair, Esq., Solicitor-General, State Papers, Scotland, 1793

consists of argument I have enclosed it in a reference I have just made to the Lords of Justiciary, addrest to Lord Justice-Clerk. As the great object is to make the business a subject of parliamentary discussion, it must be attended to in that view. I therefore trust the judges will make their report with their first convenience. At the same time, for their own sakes, and for the sake of the law of the country, which must be upheld, I hope the report will be ably and scientifically drawn up. *You may communicate this letter privately to the judges.* In the representation presented to me by Messrs. Lauderdale, Grey, and Sheridan, they state their intention to bring the business before Parliament. It is not, however, my intention to gratify them in that respect, for if the judges' Report expresses no doubt upon the subject, I will carry the sentence immediately into execution, and meet their clamour in Parliament without any kind of dismay.

There is no foundation for the report you have heard of any particular severity to Muir and Palmer. I send you the note I have just received from Mr. Nepean.—Yours faithfully,

HENRY DUNDAS.

MR. SECRETARY DUNDAS *to the* LORD ADVOCATE.

LOND. 11*th Decr.* 1793. *Five o'clock.*

DEAR ADVOCATE,—I have within this hour received a visit from Lord Lauderdale, Mr. Grey, and Mr. Sheridan to state that they were advised that the conviction and confinement of Mr. Muir and Mr. Palmer was illegal, and that they meant to take measures to try the question, and, at any rate, to make a motion for a bill in Parliament, with a retrospective clause, and that they had called upon me to give me this intimation, trusting that I would take care that in the meantime they were not sent off. I told them that if they had any communication to make on the subject, they must do it in writing, and I would consider it. Lauderdale, who was the chief spokesman, said that it was Leasing-making, and that the punishment of that was defined by an Act in 1703.

You get great credit here for your attack on the Convention. I desired Nepean to send you a perusal of the King's note to me on the subject.—Yours affectly.,   HENRY DUNDAS.

MR. SECRETARY DUNDAS *to* MR. SMITH.

WHITEHALL, 23*d. Decemr.* 1793.

SIR,—I have received your letter enclosing one from Mr. Muir at Glasgow.

It has always been with me an invariable rule to refer every application for an extension of the Royal mercy to the judges who presided at the Court where the sentence was pronounced, in order that they may give their opinion whether previous to, or during the course of the trial, or subsequent to the conviction, any circumstances appeared, or have come to their knowledge which would justify a mitigation of the sentence of the Court.

No such application has been made to me by Mr. Muir. I can therefore only join with you in that sympathy which must arise in the breast of every friend to humanity when called forth by the afflictions of parents, who, by the crimes of their offspring, are plunged into that distress which the parents of Mr. Muir have stated to you.—I have the honour to be, Sir, your most obedient, humble servant, HENRY DUNDAS.

Wm. Smith, Esq.

As soon as it became certain that the trials of Muir and Palmer would be discussed in Parliament, Mr. Henry Dundas wrote to Lord Braxfield, requesting a report on the subject. His Lordship sent up to Downing Street a unanimous opinion, by all the judges, that the sentences were legal,[1] and enclosed a confidential note from himself urging that no mercy should be shown to the prisoners.

In writing to the Lord Advocate, on the 11th of December, Mr. Henry Dundas says, "You get great credit here for your attack on the Convention."[2] What had taken place was this. In December another convention assembled in Edinburgh, at which delegates from various societies, having aims similar to those of the Friends of the People, attended. It was rumoured that the law officers of the Crown in Scotland were to be intrusted with exceptional powers; and there can be no doubt that the members of the Convention, undaunted by the fate of Muir and Palmer, had actually discussed the possibility of resisting the law by force of arms. The Lord Advocate and Solicitor-General determined to arrest the ringleaders; and, in the course of a few days, Gerrald, Margarot, and Skirving, three prominent delegates, were in custody.

---

[1] This report is in the Record Office, dated 27th Dec. 1793.
[2] *Supra*, p. 240.

LORD ADVOCATE *to* MR. SECRETARY DUNDAS.

EDINR., *6th Decr.* 1793.

MY DEAR SIR,—Last Tuesday's *Gazetteer*, containing a further account of the proceedings of the Convention, appeared to the Solicitor and me so strong, that we agreed to take notice of them. The proper warrants were accordingly obtained, and early yesterday morning put in execution, against Margarot, Gerrald, Callender, Skirving, and one or two others, and with such effect that we have secured all their minutes and papers. And tho', of course, the precognitions are not yet completed, and not laid before me, my information is that we shall have no difficulty in making good a charge of sedition ag^t them, and trying and convicting them all. It gives me much satisfaction to state to you that their conduct has excited universal detestation, and, indeed, alarm, and that the strong measures taken by us are as warmly approved. It was concerted that if, notwithstanding what passed in the morning, they should presume to meet in the evening at the usual hour, the provost should interfere, and disperse them. They did accordingly meet; and last night, about seven o'clock, he proceeded with about thirty constables to the place (Blackfriars Wynd), where about one hundred were assembled, and went up to the President's chair before they had time to recollect themselves, and ordered him out, and the others to dismiss. The President skulked off. But Brown, the Sheffield delegate, took his place, and, after expressing his determination not to move, in which he was joined by the majority of his associates, the Provost called in the constables, and turned Brown, with his own hand, from the chair. On this they dispersed, without further noise. I have been informed that they again intend re-assembling this evening in a different place, in the Canongate. If they do, we have settled that the same conduct shall be followed, and that the person found acting as Preses shall be committed for the night to the guardhouse. No time shall be lost in bringing on their trials. The copy of last *Gazetteer* is in the office, but I shall cause it, and a copy of the former one, to be sent you by tomorrow's post. I trust that on perusal you will think that we have law and fact both sufficient on our side, and that you will approve of the measures which have been taken. One of their presidents, a shopkeeper named Hart, of Glasgow, returned there on Tuesday last. Wednesday evening he appeared in the Public Coffee Room, to which he is a subscriber, and, after receiving a hiss from the whole company, was, with rather too much violence, kicked out of the room. Mr. Orr has wrote me on the subject, as the party injured has applied to the magistrate for redress. I mention it chiefly to show you that, wild as we have been in this country, our senses are beginning to return, and that even reformers are not ripe for equality, and a convention modell'd on that of France.

We are all anxious in the extreme to hear of Lord Howe.—Yours ever, R. DUNDAS.[1]

LORD ADVOCATE *to* MR. SECRETARY DUNDAS.

EDINR., 11*th Decr.* 1793.

MY DEAR SIR,—You will receive with this a copy of the Edinburgh *Gazetteer* of last night, and you will attend to the story of the "Cobler of Messina." In spite of this allusion we shall continue the strong measures adopted. And as the advertisement signed by Skirving, calling a meeting to-morrow, appears in the face of the proclamation of the magistrates and sheriff, he is to be taken up this day, and will either be committed to prison, or obliged to find bail for his good behaviour. To-morrow the peace officers are to assemble at the appointed place of meeting, and to prevent its being held there. The precognitions still go on, and, I have every reason to believe, will be completed before Saturday, and the indictments immediately prepared. I shall communicate to you the result.

The publisher of the *Gazetteer* had the impudence or the insolence to write me a letter yesterday, requesting my allowing his paper to go under my frank at the post-office, as Colonel Macleod had refused to continue his permission any longer. Of course I gave him no answer.

I understand from several quarters that the general opinion of the inhabitants here is that Muir and Palmer ought only to have been confined till the opportunity of transporting them offered; and that their being handcuffed, or obliged to work like other felons, is made the handle of much clamour, and which may have a bad effect. If you think it proper to show them any distinction from the case of other convicts, it appears to me your doing so would be of service. If the juries here take it in their heads that more is done to these gentry than is absolutely necessary, they may acquit where they would otherwise have convicted.—I am, Yours very faithfully, R. DUNDAS.[2]

---

[1] State Papers, Domestic, Scotland, 1793.   [2] *Ibid.*

The arrest of the ringleaders put an end to the Convention, Skirving and Margarot were tried, and sentenced to fourteen years' transportation, in January 1794.[1] In March Gerrald received a similar sentence.[2]

The threatened discussion in Parliament, on the subject of the trials of Muir and Palmer, took place in January. Lord Stanhope, in the House of Lords, moved for an inquiry; but his motion was defeated by a large majority. In the Commons there was a hot discussion, during which Lord Advocate Dundas had to defend himself against an onslaught in which both Mr. Fox and Mr. Sheridan took part. But the Government was supported by an overwhelming majority.

In autumn a commission of Oyer and Terminer was held in Edinburgh.[3] The principal case was that of Robert Watt, who, as we have already seen, had at one time acted as a Government informer.[4] He was now accused of high treason, the chief overt act being a conspiracy to upset the Government by setting Edinburgh on fire, attacking the castle, sacking the banks, and imprisoning the judges. That such a conspiracy existed there could be little doubt from the evidence. But Watt's defence was that he mingled with the conspirators in order to obtain information which he intended to communicate to the Government. Lord Advocate Dundas had to appear both as public prosecutor and as a witness for the prisoner. For Watt subpœnaed him in order to bring out the fact that he had been in communication with his Lordship and Mr. Secretary Dundas. But it was proved that for a long time he had ceased either to see, or correspond with, the authorities. The jury returned a verdict of guilty, and he was condemned to death. In prison, the night before his execution, he wrote a long declaration, in which he admitted his guilt.[5]

The year 1795 was a miserable year in both England and Scotland. The state of public feeling went from bad to worse. Dear food, increasing taxation, a bad harvest, and constant

---

[1] *State Trials*, vol. xxiii. pp. 391-778.
[2] *Ibid.* pp. 803-1012.
[3] In 1709 the Treason Law of Scotland was abolished, and that of England substituted for it. All prosecutions for treason in Scotland must be held before a commission of Oyer and Terminer; and a grand jury must find true bills before the trials can proceed.
[4] *Supra*, p. 233. [5] *State Trials*, vol. xxiii. pp. 1167-1404.

political agitation excited the discontent of the working classes to a dangerous point. In October the king was mobbed and insulted on his way to open Parliament. The Government retaliated by bringing in two bills, one for the prevention of seditious meetings, and the other for the preservation of the royal person against treasonable attempts. The terms of these measures were of such a nature that the Opposition did all in its power to defeat them. At Edinburgh a meeting was held to petition Parliament against the bills; and at this meeting Henry Erskine, the Dean of Faculty, moved a series of resolutions, which declared that the bills struck "at the very foundations of the British Constitution." His conduct was bitterly resented. The question of discovering whether he could not be dismissed from his official position, as head of the Scottish Bar, was taken in hand by a small committee consisting of eight advocates. These gentlemen soon found that a majority of the Faculty would support the Lord Advocate in opposition to Mr. Erskine; and the Dean was, accordingly, informed that his election for the ensuing year was to be opposed.

For some years the goodly fellowship of the Bar of Scotland had been broken up. On the one hand were the supporters of Government, a powerful party supported by the approval of the Bench and the sympathy of society. On the other hand were the supporters of the Opposition, few in number, regarded with distrust by the judges, and, many of them, suffering in social and professional life from the unpopular views which they had adopted. Thus the election of a Dean for the year 1796 became a purely party question. The election took place on the 12th of January 1796, when 123 voted for Lord Advocate Dundas, and 38 for Mr. Erskine. The opinion of the Faculty was clearly expressed. But it is to be regretted that so great a slight should have been done to so good a man as Henry Erskine, and that an honour, which Mr. Dundas was in every way entitled to receive, should have been bestowed upon him rather to signalise the triumph of a faction than to express the personal respect of his brethren at the bar.[1]

---

[1] The reader will find a full account of this transaction in Colonel Fergusson's *Life of Henry Erskine*, pp. 354-366, and pp. 544-551.

On the 6th of June the Lord Advocate was again returned for Midlothian; and the following account of the election proceedings, taken from the *Edinburgh Herald*, gives a good idea of how those matters were conducted at the close of last century.

"Yesterday, June 7th, a very numerous attendance of the Freeholders of this county took place in the Parliament House in order to elect their representative for the ensuing Parliament. After the customary forms had been gone through, the Lord Advocate proposed Sir John Inglis of Cramond, Bart., to be their Preses, and James Newbigging, Esq., to be their Clerk, and these gentlemen were accordingly unanimously elected. The roll of freeholders was then adjusted by striking off those who had died since the roll was last made up, and adding to it those gentlemen whose claims for enrolment were sustained. Upon these matters being settled, the Lord Advocate informed the meeting that having either personally or by letter solicited the favour of every freeholder of again representing the county in Parliament, he was extremely happy to see so numerous and respectable an attendance, and should be proud of being once more returned. His Lordship was accordingly elected without a dissentient voice. After which he returned them thanks in a very elegant speech, declaring that as it was his early ambition to arrive at that high honour, so his having been so frequently thought worthy of it by gentlemen among whom he had been born and bred, could not but fill his mind with the deepest sense of gratitude.

"The electors with a great number of persons of the first distinction afterwards dined with his Lordship in the George Street Assembly Rooms."

The election dinner was an almost invariable part of the programme upon such occasions. No account has been preserved of the expenses connected with the election of 1796; but the bill for the election dinner given by Lord Advocate Dundas to his supporters, on his return for Midlothian three years later, was as follows:—

LORD ADVOCATE'S ELECTION DINNER.

11th October 1799.

John Bayll's bill for dinner, etc., provided for 180,			£106 15 8	
Trotter & Co., confectionery,	£43	0	0	
Young, Trotter, & Co., putting up the tables,	22	0	0	
For the use of the Assembly Rooms,	10	17	6	
Alexr. Williamson, furnishing glasses,	3	0	0	
Given to the waiters,	3	0	0	
Gratuity to Mrs. Bayll,	2	2	0	
				83 19 6

Doz. Bs. Wines.

11	4 Claret,	5/6,	£37	8	0
6	1 Port,	2/10,	10	6	8
3	4 Sherry,	3/,	6	0	0
3	3 Madeira,	5/3,	10	4	9
1	0 Rum,	3/8,	2	4	0
0	6 Brandy,	4/6,	1	7	0
1	0 Claret for the clerks,		3	6	0

26½ dozens.   70 16 5

Bill for the clerks,	£12	6	0	
For the musicians,	10	10	0	
Election fee, £5 5 0				
Doorkeepers, 3 18 6				
	9	3	6	
				31 19 6
				£293 11 1

These election dinners very often became mere debauches. Lord Advocate Dundas, himself a very temperate man, wished to check the orgies in which many of his supporters delighted; and on one occasion he arranged, with the gentlemen by whom he was supported at the head of the table, that the party should break up at an early hour. But it was no use. On rising to leave the room, they were greeted with shouts from the croupiers' end of the table of "Na, na, Mr. Dundas, we're no a' slockened yet!" Mr. William Dundas, for many years member for Edinburgh, used to relate that at one of his election dinners a voice from beneath the table was heard hiccuping, " I dinna like thae Dundases; they dinna pay weel." " Brute," replied the member, " drunk with my claret, and yet abusing my family."

NORTH FRONT OF ARNISTON, AS ORIGINALLY DESIGNED.

The front door at Arniston, as designed by Adam, its architect, was approached by a wide flight of steps, ending with a broad landing, and with a massive stone balustrade. Adam, who had drawn his inspiration from Italian sources, had overlooked one material fact, the difference between an Italian and a Scotch climate. His outside flights of stairs, though very handsome, were unsuited to Scotland, and in many instances, Arniston included, have of late years been replaced by covered porches—less handsome, but better suited to a Scotch winter.

CHAPTER XII.

LORD CHIEF BARON DUNDAS—*continued*.

IN the summer of 1797 the memorable mutiny in the British fleet took place, when Admiral Duncan, by his firmness combined with moderation, kept the crews of the " Venerable" and " Adamant" true to their colours. These events were watched by the Arniston family with peculiar interest, from the fact that the Admiral had married Henrietta, second daughter of the Second President Dundas; and the following letters relate to the decisive victory, which, in the following autumn, he gained over the Dutch at Camperdown :—

LORD ADVOCATE DUNDAS *to* MRS. DUNDAS.[1]

MY DEAREST BESS,—I have this moment your letters of Sunday and Monday. Be you mistaken or not is to me immaterial, for whilst you write me as you have done, and wind yourself about my heart so closely as you are doing, my happiness is beyond the reach of any circumstance to alter. Three successive days have I been fighting these Scots members, and at last have beaten the brutes among them to silence. This day I am going to ride out, and stay all night with your father, and return to-morrow to finish my last cause in the House of Lords, as I hope. And as I possibly will not have time to write you to-morrow, I write you these few lines with the chance of their reaching you on Sunday. But chiefly that a sea officer was here within this hour searching for your father, and if Lamb, who came in with a face of amazement and folly mixed, when he presumes to commence a conversation with me, states that the Dutch fleet are *all* taken.[2] Now, this may

---

[1] Undated.
[2] This sentence is printed exactly as it is expressed in the original; but it is evident that something is wanting.

be true, tho' unlikely. But if true, the news will come by the post as soon as you receive this. If not, burn this note. Probably Duncan may have fallen in with, and taken, a ship or two. And, if so, I rejoice in his success and the joy it will give Mrs. Duncan. Mr. Gardner and I will arrange about the trees this evening. Such of your bills as I can pay shall be paid. I will leave nothing in my pocket of my fees here, but what is necessary to bring me down to Arniston. If the Scots bill passes Monday I will write you certainly my motions. I confide entirely in your prudence, my dearest, and believe me,—Yours most truly, R. D.

ADMIRAL DUNCAN *to the* LORD ADVOCATE.

MY DEAR ADVOCATE,—As I am sure no friend will rejoice more at any good fortune that attends me than you will, I write you these two lines to say I hope the action I have had with the Dutch, who fought with their usual gallantry, is not exceeded by any this war. We have suffered much. The returns I have had, and have not had, half exceed 191 killed, and 565 wounded; from only two Dutch ships, 250 killed, and 300 wounded. We were obliged, from being so near the land, to be rather rash in our attack, by which we suffered more. Had we been ten leagues at sea none would have escaped. Many, I am sure, had surrendered, that got off in the night, being so near shore. We were much galled by their frigates, where we could not act. In short, I feel perfectly satisfied. All was done that could be done. None have any fault to find. I have now in my possession three admirals Dutch, an admiral De Winter, Vice-ad. Reuter, Reer-adm. Meame. The admiral is on board with me, and a most agreeable man he is. He speaks English well, and seems much pleased with his treatment. I have assured him, and with justice, nothing could exceed his gallantry. He says nothing hurts him, but that he is the first Dutch admiral ever surrendered. So much more credit to me. He tells the troops that were embarked in the summer were 25,000 Dutch, destined for Ireland, but after August that expedition was given up. The government in Holland, much against his opinion, insisted on his going to sea, to show they had done so, and was just going to return, when I saw him. I am sure I have every reason to be thankful to God Almighty for his kindness to me on this occasion, and all others. I believe the pilot and myself were the only two unhurt on the quarter-deck, and De Winter, who is as tall and big as I am, was the only one on his quarter-deck left alive. After all my fatigue, I am in perfect health, and my usual spirit.—Believe me, most faithfully yours,

ADAM DUNCAN.[1]

'VENERABLE,' getting up to Sheerness,
  Sunday, October the 15th, 1797.

LADY MARY DUNCAN[2] to HENRY DUNDAS.

HAMPTON COURT GREEN, Oct. 18th, 1797.

SIR,—Tho' I have not the honour of being personally known to you, I can't resist giving you joy of the signal victory. Report says my nephew is only made a Viscount. Myself is nothing. But the whole nation thinks the least you can do is to give him an English earldom. From the multiplicity of your business, you may have slipt what I am going to lay before your eyes. Please to recollect what a chicken-hearted way all the nation was in, low spirited by the war, murmuring at taxes (tho' necessary), grumbling and dissatisfied in every county.

Now comes my hero, the first that attempted to quash the rebellious seamen, locks up the Texel for nineteen weeks, when he could no longer remain. They came out. He flies after the Dutch; completely beats them, though they resisted like brave men. I know the little etiquette of not raising gentlemen, but by degrees, a very proper distinction for those thirteen gentle lords you made last week. But what has that to do with a conqueror? What a different situation all your ministers are in at the opening of the Parliament. The nation joyful. Not a black democrate dare open his mouth. Even our cowardly allies will be ashamed to have deserted us. All success, under God, owing to my nephew. Lord St. Vincent is a brave man; he merited it; was made an earl. I leave to you the comparison. All my ancestors only rose by their brave actions, both by land and sea. Makes me think it is the only great way of rising. Am sure, were this properly represented to our good king, who esteems a brave religious man like himself, would be of my opinion. Therefore, I hope to hear soon of his being made Earl of Lundie, Viscount Texel, and Baron Duncan.

The first and last titles he owes to his ancient family, the

---

[1] Admiral Duncan was the younger son of Alexander Duncan of Lundie.

[2] Lady Mary Tufton, daughter of the seventh Earl of Thanet. She married Sir William Duncan, M.D., younger brother of Alexander Duncan of Lundie, father of Admiral Duncan.

Viscount for his successor to remember the great man, who locked up the Dutch, and bravely defeated them. Don't doubt you are proud, as I am, of being related to Admiral Duncan.—I have the honour to be, your most ob. humble servant, MARY DUNCAN.

In recognition of his great services, the Admiral was created Viscount Duncan of Camperdown, and Baron Duncan of Lundie, to which estate he had succeeded by his brother's death. He lived for nearly seven years after the victory at Camperdown; and the following letter conveying the news of his death to Mr. Dundas, who in the meantime had become Lord Chief Baron, may be inserted here:—

MR. J. ANDERSON *to* CHIEF-BARON DUNDAS.

CORNHILL, *Aug.* 4, 1804.

. . . I am very sorry for the melancholy occasion which is the immediate motive of my writing to you at present. This morning early I was awoke by an express from Lord Duncan's butler announcing the melancholy intelligence of his master having died suddenly this morning at one o'clock, in the inn at this place. I lost no time in coming here, and it will, I am sure, afford you consolation to know that he died in the most tranquil manner, and with suffering as little pain as possible. He had arrived here about six in the evening, and after eating a moderate dinner, and taking his pint of wine as usual, he went to bed about ten in good spirits, after expressing to his servant the satisfaction he felt at the prospect of dining with his family to-day. He slept for more than an hour, and then awakening with a sensation of pain in his stomach, he rang for his servant, who having given him a few drops of laudanum, left him for a little, but was soon after alarmed with another ringing of the bell. On his return he declared to his servant he was gone, and that he only regretted dying without seeing his family. The servant sent immediately an express for the surgeon at Coldstream, but before he could arrive his Lordship had expired, and both the servant and the landlady assure me that it was in the easiest manner possible. Your friend Mr. Buchan[1] of Kelloe, who is now here, has written to Lord Melville and to your brothers. An express was sent early

---

[1] George Buchan of Kelloe, in Berwickshire, married Anne, fourth daughter of the second President Dundas by his first wife, Henrietta Baillie of Lamington.

this morning to Mr. Duncan, which would probably reach him about ten, and I sincerely hope that Lady Duncan may be enabled to sustain herself with fortitude under this severe trial.

In March 1801 Mr. Pitt's Administration, which had now lasted for seventeen years, came to an end in consequence of the king's refusal to sanction a policy of Catholic Emancipation, and the Addington Ministry was formed, after a crisis during which his Majesty suffered from a return of his mental illness, and was at one time in great danger of his life. Mr. Henry Dundas, of course, retired with Mr. Pitt, but, though out of office he was still in power, and able to give a helping hand to his son-in-law the Lord Advocate. Mr. James Montgomery of Stanhope was at this time Lord Chief Baron of the Scottish Court of Exchequer; and in April Mr. Dundas writes to him:—" Retiring myself from office, it is natural for me to wish to see the near branches of my family completely settled, and the Advocate naturally forms an essential object of my consideration in that point of view. If the king had lately died, as there was too much reason for two days to expect, I should not have felt comfortable if Mr. Erskine, or any other person connected with a new Government, had been in the predicament of looking forward to be your successor. I wish now to put that point out of risk." Joined to the wish to be of service to a near relation there existed likewise a feeling of distrust of the new Ministry of a kind which it is difficult now to realise, and a dread of seeing the great offices of State placed in the hands of their adherents.[1]

Lord Chief Baron Montgomery was desirous of retiring, and (as subsequent events showed with too good reason) Lord Advocate Dundas thought his own health unequal to the work which his promotion to the Bench would have entailed upon him, and was anxious for the comparative retirement of the Court of Exchequer. Under these circumstances, arrangements for the retirement of Chief Baron Montgomery were easily brought about. He resigned, and the Lord Advocate succeeded him. Mr. James Montgomery became Solicitor-General; and, in the following July his father, the late Chief Baron, was further rewarded for his services by being created a baronet.

---

[1] See Mr. Canning's letter to the Chief Baron, *supra*, p. 264.

Some of the new Chief Baron's friends thought that he should have aimed at being Lord President, as his father and grandfather had been before him. Mr. Blair of Avonton, then Solicitor-General, wrote regretting "that you should accept a situation which will fix you for life in an office of much less importance than the one which, you know, I had allotted to you from a firm conviction that there is not a man in our profession who is, in all respects, so well qualified to exercise the duties of it." But Mr. Dundas's health had been failing for some time, and he had every reason to welcome a means of escape from the constant worry and annoyance of public life.

Having been advised on account of his health to pass the winter out of England, Chief Baron Dundas in 1804 and 1805 spent six months in cruising with the fleet at sea, and in visits to Lisbon and Madeira. In his journey from Mamhead, where he had been residing, he was accompanied by Mrs. Dundas and their niece Eliza Drummond[1] as far as Plymouth, where he embarked on board the "Illustrious," 74, Captain Sir Charles Hamilton.

On the 22d of November the "Illustrious" weighed and stood out to sea followed by the "Glory," 98, and the sloop "Rosario." Sir Charles was ordered to put his passenger on board the "Naiad," 36, cruising off Brest, which was to carry him to Madeira. In standing in towards Brest, the "Defiance," 74, Captain Durham[2] passed the "Illustrious" within hail. A heavy gale from the north-east, however, prevented the "Illustrious" joining the "Naiad" off Brest, and after battling against it for three days Sir Charles agreed at the Chief Baron's request to bear away for Ferrol, off which they arrived on the 4th of December. Admiral Cochrane's fleet was lying off Ferrol, and the Admiral agreed to send the Chief Baron to Madeira in "l'Egyptienne," Captain Fleming,[3] who was to sail next day on a cruise. On the first few days of the cruise, a variety of strange sails were sighted and chased by "l'Egyptienne," but all of them on being overhauled proved to be merchantmen under neutral flags. On

---

[1] Afterwards married to John Portal, Esq. of Laverstoke, Hants.
[2] Subsequently Admiral Sir Philip Durham.
[3] Subsequently Admiral The Hon. Charles Elphinstone Fleming.

the 13th of December, the wind being favourable for Lisbon, Captain Fleming, much to the Chief Baron's delight, agreed to run in for a few days. Their patience was, however, severely tried by the delays caused by the formalities attending the admission of the ship to pratique, by which nearly a week had to be passed at the anchorage of Paço d'Arcos, and it was not until the 22d of December that the Chief Baron and Captain Fleming landed at Lisbon.

The frigate remained at Lisbon until the 31st of December. The Chief Baron passed the time in visiting the objects of interest in the city and its neighbourhood. At daylight on New Year's Day 1805, "l'Egyptienne" weighed and dropped down the Tagus, accompanied by a fleet of merchantmen, and again put to sea. After about a week's run, the anchor was dropped, on a lovely evening, in Funchal Bay, and on the next morning, the 7th of January, the Chief Baron left the "Egyptienne" and landed at Funchal under a salute of thirteen guns. His cousin Sir James Suttie and Lady Suttie were passing the winter at Madeira, and near them a small house standing in a beautiful garden was taken for the Chief Baron. It commanded an extensive view of the town, the sea, the Desertas, and the mountains behind Funchal. The Chief Baron remained at Madeira from the 7th of January to the 12th of March 1805, and during that time suffered much from an attack of fever. He was fortunate in finding himself near his cousins the Sutties, from whom he received the kindest attention. Not having derived the expected benefit from his residence at Madeira, he became impatient to return home, and looked anxiously for Captain Fleming's return from his cruise. At last he was made happy by the arrival of Captain Fleming and his frigate on the 9th of March. Next day his journal records: "A squadron of large ships seen off the south end of the Desertas, and being suspected to be French, the Indiamen and frigates formed in line across the bay, a beautiful sight, the day being fine and calm. At noon, a breeze springing up, the distant ships approached, and by signals were ascertained to be English. At night, the Admiral's ship burned blue lights as signals to the other ships, which from our windows had a fine effect."

"*March* 11.—The bay filled with the squadron and Indiamen, a beautiful morning, and a splendid sight. The squadron consisted of the 'Northumberland,' 74, flagship of Admiral Cochrane, 'Atlas,' 74, 'St. George,' 98, 'Spartiate,' 74, 'Eagle,' 74, 'Veteran,' 64, and was bound to the West Indies in pursuit of the Rochefort squadron. There were also five Indiamen under convoy of the 'Mediator,' 44. After breakfast, Captain Fleming, Sir James Suttie, and I went on board the 'Northumberland.' The Admiral ordered the 'Egyptienne' to follow him to the Canaries, and thence to go to England. In the evening the fleet sailed for the Canaries.

"*March* 12.—Went down to the Loo to embark, but midday before we got off. Blowing hard, the 'Egyptienne' had dragged her anchors, and knocked away the bowsprit of the 'Ruckers,' Indiaman, and was in danger of drifting on the Brazen Head. She filled in time and got clear, then tacking back, took us on board, after having had a most dangerous trip of it in the boat. Made sail, and at dusk were off the south end of the Desertas.

"*March* 13.—Calm. Standing in all day towards Funchal.

"*March* 14.—Standing in towards the Cruz with a fine view of Funchal and of the island. Sent a boat on shore for Sir James, Mr. Pringle, and the servants. They dined on board, and agreed that I should go on with Captain Fleming to the Canaries, and then return; by which time he and Lady Suttie would go with us to England. Got the stock on board, and, after parting with our friends, stood out to sea.

"*March* 16.—A hurricane of wind, and a tremendous sea; it broke in at the quarter gallery window, and floated the cabin.

"*March* 17.—In the channel between the islands; all around still cloudy and stormy. About noon, the clouds clearing away a little, the top of the Peak made its appearance. It was long ere I observed it, never looking high enough in the air for this stupendous summit, which far exceeded anything my imagination had figured. It had the appearance of a snowy island up in the heavens, unconnected with either land or ocean. Stood in all day, and by evening were within six miles of the land."

After a few days at the Canaries, "l'Egyptienne" made sail for Madeira. After a week passed in Funchal Bay, on the 7th of April Sir James and Lady Suttie came on board, and after a farewell to the hospitable friends who had accompanied them on board, the frigate stood out to sea. A couple of days later the Chief Baron and the Sutties had the sight of a man-of-war cleared for action. On the 9th of April three sails were seen by the light of the moon bearing down upon them. On board the "Egyptienne" the men were at quarters, the guns loaded, and the lights uncovered, the most impressive sight, the Chief Baron remarks, he had ever witnessed. The strange sail, however, proved to be English letters of marque. After a run of about six days from Funchal, the "Egyptienne" anchored in Delgado Bay, about dusk on the 18th of April. During a two days' visit to the Azores the party landed and rode and drove over the beautiful island. The Chief Baron also consented to declare a young couple man and wife according to the law of Scotland on board the frigate. They had been betrothed four years, but had never had a chance of being married by a clergyman, and were too happy at a termination being put to the delay. The "Egyptienne" left Delgado Bay on the 21st of April, and after a passage of fourteen days, on one of which the frigate ran 251 miles in twenty-four hours, cast anchor off Weymouth.

On the 3d of May the voyage came to an end, and after bidding farewell to the officers, the Chief Baron, Sir James and Lady Suttie landed in the barge, the crew manning the yards, and giving them three cheers as they left. Next day, after a six months' absence, the Chief Baron rejoined his family at Mamhead Cottage.

Among the Arniston papers there are numerous journals and memoranda connected with the trips taken by the Chief Baron and his family. The following account of a journey from Arniston to England is from the pen of the late Mr. William Pitt Dundas :—

"Subsequent to my father's return from Madeira and taking up his residence in Scotland, the chief incidents which I remember are the almost annual journeys which he took between Arniston and some English watering-place, generally Bath. Their usual fashion was on this wise. He started in an huge yellow coach after the fashion of the day, drawn by four very good horses, with a fifth by way of outrigger, with another servant. I well remember one of these journeys in which I accompanied him, along with your father and Ann, of which one incident was that the present Gala Water Road was in process of construction, we left the carriage at Bankhouse, and walked down to inspect the works, followed by Caro the poodle and Moidy the terrier. The latter not liking the aspect of affairs, as soon as he reached the workmen, turned his face towards Arniston, and never stopped till he reached it. Sir Walter Scott's *Waverley* had just appeared, and my father was reading it. I quite recollect that he stopped, and giving a great shout, exclaimed, 'This is Walter Scott!' the passage which had so attracted him being the arrival of the Englishman at the Baron of Bradwardine's, and his surprising the maids in 'the boukit washing,' and their exclamation of 'Hech, sir.' Farther on, in the same journey, my father paid a visit at Welbeck, where, for the first time, I saw the celebrated Greendale Oak, from the acorns of which so many descendants are now flourishing in the Arniston woods. Another visit we paid, not to Lord Lyttelton, but to the grounds of Hagley, for which my father had a great admiration. Lord L. was from home, but we saw everything; and it was from a bridge in the park that he took the idea of Horace's Bridge and the Inscription. The two were not identical, but the idea was supplied at Hagley.

"About 1806-7, being at Mamhead (previous to what I have described above), I recollect a visit my father received from the Princess of Wales. The only lady that I remember accompanying her was Lady Hester Stanhope. I was five or six years old, and extremely disgusted at being brought in from my outdoor play, and dressed in my best clothes for the occasion, and I believe I behaved very ill, but the moment Lady Hester heard my name she took me on her knee, and for the visit we were great friends. She was in mourning for Mr. Pitt."

THE PRINCESS OF WALES *to* CHIEF BARON DUNDAS.

The Princess of Wales has, since she had the pleasure of seeing the Chief Baron at her house, been informed that all the worthy and true Pittites intend to have every Wednesday, in commemoration of their immortal friend, a social dinner. The Princess thinks that perhaps she might intrude upon the Chief Baron in asking him and his friends to come on that day to Blackheath; tho' the Princess is proud to name herself a Pittite and sorry for not being a Scotchwoman, *for many reasons* (which the Chief Baron may easily guess), she would never forgive herself to deprive any of these true disciples from enjoying the recollection of their departed friend. As the Princess does not dare to preside at such a meeting, she can only offer her best wishes to the whole society, and that the Pittites may reign for ever and ever, and that their toast may be drunk with success to a certain *Illustrious Personage*.

A guinea for ever.
A crown for never.

The Princess will be very happy to receive the Chief Baron and Mrs. Dundas, if she is arrived, on Sunday the 19th to dinner. She will try to summon some more of the Scotch friends of the Chief Baron to meet him on that day. The Princess flatters herself that the Chief Baron can never doubt of the high regard with which she remains for ever,   C. P.

BLACKHEATH, *April* 11, 1807.

My narrative has here anticipated two important events, the death of Mr. Pitt and the impeachment of Lord Melville. In 1802 Mr. Henry Dundas had been raised to the peerage as Viscount Melville and Baron Dunira; and, on the formation of Mr. Pitt's second Administration in 1804 he had been appointed First Lord of the Admiralty.

Lord Melville was working hard at the Admiralty when his official career was suddenly brought to a close. The Tenth Report of a Commission which had been appointed to inquire into certain frauds and abuses, which were said to exist in the management of the affairs of the Navy, was published in February 1805. It contained grave charges against Lord Melville, and afforded the Opposition an opportunity of accusing him of having been guilty of malversation in the office of Treasurer of the Navy, which he had held for some time subsequent to the year 1782. Nor were Lord Melville's opponents to be found only in the ranks of the Opposition. He had contributed materially to the downfall of the Addington Ministry; and Lord Sidmouth—by which title Mr. Addington was now known—was thirsting for revenge. Mr. Pitt stood firmly by Lord Melville. But he was unable to command a majority against Mr. Whitbread, who moved a series of resolutions in which Lord Melville was accused of a gross violation of the law and a high breach of duty. The division took place on the 8th of April, when 216 voted on each side. The speaker gave his casting vote in favour of Mr. Whitbread's motion. Lord Melville at once resigned office. His name was removed from the list of Privy Councillors. But enough had not been done to satisfy the Opposition. After several debates in Parliament, during which various modes of procedure were discussed, it was resolved that Lord Melville should be impeached, before the House of Lords, of high crimes and misdemeanours.

The trial did not take place until April 1806; and before that time Mr. Pitt was dead. His constitution, long enfeebled by gout, had given way under the enormous burden of his public responsibilities; and there can be little doubt that the mortification which he felt at the charges against Lord Melville had helped to injure him. "I have ever thought," says Lord Fitzharris, "that an aiding cause in Pitt's death, certainly one that tended to shorten his existence, was the result of the proceedings against his old friend and colleague Lord Melville." He died on the 23d of January 1806.

The trial of Lord Melville began on the 29th of April, and ended on the 12th of June, when he was acquitted on all the articles of impeachment. This is not the time to narrate, or examine in detail, the charges against Lord Melville; but the almost universal opinion of his contemporaries, even of those who bore him no goodwill, was that he was personally innocent of anything in the shape of peculation.

In the Arniston collection are a number of letters congratulating the Chief Baron upon Lord Melville's acquittal. There can be no doubt that apart from the importance of the acquittal as the defeat of a party attack upon Mr. Pitt's government, the failure of the impeachment gave general pleasure in Scotland, where Lord Melville was popular, not only on personal grounds, but from the way in which his paramount influence had been exercised on behalf of his countrymen. A political opponent, Lord Minto, has remarked there was scarcely a family in Scotland which had not been under obligations to him. "Oh, Pitt!" writes Mr. Dallas from Dawlish, "had you lived, how you would have enjoyed this triumph! But all is for the best. It can no longer be said that Pitt's influence, and the power of his Ministry, deprived public justice of its victim."

CHIEF BARON DUNDAS *to his* WIFE.

EDINBURGH, 16 *June* 1806.

MY DEAR ELIZABETH,—It would do your heart good to have witnessed what I have done yesterday and to-day, the universal joy of all persons here on your father's acquittal. I really could hardly get along the streets, being stopped by every person I met. Whether they will illuminate or not is uncertain, as the magistrates have recommended to the inhabitants not to do so, and I think, for the reason stated, most rightly. But I suspect the people will not acquiesce in the prohibition. I shall not close this till to-morrow morning. To-day I dined at home for the first time this fortnight. Yesterday I dined at Fortune's with twenty-one gentlemen, and you will see in the Edinburgh papers an advertisement for Friday night, which I believe will be more generally attended than any meeting of the kind ever was. Our varlets are at present hanging Mr. Whitbread in effigy in Mr. Blair's back court, with a half dozen companions, and a bonfire blazing, to their inexpressible delight. At the High School to-day, the play was given for the afternoon on this account, to the universal joy of the youth of the city. At Leith the seamen are employed as our boys are, with the addition, I understand, of a porter cask, in which the effigy of the porter brewer is to be consumed.

EDINBURGH, 26 *June* 1806.

An engagement having gone off by accident, I dined to-day at home with the varlets and Anne,[1] Mrs. Hamilton[2] being gone to Luffness, whence she returns to-morrow. I have therefore the evening of a day as cold as Christmas to myself, and employ it in writing to you.

I went to-day to the last meeting of the committee and stewards at Fortune's; 490 names stood then on the list, and I fear more may be expected this evening and to-morrow forenoon. By every exertion 550 can be accommodated, but it will require sitting close. I should be vexed if any dissatisfaction arose from people

---

[1] His eldest daughter, wife of Mr. John Borthwick of Crookston.
[2] His sister, wife of Colonel Hamilton of Pencaitland.

being obliged to go away for want of room. To-day has produced a great number of the most respectable gentlemen from the country, who come on purpose—Wemyss, Oswald, Stirling of Keir, Houston, etc., and numbers of the like sort. It will be a proud day for your father. Such a meeting as never on any occasion existed before, assembling on purpose to celebrate his acquittal. We are to have fireworks in the evening at half-past ten in St. Andrew Square, and I suspect that many will again illuminate. The provost has ordered all the bells to ring in the evening, bells not being within the letter of "*His Majesty's Solicitor-General for Scotland in absence of the Lord Advocate's*"[1] Proclamation. The Writers to the Signet addressed on Tuesday, after a battle, in which, after every exertion of the new Ministers, the division was 122 to 38, and, of course, all holding offices during pleasure were not present.

The Earl of Hopetoun *to* Chief Baron Dundas.

Hopetoun House, 14*th June, Saturday,* 1806.

My dear Lord,—Yesterday the Justice-Clerk showed me your very agreeable information of Wednesday, and delivered your kind message of your intention to pay us a visit here soon—which I am obliged to request your Lordship to delay till the end of your ensuing term, as next week is our sacrament week here, and the week following we have promised my brother John to go to Rankeillor. By this time I trust Lord Melville has been most fully and honourably acquitted, to the joy of his friends, which all honest men are, and to the shame and confusion of his persecutors, and that we shall again have ground of rejoicing in his perfect health and comfort restored.—My dear Lord, yours faithfully, etc., Johnstone Hopetoun.

The Comte de Vaudreuil *to* Chief Baron Dundas.

Mon cher Milord,—Je n'ai jamais douté de l'heureuse issue qu'aurait l'affaire de Lord Melville ;—la voilà terminée, avec une si grande majorité en sa faveur que le jugement peut être regardé

---

[1] "His Majesty's Solicitor-General for Scotland, in absence of the Lord Advocate." The allusion is to the spiteful conduct of Mr. John Clerk, the Solicitor-General, who took upon himself, "in the absence of the Lord Advocate" Erskine, to write to the provost and magistrates of the city, warning them of the consequences which might arise in the event of a riot on the occasion of the illumination, with which it was proposed to celebrate the acquittal. The magistrates allowed themselves to be bullied, and recommended the citizens to abstain from the illumination. Mr. Clerk's letter to the magistrates is printed at length in the *Court of Session Garland*, Edinburgh, 1871.

comme un triomphe complet. Je m'empresse de vous en faire
mon bien sincère compliment et à Madame Dundas en mon nom
et en celui de Madame Vaudreuil. J'espère, mon cher milord, que
vous êtes bien sur de tout notre intérêt pour ce qui vous touche de
près ou de loin. Les marques d'amitié que nous avons éprouvées
de votre part, et de celle de Madame Dundas, vous ont acquis à
jamais des droits à notre reconnaissance, et à notre tendre attache-
ment. Agréez que je vous en renouvelle l'hommage et celui de
la haute considération avec laquelle j'ai l'honneur d'être,—Votre
très-humble et très-obéissant serviteur,

LE C^{TE} DE VAUDREUIL.[1]

Le 14 *Juin* 1806,
No. 23 BRYANSTON STREET, LONDON.

Mr. GEORGE ABERCROMBY *to* CHIEF BARON DUNDAS.

MY DEAR LORD,—Most sincerely do I participate with you in
the joyful intelligence of Lord Melville's acquittal, an event not
only important to himself and to his friends, but to every man
who is capable of feeling for the character and reputation of his
country. The feelings of the country will not and ought not to
be suppressed on such an occasion. Our enemies have been abundantly triumphant for these fifteen months. Let them now feel
that their victory is turned into a defeat, and that it is now less a
reproach to have been convicted with Lord Melville than with
Mr. Fox.

On receiving the account last night I formed the resolution of
riding into Edinburgh this forenoon to see the fun, but on
receiving your letter, and one from Boyle, I will delay it until the
day fixed for the public fête. If you are to be at Arniston on
Sunday I will join you there.—Yours most sincerely,

GEORGE ABERCROMBY.[2]

General John Scott of Balcomie married Margaret, daughter
of the second President Dundas, by whom he had three daughters.[3]
The eldest, married to Lord Titchfield,[4] inherited General Scott's

---

[1] The Comte de Vaudreuil, along with the Duc de Grammont and others, accompanied the Bourbons into exile at the Revolution. During his residence in Scotland the Comte de Vaudreuil was much at Arniston.

[2] George Abercromby, afterwards the second Lord Abercromby, eldest son of Sir Ralph Abercromby, and Mary, daughter of John Menzies, Esq. of Fern-tower. He married the youngest daughter of Lord Melville.

[3] *Supra*, p. 188, note.

[4] Lord Titchfield, subsequently fourth Duke of Portland, born 1768, died 1854.

large fortune, the two younger sisters, Lady Moray and Mrs. Canning, receiving each £100,000 as their portion. In the case of Mr. Canning, his wife's fortune was of invaluable service in meeting the expenses of a political career. Lord Titchfield and the Chief Baron were Mrs. Canning's marriage trustees, and between the years 1801 and 1810 a variety of letters upon Mr. and Mrs. Canning's private affairs are in the collection at Arniston. At that time Mr. Canning seems to have been upon terms of intimacy with his wife's relations, which continued down to the unhappy schism of 1828.

Among the letters at Arniston is one from Mr. Canning to the Chief Baron, which, although primarily upon his private affairs, at the same time shows the feeling of insecurity prevailing, in their circle, as to the course which might be followed by the new Ministry:—

Mr. Canning to Chief Baron Dundas.

Somerset House, *Feb.* 26, 1806.

My dear Lord,—You may depend upon it that no use will be made of the powers which you have signed, but such as is strictly conformable to the purposes of the trust for which you are responsible. Very probably they may not be used at all. The alarms (which had reached us some time before it became public) of an intention on the part of the new Government[1] to appropriate a part of the Sinking Fund to the supplies of the year, induced us to wish to have it in our power to escape from the ruin which such a measure would bring upon all funded property, but that for the present at least is past by.

Many thanks, my dear Lord, for your kind expressions, which be assured I feel as I ought to do. It is indeed a comfort and consolation to me (and the only one which such a loss admits[2]) to reflect that I have at least endeavoured, on all occasions, to discharge faithfully the duty which I owed him both as a public and as a private friend. That the loss is, in both views, irreparable, no man can feel more painfully than I do. Yet even amidst my own keen regrets I cannot help turning aside now and then to compassionate what must be, under all the complicated misfortunes to which this last and heaviest has been added, the sufferings of poor Lord Melville.

---

[1] All the Talents.
[2] Mr. Canning's allusion is to the death of Mr. Pitt.

Joan (Mrs. Canning) left town last week. I quit my quarters here on Friday, and shall then go to ———[1] for a day or two, but must return again to attend the House of Commons.

Our best wishes ever attend you and yours, and I am ever, my dear Lord, most sincerely and faithfully yours,   GEO. CANNING.

In September 1809 the Portland[2] Ministry came to an end; and on the 22d of September, Mr. Canning and Lord Castlereagh, having resigned their offices a few days previously, brought their long differences to a head by fighting a duel. Lord Castlereagh believed that Mr. Canning had intrigued for his removal from the ministry on the score of incompetence. This on the part of a brother Cabinet Minister he resented as a personal insult, and accordingly sent a challenge to Mr. Canning, by whom it was accepted. They met, and at the second discharge Mr. Canning received his adversary's bullet in his left thigh, when the affair terminated.

Five days later Mrs. Canning wrote to her uncle the Chief Baron, expressing her feelings upon what had passed between her husband and Lord Castlereagh:—

MRS. CANNING to CHIEF BARON DUNDAS.

GLOUCESTER LODGE, *Wednesday, April* 27.

I am really quite concerned at not having been able to write to you sooner, as I'm sure you will be anxious to hear how Mr. C. is going on. The truth is that what with anxiety of mind, and the number of people I had to see and to write to in order to save him from fatigue as much as possible, I really had not for the first few days after my arrival here a moment to recollect myself. He is now (thank God) so well that all my anxiety as to the result is at an end, and I have assurance that in ten days more he will be well.

That such an event was as little to be expected by Mr. C. as by any one else, the statement which I inclose is sufficient proof; as likewise that he could not act otherwise than as he did. I must forbear making any comment on the conduct of his adversary, as I cannot help feeling unchristian like on the subject; but when to the inclosed statement of facts I add that Lord C. was perfectly

---

[1] Illegible.

[2] The Prime Minister, the third Duke of Portland, only survived the termination of his official career by a few days. He died on October 30, 1809. He was succeeded by his son the fourth Duke, husband of Miss Scott, and co-trustee with the Chief Baron under Mr. and Mrs. Canning's marriage settlements.

informed of all that is there mentioned, and even more, if not *before* he sent his letter, at least certainly *before* he went out to fight, and that knowing himself therefore to be so perfectly in the wrong, and knowing himself likewise to be the best shot in the country, he insisted upon *twice* aiming at the life of the person upon whom he chose to exercise his revenge—you will I think agree with me that no terms are too strong to express one's horror of such conduct. Pray give my kindest love to Mrs. D., and believe me ever most affectionately yours, J. CANNING.

Next year, 1810, the Duke of Portland again writes to the Chief Baron for his opinion respecting the investments which Mr. and Mrs. Canning were desirous of making.

DUKE OF PORTLAND *to* CHIEF BARON DUNDAS.

FULLARTON, *Aug.* 13, 1810.

. . . I understand the case to be this:—

Huskisson, ever since he has been out of office, has had a very bad opinion of the finances of the country, and has persuaded Canning (who knows nothing about the matter) that the report of the Bullion Committee would lower the funds ten per cent. At this Mr. and Mrs. Canning have taken alarm, and the more, as other events (which I believe have no connection with the subject which was before the Bullion Committee) have seemed to justify Huskisson's predictions, and they now have it in contemplation to lay out their money in land, and in the meantime they are anxious to anticipate the expected fall of the stocks.

By-the-bye, in case a purchase of land should be made, I suppose we ought to have a good professional opinion, that the money is well laid out, as, though I suppose we cannot be expected to contrive that the money should receive as good interest from landed security as from the funds, we are bound to use ordinary diligence and attention to see that it is not improvidently invested.

We shall be very happy to see you and Mrs. Dundas and the General,[1] either the end of this month or the beginning of next. I am afraid we shall not be able to lodge you as well as we could wish, but if Mrs. Dundas will put up with such accommodation as this house, which is a very bad one, will afford, we shall be very happy. I hope you will find Lord Melville looking as well as when he was here about ten days ago.—Ever, my dear Lord, yours sincerely, SCOTT PORTLAND.

---

[1] General Francis Dundas, the Chief Baron's brother.

Several other letters upon the same subject follow in the Arniston collection, but they are confined to the legal aspect of the business. In one of them Mr. Canning fully explains to the Chief Baron his wishes with regard to the trust funds. But these letters are of no general interest.

On the 21st of May 1811 the citizens of Edinburgh were startled by hearing of the sudden death of Robert Blair of Avontoun, the President of the Court of Session. The previous day, being a Monday, was a Court holiday, and the President had taken, according to his usual custom, a walk before dinner round Bruntsfield Links. On reaching his house, No. 56 George Square,[1] he complained of feeling unwell, and almost immediately expired.

Chief Baron Dundas to his Wife.

Monday Evening, 20th May 1811.

My dear Elizabeth,—Returning home a little after three I met Betsey Robertson[2] at my door, and while we were talking I saw the President coming up from his walk and go into his house. We dined *en famille* a little after four, and before I had finished my dinner, John Wauchope called me out and informed me my most excellent and honourable friend had that moment breathed his last. A cramp in the stomach, so rapid in its progress that ere medical aid could reach him, he was no more.

Accustomed as I have been to consider for a long time my own end as not far distant, the idea that he who a few minutes ago I saw in health and vigour far superior to mine, is now a breathless corpse, and thrown in a few minutes into eternity, could not but strike me with some degree I had almost said of terror. To his family and to Scotland his untimely end is an irremediable loss.

I have sent an express to Dunira, who will be there to-morrow forenoon, and I think it next to certain your father will come here, and possibly sleep here, Wednesday (May 22d) night. Of course I shall have his apartment ready. I have therefore sent the chaise, as I think you may, and I think ought, to come to town on Wednesday. The funeral in all probability will be a public one, as

---

[1] The Chief Baron's house was next door, No. 57.
[2] Daughter of Mr. David Robertson, owner of Loretto, near Musselburgh. She is said to have been a charming person, and deservedly popular in Edinburgh society.

such a man, so universally and so justly and highly respected, will not be suffered to be for ever placed in the grave without some mark of the regrets and the sorrow of his countrymen. My motions therefore for the present are uncertain. You should now I think bring Anne (her eldest daughter) with you, as it is not likely I shall accompany you back to Arniston the end of this week, or require a place in the chaise.—Affectionately yours,

R. DUNDAS.

To this letter is appended the following memorandum in Mrs. Dundas's handwriting :—

" I went to Edinburgh and found my father arrived there in great distress for his friend President Blair's death. I stayed in Edinburgh with the Chief Baron and him till Sunday (May 25th) evening, when I returned here (Arniston) with my father. He spent all Monday, 26th, with me and the children, and seemed much gratified by riding about the place all the morning, and walking with me in the evening. Next morning (Tuesday 27th) he desired Anne to give him his breakfast early, previous to his going to Edinburgh. The President's funeral was to be next day, the 28th. Contrary to my usual practice I felt an irresistible desire to be up in time to see him before his departure. I did so, and he flattered me with hopes of returning Thursday or Friday. He went to Edinburgh, dined and spent the evening with the Chief Baron, cheerful and well, went to bed, where he was found by his servant lifeless next morning, the 28th. He died almost upon the birthday of his great private and political friend Mr. Pitt."

There is also among the Arniston papers a brief note, indorsed in the Chief Baron's handwriting, as written to him by Lord Melville on the day of his death. It begins with a line from the Chief Baron :—

" MY DEAR LORD,—I have not a scrap from London, either yesterday or to-day. Do you dine at home?—Yours,

R. DUNDAS."

In reply, Lord Melville wrote at the foot of the page :—

" I have not a line from anybody; you are engaged to dinner, and I would not wish you to break your engagement, for this is a day on which I have no objection to dine alone. The circumstance which occurred in January 1806 has a strong and striking resemblance to what has recently happened.[1]—Yours, M."

---

[1] The allusion is, of course, to the death of Mr. Pitt.

1st Lord Melville

However, as Mrs. Dundas mentions in her memorandum, the Chief Baron put off his dinner engagement, and Lord Melville spent his last evening in his company. Above a quarter of a century had passed since Harry Dundas had concluded one of his confidential letters to his brother the President by requesting that it might be shown to his nephew Robert, of whose good sense and discretion he had formed a high opinion. After the father's death the correspondence was continued with the son. To this long and unbroken friendship the evening of the 27th of May formed a singularly appropriate ending. From Lord Melville's allusion to January 1806, old times were on that afternoon uppermost in his mind, and they doubtless formed the topic of conversation between him and the Chief Baron on that the last evening of his life—a peaceful sunset to so long and stormy a day.

Thus died, in the seventieth year of his age, Henry Dundas, first Viscount Melville. He had been called to the Bar of Scotland in February 1763, and no one had ever put on a wig and gown in the Parliament House with more brilliant prospects of success. His father had been Lord President; and, in 1763, his elder brother, after filling the highest positions as a law officer of the crown, had been for three years at the head of the administration of the law in Scotland. By nature Henry Dundas was endowed with qualities which fitted him, in a singular degree, for turning these advantages to the best account. Though not a profound lawyer, he was sufficiently possessed of the legal capacity necessary for the career of an advocate. Though never a polished or eloquent speaker, he had an ample command of language, great readiness, and the most complete self-confidence. He had a tall and commanding figure, and a handsome face. His manners were frank and open; and his social qualities made him a fascinating companion in private life.

Dundas seems to have come to the Bar with no other intention than to practise in Scotland, and, if he could, rise in his profession as his ancestors had done before him. But when he had been only three years at the Bar he was hurried into official life, having been appointed Solicitor-General in June 1766, at the age of twenty-four; and in 1774 he was returned to Parliament as member for Midlothian. The Arniston family had been Whigs before and since the Revolution; and it was by the Whig Ministry of Lord Grenville that he had been appointed Solicitor-General. He had, between 1766 and 1770, held office under Lord Rockingham and the Duke of Grafton. In 1770, the Duke of Grafton resigned, and Chatham, who had been the guiding spirit of his administration, attempted to form an alliance with the Bedford section of Whigs. In this he failed; and the seals were handed to Lord North, who remained in power for the next twelve years.

It was during the latter part of Lord North's tenure of office that Henry Dundas entered on that political career in which he afterwards rose so high. In 1775 he became Lord Advocate; and his politics and those of his family gradually assumed a Tory hue. But this was not in compliance with the wishes or policy of Lord North. At that time the spectacle, almost unknown at the present day, of ministers opposing each other openly on the floor of the House of Commons, was frequently seen; and Dundas never hesitated to oppose, when he thought fit, the measures of the Government. His first speech in the House had been against Lord North's motion in favour of a reconciliation with America; and after he became Lord Advocate he continued the same independent line of conduct. So strong and consistent was he in adhering to the view which he took, and in which he was undoubtedly wrong, of the policy which ought to be pursued towards the Americans, that the King was extremely annoyed. "The more I think," he says in one of his innumerable letters to Lord North, "of the conduct of the Advocate of Scotland, the more I am incensed against him. More favours have been heaped on the shoulders of that man than ever were bestowed on any Scotch lawyer; and he seems studiously to embrace every opportunity to create difficulty. But men of talents, when not accompanied with integrity, are pests instead of blessings to society; and true wisdom ought to crush them rather than nourish them." This was in 1778; but a year later, finding it was impossible to "crush" Mr. Dundas, his Majesty thought it wiser to "nourish" him, and use his talents to confront the Opposition. Let him be gained, he said, to attend the House constantly, and "brave the Parliament."

It was in January 1781 that Mr. Pitt first took his seat

in the House of Commons. The long struggle against the Americans was now drawing to a close. Three years before Mr. Pitt's great father had made his last speech, in opposing the Duke of Richmond's motion to recognise the independence of the United States, and before long his son rose to explain what he believed to have been his father's views. Dundas followed him, and was loud in his admiration of the young Whig statesman. "I find myself," he exclaimed, "impelled to rejoice in the good fortune of this country and my fellow-subjects, who are destined in some future day to derive the most important services from so happy a union of first-rate abilities, high integrity, bold and honest independency of conduct, and the most persuasive eloquence." This eulogy was well deserved; but few of those who heard it could have imagined how close an intimacy, in politics and private life, was soon to be established between Dundas and the new member of whom he spoke.

After the fall of Lord North, Dundas continued to hold office as Lord Advocate in the Rockingham Administration, in which Lord Shelburne and Mr. Fox were the Secretaries of State; and it was at this time that he first came forward as an authority on the affairs of India. He had been appointed chairman of a Secret Committee, which was to report on the causes of the war in the Carnatic, and the state of the British possessions in that part of India; and, in April 1782, he addressed the House on the momentous question of Indian policy in a speech of three hours. "It was then, perhaps," says Lord Mahon, "more than on any previous occasion that he fully showed, or saw acknowledged, the mastery of debate which he so long retained." When, in May 1782, Mr. Pitt brought forward the subject of Parliamentary Reform, he was opposed by Dundas, who declared that the constitution had for ages been pure, and that that was not a proper time to think of altering it. The motion was lost by twenty votes, although Mr. Fox had supported it; and, as Lord Macaulay says, "the reformers never again had so good a division till the year 1831." On other questions besides that of Parliamentary Reform, the members of the Government failed to agree; and, in particular, there was bad blood between Mr. Dundas and Mr. Fox. The death of Lord Rockingham brought matters

to a crisis ; and when he was succeeded as Prime Minister by
Lord Shelburne, Mr. Fox and other ministers resigned. Mr.
Pitt entered the Cabinet as Chancellor of the Exchequer ; and
Dundas retained his place as Lord Advocate. His attendance
in the House of Commons was not, however, for some time so
regular as usual ; and the character which he had now acquired
as a debater is proved by the fact that, in order to secure his
support, Lord Shelburne offered him the offices of Treasurer of
the Navy and Keeper of the Scottish Signet for life. At the
same time he continued to retain his place as Lord Advocate.
But this was not all. During the forty-four years which had
elapsed since, at the close of the last Jacobite rebellion, the
office of Secretary of State for Scotland was abolished, the
privilege of nominating the persons who were to receive
appointments in Scotland had been partly in the hands of the
Secretaries of State and partly in those of some public man
who, whether in office or out of office, was in the confidence of
ministers. A large part of the patronage of Scottish places
had, indeed, been enjoyed for many years by the members of
the Arniston family ; but this had hitherto been the case
without any formal arrangement. Now, however, Dundas
received and, of course, accepted a formal offer of the
entire patronage of all places in the public service in Scotland.
Thus it was that, in the words of Lord Cockburn, "to his nod
every man owed what he had got, and looked for what he wished."
He was King of Scotland in a far truer sense than John, Duke
of Argyll, to whom that epithet had been given at an earlier
period of the century, had ever been. Argyll had always been
opposed, and often with success. Dundas, for many years,
was seldom opposed, and almost never with success. Whether
the possession of so much power was a source of pleasure to
Dundas may well be doubted. The burden became heavier
and heavier with each succeeding year. A shade of melancholy
pervades his letters, the melancholy and dissatisfaction of a
man who is constantly brought in contact with mean and
greedy placemen, who is fast losing faith in the purity of
motive, and even the common honesty of those he has to deal
with, and who can never be sure that ulterior views do not lurk
behind the common civilities which he receives even from his
friends. His enormous correspondence, still preserved at

Arniston and Melville Castle, teems with applications, couched in every variety of expression, for the honours and offices at his disposal. Peers and peeresses, judges, officers of the army, clergymen, members of every rank and every profession, write to him; and the burden of every letter is the same—a lord-lieutenancy, a marquisate, a pension, the command of a regiment, a better living. With so many grasping hands constantly stretched up to him, it is little wonder that Henry Dundas, as years went on, grew somewhat cynical. The wonder rather is that he retained any generosity of feeling or sympathy with the wants of others. But that he did so there can be no doubt. His kindly nature seems never to have been soured, even by ingratitude, which, on more than one occasion, he certainly felt keenly. One story, in which there is a touch of romance, of the way in which he exercised his patronage, has already appeared in print. Riding one day in the Highlands he called at a friend's house, when a young lady asked leave to speak to him alone. "Mr. Dundas," she said, "I hear that you are a very great man, and, what is much better, a very good man. I will venture, therefore, to tell you *a secret*. There is a young man in this neighbourhood who has a strong attachment to me, and, to confess the truth, I have a strong regard for him." She then explained that her lover had been bred to the medical profession, and was anxious to obtain a situation in India, when he would be able to marry her. Dundas, according to the story, took her by the hand, and said, "My good girl, be assured, if opportunity offers, I shall not forget your application." Some time after he was dining with a director of the East India Company, who mentioned that there was an appointment as surgeon in the service vacant, and that it was at his disposal. "The very thing I most anxiously wished for," said Dundas, and the appointment was at once conferred on the doctor from Scotland, who married the young lady, and had a successful career in India.[1]

On the formation of the Coalition Ministry, which came into power on the resignation of Lord Shelburne in 1784, Dundas did not at once resign the office of Lord Advocate; and, indeed, he is said to have declared that "no man in Scot-

---

[1] *Correspondence of Sir John Sinclair*, vol. i. p. 144.

land will venture to take my place." But his intimacy with Mr. Pitt aroused the suspicions of Mr. Fox, who had never liked him, and who now resolved to get rid of him. "It began," Fox writes to Lord Loughborough, "to be seriously credited that it was not permitted to them[1] to remove any person (in Scotland) protected by Dundas." The Lord Advocate was, accordingly, dismissed from office, and speedily allied himself openly, and once for all, to Mr. Pitt.

In the Administration of Mr. Pitt, which was formed on the downfall of the unpopular Coalition Ministry, Mr. Dundas became Treasurer of the Navy. His appointment was severely criticised by the opposition journals.

"Mr. Henry Dundas," said the *Morning Herald* of the 1st of January, "has had the modesty to accept of the sinecure place of Treasurer of the Navy; a place which, in a debate during the last sessions of Parliament, he acknowledged to be very improper for him to accept, particularly on account of his profession as a lawyer. However, his young friend, Mr. Pitt, notwithstanding the dislike he professes to have for a coalition, has prevailed upon the late Lord Advocate of Scotland to coalesce with the Treasurer of the English Navy, and to act in future as one man. It is said, however, that the learned gentleman did not long stand out against the persuasion of his young friend, as he felt in his breast a very strong inclination to such a coalition.

"Mr. Dundas, in getting into the office of Treasurer of the Navy, has by no means obtained the ultimatum of his wishes: he has condescended to accept of £3000 a year *ad interim*, until something better can be found for him; and that something better he has already fixed his eye upon. It is a part of the new minister's plan to appoint a new secretary of state, who is to have India for his department; and if this plan should be adopted by Parliament, Mr. Dundas is certainly to be placed in that department, for which his attendance as chairman of the Committee of Secresy has particularly well fitted him."

But Dundas was well entitled to a high place in the Government; for during the next three months, when Mr. Pitt and his colleagues had to contend night after night against a hostile majority on the opposition benches, Dundas did yeoman service. The majorities against Government gradually dimin-

---

[1] The Administration.

ished, until at length the crisis was reached on the 8th of March, when Mr. Fox's motion to address the King for the removal of the Ministers was carried by only one vote. "Seldom," says Wraxall, "have I heard Dundas, during the course of his long and brilliant career, display more ability or eloquence than on that evening, which may, in fact, be regarded as having terminated the contest between Pitt and Fox, between the Crown and a majority in the House of Commons." Soon after this Parliament was dissolved; and the result of the general election was the complete triumph of Mr. Pitt.

Such were the leading facts in the life of Henry Dundas prior to the commencement of Mr. Pitt's long term of office. Beyond this, even a meagre outline of his life could not be given without entering upon a multiplicity of topics which would be out of place in a volume of family history; for the career of Henry Dundas henceforth was that of a British Minister. He managed the affairs of India for a number of years. He was at the Home office during the troublous times which followed the outbreak of the French Revolution. At another time he was charged with the conduct of the war. He was afterwards First Lord of the Admiralty. He was responsible for the transactions which culminated in the abolition of the Irish Parliament and the passing of the Act of Union. He was deeply engaged in the events which led to the resignation of Mr. Pitt in 1801, and still more deeply engaged in those which led to Mr. Pitt's return to power in 1804. The charges brought against him by the opposition in the following year, and his impeachment during the Ministry of All the Talents, have already been alluded to. Of the charges then brought against him he was acquitted; but his official life was at an end. Nevertheless his correspondence proves that within a year after the termination of his trial, he was once more virtually the Minister for Scotland. Judging by the letters which were addressed to him by members of the Duke of Portland's Ministry and by the public in Scotland, he had almost as much power, from the year 1807 until his sudden death in 1811, as he had enjoyed during the old days when he and Mr. Pitt sat side by side on the front bench of the House of Commons.

The character of Lord Melville was, during his lifetime, the subject of severe criticism by one party in the State, while by

another party it was the subject of fulsome eulogy. By one
party he was represented as an unscrupulous adventurer who
cared for nothing but his own advancement, who was ready to
adopt any policy which promised success, and who had achieved
his high position by an utter want of principle. By another
party he was, in Scotland at all events, regarded as a great and
powerful Minister, whose chief claim to distinction was his lofty
independence of character, and whose success in life was solely
the result of merit. The truth probably was that he entered
public life with rare advantages, and did himself full justice.
His age and experience made him an invaluable ally to Mr.
Pitt. His business habits and readiness in debate were sufficient
to have secured him offices of Cabinet rank, even had they not
been combined with an extraordinary political foresight, amount-
ing to a special talent, by which he was able to perceive, almost
by intuition, what were the exact chances of party warfare.

This combination of qualities enabled Henry Dundas, the
younger son of a house which had already for a long time
enjoyed great political influence, to rise higher in the service of
the State than any of his family had done before him. His
death made a great blank, not only on account of the experience and knowledge of affairs which passed away, when he was
laid in the grave; but because, whatever his faults may have
been, he had always proved himself a staunch friend and a
reliable kinsman. In his own home at Melville, or riding about
the woods at Arniston, he was simple-hearted and kindly,
taking an interest in country pursuits, fond of meeting old
friends and neighbours, and displaying none of that arrogance
which was sometimes, perhaps not unnaturally, attributed to a
man of whom it has been said that there was a time " when the
streets of Edinburgh were thought by the inhabitants almost
too vulgar for Lord Melville to walk upon."

Immediately after the Arniston family had lost their most
distinguished member, a question arose in deciding which his
advice would have been invaluable; for on the death of
President Blair,[1] the Prince Regent and the Ministry were
most desirous that the Chief Baron should accept the President's chair. He had lately been suffering from ill health,

---

[1] *Supra*, p. 267.

and was averse to the proposal, but it was repeatedly pressed upon him. The correspondence upon the subject is lengthy, but enough of it is here given to explain the bearings of the case.

(SECOND) VISCOUNT MELVILLE [1] *to the* CHIEF BARON.

WIMBLEDON, *1st July* 1811.

DEAR CHIEF BARON,—You will be surprised at receiving from me, so soon after your peremptory refusal of the President's Chair, a repetition of that suggestion under circumstances which perhaps may incline you to depart from your resolution. I will state to you as concisely as possible, but without reserve, what has occurred, and the present situation of affairs with regard to that question. It is for your own private information, unless you choose to show it to the Justice-Clerk,[2] but I shall communicate to Mr. Perceval your reply to this letter, unless it goes into other matters separate from your own concern in the business.

In the course of last week the Prince Regent saw the Lord Chancellor and stated to him his own anxious wish that you should go to the President's chair, unless you preferred the Justiciary, and that Mr. Adam[3] should succeed you as Chief Baron. Next day Mr. Adam came to me and stated that the Prince Regent had made a similar communication to him, and had desired him to wait upon me, and to intimate the desire of his Royal Highness that I should see him on the subject next day. I mentioned immediately to Mr. Adam that independently of any other consideration in this matter, it happened that the proposal of your going to the President's chair had very recently been under your consideration, and that for the reasons which I stated to him (as I had also previously explained to Mr. Perceval) you had positively refused.

When I waited upon the Prince Regent next day, he began

---

[1] Robert Dundas, second Viscount Melville, son of Henry, first Viscount, and Elizabeth Rannie. Born 1771; President of the Board of Control, 1807, with a seat in the Cabinet; Secretary of State for Ireland, 1809; Privy Seal for Scotland, 1811. He subsequently held various offices, including that of First Lord of the Admiralty, until 1830, when he retired into private life. Died 1851.

[2] The Right Hon. Charles Hope, afterwards Lord President.

[3] The Right Hon. William Adam of Blairadam. Born 1751. He became a member of the House of Commons in 1774, and held office under Lord North, in defence of whose policy he fought a duel with Mr. Fox in 1780. He was afterwards Attorney-General to the Prince of Wales. In 1816 he was appointed Chief Commissioner of the Jury Court in Scotland, and, having prospered under every ministry during fifty years, died in 1819. His wife was the Hon. Eleanor, daughter of the tenth Lord Elphinstone.

by adverting to all that had occurred for some years in regard to my father. He also reminded me of what had passed between us on a former day on the subject of the Privy Seal, and of Lady Melville,[1] on which latter point he certainly had gone much beyond anything I had in contemplation, especially in the mode of doing it, which I could not conscientiously, as one of his servants, approve, viz., a message from himself to the two Houses of Parliament. He also adverted to my father's intimacy with the late President Blair and their mutual friendship, and his own earnest desire to confer an adequate mark of his own and of public esteem for Mr. Blair's character by providing adequately for his family. He then mentioned my father's and my intimacy with Adam, and the zealous and able professional assistance which the latter had afforded on the impeachment, and how gratifying on that point of view any mark of favour conferred upon Adam would probably be at the present moment.

His Royal Highness next explained the nature of his own connection with Adam, and the obligations he felt himself under to him, both on his own and the Duke of York's account, and the unjust obloquy to which Adam had been exposed in the clamour against the Duke (of York), and he expressed his strong and anxious wish that Adam should be appointed to the Chief Baron's chair in Scotland, by your accepting the other situation. He concluded by stating his belief that if the arrangement took place it would enable Adam, from his good sense and principles, to put down or at least keep in order a parcel of shallow-pated reviewing Reformers at Edinburgh, who were meddling in matters which they did not understand, but who were doing much mischief.

I stated to his Royal Highness what had passed lately with you on the subject of your removal to the Court of Session, and my apprehension that the same reasons would still operate to prevent your agreeing to it now. But he desired positively that it should be again put to you, and that his strong and anxious wish should be conveyed to you; a duty which I have accordingly discharged by repeating to you, in farther proof of his earnestness on the subject, the grounds on which he placed it. I need scarcely add that the whole was conveyed in the most gracious manner to myself, and with every expression that could be gratifying, and I will only mention farther that the Chancellor gave the same report of the Prince's earnestness and anxiety on the subject.

---

[1] Lady Jane Hope, widow of the first Lord Melville, subsequently married to Mr. T. Wallace, created Baron Wallace.

I need scarcely add, that we (the Ministry) are strongly impressed with the conviction that the most beneficial as well as satisfactory appointment to the President's chair will be by your acceptance of it.—Yours sincerely, MELVILLE.

The above letter was followed on the 13th of July by a formal offer of the President's chair, through Mr. Ryder, Home Secretary, by command of the Prince Regent, which was declined, on the score of ill health. But as an immediate decision was not pressed for, the matter was allowed to stand over for maturer consideration. Besides the grounds of advantage to the public from the President's chair being filled by a man of the Chief Baron's long experience and knowledge of public business, Lord Melville urged upon him the advantages arising from the appointment both to his party and political adherents in Scotland, and to his own family.

On the 1st of August he wrote:—

"I have nothing more to say on the subject of your removal to the Court of Session, except that independently of any private or personal considerations, I am much mistaken if you are not throwing away a *public* card in Scotland which will not be recovered during your life or mine."

Again he wrote:—

WIMBLEDON, *Aug.* 11, 1811.

You are very much mistaken if you suppose that I have had in contemplation only the *public* reasons to which I formerly alluded, and I rather think that I adverted expressly and distinctly also to considerations of a private or personal nature. *Your own eldest son will be the greatest sufferer by your refusal,* and to an extent which you will never be able to replace to him, and I promise you that even *you* will admit that proposition before you quit Boroughbridge (where Lord Melville and the Chief Baron were to meet). It is quite reasonable that under any circumstances neither you nor your family should be the sufferers, and nobody ever dreamt of such a proposition, but directly the reverse. But, however, *quem Deus vult perdere,* etc. etc. I shall at least have done my duty both to the public and to yourself, and shall not be responsible for the consequences.

On the 14th of August the Prince Regent wrote to Lord Melville again, expressing his "most anxious wishes for the accomplishment of the arrangement which has been proposed to the Lord Chief Baron of Scotland; an arrangement so important to the judicature of Scotland, about which my anxiety is such that I have thought it right to write you with my own hand."

If the matter had been left in Lord Melville's calm and judicious hands, the Chief Baron would apparently have consented "to obey the commands and gratify the wish of his Prince." But unfortunately his brother William[1] seems to have taken it in hand, and not satisfied with the intimation of the intentions of ministers, as expressed in Lord Melville's letter of the 11th of August, wrote to Mr. Perceval to know "if he had any objection to the proposition being submitted for the consideration of H.R.H. to give the Chief Baron a seat in the House of Lords," an injudicious step which produced a lengthy refusal from Mr. Perceval.

There is no doubt that as Lord Melville was a Cabinet Minister, and in direct communication with the Prince Regent himself, his letter of the 11th of August should have been considered a sufficient intimation of what Ministers intended to do, in the event of the Chief Baron's meeting the wishes of the Prince Regent. But William Dundas's letter, by seeking to tie them down by an express stipulation, was in reality placing the Prime Minister in a position in which no one holding the post could submit to be placed. It is curious how an able man like William Dundas, after a long parliamentary and official life, could have been guilty of so great an indiscretion. However, his letter and Mr. Perceval's reply drew forth a peremptory refusal from the Chief Baron to listen to anything farther, and the negotiations for meeting the Prince Regent's wishes came to an end.

One of the arguments which Lord Melville used, when trying to induce the Chief Baron to become Lord President, was that the family influence would be rendered more complete if he put himself at the head of the administration of the law in

---

[1] Right Hon. William Dundas, third son of the second President Dundas, by his second wife, Miss Jean Grant. Born 1762. A Commissioner of the Board of Control, 1797; Secretary at War, from 1804 to 1806; a Lord of the Admiralty 1812 to 1814; appointed Lord Clerk Register of Scotland in 1821. Died 1845. His wife was Mary, daughter of the Hon. James Stuart Wortley Mackenzie (second son of John, third Earl of Bute), and sister of James, first Lord Wharncliffe.

Rt. Honble. W. Dundas. M.P.
Ld. Clerk Register.

Scotland. Although Midlothian was no longer represented by a member of the Arniston family, there was still a Tory majority. Sir George Clerk of Penicuik, who had succeeded Robert Dundas of Melville, when the latter became a peer on the death of his father, gives the following estimate of the political state of the county, in a letter to the Chief Baron, dated the 26th of March 1812:—

For Sir George Clerk (*Tory*),	51
For Sir John Dalrymple (*Whig*),	38
Absentees,	20
Doubtful,	17
	126

Lord Melville held the office of President of the Board of Control in Mr. Perceval's Government, and was the confidential adviser of Ministers in regard to the affairs of Scotland, as his father had been before him. The assassination of Mr. Perceval, in May 1812, led to a ministerial crisis, after which Lord Liverpool became Prime Minister; and in the new administration Lord Melville was appointed First Lord of the Admiralty, the centre of Scottish patronage being at once transferred from the Board of Control to the Admiralty.

In writing to her son Henry,[1] Mrs. Dundas thus alludes to Mr. Perceval's death:—" Your father and I have been thrown into the greatest affliction by this unexampled and atrocious murder of Mr. Perceval. It is dreadful for the poor man's family, and dreadful for the country, and they will find it a most difficult, if not an impossible task to fill his situation with as able, and above all, with as good a man. It certainly seems as a punishment for our sins that it pleases heaven to deprive us at such a moment of his services. Next to his own immediate family, I know none more to be pitied for his loss than Lord Melville, as he had always the greatest regard for him. Your father is dreadfully shocked by Mr. Perceval's death."

The following letter from the Duc de Gramont to Mrs. Dundas was written at the close of November 1813, a few weeks after the decisive battle of Leipzig and the surrender of Dresden with its garrison of 40,000 French troops. The power

---

[1] A boy at the Naval College, Portsmouth.

of Buonaparte seemed to be crumbling to pieces, and the dawn of happier times to be rising upon the long oppressed French royalists:—

THE DUC DE GRAMONT *to* MRS. DUNDAS.

HARTWELL HOUSE, *à* 29 *Novembre* 1813.

Le Duc de Gramont a l'honneur de présenter ses respects à Madame Dundas et les remerciements du roi pour la boite de grouses qu'elle lui a envoiée ; elle a été reçue hier ; on en a servi deux sur la table du roi qui les a trouvé excellentes, et meilleures qu'il n'en avait encore mangées. Le roi désire que Madame Dundas fasse parvenir au Lord Chief Baron ses remerciements de son aimable attention.

Le Duc de Gramont remercie Madame Dundas de la part qu'elle veut bien prendre aux espérances que cette continuité de bonnes nouvelles peut nous permettre ; nous n'avons cependant nous y trop livrer. Il faut cependant espérer que le ciel cessera de nous persécuter, et que la bonne cause finira par triompher.

Le Duc de Gramont a l'honneur de renouveler à Madame Dundas l'assurance de ses sentiments respectueux.

DUC DE HARCOURT *to* CHIEF BARON DUNDAS.

Duc de Harcourt presents his respects to the Lord Chief Baron, and returns his most sincere acknowledgments for the polite note he has been favoured with. Nothing can be of a more favourable omen for the cause of the Bourbons than to see it supported and hailed by the first magistrate of a country, to which the French princes are so much indebted for its noble and kind hospitality.

Wednesday Evening, 6 *April* 1814.

Duc de Harcourt begs to be respectfully remembered to Mrs. Dundas.

The correspondence closes with a few lines from the Chief Baron, dated Bath, April 11th, to the Duc de Gramont for transmission to the King of France, hoping that his Majesty may long continue to reign over a brave and loyal people, and that the prosperity of his Majesty's future life may in some degree compensate for the unmerited and severe calamities sustained, through so many years of adversity, with a magnanimity worthy of his illustrious name.

On leaving Scotland the Comte d'Artois sent to the Chief Baron his portrait, to be added to the pictures at Arniston, in recollection of the attentions he had received while living at Holyrood, and also a backgammon box, probably as a souvenir of various games with the Chief Baron.

The termination of the war against France, in 1815, once more opened up the continent of Europe to travellers; and it was with feelings of curiosity and pride that Englishmen and Scotsmen visited the scenes of the memorable struggle against Napoleon.

MR. ROBERT HALDANE [1] *to the* CHIEF BARON.

DUNKELD, 14*th Sept.* 1816.

MY LORD,—I lately went to visit the field of Waterloo, and in the true spirit of a pilgrim, wished to carry away with me some relics from that interesting spot. The things which are sold by the inhabitants as memorials of the battle cannot be depended upon as genuine. I therefore resolved to purchase nothing which might have been fabricated for the purpose of imposing upon credulous travellers, but cut for myself staves from the garden of Hugomont, and from the edge of the wood of Bossy, at Quatre Bras, where so many of our gallant countrymen fell. I was loath to lay profane hands upon so interesting and venerable an object as Lord Wellington's tree, which had been splintered by shot on the day of action, and *since* sadly mutilated by the knives of merciless travellers. But, observing some scraggy branches near the top almost broken off, I made Lacorte's son climb up and bring them to me. I wrapped up all the sticks, sewed carefully in a cloth, and they formed a parcel so singular in appearance, as to excite much astonishment wherever I went, particularly amongst the custom-house officers, who do not know what to make of them. Little as this package was thought of by others, I put much more value upon it than all my luggage besides, and was always much more afraid of losing it than my portmanteau. I left the staves in Edin[r] to get them dressed and made straight, and gave the charge of them to Dr. Grant, with proper injunctions to secure their identity. He writes me that they are now ready, and I have requested him to carry the handsomest-looking one to your Lordship's house in George Square, and you will gratify me highly by

---

[1] Professor of Mathematics in the University of St. Andrews, and subsequently Principal of St. Mary's College there. Moderator of the General Assembly in 1827.

accepting of it. Had I not been under the necessity of coming directly north to look after some little affairs here, it was my intention to have done myself the honour of waiting upon your Lordship at Arniston, to have given you some account of my excursion, and to have delivered this Waterloo trophy into your own hands. I am not sure that I have fixed upon that sort of present which your Lordship may value most highly, or deem the most appropriate that could have been thought of. But of this I am certain, that I could not offer any memorial of the battle of Waterloo to one in the kingdom who felt more unmingled joy than you did at the glorious issue of that tremendous conflict, or who was more truly proud of the matchless feats which our heroes, and especially our *Scottish heroes*, there achieved.

From the numerous and accurate descriptions which have been published, every person may form a very good idea of the ground on which the battle was fought, but it is impossible to describe the feelings which a person experiences when for the first time (having advanced a little way in front of the farm of Mont St. Jean, to the edge of the ridge), the whole field of battle bursts upon his view, and he feels himself standing on the ground where lately the fate of the world was decided. . . . Yours truly,

Rob. Haldane.

In the summer of 1817 the ill health of the Chief Baron was a cause of grave anxiety to his family. And with the hope of regaining some measure of strength, he was induced to make a tour upon the Continent, and try the effects of a better climate than that of home. He was accompanied by two intimate friends, Sir William Rae[1] and Dr. Haldane of St. Andrews, by his brother General Francis Dundas, and by his eldest son Robert, then a youth of twenty years of age.

The lighthouse yacht was placed at his disposal to take him across to Holland, and on Friday, the 25th of July, the party embarked on board the cutter in Leith Roads, where she lay in readiness to receive them. Sail was at once made, and the vessel ran down the Firth before a fair wind, and soon got out to sea. During the voyage, when adverse winds prevailed, against which little progress could be made, their presence was taken advantage of for visiting places of interest along the coast; instead of beating all day against a head wind. In that

---

[1] Appointed Lord Advocate in 1819.

way Holy Island, Bamborough, Scarborough, and other places were visited, and it was not until Thursday the 31st, that the cutter came to anchor off the harbour of Helvoetsluys.

After a night's rest, the party started next day in two coaches for the Brille, where for the first time they saw a Dutch town in perfection, with canals, streets, and trees interspersed. The same afternoon they embarked on board a *schuyt* for Rotterdam, and wind and tide being with them, had a pleasant run of three hours up the noble river to Rotterdam.

From Rotterdam the tour of the chief Dutch towns was made, always travelling, and with much pleasure, by canal.

Why Holland had been selected for the Chief Baron's first tour abroad, the journal does not say. Probably the old educational connection between Scotland and the Dutch universities had to do with it.[1] His father and his grandfather had been educated in Holland, and he had been brought up in a house where the library shelves were stored with Dutch editions of the classics which they had collected; and apart from the other sights of Holland which would strike any stranger, he regarded the University towns with peculiar interest. For instance, on arriving at Leyden, he goes straight to the chief bookseller's shop, where he sees many editions of the classics for sale, and on his walk through the town, student life appears through the notice in Latin on the walls of the houses, *Cubicula locanda*. It was vacation-time at the University, but Dr. Haldane purchased a copy of the Prospectus of Lectures about to be delivered, with the days and hours, all in Latin. They visited the Museum, College Hall, and Library, where the librarian wondered at the Chief Baron's repeating part of the Proemium of Justinian's Institutes, and said he must be an adept in civil law.

At Haarlem, besides the great organ, the Chief Baron's affections were divided between the copy of Coster's *Speculum Christianæ Salvationis*, printed in 1440, and a collection of tulip and Hyacinth roots, "all very high priced," which he bought for the garden at Arniston.

In Amsterdam, the hotels in 1817 bore the same character for high charges they still maintain, the bill at the Doelen

---

[1] On this subject, see *Dr. Carlyle's Autobiography*, Chapter IV.

being pronounced "enormous and extravagant." Besides the ordinary sights of the town, the Chief Baron's country gentleman's instinct led him to visit the prison, a thing which few travellers at that day would have done; and he seems to have been much struck with its bad management.

The party left Amsterdam by canal as usual, the boat coming under the windows of the hotel to take them and their luggage on board. "We dined," says the journal, "at Slostendam, a nice country inn on the side of the canal, and thence passed through a succession of gardens, villas, and trees; most enchanting; the families were all in their summer pavilions on the bank of the canal, drinking their coffee, and we bowed to each other as we passed. Let not the Dutch taste be ignorantly vilified and despised, as it is by fools among us at home. In such a country it is undoubtedly not only the best, but the only possible style of ornamental gardening. Also let no one think of travelling in Holland in summer or in fine weather in any other way than by water, the beauties of the country can be seen in no other way." After sailing or tracking through shrubberies and pleasure grounds, on a beautiful evening the party reached Utrecht after dusk. The gates were shut, but a trifle opened them, and they tracked along the canal to the landing-place, close to the hotel where beds had been secured for them.

At Utrecht, the pleasant tracking along canals, through shrubberies and pleasure grounds, came to an end, and the journey to Rotterdam, through Gouda, was performed by road.

At Rotterdam, General Dundas and Sir William Rae quitted the party, and embarked at the Brille on their return to Scotland, while the others, in a barouche with three horses, started with the intention of making their way to Berlin. But at Gorcum the Chief Baron became so unwell that the journey to Berlin had to be given up.

The party, now reduced to the Chief Baron, his son, and Dr. Haldane, travelled leisurely, halting at Antwerp, Ghent, and other places of interest, and arriving at Brussels at the end of August.

They found Brussels so full of strangers, that they had some difficulty in finding apartments—crowds of English, and visitors from all parts of Europe. On the morning after his arrival, the Chief Baron notes that he met Cambaceres, Sieyes, and David walking together, the first being the most abominable-looking ruffian he had ever set eyes on.

After a short halt at Brussels, the party went on to Waterloo, to which a long visit was paid. At this distance of time a flying visit on a fine summer day is usually all that is devoted by the traveller to his excursion to Waterloo. But a visit to the field, coming so soon after the great battle itself, by people who were deeply sensible of the relief the overthrow of Buonaparte had given to their country, and who felt the blessing of the cessation of the struggle for existence in which it had been so long engaged, together with sorrow for the death of friends, yet fresh, made a visit to the field of Waterloo a subject of the deepest interest.

It will not be surprising, therefore, that the Chief Baron spent the afternoon of the day of his arrival at Waterloo, the whole of the next day, and half of the following day, in tracing the course of the struggle, upon the ground, and that the record of the impressions made upon him occupies a large space in his journal.

The two nights of their stay near the battle-field were spent at the little inn, the Roi d'Espagne, at Gemappes, whose landlord was a farmer, and the inn the farm-house and offices. At the time of the battle the Roi d'Espagne underwent rapid changes of occupants. On the 16th of June the Duke of Wellington slept in it, on the 17th, Jerome Buonaparte, and on the 18th, at ten at night, arrived the veteran Blucher, and took up his quarters in it. He supped and then smoked his pipe until two in the morning, when he went to bed. He rose late, not until after ten next morning, and immediately marched with the Prussian army.

After the visit to Waterloo the travellers continued their journey to Spa, which, like Brussels, was full of English visitors, all enjoying the opening up of the Continent, from which war had so long excluded them.

After a fortnight at Spa spent among the many friends he met there, the Chief Baron, his son, and Dr. Haldane, travelled on to Frankfort, and thence to Mayence, descending the Rhine in a boat, a voyage to which a word or two may be given.

The Journal says:—

"*Mayence, Sept.* 28.—Hired a boat with two boatmen to carry us down the Rhine to Cologne for five louis-d'or.

"*Sept.* 29.—Weather fine. Sailed in our canoe from below the bridge, and had a delightful day gliding down the stream of this noble river. Below Bingen we passed one of the falls of the Rhine; the current is strong and rapid, and from the rocky bottom of its bed causes a strong and tumultuous stream like a mill-race. We passed this, and several smaller falls lower down with great rapidity, but no danger, our boatmen always keeping near the shore, and out of the surge of the river. We landed at Caub, thirty miles from Mayence, six hours sail, and slept there. Several Rhine vessels going upstream passed us to-day; one towed by thirteen horses arrived this evening and moored under our windows.

"*Sept.* 30.—Cold wind and heavy rain which lasted all the way to Coblentz. Below St. Goar we passed through a strong fall of water, eddy and whirlpool, dangerous to boats such as we were in, if not well managed. It seemed to me to resemble the fall of the Thames at London Bridge near low water.[1]

"*Coblentz, Oct.* 1.—Rain falling so heavily that it was eleven o'clock before we could embark, when it cleared a little, and we proceeded on our voyage. At Andernach there was a toll of one franc to pay. The toll-keeper's office was shut, and he was gone to his dinner. We went to his house a few doors off with the franc, but he refused to take it, and kept us waiting until he opened his office two hours later. The rain continued to fall, but that did not prevent our enjoying the scenery from Andernach down to Lintz, where we landed for the night. The host of the inn, a German, had been seized during the war by the French as a conscript, and sent to serve in their army in Spain. At the peace he was discharged, and had returned to his native village. He and his wife were civil people, but the fare at their house was bad; a piece of stinking chevreuil, a starved chicken, and two snipe, formed our dinner, but the bread was excellent, and the red Aar wine good of its kind.

"*October* 2*d.*—Left Lintz in the canoe this morning. The wind was strong from the north, and dead against us; we

---

[1] The bed of the Rhine has been greatly improved since 1817, by the removal of the dangerous rocks which caused the falls. Of course the reference is to Old London Bridge.

suffered much from cold. Landed at Cologne after a six hours' sail, where our coachman had arrived on the preceding evening, and had secured rooms for us at the Cour Impériale."

On his way from Cologne to Calais the Chief Baron halted a few days at Valenciennes, round which the British army of occupation was quartered, and had the good fortune to come in for a grand review of the troops. He says:—

"*Oct.* 15.—Set out at nine for the review. About eleven reached Douchy, where we saw the army drawn up on the height between that village and Bouchain. At half-past eleven the Duke appeared on the field, and after he had ridden up and down the line, the manœuvres began. We drove to the knoll above Douchy, from which we had, on a fine day, a full view of the most impressive sight I have ever witnessed. About thirty thousand men were on the field, all in the highest order, and mostly the troops which had fought at Waterloo; the sight was one which it is impossible either to describe or to forget.

"The Duchess of Richmond presented me to the Duchess of Wellington, and I had an invitation from the Duke to dine with him that day at Cambray, which, from the lateness of the hour at which I returned to Valenciennes, it was out of my power to accept."

From Valenciennes the party made their way to Calais, where Dr. Haldane quitted them to return to Scotland.

The Chief Baron had obtained leave of absence to winter in Italy, and it had been arranged that Mrs. Dundas and his two daughters should meet him at Calais on the way there. He had written her full directions about what was wanted for the journey, some of which sound amusing now.

She is told to bring as little baggage as possible with her. If she can do without the Imperial, or half of it, they would be enabled in the South to keep the carriage open, which would be a great pleasure to them all. Clothing of all kinds, except linen, was to be bought abroad as needed. She was told to bring two or three large tea-cups with her, for in Italy "they have no cups larger than a thimble; the case of knives and forks is also most requisite."

Armed with these instructions, Mrs. Dundas and her

daughters made their way to Dover, embarked in the packet on one day at noon, and after knocking about all night off Calais, got into the harbour on the following morning. She had brought with her the family coach, a ponderous vehicle; in addition to which a calèche was bought at Calais, and with these conveyances the family began the journey to Rome.

The journey from Calais to Paris occupied four days, on the last of which, from Breteuil to Paris, they were in the carriage from half-past seven in the morning to seven at night, with only a few minutes' halt at a cook's shop at Lesarches, where for five francs they had as much as they could eat.

After a week spent in Paris, in sight-seeing, theatre-going, and visiting friends, the journey was recommenced on the 31st of October, when, owing to a breakdown of the calèche, Essonne was the limit of the first day's journey. Turin was reached on the 14th of November, a fortnight's journey from Paris, devoid of incident beyond the squabbles with postilions and the differences with postmasters as to numbers of horses to be taken, matters of course in pre-railway days. Up the steep road over the Mont Cenis, the modern road in some places being only in course of formation, the family coach was dragged by a team of eight horses, a novel sight to travellers whose longest journeys had been from Scotland to Devonshire.

Southwards from Turin, the route followed was by Bologna and the shores of the Adriatic to Loretto, encountering the furious blasts of wind and rain frequently met with towards the close of autumn in Italy. Swollen by the rain the torrents which had to be forded were coming down like broad and impetuous rivers. Two visits were paid to the Santa Casa at Loretto, lately robbed by the French of its ancient treasures, even down to the candlesticks required for the church service.

From Loretto the journey was continued to Tolentino and across the Apennines to Rome; and at the mountain inns they met with very indifferent accommodation. "On one evening," the Journal narrates, "we reached Valcimara, a most miserable place, but where we had to halt for the night. We got some weak soup and hard mutton for dinner—the wine was execrable, and they had no spirits of any sort, no milk, nor sugar, only some indifferent coffee. There was no firewood beyond roots of vines, and some sticks plucked from a dead fence near the inn door. The filth of the house was extreme, no glass in the window, and this on a cold frosty night, with the mountains facing us covered with snow, and in my room neither fire nor fireplace. We retired to the abominable beds longing for next day."

At that late time of year, the last days of November, the higher parts of the road were covered with ice and beaten snow, slippery and glassy, and very unpleasant for travelling upon. The plain at the summit of the mountains was deep in snow, in some parts so deep that the postilions had to leave the road and drive over the open ground; in others nearly as high as the windows of the carriage. But at last the mountain was crossed, and in three days more the party reached Rome, the time occupied on the journey from Paris to Rome, short halts included, having been a few days over a month.

Naples was intended to be the halting-place for the first half of the winter, so after a week's rest in Rome, the party were again upon the road. They slept at Terracina, where were also their friends Colonel Herries and Captain Gordon. The two latter, instead of sleeping at Terracina, set off about seven in the evening to travel all night to Naples. Soon after leaving Terracina, and half way between two picquet guards posted only half a mile apart, Herries and Gordon were attacked by five robbers, who fired at the carriage, and dangerously wounded the postilion, stripping the gentlemen of their money and watches.

Next morning the Chief Baron and his family left Terracina, and on coming up to the place where Colonel Herries had been robbed, found the wounded postilion still there. A little later a soldier brought a letter from the Colonel mentioning the affair, and saying he had got on to Fondi. On arriving there, the Chief Baron found him, and supplied him with money for continuing his journey.

And here the extracts from the Journal may cease. They have been made with the object of showing how a Scottish family made its way across the Continent seventy years ago.

But the object of the journey, the restoration of the Chief Baron's health, was unsuccessful. He spent the winter at Naples and Rome, returning homewards in the following summer through Switzerland, a suffering invalid.

Early in the summer of 1819, and not long before his death, the Chief Baron resigned his office. Lord Sidmouth, who was then Home Secretary, in acknowledging the resignation, expressed his regret that the state of Mr. Dundas's health obliged him to deprive the public of his services.

After this he grew rapidly worse, until, on the 17th of June 1819, he died quietly at Arniston.

Besides his eldest son, Robert, who succeeded him in the family estate, he had four children—Anne, married to Mr. John Borthwick of Crookston; Henry, Vice-Admiral in the Navy; William Pitt, Deputy Clerk Register of Scotland; and Joanna, wife of Mr. George Dempster of Skibo.

The personal appearance of Chief Baron Dundas has been already described.[1] His portrait, painted by Raeburn in 1795, bears out the description. His statue, from the chisel of Chantrey, stands in the north-east corner of the Parliament House, almost under the shadow of that of his famous uncle Henry. But in the statue there is an expression of pain, or, at all events, of weariness, which his features did not wear during the active period of his life. "If Chantrey ever saw him," says Lord Cockburn, "it must have been when he was dying, a state which lasted some years."

But about Chantrey's having seen Chief Baron Dundas, there is no doubt, for he visited him at Arniston, though, as Lord Cockburn correctly states, it was when he was in failing health.

Throughout his life, apart from politics and from official duty, the main subject of interest which engrossed the mind of Chief Baron Dundas was the improvement of the family estate and the adornment of its pleasure grounds. He farmed largely himself, and, independently of the home farm, frequently had other farms on hand which he improved and remodelled before letting them to tenants. Nor were his efforts for the improvement of agriculture confined to what was doing on his own estate. As a public man he employed the personal influence he possessed in furthering the plans which from time to time were proposed for the improvement of the country. And in particular it may be noted that Chief Baron Dundas was one of the original Vice-Presidents

---

[1] *Supra*, p. 219.

Edinr. 23d March 1795 Received from the Lord Advocate the Sum of Eighteen Guineas for a Portrait of himself

Henry Raeburn

RECEIPT BY RAEBURN.

of the Highland and Agricultural Society at its formation in 1784.

The time during which Chief Baron Dundas was possessor of Arniston, from 1787 to 1819, happened also to be peculiarly favourable for agricultural improvement, and, under the stimulus of war prices, the progress of agriculture in the Lothians was rapid beyond example. In less than a quarter of a century the face of the country was so to speak remodelled, and it became difficult to recognise in the large farms with symmetrical enclosures, and substantial buildings sheltered by thriving plantations, the land of treeless waste and turf-covered hovels. The no less rapid march of mechanical invention hastened the separation of manufactures and agriculture, which by the beginning of the nineteenth century may be said to have been complete. "In nothing," writes the author of the *Survey of Midlothian in* 1793, "is there a more striking contrast than in this, that every article of family maintenance which was formerly maintained at home is now purchased in the market or in the shop. Not only the different articles of clothing, but bread, beer, and butcher's meat are all had from the town." This change of circumstances was not confined to the farmer and his family, but extended to their labourers as well. The old farm-house in which master and servants lived together was replaced by a dwelling-house, suitable for the accommodation of the master and his family alone, the labourers being lodged in houses detached from the farm, and "larger, better lighted, and warmer" than the cottages of former days. These new cottages were "built of good mason-work seven or eight feet high in the walls, and neatly thatched with straw, in some cases with a ceiling and timber floor, a refinement which in the present spirit for convenience and embellishment is likely to become general. In size these houses are from 16 to 18 feet square, which is found sufficient to hold the furniture commodiously."

The buildings for the shelter and accommodation of the stock underwent a similar change. The introduction of green crop and sown grasses into the rotation of the farm, and the improvement in the breeds of cattle and sheep called for a more commodious class of farm-steading. Sheds and courts for turnip feeding became indispensable, and well-built barns for

Chief Baron Dundas.

containing the threshing machines now coming into general use in the south of Scotland. The old buildings of rough stone, thatch covered, and plastered with clay or mortar, were replaced by regular mason-work, with tile or slate roofing, the improvements on the internal fittings being on a corresponding scale.

Chief Baron Dundas lived to see the completion of one great improvement upon his estate—the enclosure of the arable land. In the Charter-room at Arniston there is a beautifully executed map of the part of Midlothian lying between Dalkeith and Heriot, drawn by General Roy, and presented by him to President Dundas sometime about the year 1755, on which all the enclosures then existing are accurately laid down. At that time Roslin stood upon the edge of the enclosed land, and although, owing to the close succession of mansion-houses upon the North Esk from Roslin down to Dalkeith, and with Dalhousie and Newbattle on the South Esk, only a short distance from them, parks and home farms covered that district with enclosures, yet a large extent of ground is shown as unenclosed even so low down the country as Loanhead and Lugton. Arniston with its enclosures stood like an oasis in the midst of the high country desert of bare unenclosed land.

Systematic land drainage cannot be said to have existed, in Scotland at least, until the time of Smith of Deanston; but along with the work of enclosing and building, a considerable amount of drainage work was done in Midlothian towards the close of last century, principally in marshy places where outlets could be got for the springs. From the Arniston estate books the drains would seem to have been from two to three feet deep, half filled with small stones, covered with a layer of straw, the cost for cutting being 3d. to 4d. per rood of six yards. The main drains were built conduits of stone, carefully formed, and in many instances running as clearly now as when first built. But it was still thought more profitable to plant poor wet land than to improve it for agriculture. In a plan of Arniston made in 1791, the damp land is described as " poor wet land which ought to be planted," any land being thought good enough for trees.

Of course these outlays upon enclosing, building, planting, and draining were not made without a heavy outlay. But prices of produce were high, rents rose, and landowners and farmers both prospered.

The narrative which Chief Baron Dundas wrote of the improvements made by himself and his predecessors, and from which quotations have frequently been made in the earlier pages of this volume, is prefaced with the following remarks:—

"Having collected, when a boy, from my father's conversation, and to the accuracy of whose memory I can (as Arnot does in his *Criminal Law*) bear the fullest testimony, a variety of particulars relative to the age of the different woods, plantations, and trees at Arniston, I have felt it right and proper to commit these to paper, and to leave this book in the Charter Room there, not only for the information of our posterity, but that they may, I hope, be encouraged by the example of their ancestors, to continue to protect those to which they have succeeded, and to extend them as regularly and progressively as we have done: assuring them most solemnly that, after thirty years' experience, no pleasure is to be compared with that which a man enjoys in contemplating the woods he has planted, and sees yearly advancing in their progress, especially if to that is joined a taste for, and cultivation of, literary pursuits, and a conscientious endeavour to discharge the duties of life honestly and virtuously. I have subjoined to this narrative an exact account since the year 1800 of all the timber I have cut and disposed of, with the sums of money I have actually received, that my descendants may see that their own interest is deeply concerned in continuing that attention to their woods, which I earnestly recommend. They will reap the benefit of those acorns I am now committing to the ground, and receive the value of those seedlings which are now planting out from my nurseries, as I am now enabled to defray all the expenses of these and other more extensive embellishments and improvements by the sale of trees planted by my great-grandfather, who above a century ago commenced those plantations, which his son and his grandson so wisely cherished and extended."

At the close of last century, when the Chief Baron was carrying out his improvements, the old Parliament House at Edinburgh was being rebuilt. No care was taken to preserve the characteristic carvings with which its masonry had

GARDEN GATE BUILT OF STONES FROM THE OLD PARLIAMENT HOUSE
(*except the Mask on the top*).

been enriched. These were treated as mere rubbish. But the Chief Baron, in order to preserve a part at least of that old building with which his family had been so long connected, brought many cartloads of the old stones to Arniston, where they were used for ornamental doorways and bridges about the pleasure grounds. In particular, the Royal Arms were built into the new pediment by which the tame and unbroken outline of the south front of Arniston house was being relieved.

The Chief Baron's love of old associations also led to the erection of the pillars of which a woodcut is given below. "The pillars of that gate," he writes in his MS., "with the two

BEECH AVENUE GATE, WITH PILLARS TAKEN FROM NICOLSON STREET.

lions on the top of them, stood in front of Mr. Mitchelson's, afterwards Dr. Bennet's, house, in Nicolson Street, and were purchased by me for twenty guineas. They were erected when I was a boy at the High School about 1766 or 1767, and it was one of the first houses in that street." He had to pass the pillars on his way to school, and as Edinburgh grew, the house to which they belonged was pulled down, and so he bought his old friends and put them up at Arniston.

THE CHURCH OF BORTHWICK.

The old church of Borthwick, which, as we have already seen, had fallen into a ruinous state when the vestry was bought by Sir James Dundas in 1606,[1] was destroyed by fire about the year 1780. The church which was erected, after the fire, to replace the old building, was a hideous barn-like structure, relieved outside by a pitiful little belfry. Inside, this second church was as bare as a barn, a gallery at each end, the pulpit in the centre of the south wall, and facing it a platform on which was placed a large pew with chairs and a fireplace for the Arniston family. A monument to the second President Dundas stood over the chimney-piece.

On the church wall were fixed, on each side of the pulpit, large frames containing the Ten Commandments, Lord's Prayer, and Creed, and on the back panel of the pulpit there was painted a cross about two feet high. The following anecdote in the *Life of Barham*, author of the *Ingoldsby Legends*, explains how these came to be part of the fittings of a Scottish Church:—

"Meg Dodds, described in *St. Ronan's Well*, is a Mrs. Wilson, who keeps the inn at Fushie Bridge, the first stage from Edinburgh on the road to Abbotsford.[2] She adores Sir Walter (Scott), and when Dr. and Mrs. Hughes were detained for want of horses, finding out accidentally that they were friends of his, she without any scruple ordered those which were bespoken for a gentleman, then on his way to dine with Lord Melville, to be put to their carriage. Mrs. Wilson is a strict Presbyterian, and once complained to Sir Walter that 'tho' he had done just right by being so much with Arniston,'[3]

---

[1] *Supra*, p. 6.

[2] "Dined at Fushie Bridge. Ah! good Mrs. Wilson, you know not you are likely to lose a good customer!" wrote Scott in 1827, to which Lockhart adds: "Mrs. Wilson, landlady of the Inn at Fushie—an old dame of some humour, with whom Sir Walter always had a friendly colloquy in passing. I believe the charm was, that she had passed her childhood among the Gipsies of the border. But her fiery Radicalism latterly was another source of high merriment."—Lockhart's *Life of Scott*, vol. vii. p. 86.

[3] "The Chief Baron, my early, kind, and constant friend, who took me up when I was a young fellow of little mark or likelihood."—Lockhart's *Life of Scott*, vol. iv. p. 336.

yet that the latter had grievously offended her. 'He had pit up,' she said, 'in the kirk the Lord's Prayer and the Ten Commandments, and when a remonstrance was sent to him against such idolatry, he just answered that if they didna let him alane, he would e'en pit up a Belief into the bargain.'"[1]

[1] *Life of Barham*, vol. i. p. 130.

BRIDGE MADE OF STONES SAVED FROM THE OLD PARLIAMENT HOUSE.

CHAPTER XIII.

ROBERT DUNDAS OF ARNISTON.

Robert Dundas, eldest son of the Chief Baron Dundas, was born on the 19th of June 1797, at his father's house, No. 57 George Square, Edinburgh.

He was educated at the High School of Edinburgh, and at Dr. Bond's at Hanwell, as were also his brothers Henry and William, a favourite school at that time for Scotch boys. During short holidays, when the length of the journey did not permit of Robert going home, he and his brothers used to visit their relations; Lord Melville at Wimbledon, William Dundas in Grosvenor Street, and old Sir David Dundas at Chelsea Hospital. Lady Dundas was very kind to the boys; and a portrait of her husband the General, now at Arniston, was given by her to the Chief Baron in exchange for a water-colour of the boys.

After leaving Hanwell Robert Dundas completed his studies by a course of lectures at Edinburgh University.

From his earliest days he was passionately fond of field sports, although at the beginning of the present century there was but little sport to be had in the lowlands of Scotland. For nearly four hundred years an Act of Parliament had been nominally in force which forbade the slaughter of partridges, muirfowl, and some other birds from Lent till August. But the close-time thus ordained seems to have been but little observed. In the Arniston house-books there are entries of payments for partridges in March, and for muirfowl in July. The first President Dundas, writing from his Highland quarters in June 1743, says, "Fishing goes on, and Tom hath taken a little touch of shooting, but Currie's and Vogrie's dogs seem good for nothing."

The first mention in the papers at Arniston of pheasants

there is in 1757, when the following entries occur in the account book of the Second President Dundas:—

Feb. 6, 1757.	16 Pheasants,	.	£7 4	0
	10 Pheasant hens,		4 10	0
1758.	18 Pheasants,	.	7 16	0
1759.	Pheasants,	.	6 16	6

In the house-books are frequent entries of barley given out for the "pheasant fowls." But want of shelter and absence of protection from vermin rendered unsuccessful this first attempt at naturalising pheasants in the Arniston woods.

Towards the close of the eighteenth century greater attention was turned to the systematic preservation of game. Notices were published in the newspapers by many of the landed proprietors, among others by Lord Advocate Dundas of Arniston, warning poachers that they would be prosecuted according to law, and hoping that no gentleman would hunt or shoot upon their lands without leave. An association of Midlothian Heritors was formed about the same time for the prosecution of persons trespassing in pursuit of game.

The winter of 1794-5 was very severe, occasioning great destruction of the breeding stock of game, at that time small at the best. At a meeting of the Heritors of Midlothian held within the old Justiciary Court-room on 11th July 1795, it was resolved that a Jubilee should be given to the game during the ensuing season. The meeting also resolved to enforce the law for the observance of close-time, and that all persons transgressing the law in that particular should be prosecuted, without distinction. In the advertisement announcing the Jubilee, muirfowl and partridges are specified but not pheasants.

The summers of 1795 and 1796 did not suffice for repairing the damage done to the game by the severe winter of 1794, for on August 3d, 1796, the Midlothian Heritors were again obliged to resolve, "that as from all appearance a good deal of corn would remain uncut on the first of September, and that the partridges were very scarce in most parts of the county, having not yet recovered the inclemency of winter 1794, the heritors postpone the commencement of the time for killing partridges to the 1st of October, instead of the 14th of September."

In the following year, 1797, pheasants were turned out in

Dalkeith Park,[1] and proper measures having been taken for their preservation, they soon spread over the adjoining country. The assistance of the neighbours was asked by an intimation—

"That a few pheasants have lately been turned out in Dalkeith Park with an intention to encourage their breeding in this part of the country, and as some of them have already been seen at a distance from the park, it is earnestly hoped that the gentlemen in the County of Midlothian and the neighbourhood will give orders to their gamekeepers and servants not only not to molest the birds, but to afford them all the protection in their power—28th October 1797."

At Arniston, in the upper district of Midlothian, pheasants were, in 1812, turned out into the woods above the meeting of the South Esk and Fullerton Burn; and for many years afterwards a pheasantry for providing a breeding stock of birds was kept up at Temple Mill. But from the entries in a sporting diary kept by Robert Dundas in 1816, the pheasants must have increased at a very slow rate. From the 12th of August to the end of October, the game killed by his own gun were 46 grouse, 4 blackgame, 2 snipe, 78 partridges, and 2 pheasants. Hits and misses are both recorded in the diary; and the sportsman seems usually to have had from six to twelve shots in a day, seldom more, and frequently less.

The following letter will serve to illustrate how scarce grouse were on the Midlothian and Peeblesshire hills at this time:—

ROBERT DUNDAS *to his Brother* HENRY.

MY DEAR HEN.,—According to my promise, I now sit down to inform you of my success at the muirs this year. On Saturday the 12th Lord Robert Kerr[2] and I set out from Arniston at 6 in the morning, and went to Outerston Moss. We hunted all the Moss and grounds near it, but found that some rascal had been there before us, for all the birds were scattered about. We got very few shots, and each slew a bird. We then breakfasted on a bottle of beer and a cold duck, and then crossed the hills. We hunted till twelve o'clock, and I killed another bird. We lay from 12 till 1 on the ridge of the hills in the most pelting shower I was

---

[1] During the lifetime of Henry, third Duke of Buccleuch.
[2] Born 1780. A lieutenant-colonel in the army.

ever out in. We dined at 4, and after dinner Lord R. killed an old cock bird, and we both mauled a leveret; his shot struck its head and mine its tail. It was close to us, and was killed quite dead. We were not home till 8. On Sunday George Suttie and I went to Colquhar.[1] It rained all Monday till 4 o'clock, but we killed 2 brace in the evening. On Tuesday the high wind made the birds so wild that we only killed 2 brace, and on Wednesday I returned to Arniston to shoot with General Wynyard and Lord R. Kerr. I met them near Castleton, but the day was so bad that Captain Napier killed but one bird, I killed one, General Winyard a hare, and Lord Robert 3 brace. On Monday Mr. Hepburn[2] and I went out; we had bad sport. I got but one shot, he got 3, and killed a brace. Bravo has proved himself to be an incomparable good dog for muirfowl. He did not commit two faults the whole time. I have likewise got the loan of two very fine dogs from Baron Clerk called Sal and Ponto. There has been a change in the stud here; Ann has got Caleb, and I have got young Hap Hazard: he is not so good a horse as Caleb, but a better hunter. Papa desires me to say he will write to you in a day or two. We go to the Highlands on Tuesday.—Believe me, dear Hen., ever yours, R. DUNDAS.

ARNISTON, *Thursday*.

The Midlothian Coursing Club, an institution for some time intimately connected with the social life of the county, deserves a passing notice in these Memoirs. For many years it discharged the double duty of bringing county neighbours for sport, and for the dinners which formed an important part of the business of the meetings, and which usually took place at the Fushie Inn or at Dalkeith. One of the club programmes for the year 1815 is among the Arniston papers, from which it appears that the Duke of Buccleuch was President and Lord Dalhousie Vice-President. The spring meeting of the club, it states, is to be held at Esperston on Tuesday the 21st, and at the Roman Camp on the 22d, of February. "The club will breakfast at Foushie Bridge on the morning of the 21st, and will dine that day at Davidson's Inn, Dalkeith, at five o'clock;

---

[1] Sir James Suttie's shooting lodge in Peeblesshire. George Suttie was his eldest son.

[2] Mr. Hepburn of Clerkington. Clerkington was soon afterwards sold to the Earl of Rosebery, from whom it received the name of Rosebery.

and on the 22d at Morrison's Inn, at the same hour." Among those who owned and ran greyhounds were the Chief Baron Dundas, Sir John Pringle, Sir John Dalrymple, The Marquis of Lothian, Sir John Hope, and other county men. There was a club prize of fifteen guineas at each meeting, sweepstakes of one guinea each, and private matches. In the early days of the club, friends connected with the county by relationship or other ties were admitted as honorary members. But latterly, when, from various causes, fewer of the county gentlemen kept greyhounds, it became necessary, for the purposes of sport, to admit as honorary members greyhound owners from any part of Scotland. The meetings were good as coursing meetings; but, owing to the gradual withdrawal of the county gentlemen, they ceased to be the social gatherings they once had been. At last it was resolved to dissolve the club, which, after a prosperous existence, had outlived the purpose for which it had originally been founded.

The following letter was written while the meetings were in full swing, in the year 1815, and gives an account of the sixth meeting of the club, when the cup was won by Mr. Robert Græme's Needle. Mr. Græme was, like the Chief Baron's sons, a keen courser, and his sister, Mrs. Maxtone of Cultoquhey, used, in after years, to tell how, on one occasion, he rode from Cultoquhey to Eskbank, a distance of between forty and fifty miles, at midnight, returning in time for breakfast, simply " to see a litter of Needle's puppies."[1]

ROBERT DUNDAS *to his Brother* HENRY.

31 GEORGE SQUARE, *February* 12.

MY DEAR HEN.,—It is a very long time since you and I have corresponded. Now I think it would be better for both parties that the said correspondence were renewed, so without saying who broke it off, I thus begin it again. Yesterday being mild and

---

[1] The inscription on the cup, now in the possession of Mr. Maxtone Graham of Cultoquhey, is as follows: " At the sixth meeting of the Midlothian Coursing Club, begun at Esperston on the 8th November 1814 and continued, by several adjournments, to the Roman Camp, till the 11th February 1815, this cup was won by Needle, the property of Robert Græme, Esq., Advocate." Mr. Græme (who adopted the " Graham " mode of spelling his family name) afterwards succeeded his cousin, Lord Lynedoch, in the estates of Balgowan and Lynedoch, and died in 1859.

soft enough for coursing, the Cup was at length decided in favour of Mr. R. Graeme of Eskbank. We met at the Roman Camp, and there were between 1 and 200 horsemen. Our bitch Wasp was beat by Captain James Dalrymple of North Berwick's dog Czar. The course was a desperate one, but we were fairly beaten; the hare went away with her fud cocked. She never was turned, and seemed not to give a d—mn for either Wasp or Czar. This was the second course. The first was between Mr. Graeme's Needle and Baron Clerk's Salamanca. Salamanca was beat. The last course was between Needle and Czar. I never saw two more beautiful dogs. Czár was beat, though the best dog, owing to a fall in a ploughed field. The unfortunate hare was encountered near the wood, and slain by a mob of fellows (about 80 or 90), who would not keep back their horses, but charged the dogs, and hare, and all. The hare was slain, the dogs, for a wonder, were not. The spring meeting takes place next week. I must write to Pitt to tell him that Wasp was beat, so adieu. Write to me when you have time.—Ever yours affec^{ly}., R. DUNDAS.

In the autumn of 1817 Robert Dundas went abroad with his family, the object of the journey being the hope, however faint, of the Chief Baron deriving benefit from a winter spent south of the Alps; and in the summer of 1818 he had a run through Greece and Turkey. A few of his letters to his mother are still at Arniston:—

ROBERT DUNDAS *to his* MOTHER.

PATRAS, *May 3d*, 1818.

A brig is to sail from this in a few days, and I shall send this letter by her to London. In the way of news I have little to add to my letter from Corfu, dated, I think, 26th April. We[1] sailed from Corfu on the 27th along with Mr. Bonnar. I left Corfu with regret. It is a lovely spot, and I had been treated by every person there with the greatest kindness. We passed the islands of Paxu and Antipaxu, and on the Albanian shore the small town of Pargo. We crossed the gulf of Actium, and landed at Santa Maura. We landed at the fort, and the ship sailed round, and anchored on the other side of the neck of land. We were

---

[1] He was travelling with two friends, Wyse, afterwards the Right Hon. Thomas Wyse, and a Mr. Godfrey.

received most kindly by Colonel Ross of the 75th. He gave us quarters in the fort to sleep in, and insisted upon our living with him.

The third day after our arrival we sailed to Previsa to see Ali Pacha, the rest of the party meaning to proceed to Janina, across Pindus. We met a brig coming out of Previsa, and knowing her to belong to Sir Thomas Maitland,[1] we went alongside. We found Sir Frederick Adam[2] on board of her. Sir Thomas sent an officer in this vessel to wait for Sir Frederick at Previsa, and to give him the despatches which I am to take to Constantinople.[3] Sir Thomas had written to say that I must leave Santa Maura as soon as possible, and get to Constantinople as quickly as I could; I might choose the road I liked best, and stay a few days at Athens. I, of course, acted as he told me, and returned that evening to Santa Maura alone, leaving Godfrey and Wyse at Previsa; they mean to cross Pindus, and pursue the original plan. Next day I sailed; we passed the Lover's Leap at sunset, and were close to Ithaca all night, and part of next morning. The breeze then sprang up, and we reached Patras about two in the afternoon. I was received here by the consul, in whose house I am. He recommends me to go to Athens, through Delphi and Thebes. To go by Corinth I must have a passport from the pacha, who lives near Sparta, involving five or six days' delay. Besides, Colonel Ross told me that the Bey of Corinth has orders to stop all despatches going across the Isthmus.

ROBERT DUNDAS *to his* MOTHER.

BRITISH PALACE, CONSTANTINOPLE,
May 25, 1818.

My last letter was sent from Patras in a currant ship, which was to sail in a few days. At Patras I found it was necessary to have a passport from the pacha of the Morea, who resides at Tripolitza, not far from Sparta. This pass is not demanded until the traveller arrives at the Isthmus of Corinth. As I did not think myself justified in detaining the despatches (which I knew were

---

[1] Sir Thomas Maitland, Governor of the Ionian Islands; died 1824. He went by the nickname of *King Tom*.

[2] Sir Frederick Adam, a general in the Army. Commanded a brigade at Waterloo, where he was wounded. Sir Frederick was appointed Lord High Commissioner of the Ionian Islands at the death of Sir Thomas Maitland in 1824.

[3] Sir Thomas Maitland, during Mr. Dundas's visit to Corfu, had asked him to convey some despatches to Sir Robert Liston, Ambassador at Constantinople.

important) for three days till a courier could procure me the passport, I got a boat to convey me to Salona, meaning to follow Mr. Wood's route to Athens by Delphi, Thebes, and Livadia. My luggage was in the boat, and all was ready, when the consul's deputy came running to inform me that the plague was raging at Livadia and Thebes, and that I should have a quarantine of twenty days at Athens. I was, of course, forced very unwillingly to give up this route, and I embarked for Corinth. It blew very hard. The voyage is usually performed in two or three days, but we were within twelve miles of Corinth in eight hours. The wind fell, and the sailors insisting that it was contrary, ran the vessel, a small open boat, into a creek near the ancient Sicyon. As I was yet unaccustomed to the ways of the Greeks, I allowed them to do so, and lay down in my cloak upon the shingle, where I slept for four hours. Next day the consul told me that a friend of his had agreed to give me a passage to Constantinople; that I would find him to be the best of his countrymen. I accordingly embarked in a noble ship, 550 tons burden, 25 guns, and 66 men. I saw Captain Murray, whom I am to meet at Smyrna on the 15th June, when he will take me to Malta. In three days we were within 20 miles of this place; there we were becalmed, so I left the ship with regret, and rowed up here.

ROBERT DUNDAS *to his* MOTHER.

VIENNA, *Aug.* 5, 1818.

Thank Heaven, here I am in a Christian country. I have got out of Turkey, and I assure you I shall not enter it again without some very good reason. I arrived here from Constantinople by Bukharest, Hermanstadt, Temeswar, and Buda on the 25th July. As far as Bukharest my health was perfectly good, but there I began to be unwell much as I was at Spa last year. Fearing I was about to have the same sort of bilious fever, I stopped at the Convent of Argis, a small hamlet in Wallachia at the foot of the Carpathian mountains, half way between Bukharest and Hermanstadt, halting there two days for rest and medicine.

His illness had been no light matter; and that he thought himself in great danger is shown by a curious memorandum among the papers of this period. It is indorsed, "Sealed at Argis 12th July 1818, opened at Arniston, September 11, 1821," and is headed:—

Reflexions written when confined by illness at the Greek **Convent** *between Bukharest and Hermanstadt.*

ARGIS, *July* 12, 1818.

Where am I now? What am I? I am a poor, feeble wretch, near three thousand miles from his native home. Such was the question and answer which awakened me from the dream which for the last hour has so pleasantly occupied my wearied mind. I dreamed of home. I was seated at Mrs. Wm. Dundas's cottage planning some new improvements. The company who were there assembled at tea were my father and mother, Wm. and Mrs. D., all my brothers and sisters, and uncle Francis. I saw plainly Philip playing with Ripon and Texel on the green. I hear distinctly the distant sound of Braidwood Cascade. Hark to Windsor yelping in the wood, and see Brown with his gun returning slowly home. The sun is setting in glory over the Pentlands, and the whole scene is nothing but peace and joy. Such is the painting which for this hour past has occupied my mind's eye, delineated in richer colours than Claude or Titian ever imagined. But is the real scene before you? The plain white-washed cell of the Monastery of Argis, with its single print of some favourite saint. These figures that through the half-shut door watch the couch which supports your faint and feverish limbs, are they your relations? 'Tis Alexander, Mustapha, and a monk with your provisions. Is the scene without splendid and peaceful? It is still and sublime. The distant thunder is grumbling near and more near, while the sun darts his hot reflected ray on the gloomy ridge of the Carpathian mountains. The torrent is brawling past with ceaseless din to mix its waters with those of the Alt. The storm is passing away over the wide interminable plains of Walachia, and mingling its hollow murmurs with the distant bay of the watch-dog. And this place is 3000 miles from home!!!!

But God is everywhere. His arm upheld, and if he pleases will still uphold me. By his infinite goodness and mercy I have passed through banditti, through storms, through fatigues and pestilence. He was with me at Terracina and Bovino. In the Gulf of Corinth 'twas he that took my skiff through the tempest. The plague at Athens touched me not, neither did the fatigues of my journey overcome me. To Thee, oh my God, I deliver up myself in perfect trust, restore health of body and mind, and send me *home* in safety through Jesus Christ.

The devotion of his servant, and a good constitution, did wonders; and he was soon able to travel on to Vienna.

Arrived there he was placed in the hands of an able physician, who ascribed his illness to over-fatigue, aggravated by the improper medicines he had taken. He soon recovered under proper treatment.

From Vienna, he returned by Salzburg and the Tyrol to Northern Italy and Florence. By that time his family had left Italy on their way home. In a letter of the 8th of September, he mentions having seen Lord Lauderdale and Lord Maitland, who had just arrived from England, and who had given him every kind of news which they thought would interest him. Lord Lauderdale, owing to the accounts he had received from Lord Melville, had gone to Lausanne to see the Chief Baron, and found him sufficiently recovered to undertake the journey home.

At Florence he met his friends Pringle[1] of Yair, and Alison,[2] both of them his seniors by five years, and members of the Scotch Bar. They told him of the successful start his most intimate friend John Hope[3] had made at the Bar, and said that they looked to Hope and to him as their leaders for the future, and urged him to follow Hope's example without further loss of time.

"I inquired," he writes to his mother, "how J. Hope was coming on. Alison said, 'he has now been but eighteen months at the Bar. He is become Advocate Depute, and is making at least £700 a year. You will have tight work to come up with him, for we all settled that you and he are to be our leaders, the one Advocate and the other Solicitor. So see you don't disappoint us.' I took this as a way of talking, and smiled; when Pringle said, 'I assure you we are quite in earnest, for, as Alison says, it is you and Hope that we all look to, so you must stand to your tackle, Dundas.'"

This conversation seems to have left an impression on his mind, and, along with the accounts of his father's failing health, induced him to give up his foreign travels, and return at once to Scotland.

---

[1] Alexander Pringle of Yair, afterwards M.P. for Selkirkshire, and a Lord of the Treasury in Sir Robert Peel's ministry.

[2] Archibald Alison, author of the *History of Europe*.

[3] John Hope, afterwards Lord Justice-Clerk.

The Chief Baron died on the 17th of June 1819; and young Robert Dundas succeeded to the estate of Arniston.

The county of Midlothian at this time had a regiment of Yeomanry Cavalry of whose efficiency it was proud. Sir Walter Scott had once been an active member of the Edinburgh troop. Robert Dundas was now Captain of the Dalkeith troop, and devoted to his regimental work. In the year 1820, the regiment was called out, and marched, in the middle of a winter night, to the west of Scotland to take part with the regular and volunteer forces in maintaining order. That year was a season during which the spirit of disaffection, for some time prevalent throughout Great Britain, had become threatening to the peace of the country. Vigorous measures had to be taken for keeping the restless, and partially armed mobs within bounds. At Glasgow it was necessary to keep the regular troops ready for instant action, and to call to their assistance the yeomanry of the neighbouring counties. It was a matter of deep regret to Mr. Dundas that he was unable to accompany his regiment to the west. In a letter to him from his friend Alexander Pringle of Yair, the experiences of the yeomanry are narrated :—

Mr. Pringle *to* Robert Dundas.

Glasgow, *Tuesday morn., April* 11, 1820.

My dear Dundas,—Since you are denied the pleasure of a visit to the land of Radicals, I know you will like to hear what we are about. I can only say that we lead a life of constant uncertainty and expectation, which is abundantly interesting, and I wish much you were with us, for I am sure you would enjoy it. A few days ago I envied you the near prospect of your march, but now I have the advantage of being in the midst of duty, and well and able for it. Every day, or rather every night, brings some new event, and we are kept constantly on the alert. To give you some idea of it: last night two parties of our troop were roused out of bed at a moment's notice. The one is just returned after a march half way to Paisley, to attack a house where there was information of a committee of Radicals sitting. When they arrived, the committee had decamped, and left the door locked, which Home forced with his pistol. They only got one man and a few papers. The other party has not returned yet. Besides these we have a

picquet of 20 constantly on duty, with as many of the hussars and of the Glasgow troop. So you see we never know what we have to do the next hour. There is a report to-day of something having happened at Hamilton, but we have no particulars. The numbers taken up now are immense, and the lawyers are all very busy at the Star. I am living in capital quarters, a guest of the Lord Provost. We had a letter this morning from Lord Sidmouth offering a reward of £500 for the discovery of the authors of the April placard.[1] I have just seen a letter from Greenock with some particulars of the row there, of which you must have seen an account in the newspapers. The Volunteers at first fired over the heads of the mob, which only incensed them. At the second fire their officer told them to level low, and the consequence was that the persons shot were some of the very worst. It is ascertained that there were among them many Radical incendiaries from Paisley. Of the nine who are dead, seven are known to have been *mauvais sujets*, and the other two nobody will own, so it is supposed that they are stranger incendiaries. The only other troop of yeomanry here now are the Glasgow; those of Ayrshire and Dumbartonshire are sent home. In every village of importance there are some quartered. Sir C. Lockhart's and Sir Samuel Stirling's are at Hamilton, Shawfield's at Airdrie, etc. I understand that those still out are the Lanarkshire, Stirlingshire, Clackmannanshire, Linlithgowshire, and our own. All your acquaintances here are well, and in constant spirits. Such as had colds, etc., sore throats, etc., recovered in the night marches. They had very hard work indeed till they came here. I have time at present for no more, but that I remain, dear Dundas,—
Your sincere friend, ALEX. PRINGLE.

The most serious event of what was known as the Radical War, had taken place six days before the date of this letter. There had actually been a skirmish at Bonnymuir in Stirlingshire, between a band of the misguided men who imagined they could obtain Reform by force of arms, and a troop of the Stirlingshire Yeomanry. Shots were fired. Several men were wounded. Ultimately twenty-four persons were found guilty of high treason, and sentenced to death. Only three, however,

---

[1] A placard which was posted up in the streets of Glasgow, Paisley, and other places in the west of Scotland, calling on all persons to stop work, on and after the 1st of April, and "attend wholly to the recovery of their rights."

were executed; and these were the last treason trials which have taken place in Scotland.

On the 16th of December 1820, Mr. Dundas was called to the Scottish Bar, with the intention of following in the footsteps of so many generations of his family who had made the Scottish Bar their first step in political life. His abilities peculiarly suited him for such a career. It was one in which he took a keen interest, and the political influence of his family was still strong enough to ensure him a favourable start in the race he was anxious to run.

The representation of Midlothian in Parliament had been enjoyed by so many members of the Dundas family as to make it seem a sort of hereditary seat. By the death of the first Viscount Melville in 1811 a vacancy was caused in the county, and Sir George Clerk [1] of Penicuik was elected in place of the Honourable Robert Dundas, who succeeded his father as second Viscount Melville. A better choice could not have been made; Sir George was one of the largest landowners in the county, and a man, as was shown by his subsequent career, in every way suited to the post. But at Arniston and at Melville he was looked upon as a sort of stop-gap, whose duty it would be to make way whenever the family might require the seat, and this feeling was by no means confined to the family, for many of the county gentlemen were desirous of seeing Midlothian represented as it had so long been. Soon after he returned home from his foreign tour, the Lord Advocate [2] spoke to Robert Dundas on the subject, and told him that although he and the principal freeholders had hitherto supported Sir George Clerk, they nevertheless meant to withdraw their votes as soon as he should come forward as a candidate. The Lord Advocate added that he and several of the principal people of the county meant to inform Sir George of their determination. In reporting this conversation to his uncle Lord Melville (March 15, 1819), Robert Dundas adds his own views upon the impolicy of his pledging himself *then*, as to what steps he might take six

---

[1] Sir George Clerk, sixth Baronet of Penicuik. Represented the county of Midlothian in Parliament, and subsequently the boroughs of Stamford and Dover. After filling various subordinate offices he was appointed Master of the Mint, and Vice-President of the Board of Trade, and a Privy Councillor in 1845. Sir George died in 1867.

[2] Mr. Alexander Maconochie, afterwards the second Lord Meadowbank.

or seven years hence; adding that if ever the train of events and the wishes of his friends should lead him to stand for the county, he would come forward fairly and openly and tell Sir George he meant to dispute the field with him, but until that time should arrive he would have nothing to do with the matter.

In reply, Lord Melville writes:—

"ADMIRALTY, 20 *March* 1819.

"I do not recollect to have received any similar communication with more pleasure than your letter of March 15; the good sense and proper feeling which pervade every line of it were very gratifying to me, and it is scarcely necessary for me to add, that I entirely concur in your views of the subject to which it relates.

"It would have been quite unnecessary to announce to Sir George Clerk that when he was elected for Midlothian there was no pledge either expressed or implied that those who supported him were bound to him for the rest of his life. Whenever a dissolution of Parliament shall take place, you will be at full liberty to come forward if you choose it, and if it shall be in other respects convenient or agreeable to you, and I have no doubt you will find the county as well disposed to yourself, as they have been for a century past to others of your family who have gone before you."

On the 9th of April 1822 Robert Dundas married Lilias, daughter of Colonel Durham Calderwood of Polton, a descendant of the famous Sir Thomas Hope, Lord Advocate in the reign of Charles the First, and also of Sir James Stewart of Goodtrees, Lord Advocate to King William and Queen Anne. Mrs. Dundas notes in her diary, "April 9th, went to dinner at Polton. After dinner, Robert and Miss Durham were married, and went to Arniston."

Two years later, in 1824, he obtained his first promotion at the Bar, being appointed Advocate-Depute in room of his friend John Hope, who became Solicitor-General.

The second Lord Melville, who held the office of first Lord of the Admiralty in Lord Liverpool's Administration, was at this time the Scottish Manager. "The rise," says Lord Cockburn, "of Robert Dundas, Lord Melville's son, was an important event for his party; for, without his father's force, or power of debate, or commanding station, he had fully as much good sense, excellent business habits, great moderation, and as much candour as, I suppose, a party leader can practise." The first symptoms that his influence was waning were seen in 1826, when the Government, alarmed by the commercial crisis of the previous year, resolved to bring in a bill to prevent the issue of bank-notes for a smaller amount than £5. In Scotland, where a greasy £1 note was received with greater confidence than a brand-new sovereign or a crisp Bank of England "fiver," this proposal was most unpopular. Mr. Downie of Appin, member for the Stirling burghs, gave a significant answer when Mr. Canning asked him if the one-pound notes were not very dirty. "Very," he said, "and if you meddle with them, you'll foul your fingers."

Lord Melville supported the obnoxious measure, and was roundly abused for doing so. But the measure might have become law had not Sir Walter Scott, one evening in February, suddenly thought of taking up the cudgels against the Government. "I am horribly tempted," he writes in his diary, "to interfere in this business of altering the system of banks in Scotland." Next morning, the 18th of February, he set to work; and on the following day the first letter of Malachi Malagrowther was finished. A second and a third followed. As is well known, these famous letters created an enormous sensation. They appeared in the *Edinburgh Weekly Journal* in February and March, and were often quoted during the discussions which afterwards took place in Parliament. The proposed measure was, so far as Scotland was concerned, abandoned; and the fact that the Scottish banks retained the privilege of issuing £1 notes was universally said to be the work of Sir Walter Scott.

The Government was seriously annoyed. "The Ministers," Lockhart wrote to Sir Walter, "are sore beyond imagination at present; and some of them, I hear, have felt this new whip on the raw to some purpose." No one was angrier than Lord Melville. "Sir Robert Dundas," Scott writes in his diary, "to-day put into my hands a letter of between twenty and forty pages, in angry and bitter reprobation of Malachi, full of general averments, and very untenable arguments, all written *at* me by name, but of which I am to have no copy, and which is to be circulated to other special friends, to whom it may be necessary to 'give the sign to hate.' I got it at two o'clock, and returned it with an answer four hours afterwards, in which I have studied not to be tempted into either sarcastic or harsh expressions."

Among the papers at Arniston are Lord Melville's letter written *at* Sir Walter Scott, and Sir Walter's reply through Sir Robert Dundas :—

Lord Melville *to* Sir Robert Dundas.

Private. ADMIRALTY, 6 *March* 1826.

My dear Sir,—I received in due course your letter of the 10th ulto., with its enclosure, and I have since seen various applications from other clerks in the Law Departments in Scotland for increase of salary. I hope the salaries of the Judges will be increased, and at any rate I shall use my best endeavours for that purpose, because I think it of great importance to the respectability of the Bench in Scotland, as well as in England, that the salaries of the Judges should be to such an amount as will induce well-employed competent lawyers to accept the situation. Since the salaries of the Judges in Scotland were fixed on their present footing, the emoluments of the Bar, as I am informed, and indeed know to be true, have increased out of all proportion. With regard to the Clerks of Session and sundry other and inferior clerks, and even judges (the commissaries for instance), there does not appear to me to be the slightest ground for any such increase, and if my opinion is asked, I shall give it accordingly. There is no lack of candidates for those situations, and of the first abilities, or at least fully adequate to the duties they have to perform.

In your same letter of the 10th ulto. you advert to the question of the Paper Currency in Scotland, and you state, as others have since done, that the introducing a metallic circulation into that country in lieu of their small notes would be injurious to its interests. I cannot pretend to any great depth of knowledge on that subject, but it is not new to me as far as regards Scotland, and I have no difficulty in saying that my opinion has long been at variance with that doctrine. It has appeared to me for several years that the extent and facility of banking credit in that country and the speculations of all kinds, agricultural, commercial, and manufacturing, to which it has given rise, are hollow and unsafe. It is true, as you state, and for reasons which you assign, that the banks in Scotland as a body, are more solid and more worthy of confidence than is generally the case in England ; but if they had not hitherto been, and were not still, in an implied league to support each other, I do not believe that they could with justice have been so much extolled for their solidity. I know a few anecdotes on that subject which would sound ominously if published to the world, and I am confident that for their own sakes they had better not provoke too much probing of the system. On the other hand, there can be no question that as far as regards the granting of cash credits, anything which would suddenly derange that system would not only be injurious to Scotland now, but would affect her permanently if it is (as they assert) necessarily interwoven with the power of issuing notes under £5. I say nothing so much of the banking system as relates to the discounting of bills or to deposits, as these branches are common to all bankers in this kingdom as well as elsewhere, except that the allowing of interest on deposits is not peculiar to Scotland, but is common in England, independently of any circulation of small notes. Sundry delegates from the Scotch banks have recently come to London, and if they can make out that the abolition of small notes will necessarily and unavoidably have the effect of putting down altogether the system of cash credits, I think they will establish a case which will call for a different course to be adopted in Scotland from what is contemplated for England. I am by no means satisfied from anything I have yet heard, that such a consequence would follow, even at Glasgow and other manufacturing districts where small notes (or sovereigns) are required for the payment of their workmen, and still less do I believe that it would follow in the eastern parts of Scotland, where the notes of £5 and £5, 5s. would to a considerable extent supply the place of small notes. I have heard and believe that a much greater proportion of the Royal Bank circulation (which is considerable in Glasgow) is in small notes, than of Sir William Forbes' House, which is chiefly at Edinburgh and the neighbouring counties.

But whatever may be the real state of the case in that respect, you will observe that I have herein adverted to Scotch concerns only; though there is another part of the subject equally deserving of consideration, viz., how England may be affected. And here I cannot help reminding you of the profound and total silence of every resolution and petition on this point; the people of North Britain who have lately come forward have either overlooked it altogether, or have thought, as a matter of course, that England was bound to submit to every inconvenience and loss which Scotland might think fit to impose upon her. I presume it will not be denied that a pressure on the money market, or any commercial difficulty, is likely to affect both countries at once, and not one exclusive of the other. If that is the case, and supposing England to have a considerable gold circulation, and Scotland none, it is quite clear that whenever such pressure arises, Scotland must depend, and be a dead weight upon England, for whatever gold coin she may require over and above what she ought to have, and what she would have if her small notes were extinguished. This inconvenience is unimportant in ordinary times, but at pinching periods it might be most serious, and it would affect the money market much beyond the difference between the ordinary metallic circulation of England and of Scotland. If the banking delegates from the north can point out any mode by which England can be protected from such an invasion on her circulation, they will undoubtedly remove one of the objections to a continuance of small notes in Scotland.

I have perused within these few days two letters in the newspapers from a certain Mr. Malachi Malagrowther, and I should not now have mentioned them if I had not heard with sincere regret that they are from the pen of Sir Walter Scott. I know the people of Scotland as well as he does, and I also know full well how they ought to be dealt with; and I am much mistaken if the period is far distant (if it has not already arrived) when every person in that country, whose good opinion he would most wish to cultivate, will not join with me in condemning, on public grounds (I will not condescend to advert to private feelings), the style and tone of those letters. I do not quarrel with his opinions on the Scotch banking system and paper currency; many of his observations and arguments on those matters are very much to the purpose, and deserving of great consideration, and if they are not altogether new or original, it would be very unreasonable to find fault with him merely on that account. But I do quarrel with him, first for the inflammatory tendency of his letters, secondly for the gross misrepresentations which are to be found in every paragraph, and almost in every line of them, except where he discusses exclusively the professed subjects of the letters; and thirdly for his insulting taunts and unfounded attacks on the present Government.

Before adverting to these points separately, it may be worth while to inquire what foundation there is for the allegation, not only in these letters, but in almost all the resolutions and petitions which I have seen, where we are told with an air of triumphant superiority, that the permission to issue small notes has existed in

Scotland above a century, meaning thereby to apprise the uninformed lieges (as I understand the matter) that England has not had the same happy lot. Now, it so happens that with the exception of twenty years, viz., from 1777 to 1797, the law in that respect has been common to both countries from the earliest periods to the present time; and yet (to show the extraordinary extent of misconception on that point) no less a person than Mr. Kirkman Finlay informs us in a set of resolutions adopted by the Merchant Company at Glasgow that " the permission to English banks as to the issue of notes under £5 is of very recent origin, whereas in Scotland it existed before the Union," etc. I trust that the Government whose proceedings are animadverted upon by Messrs. Malagrowther, Finlay, and others, are not so ignorant of the laws and history of their country on these matters as their said assailants.

But to return to Mr. Malachi's letters, I am persuaded you will agree with me that I am fully justified (on the first point) in stating that they are of an inflammatory tendency, and it is difficult to conceive that such was not the meaning and intention of the writer. The questions as to paper currency, or the advantages or otherwise, of a metallic circulation, do not belong exclusively to Scotland, or to England, or to France, or to any other country, and therefore the attempts to persuade uninformed persons on the north side of the Tweed that these questions are part and parcel of the ancient and fundamental laws of Scotland, and that the meddling with them by the Imperial Parliament, or with anything that could possibly affect "cash credits," would be a violation of the articles of the Union, is so preposterous, that it is impossible to receive these remarks as arguments addressed to reason and common sense: they are directed to the passions of the ignorant and the illiterate. I little thought, if Sir Walter Scott is really the author of these letters, that *he* would ever have been found to be dabbling in such an impure stream. The honest claymore to which he appeals had but one edge: popular inflammation is a two-edged weapon, and is seldom resorted to by those who really wish well to their country.

On my second head of charge, the plentiful crop of misrepresentation which may be gathered in these letters, I really know not where to begin with instances, and still less where to end with them, unless I were to copy and animadvert upon every separate paragraph of the letters. Almost all that is stated as to the changes in the jurisprudence, and in the revenue system of Scotland, and in the motives of those who originated or acquiesced in those charges, is, to my certain knowledge, absolutely untrue. Even in minor instances, and which he professes only to quote as proofs of a contemptuous *animus* towards Scotland in recent years, he is equally at variance with the fact. For instance (to begin from my own shop), he tells us that "till of late, there was always an Admiral on the Scotch Station." I never heard of an Admiral on that Station till after the renewal of the war in 1803, and Mr. Malachi's memory, if he is as old as Sir Walter and I, *must* have told him so. The assertion I believe to be wholly unfounded, and *I* am the only person who ever left an Admiral there during peace, and I only withdrew him when the Revenue Cruisers were taken from under our orders. Again, we are told "that till of late years there was always a Commander-in-Chief, with a Lieutenant-General and two Major-Generals under him." I believe this assertion to have as much foundation as the other, as far as relates to periods of peace; and I observe in a Scotch Almanac of 1783, when the war was scarcely ended, and before the Definitive Treaty was signed, that the Scotch staff then consisted of two Generals, viz., Mackay and Skene. The next instance, as to the Scottish Yeomanry (for he alludes to them exclusively) having been deprived of their allowances, is, I believe, equally untrue, with the additional demerit of being very mischievous. I understand, on the contrary, that the Yeomanry Allowances have lately been increased. Mr. Malachi says truly that these instances are perhaps trifling, but he adds that they display the *animus* towards Scotland. I am not conscious of being prone to ascribe improper motives to any person, especially to one for whom I have felt an affectionate regard; but really if Mr. Malachi had only the *animus* of misrepresentation, it would be difficult for him to stumble on a more unfortunate collection of assertions than are to be found in those letters, always excepting where he is discussing only his proper questions of banks and currency. Perhaps it might only be intended as a correct representation of the Malagrowther character, in like manner as a very honest gentleman may without offence, or any imputation on his morality, go to a masquerade in the character of a highwayman. If that is the case, I shall regret having misconceived Mr. Malachi's meaning and intention; but I must, in that event, be permitted to remark that in these letters the part is greatly *over-acted*.

These last observations apply equally to my third head of charge, viz., his unfounded attacks on the present Government. He assumes, or rather asserts broadly, that the intention to abolish small notes in Scotland was entertained by the Government on the sole ground of establishing a system of uniformity with England, and not with any view to the advantage of Scotland; and also that the resolution having been adopted to make it simultaneous with England, or at the end of six months, such resolution had subsequently been abandoned, and the period extended to six years, therein manifesting a "temporising and unmanly vacillation." Possessing, as you will readily believe, full knowledge as to everything that has been done, or intended to be done, by the Government on those several points, I deny flatly and unequivocally that there is the slightest foundation for any of the above assertions or insinuations; they are wholly and absolutely untrue. Our first impression was to leave Scotland untouched, and to comprehend in the measure only England and Ireland. On further discussion at a subsequent period, and after the receipt of information of which some amongst us had not before been in possession, it was judged advisable to include Scotland—not for the sake of uniformity, which no one ever dreamt of as a reason for such a change, but because it was thought for the permanent interest of that country, though it was deemed to be inexpedient that it should take effect there as soon as in England, or at an earlier period than six or seven years. Such are the real facts, and I need not point out to you how totally at variance they are with the assertions of the Malagrowther. Our decision may have been wise or the reverse; but here again a course was adopted the more effectually to guard against the risk or the evil effects of its having been erroneous. I wrote myself repeatedly to request that some well-informed gentlemen from the different banks might come to London in order to afford the fullest information on the subject, because it might very well happen that in legislating on a measure of that description various details which might be applicable to one part of the kingdom might be inapplicable and injurious to the others, and in the meantime everything relating to the Scotch question (and indeed the Irish also) was suspended. These gentlemen are now come to London, and I presume that in a few days, or at least an early period, proper opportunities will be afforded to them of explaining at full length everything they may think fit to urge upon the question.

I have now performed a task painful from deeply rooted feelings of regard and attachment to the individual whose assertions I have been compelled to notice, but *his* name having been ostentatiously put forth on the occasion, it has been impossible for me to avoid dealing with these assertions as they really deserve. I must request that you will communicate this letter *in extenso* to Sir Walter Scott, and you are at liberty to do the same if you chuse to any others of my private friends, only taking care that no copies of it are taken.—I remain, my dear Sir, yours sincerely,

(Signed) MELVILLE.

Sir Robt. Dundas, Bart.

Sir Walter Scott *to* Sir Robert Dundas.

My dear Sir Robert,—I return you Lord Melville's letter, and as it is chiefly intended for my perusal, I am under the necessity of adding a few observations.

My Lord Melville is fully entitled to undervalue my arguments and contravene the facts which I have aired. Very possibly the former may not be worth minding, and the latter in some degree incorrect, though I believe the general statement will be found substantial.

But I think it hard to be called a highwayman for taking the field on this occasion when God knows I had no personal booty to hope for. I think Lord Melville might have at least allowed the credit of Don Quixote, who took the field as an imaginary righter of wrongs.

Twice in my life I have volunteered in public affairs. Once about twenty years ago when, with zeal if with little talent, when I did so on behalf of an honoured friend and patron. By doing so I gave great offence to persons then high in office, some of whom thought it worth while to follow up the debit with something like persecution, insisting that I should be sent to Coventry by every friend I had connected with that side in politics. I have never regretted that I did this, though the result was painful.

In the present case the concern, which as an individual I am bound to take in the welfare of my country, has appeared to me to dictate another interference at which, to say truth, I did expect from the beginning some of my great friends would be displeased.

I cannot complain of the consequences in either of the cases, since I incur'd the risque of them voluntarily. But I think the motive leading me to a line of conduct which is at least completely disinterested, ought to have been considered.

I am perfectly aware that the pamphlet was warmly written, but its subject was warmly felt, and I would not term a blister inflammatory merely because it awakened the patient.

So much for intention and manner of expression. I have not the vanity to think Lord Melville wished me to enter into argument on the subject. Were I to do so with a view to his Lordship's private information, I could say very much connected with matters in which he is deeply interested to show why the course I have taken is beneficial to Scotland and to his Lordship as the guardian of her subjects. But the mode in which his Lordship has intimated his sentiments renders this impossible.

I might, I think, complain that so long a letter is sent for the purpose of being shown to his Lordship's private and confidential friends, and is not to be copied—although I am so deeply implicated—or even a copy of it permitted to remain with me, the person al, though not to whom the whole is written. Most of these individuals must in our little and limited circle be my friends also, and it seems hard that where such sharp language is used I am to be deprived of the usual privilege of putting myself on my own defence, and that before such a special jury.

The circumstances respecting the Naval Station and Military force are not written by me on my own authority, for I know nothing of the matter, but were inserted on the information of a personal friend, no less of mine than of Lord Melville, and they really are not founded on anything of much importance, and the general statement is not I think untested. The clubbery of our great Officers of State is certainly accurate. The facts alluded to by Lord Melville respecting something like insecurity of the banks I certainly never heard. But who was more distressed during the changeful events of the last war than the Bank of England? And so must every great commercial body during such extraordinary circumstances—it is not for such but for the ordinary state of commerce that laws are made. When danger comes according to circumstances Marshal Law is proclaimed. The Habeas Corpus is suspended, and the issuing of specie from the bank is dispensed with. But these, like the appointment of a Dictator in Rome, on the dictates of stern necessity. Legislators do not make laws for them.

I must with whatever pain to myself understand the circulation of such a paper without any copy being permitted as a general annunciation to Lord Melville's friends that Malachi is under the ban of his party. I am not surprised that Lord Melville parts lightly with a friendship which, however sincere, cannot be of any consequence to him. He cannot prevent me from continuing the same good wishes to him which no man has more sincerely entertained, and which no endurance of his resentment can alter.

Other times may come before we are either of us elsewhere, and he will find Walter Scott just where he was, without any feeling of animosity, but with the same recollection of former kindness.

I own my intention regarded the present question much less than to try if it were possible to raise Scotland a little to the scale of consideration from which she has greatly sunk. I think that John Hume mentions that Hepburn of Keith, a private gentleman of pleasant manners and high accomplishments, was regretted by the Whigs as having induced him to sacrifice himself to a vain idea of the independence of Scotland. With less to sacrifice and much fewer to regret me, I have made the sacrifice probably as vainly. But I am strongly impressed with the necessity of the case, and I know that not a man will speak out, but one who like myself is at, *above* and *below* consequences. Scotland is fast passing under other management and into other hands than Lord Melville's father would have permitted. In points of abstract discussion, quickness of reform, etc., the Whigs are assuming an absolute and undisputed authority. Now here was a question in which the people might be taken absolutely out of their demagogues, and instead of that our numbers strengthen the hands of these men with ministerial authority to cram the opinions of these speculative economists down the throat of an unwilling people, as they have crammed a dozen of useless experiments already. I could say more of this and to the same purpose, but I need not make both Whigs and mistaken Tories alike my enemies. And yet, if I could do good by doing so, I would not care much for any personal consequences.

Concerning the first part of Lord Melville's letter you are, I am sure, aware that individually I rather discouraged the application of the Clerks of Session for an augmentation, and signed the memorial in deference to the opinion of my brethren who, entertaining such a sense of their pretensions, I did not think I had any title to withdraw myself from their body. I certainly consider that we were and are harshly treated in the case of our brother Ferriar. As to the argument that good men will be got to fill our offices at less than our emoluments, I will engage that if every public office were exposed to auction on the Dutch principle that every man should underbid instead of overbidding each other, and preferring the lowest bidder, they would be all reduced to a very moderate standard. Old Fleming offered to be a King for £500 a year. How far this would lead to the improvement of the country is *de quo quæritur*, the improvement would be a radical one.

I have written a great deal more than I intended, and still I could write much more fully in the controversy, but I am conscious that I am a rash cudgel-player, and incapable of expressing regret. When I have no feeling except of sorrow, I think it is better to stop as I am.

When I say that I regret Lord Melville's alienation, I hope his Lordship will understand it is that of the friend and early companion, not of the Minister. In the latter capacity I have always found Lord Melville more kind and attentive to my personal concerns than I had any title to expect, and I think his Lordship will do me the justice to say I have seldom troubled him with personal requests. If I have been frequently an intrusive solicitor for others it has been for persons recommended either by talents, by distress, or by merits towards Government.

I wish you may be able to read this, but by candle-light I cannot write so distinctly as usual. I request you will transmit to Lord Melville. I have read it once over and keep no copy. But I should think it fair, with his Lordship's permission, that it should be shown to these friends to whom he wishes you to show his own letter. If I am wrong, I have a title that men should know that I have erred from honourable and patriotic motives. The event will show whether I have erred or not. If I have, there is not much harm done; and if I have not, I am sure I do not know whether I ought to be glad or sorry for it.—Adieu, dear Sir Robert, I am always affectionately yours,

WALTER SCOTT.

CASTLE STREET, 9 *March* 1826.

The Malagrowther letters treated of a subject on which Scott was ignorant; and he remarks in his diary, while writing the second letter, "Had some valuable communications from Colin Mackenzie which will supply my plentiful lack of facts." The Ministers were, not unnaturally, "sore beyond imagination" at such an attack; and Lord Melville's letter was their reply, one result being "a quarrel in all the forms" between Sir Walter's old friend and himself. It was not, however, permitted to last long. A message from Lord Melville was sent to Scott, through Sir Robert Dundas, expressing the assurance that however strong Lord Melville's dissent from Malachi's views on the currency might be, it would not be allowed to interrupt his affectionate regard for the author; and this message was accepted by Sir Walter in the spirit in which it was sent.

At one period of the struggle Sir Walter had had to encounter the keen wit and practised irony of Mr. Croker, who replied to the Letters of Malachi Malagrowther in the

Courier newspaper under the assumed name of "Edward Bradwardine Waverley." Mr. Croker's tone was highly provoking, and although, as his biographer candidly admits, the victory rested with the author of *Waverley*,[1] nevertheless some of his observations were sharp, and extremely well calculated to irritate his antagonist. Perhaps his best point was made in answer to Sir Walter's allusion to the edges of the Scottish claymores. "I shall not," he wrote, "stop to inquire whether the *edge of a claymore* is a good argument in a question of legal improvement or civil administration, nor will I insist on the obvious retort that if *claymores* had *edges* at Prestonpans, *bayonets* had *points* at Culloden." Often during his long literary career was the pen of Mr. Croker dipped in gall, but, although he considered that Sir Walter had "attacked with great violence and injustice the administration of Lord Melville, and, indeed, of our party in general," he had too much genuine regard for him to be as implacable as usual. Sir Walter, though quite prepared for a set-to,—"As to my friend Croker, an adventurer like myself, I would throw my hat into the ring for love, and give him a bellyful," he wrote to Sir Robert Dundas—as soon as he saw that he had gained his point, was also very ready to make up the peace. "I thought it best," he writes to Mr. Croker, "not to endanger the loss of an old friend for a bad jest, and sit quietly down with your odd hits, and the discredit which it gives me here for not repaying them, or trying to do so."

In 1826 signs of the coming storm, which was about to subvert the old political state of Scotland, began to appear. The family at Arniston were startled by hearing of a plot on the part of a section of the Edinburgh Town Council to throw off their old allegiance, and to elect the Lord Provost[2] as their member, in place of William Dundas, who had represented the city since 1812.[3] At the first intimation of such a piece of

---

[1] *Correspondence and Diaries of the Right Hon. John Wilson Croker*, vol. i. p. 314.

[2] The Lord Provost was Mr. William Trotter, upholsterer in Edinburgh.

[3] The hospitalities of the Arniston family to the Town Council had continued (from the days of the first President) down till shortly before this episode. Mrs. Dundas, wife of the Chief Baron, notes in her Diary, '*Sep. 2nd*, Arniston.—The Magistrates and Council of Edinburgh dined here; Gow played during dinner in the Hall.'

treachery, Robert Dundas seems to have pounced upon the unlucky Provost, and to have brought him to book. In a letter to his uncle, Lord Melville, he describes what took place:—

Robert Dundas to Lord Melville.

Friday, June 2d, 1826.

This morning Dr Wood, one of the town-councillors, informed me that three days ago a deputation of the trades waited upon Trotter, the Provost, to offer him uncle William's seat; that he (Wood) had just found this out by accident; that Trotter wished, if possible, to accept, but felt that it was almost out of his power to do so; that he was far from having given a decided negative; and that the negotiation was still going on.

Hope [1] and I saw at once that despatch was the only remedy; so, taking T. Cranstoun [2] with me, I went straight to the Provost. *He came into the room shaking and trembling and clearly ashamed of himself.* The general tenour of the interview was that he felt most highly flattered with the offer; that, however, he was pledged to uncle William, and that the seat was in his hands (the Provost's), as there was a clear majority in his favour; that he meant to call a meeting of "the chairs" that day to consult them; that he had not mentioned it to me or to Hope, or had not written to you; that he thought the best thing for our interests was to give no decided answer, as in that case the enemy would start some one else. I answered that of course *he* was pledged, and that I did not believe in the alledged majority, and that if he really looked to our interest, or indeed to his own, he should meet all such proposals with a decided refusal.

The prompt and vigorous steps taken for suppressing the civic rebellion were successful. The councillors were canvassed; and in a letter of the 4th of June to Lord Melville, Robert Dundas reports the result as being "twenty for us, and eleven against us, and two out of town." A note is preserved of the details of the canvass, giving in pithy remarks the characteristics of each of the voters, in terms more expressive than complimentary:—

---

[1] John Hope, Solicitor-General for Scotland.
[2] Thomas Cranstoun, Esq. of Harviestoun. He was agent for the family.

LIST OF TOWN COUNCIL.

(ENCLOSED IN MR. DUNDAS'S LETTER TO LORD MELVILLE.)

THE LORD PROVOST.

WILLIAM GILCHRIST, was out of town, but said to be quite steady.

ROBERT MITCHELL, quite steady and firm.

JOHN BONAR, quite steady.

ADAM ANDERSON, do. do., useful for information.

ROBERT WRIGHT, *false* and unfriendly: a decided foe, and dares not say so.

WILLIAM PATISON, a steady friend.

AL. HENDERSON, a friend, but unsteady character.

AR. M'KINLAY, a decided friend, and true as steel.

JOHN SMITH, do. do., also useful for information.

ROBERT SMITH, was away; said to be hostile: at *best* doubtful.

PETER FORBES, hostile and dangerous.

JOHN WAUGH, a friend, tho' a Puritan.

ROBT. HALL, a friend.

DAV. CUNNINGHAM, *a friend sure.*

ADAM LUKE, doubtful, but to be gained.

JAMES LEISHMAN, a friend and an honest man. A Whig, but thinks things as they are best.

DAVID M. GIBBON, } Two zealous, active, and useful friends,
DR. W. WOOD,   }   steady and zealous.

JAMES MILNE, a clever fellow, a Whig savant not to be depended upon.

DR. D. HAY, quite friendly at present, but scarce to be trusted. A Whig in politics, and a Puritan in faith.

ROBERT LEGATE, an honest, simple man, apt to be led away, but willing to do right. Is heartily sick of the whole business. Is right at present.

WILLIAM PURVIS, a conceited Radical and enemy.

JOHN MENZIES, the same, only with less conceit and less brass, but more dangerous.

JOHN GUTHRIE, a foe, also a fool.

JAMES NASMYTH, a bitter foe.

THOMAS MILLER, all right, but a Puritan I am afraid.

JOHN CLARK, a Whig and an enemy decided.

JAMES BROUN, a friend, but not to trust to.

T. SAWYERS, the focus of discord.

ALEXANDER MURRAY, an enemy, but a "turner."

ROBERT RIDIE, a friend.

W. PATERSON, ditto to Sawyers.

LORD MELVILLE *to* ROBERT DUNDAS.

Monday, 5*th June.*

MY DEAR ROBERT,—I have received to-day your letter of the 2nd, and also one from the Lord Provost on the same subject, viz., the modest proposal to elect *him* for Edinburgh. There is not time this afternoon, before the departure of the post, but I will to-morrow send you his letter, and the copy of one I have written to him. I hope that whatever may have been the threatened backslidings of the said Provost, or the formidable weight of his vanity, when put into the scale against his honesty, the Lord Register will have behaved to him as if he had spurned the offer with the utmost indignation.—Y^r ever, M.

A few lines from the Provost closes the correspondence. He is happy to hear Mr. William Dundas's majority is so decided, and hopes the election will be unanimous, "the object he had been anxiously endeavouring to attain! As to the other matters introduced into Mr. Robert Dundas's note, it can now serve no good purpose to discuss them, and therefore, with his leave, the Provost will endeavour to forget them."

On the 17th of February 1827 Lord Liverpool was seized with a fit of apoplexy, and although he survived its effects for some time, the illness brought his public life, and the Ministry of which he had been head, to a close. After some delay, the king determined upon the 10th of April to send for Mr. Canning, and to intrust him with the formation of a new Administration, of which he was to be the head. "Mr. Canning," says Wade, " forthwith began to make his arrangements under the impression that his former colleagues would bow to his supremacy; in lieu of which, within forty-eight hours after, seven leading members of the Cabinet sent in their resignations. These Mr. Canning on the 12th took to St. James's, and laying them *en masse* before the king, said : 'See here, sire, what disables me from executing your Majesty's will.' However, *before* separating from his late colleagues, Mr. Canning had opened negotiations with the leading Whigs, and ultimately the bulk of the opposition undertook to support him, without stipulating for the immediate possession of places, merely on the ground of approval of his late policy. Under these circumstances the Canning ministry was constituted."

The seven ministers who retired were the Duke of Wellington, Mr. Peel, Lord Eldon, Lord Melville, Lord Londonderry, Lord Bathurst, and Lord Westmoreland.

Those who took office under Mr. Canning were Lord Bexley and Lord Harrowby, along with Messrs. F. Robinson, Huskisson, and Wynn. It has always been thrown in the teeth of the seven retiring Ministers that their concerted action was taken specially with the view of preventing the formation of a Ministry under Mr. Canning. But, although the point is now of but little interest, it may be said that the late Lord Melville, who perfectly remembered all that took place, was able to state that such was not the case. Their refusal to act with Mr. Canning arose entirely from their knowledge that he, previous to their refusal, had been intriguing with the Whig leaders for their support.

The Whigs who were induced to join Mr. Canning and the section of the Tory party which adhered to him, were Tierney, Lord Carlisle, and Lord Lansdowne.

Although it was hoped by the more sanguine members of the Tory party that the *Piebald Administration*, as the new Government was nicknamed, would shortly succumb between the hostility of the great body of the old Tories, and the lukewarm support which was all that could be expected from the Whigs, still the Canning schism was a grievous blow to the stability of the Tory party.

In Scotland, particularly, the blow was one from which no complete recovery was ever made. The retirement of Lord Melville from the Admiralty involved his retirement from the management of Scottish business; and this event was regarded with various feelings. "The retirement of Lord Melville," says Cockburn, "from the government of Scotland was not an event for which, *in itself*, any candid Scotch Whig could rejoice; because no man, individually, could have conducted the affairs of the country with greater good sense and fairness, or with less of party prejudice or bitterness." Dr. Chalmers, on the other hand, writes: "The great deliverance which I feel in the recent changes is the removal of Lord Melville from an influence of which I am sorry experimentally that it had a most blasting and deleterious effect, both on the interests of literature and the Church."

Robert Dundas took a most gloomy view of the position of affairs. Although, as appears from the letters which he received, some of his friends thought otherwise, there can be no doubt that he was right, and that both the Tory party, and the influence of the Arniston family, had suffered irreparable damage from the recent crisis. It was not only that Lord Melville was out of office, and had no longer the business of Scotland in his hands,—that might have changed with another change of Government; but the whole system of Scottish management was altered. The first intention of Mr. Canning had, indeed, been to hand Scotland over to Lord Binning. But some of the Whig members remonstrated; and the result was that no Scottish manager was appointed. Lord Lansdowne, who became Home Secretary, conducted the business of Scotland himself; and Whig councils were those to which, as a Whig, he naturally listened.

It was under these circumstances that the following letters were written:—

LORD ABERCROMBY to ROBERT DUNDAS.

(*About*) *Feb.* 22*d*, 1827.

MY DEAR ROBERT,—I enclose for your private perusal and Hope's a few lines which I received from Lord M. two days after Lord Liverpool's illness.

It was written under the impression that Lord Liverpool would not long survive, and if in that event the Cabinet had decided, and easily one may fairly say, to do nothing in a hurry, the prolongation of Lord L.'s life is so far a sort of relief to them, as no arrangements can very well be made till he is in a state to tender his resignation and till the King comes to town.

Had either of the contending parties in the Cabinet felt themselves strong enough to dispense with the services of the other, this would not have been the decision.

My conjecture therefore is, that we shall have no material

change, and certainly none, in my judgement, to excite any uneasiness in your mind.

The case probably would have been between the Duke of Wellington and Canning. They are both tacticians, and I think we may leave it to them to settle the point of supremacy. My conjecture is that Canning will content himself with less than *all*, and we shall see what concessions may be made from the other side.

A great difficulty remains behind, and I cannot solve it, namely, how Lord Liverpool's place is to be supplied in the House of Lords. I do not agree in opinion with your uncle (Lord Melville) upon this point; it is not likely that Canning will leave the House of Commons.

If I hear anything worth communicating I will let you know.

We shall be most happy to see Mrs. D. and you at the time you mention. I believe I must go to town to support my friend Pinkie[1] on the 12th.—Yours sincerely,   ABERCROMBY.

ROBERT ADAM DUNDAS, M.P., *to* ROBERT DUNDAS.

LONDON, *May* 31, 1827.

MY DEAR ROBERT,—Yesterday I received your letter, and although I enter in some degree into your feelings with regard to the present state of affairs, particularly with regard to Scotland yet I cannot see any reason why you should be so dreadfully apprehensive of utter ruin. I by no means consider Lord Melville's interest and yours placed in so lamentable a situation. I by no means consider your future prospects for ever checked by the late changes in the administration; and I am by no means convinced that these changes have met the approbation of the King, or the sense of the country. At the time Mr Pitt went out of office, Scotland was placed in a far more awkward predicament. What was said at Lord Melville's impeachment as to your prospects of success in public life? What was said at the death of Mr. Pitt and the changes that then took place? Every one of these changes was apparently a death-blow to all the former interests established in Scotland. At that time there were individuals in Scotland who endeavoured to establish an ascendancy there, and whom we had every reason to dread. At present the case is totally different. If Lord Lansdown were Minister to-morrow, and all of us in rancorous opposition with the Duke of Buccleuch, Lds Hopetoun and Lauderdale, who

---

[1] Sir John Hope of Pinkie.

is the most *malignant* Peer in the House with the exception of Lord Grey, the Whigs could not establish a powerful interest. From what I saw of Hope at the time he was here, it appeared to me that he was acting most judiciously. Should **Canning break faith** with him, of which I have very little doubt, **should Lansdown** as Secretary of State insist on having the patronage of **Scotland,** then you will have a most favourable opportunity of striking **your colours also.** On no account at present talk of giving up your office. As a friend of Mr. Peel it is the worst and most injudicious step you could take; he would give you no such advice. That **Canning is a rogue I am** convinced, **and were I to** give you a history of all the details of his late intrigues which are now become common topics of conversation in society, you would be astonished at the lies and tricks of the R^t Honble gentleman. I am equally certain that Hope forms a very false impression of his integrity, and the stability of his government, and that a short experience will show that he has been completely deceived. Read the debates and see what a fool the Whigs have already made of Canning. He pressed strongly on the House the **impropriety** of disfranchising Penrhyn. His emissaries were on the long trot the whole evening, every minister spoke on his side, and yet see how he was beaten. Read the squabbles every night about the **Test and Corporation Acts;** and see how weak he is with all his new adherents against him. In short there is not a great *constitutional question* on which the Government is unanimous. It is quite absurd to suppose this can go on long, and I can assure you the public opinion is becoming more decided every day against the present Administration. All that we desire is a *question* to justify *fair opposition*, and I have no doubt of Mr. Peel's power in the Commons.

I have not sat behind the Treasury Bench[1] since the late changes. Henry Scott[2] you may trust; he is with Mr Peel. In Adam Hay,[3] John Campbell,[4] and Duncan Davidson,[5] you have sworn allies. They have proved it on the Leith Police Bill Committee, and will prove it against Dalrymple and the Police Commissions to-day. Do not despair. Were you here, you would view public affairs under a very different aspect to what you do in Edinburgh.—Y^r sincerely,   R. A. DUNDAS.

---

[1] Mr. R. A. Dundas was member for Ipswich.
[2] Henry Francis Scott, M.P. for Roxburghshire, afterwards Lord Polwarth.
[3] Adam, afterwards Sir Adam Hay, M.P. for Selkirk, etc.
[4] John Campbell, M.P. for Dumbartonshire.
[5] Duncan Davidson of Tulloch, M.P. for Cromarty and Nairn.

DAVID ANDERSON OF MOREDUN *to* ROBERT DUNDAS.

MOREDUN, 9*th July* 1827.

MY DEAR SIR,—My brother Adam [1] has communicated to me the conversation you had with him two days ago respecting the state of the county politics, when you mentioned to him that in the event of an immediate dissolution of Parliament it was not impossible but that some member of your family might come forward as a candidate for the representation of the county.

I am happy to take the earliest opportunity of expressing the respect that both my brother and I entertain for your family, and of assuring yourself that if you have any thought of standing for the county you may depend upon our most zealous and hearty support.

With the members of Lord Melville's family I have but a very slight acquaintance, but entertaining as we do a hereditary respect for Lord Melville, and admiring most sincerely the high-minded feelings which have influenced his conduct during the late changes in administration, I have no hesitation in saying that were Parliament to be dissolved at present, we would give our cordial support to any son of his that might offer himself to the county.

To our present member [2] I entertain every feeling of regard and good-will, but he has attached himself to an administration which I can by no means approve of, and which, as it is supported by the most violent of the Whig party, I cannot but regard with feelings of great suspicion.—Y^r most faithfully,

D. ANDERSON.

Mr. Canning died on the 8th of August, and was succeeded as Premier by Lord Goderich. But his term of office was short. Before his death Mr. Canning had resolved to appoint a finance committee to inquire into the state of the revenue. Lord Goderich revived this project, and, on the advice of Mr. Huskisson, proposed to nominate Lord Althorp as chairman. Mr. Herries, who was Chancellor of the Exchequer, took offence because he had been passed over, and sent in his resignation. It was not accepted. But he and Mr. Huskisson were now on such bad terms that the Prime Minister found it impossible

---

[1] Adam Anderson, afterwards a judge with the title of Lord Anderson.
[2] Sir George Clerk of Penicuik.

to reconcile them; and the result was that the Administration came to an end.

The King sent for the Duke of Wellington, who, in January 1828, succeeded in forming a Cabinet. Lord Lyndhurst was Lord Chancellor; Mr. Goulburn, Chancellor of the Exchequer; Mr. Peel, Home Secretary; Lord Dudley, Foreign Secretary; Lord Palmerston, Secretary at War; and Mr. Grant, President of the Board of Trade. Mr. Huskisson was appointed, against the wishes of many among the Duke's supporters, Colonial Secretary. During Lord Liverpool's long term of office Lord Melville had been in the Cabinet as First Lord of the Admiralty; but he now consented, to the disappointment of his friends in Scotland, who wished him to insist on having one of the highest offices in the Government, to become President of the Board of Control.

LADY MELVILLE *to her Nephew* ROBERT DUNDAS.

GREEN STREET, *Jan. 21st*, 1828. Evening.

MY DEAR ROBERT,—I would have written by this day's post, but was so hurried by house visiting, and visits to particular friends, that I had no time, and I now prepare a letter as the same impediments will recur to-morrow.

I am anxious to make my confidential communications to *you*, but you must understand that they are to be confined to yourself. The statement you see in to-night's *Standard* is, I believe, correct; the appointments are as stated there, so far as I understand, and after the manner in which Lord Melville's immediate friends treated his resignation, and the allegations they made at that time in regard to the Duke of Wellington, I cannot but confess that I do sincerely regret the turn the appointments have taken, as they regard the Duke. The fact, I believe, is true that in spite of the complete secrecy which the Duke had insisted on as to his arrangements, by some neglect or worse, the projected list got into the *Morning Chronicle* the very morning that Lord Melville was to arrive, and before his opinion could be taken. When he arrived he found the Duke and Mr. Peel were in great indignation and Mr. Peel declared his perfect readiness to accommodate to any other arrangement for himself if Lord Melville had any objection to return to the Board of Control, and would take the Home Office. Lord Melville, of course, said that which office he was to fill was immaterial to him, so long as it was not incompatible with his circumstances and situation, as he had no other view than to make himself useful in the most efficient manner in which he was able. The Duke said he had given it to be understood that he considered it due to Lord Melville to leave him entirely at liberty to choose his office; but that for many reasons difficulties presented themselves. He had found it advisable to propose to Mr. Huskisson and to Lord Dudley to continue in office, though he had pledged himself to no one for any particular office till Lord Melville should arrive to make his own determination, but that the expiration of the charter[1] being likely before long to require a special consideration, he did feel it was by no means unimportant how that office was filled now, and therefore he stated his wish, without intending to fetter Lord Melville thereby. Of course Lord Melville felt that it was very unfit to be bargaining for a thousand a year or a little piece of precedence, and therefore acceded at once, but knowing as I do, the way in which it has been alledged that he had been the "dupe of the Duke of Wellington's ambition and Lord Eldon's pique," the Duke having at last taken the Premier's place, those who have made the accusation will think it substantiated, particularly as reports of Lord Melville's being intended for it had arisen (probably) from the intention manifested to wait his arrival for the final arrangements. I cannot deny that I am very much afraid that the public impression will be that the Duke has not redeemed his pledge, and I exceedingly wish that Mr. Peel had been appointed to the Premiership; but there seems to have been difficulties that could not be reconciled any other way, and there is a great feeling that the Duke's decision of character is at least something to rest upon for a ground of hope that something like a distinct line of policy will be adhered to. If therefore any abuse of the Duke or discontent at Lord Melville's not being as Lord Abercromby advised "as near the top as possible" is manifested among our friends, I beg you will take the high tone, and maintain that the confidence which has been manifested by the Duke and Peel makes it wholly immaterial whereabout he stands in the play-bill. I am very sorry any Canningites are retained, and my confidence is much shaken thereby as to stability, believing them all *to be no better than they should be*, but it seems to be thought that it is a *necessary policy*, and we must swallow the pill without making wry faces. After the manner in which all Lord Melville's friends have acted by him, the conduct of Sir George

---

[1] The East India Company's Charter.

Clerk and the Solicitor,[1] and the language I have heard from your uncle William, and know Lord Abercromby to have held, I cannot help having great anxiety for Lord Melville's vindication proving full and complete; though, in my own mind, I feel the undoubted honour of his proceedings admits of no question, and am entirely aware that all those who were politically acquainted with him here did him ample justice, the dirty conduct of the gentlemen [2] whom he had been instrumental in bringing into office, in and from the north (of whom the Advocate seems the only one who has acted with honour), has certainly made a strong and unfavourable impression upon me. If, however, their interests fail, he is not now to be charged with having broken them. The policy he pursued has so far found its level that the king has been compelled to resort again to the assistance of the statesmen with whom he had divided, and if, by having themselves depreciated the measure, they have entailed weakness and insecurity, they have only to thank the paltry love of present profit that induced them to *ask* what they ought to do, instead of confiding in the judgment of the man who had the conduct of those interests for twenty years creditably. As your interests may now be deemed decidedly to coincide with his, I have no doubt *now* about opening my mind to you. If now the measures pursued are to be changed as before and confidence denied, because much is to be objected to, the reasons of which the conductors of the business only can sift and decide upon, they must e'en go to the dogs. It is the King who has desired the Duke to take the Premiership, and, had he persevered in refusing it, he must have resisted the positive command. What is yet to be done with the army is not known. I think that a fearful point in the question, for though I think no man did ever unite so much political with such powerful military talent, the powers of man must be limited.

Sir George Clerk called on me yesterday, and (as I thought) looked so blank, that I could not help feeling as if I let him see I thought so, tho' I did my best not to do so.

I hear Lord Wharncliffe, Lady Canning, etc., etc., are furious at Huskisson for coming in with us.—Y'rs aff'ly,   A. M.

Lady Melville's letter explaining Lord Melville's reasons

---

[1] Solicitor-General Hope.

[2] The persons alluded to are Sir W. Rae, Lord Advocate, John Hope, Solicitor-General, Sir George Clerk, and William (afterwards Lord William) Keith Douglas.

for accepting the India Board was by no means unnecessary. Among many of his friends in Scotland, who looked upon him as the leader of the Tory party there, a strong feeling existed in favour of seeing him re-occupy at least as prominent a post in the Ministry as he had done under Lord Liverpool. Robert Adam Dundas in particular expressed his views strongly upon the impolicy of Lord Melville's accepting the India Board. He himself was anxious to give his services to the Government, and to work under Lord Melville in any "*creditable*" appointment. Robert Dundas wrote to Lord Melville (January 29, 1828) urging that an appointment should be given to Robert Adam. In the same letter he expresses his own views as to himself. The return of the Duke of Wellington and Mr. Peel had made him dismiss his late gloomy ideas of the ruin he supposed to be impending over the Tory party. "*Now*," he says, "considering the present political state of the Scots bar I trust I am not too presumptuous in allowing these prospects again to revive.[1] Under these circumstances I wish to make you aware that were I Solicitor-General my first step would be to obtain a seat in Parliament for the sake of doing all that my powers would permit of helping the Ministry. I should do this whether the Lord Advocate was in Parliament or not, and *that*, at any sacrifice of professional emolument, for the sake of devoting my whole time and labour exclusively to public business. The county of Edinburgh would naturally be the seat to which I should look, and I trust you will not think I am interfering with Henry's[2] interests in holding this opinion."

Lord Melville at once answered—

LONDON, *Feb.* 2, 1828.

MY DEAR ROBERT,—If your letter had arrived *one* day sooner, Robert Adam would have been an un-salaried Commissioner at the India Board. We must have two Commissioners who are not Privy Councillors, and as Lord Graham, one of those who is to receive a salary, is a Privy Councillor, I settled with Mr. Peel to let his own brother's name be inserted, being at a loss for any other person. I thought of Robert Adam, but did not choose to

---

[1] Alluding to the probable early promotion of Lord Advocate Sir William Rae to the bench, with Hope for Lord Advocate and himself for Solicitor-General.

[2] Henry, Lord Melville's eldest son, subsequently third Lord Melville. He sat for Rochester in the last Parliament of George IV.

2nd Lord Melville.

take upon myself to appoint him without his knowledge or consent, though I should have held your suggestion to be sufficient. I am very sorry it was not done, as he would have been of more use to me than any of the others.

With regard to your own coming in for Midlothian, Henry, of course, will never stand in your way, as he never dreamt of it, unless you did not choose to come forward. I only doubt the prudence of it, as far as your professional views are concerned, and it is not more than a week since I objected to having John Hope brought into Parliament, because it is most inconvenient to the public service, especially with the great increase of criminal business, that both the Lord Advocate and the Solicitor-General should be absent from Scotland for several months in spring.

Lord Melville's appointment at the India Board lasted but a short time. On the resignation of the post of Lord High Admiral by the Duke of Clarence, the Duke of Wellington replaced Lord Melville at his old quarters at the Admiralty, where his knowledge of the business of naval administration was very much wanted. The vacancy at the India Board was filled up by the appointment of Lord Ellenborough. This began his connection with Indian affairs, which ultimately led to his appointment as Governor-General, and in the end to his celebrated recall by the East India Company.

Although by the return of the Duke of Wellington to power, accompanied by most of the members of the former Liverpool Administration, the Tory party seemed to be firmly re-instated in office, the feeling against such of the Tories as had *ratted* by continuing in office under Mr. Canning was very keen. Among those who had in that way offended his party was Sir George Clerk. The Dundas influence in Midlothian had been given to him, and to Lord Melville he owed his first place in the Administration. For a man under such obligations to have deserted his party in their time of need was felt to be an unpardonable offence; and although the offence was condoned by his re-appointment to office on the Duke of Wellington's return to power, the local members of the party in the county were by no means inclined to be so forgiving, and a desire was expressed by many of the leading freeholders of showing their disapproval of his political course by refusing to return him on his vacating his seat on his new appointment in the Wellington Ministry. The correspondence on the subject at Arniston is lengthy, but enough is now given to show how matters stood.

On the 1st of February, Robert Dundas wrote to Lord Melville, putting two questions: "1st, Should I stand for the county? 2d, If not, should Henry try? As to the 1st there exists more than one strong objection against my doing it—

"1. The chance of defeat by the junction of the James Gibson party with those who might not wish to turn against Sir George after nineteen years' services.

"2. The difficulty of holding the county without residing at Arniston, which under existing circumstances is quite out of the question.

"3. The expense attending such a seat in contested votes, etc.

"4. The probability of Parliament, especially for such a seat, interfering so much with my profession as to form a bar against any future promotion therein.

"5. The fact of having another seat ready either now or whenever it may be more convenient for me to take it. If this were not the case, I should have run the risk rather than totally give up all prospect of being in Parliament.

"2d. As to the next question: Ought Henry to try? The 1st objection here also occurs, and I must candidly and openly state that I fear it exists with greater force in his case than in mine, as from constant residence I have had the opportunity of making more personal friendships and connections among the electors than what Henry can have done. In this I *may* be wrong, but I fear I am right. None of the other objections apply, and I therefore think Henry ought to try it for the following *reasons:*—

"1. If he or I cannot turn out Sir George *now*, we never can.

"2. I fear from all accounts that his present seat will not be again secured, except at an expense which he cannot bear, and far beyond what the county will cost him.

"These two reasons seem to me sufficient to induce Henry to try."

The concluding sentence of Robert Dundas's letter to Lord Melville is worthy of special notice, as illustrating the complete and thorough-going nature of the revolution soon to be effected, by the Reform Bill, in the management of the Scottish constituencies:—

"The conclusion therefore is," he says, "that he should now try the county, leaving to me, at such time as will best suit me, the less respectable, secure, and easy sent for the town which my uncle William is ready to give me whenever I please."

LORD MELVILLE to ROBERT DUNDAS.

GREEN STREET, *4th Feb.* 1828.

MY DEAR ROBERT,—I have received to-day your letter of the 1st inst., and have only to say that as far as I am concerned, I have not the least objection to your starting for Midlothian on the present vacancy. I presume the writ will be moved to-day. I should object to Henry (his son) coming forward, because it would look like a personal, and therefore an unworthy, attack on my part against Sir George (Clerk), after I had acquiesced in his continuing in office under the new administration; but the case is totally different with regard to you, whose natural position it is to represent the county, and who have much better claims to it than Sir George. I do not wish to urge, or even to recommend you to do it, because I have no personal feeling against him, and also with reference to your private concerns; but if you decide on coming forward, you have a right to my concurrence and cordial support, which most assuredly you shall have. *He* has no claim on me, and I only acquiesced in his remaining in office now, because he offered to resign in April last if I wished it, or would advise him to do so, and because I did not choose to do anything that might appear like pique or vindictiveness. His continuing to represent Midlothian is quite another affair, if you choose to oppose him, but for your own sake you ought to be tolerably sure of success before you embark in such a contest. He expressed a wish to come to the India Board with me, which I declined, as it would have had the appearance of his being *my* nominee, and I requested the Duke of Wellington to put him anywhere else if he was to continue in office under the new Government.—Ever yours affect^{ly},

MELVILLE.

On the same day Lady Melville wrote as follows :—

GREEN STREET, *Feb. 4th*, 1828.

I am clearly of opinion you *ought* to start. I certainly do not understand why, if Sir George Clerk could not remain at the Ordnance, he was to have another office; but I understand he has been trying to get himself in as Under Secretary in Husky's department, and there he would not have had to vacate his seat. They say there is a general amnesty for *Rats*.

I am so disgusted with all this year's business, that I was never in worse humour with Politics. I believe the old system of things must fail, for the *purifications* of the last half-century have made *Riches* the only available *Talent*—the last that ought to prevail if the good of the community in general is to be considered. Thus *dirt* must always be the basis of power, till some renewal of temptation to those who can use their talents with honour can be held to those who have them, that will not make honour the losing game.—Yours very sincerely, A. MELVILLE.

Robert Adam Dundas was equally explicit in expressing his feelings, that after Sir George Clerk's tergiversation, his return for Midlothian should be opposed. He says :—

ARNISTON, *Feb. 5th*, 1828.

MY DEAR ROBERT,—With regard to Lord Melville's objection,[1] I wish you to be aware that as long as Henry and I are in Parliament, the County may be assured that when your professional duties call you from London, its business will not be neglected by either of us. It is absurd for a moment to suppose that the freeholders expect you to abandon your profession. Your presence in London will not be required as much as you may naturally suppose. I beg you also to understand that as long as Mary and I can find *a corner* for you, you will make *our house* and no other your abode in London. My decided opinion is, that you *should not* allow Sir G. C. to be returned for the county.—Ever yours in haste, R. A. DUNDAS.

Ultimately, the prudent counsel of the Duke of Buccleuch, Lord Hopetoun, and, in particular, of Sir John Hope, prevailed, that no opposition at that time should be offered to

---

[1] Alluding to Lord Melville's dislike to both the Lord Advocate and Solicitor-General being in Parliament at the same time.

Sir George Clerk's return. It was felt that once, to use Lady Melville's expression, an amnesty had been granted to the Rats, it would be ungracious to oppose his return on a vacancy caused by his having been appointed to an office under the Government, of which his opponents were keen supporters. There was also the risk of the Whig party taking the opportunity of the schism in the Tory camp to carry their man. Sir George was, however, informed that abstention from opposing his return on that occasion implied no obligation of future support, and that in all probability Robert Dundas would become his opponent at the next election, whenever it might happen.[1]

The successive Administrations of Lord Liverpool, Mr. Canning, and Lord Goderich had each contained the elements of discord; and the Wellington Government suffered from the same misfortune. There was hardly a question on which the Ministers agreed. The important subjects of the Corn Laws, Foreign Policy, and Parliamentary Reform were all so many bones of contention, any one of which might at any time lead to a collapse of the Government. "The Cabinet," Lord Palmerston notes in his journal of the 22d of May 1828, "has gone on for some time past as it had done before, differing upon almost every question of any importance that has been brought under consideration:—meeting to debate and dispute, and separating without deciding." It was on a question of Parliamentary Reform that the final quarrel took place. It had been conclusively proved that the constituency of East Retford was hopelessly corrupt; and a bill was introduced by Mr. Tennyson, the member for Blechingley, for the transference of the franchise from East Retford to Birmingham. On the day on which the bill was to be considered in the House of Commons the Cabinet met. The Ministers were at variance, and separated without deciding what should be done, although the mode of proceeding which appears to have been thought most advisable was that suggested by Lord Melville, namely, that each should be free to vote as he pleased. In the House that afternoon there was a division. Mr. Peel voted in favour of a proposal to transfer the representation of East Retford to the

---

[1] Mr. Peel was of the same opinion, and felt that it was an awkward moment to choose for opposing and ousting Sir George.

adjoining hundred. Mr. Huskisson and Lord Palmerston voted in favour of transferring it to Birmingham. Mr. Peel was in a majority of eighteen. Here the matter ought to have ended; but the division led to the resignation of Mr. Huskisson, who was followed out of office by Lord Palmerston, Lord Dudley, Mr. Lamb, afterwards Lord Melbourne, and other Canningites.[1]

The following letter was written to Mr. Dundas by Sir William Rae, while it was as yet uncertain how the Ministerial crisis, caused by the division on the East Retford question, would end :—

SIR WILLIAM RAE, LORD ADVOCATE, *to* ROBERT DUNDAS.

LONDON, *May* 23, 1828.

MY DEAR DUNDAS,—You will have heard there is a bit of a rumpus in the Gov^t. I believe the truth to be this: in the Retford question, though the mode of proceeding had been adjusted in the Cabinet, Huskisson and Palmerston did not support Peel, and divided against him. Huskisson walked home with Planta,[2] who said that Huskisson should resign, and accordingly he wrote a letter to the Duke of Wellington, dated at two in the morning, resigning. The Duke went forthwith to the King, who approved of its being accepted. The Duke accordingly wrote to H. expressing general regret at losing him, and wishing him well. This brought an answer bearing that H. had only meant to place his resignation in the Duke's hands. A reply from the Duke contradicted that view of the matter, and bore that he would keep no man in the Government who chose to express a desire to leave it. A rejoinder followed, of a description as if meant for publication, and there the matter rested yesterday, and there it will rest, unless H. *asks* to be retained. In doing this he will lose character. In keeping him otherwise the Government would suffer, which, you and I will agree in thinking, would be worse. It seems strange that a man of the age of Huskisson should not have chosen to sleep upon a matter of such grave importance. If he had waited till morning, and spoke to the Duke, all would have been well, as they have all along been on very good terms.

Lord Palmerston, it seems, said something to the Duke about

---

[1] The Canningites were Mr. Huskisson, Lord Dudley, Lord Palmerston, the Duke of Portland, Lord Eliot, Lord George Bentinck, Mr. Charles Grant, Mr. Lamb, Mr. Evelyn Denison, and Mr. Frankland Lewis.

[2] Joseph Planta, M.P. for Hastings.

resigning, which his Grace hardly deigned to notice; he afterwards observed he was not going to take a cannon to kill a butterfly. All this, mind, is for your private ear.—Yours ever most truly,
W^M. RAE.

What Sir William Rae alluded to in the last paragraph of his letter was, probably, the interview which took place between Lord Palmerston and the Duke of Wellington on the afternoon of Tuesday the 20th.[1] Lord Palmerston had represented to the Duke that Mr. Huskisson had merely offered to resign if the Duke wished it; but the Duke maintained that he had actually resigned, and that it was impossible to *request* him to remain in office. Lord Palmerston then said that if Mr. Huskisson went out he must do so too. "I remarked," says Lord Palmerston, "that while I said this he raised his eyes, which had been fixed on the ground as we were walking up and down, and looked sharp and earnestly at me to see whether this was meant as a sort of menace, or a party measure."

There can be no doubt that the Duke had been anxious for some time to get rid of Mr. Huskisson; and on the 25th he was able to inform him that his successor at the Colonial Office had been chosen.

SIR WILLIAM RAE *to* ROBERT DUNDAS.

LONDON, *May* 26, 1828.

MY DEAR DUNDAS,—Huskisson is out.

The Duke sent for Lord Dudley on Saturday morning, and said there must be an end of the then state of matters, and that if he did not hear from H. before two o'clock, he would go to the King. Dudley soon after returned, and requested that the Duke would say something to smooth the way. But the Duke said no; that whatever was to be passed was to be in writing, and that whatever had passed verbally must go for nothing, but that he would wait till two.

The hour came, and no letter, so off went the Duke to the King. It is believed that a countryman of our own will be the successor in the colonial office, but I am not at liberty to say more. We shall not suffer by this change; we lose a man of talent, but a united Treasury Bench is of more importance in the House of Commons.—Yours faithfully,
W^M. RAE.

---

[1] Bulwer's *Life of Lord Palmerston*, vol. i. p. 261.

HENRY DUNDAS *to* ROBERT DUNDAS.

BROOK STREET, *May* 28, 1828.

DEAR ROBERT,—I have no doubt you will have received the news of the secession of Husky with the same satisfaction that I felt on first hearing of it. Sir George Murray is to be his successor. This is the only appointment I believe that is decided.

Charles Grant, I understand, has also resigned. Sir Henry Hardinge and Sir George Clerk have both been named as successors to Lord Palmerston. I think the latter quite impossible, and should not think he could wish to move so soon. One resignation seems much regretted, that of the *Doodley*.[1] It was not expected he would have thought it necessary to take this step, in consequence of Husky's secession, and I think, for a man of his rank and station to identify himself with such a man as Husky is much beneath him. Besides, if my information is correct, he expressed himself as thinking Husky to have acted a very wrong part, and as he seems to have given great satisfaction in his office, his resignation is rather to be regretted, particularly as it gives a sort of rallying point for the Canning party, which, had he remained, would otherwise have sunk into nothing; for as to Husky or Grant, no one cares one damn about them. The general opinion in the city when these resignations were first mentioned, was that it would have the effect of establishing the Government on a stronger footing. The Duke has got the entire confidence of everybody, and has acted very firmly and discreetly in this business. Husky wanted to retract his offer of resignation, or, at least, to explain it away as only intimating his readiness to resign, if it was thought necessary, and not as a positive tender of his resignation. This was a regular quibble, and the Duke very properly sent the second letter, as he had done the first, to the King, who, it is said, showed no dissatisfaction at the retirement of Husky, but rather the reverse.

William Lamb[2] has also resigned, for no other reason, it would seem, but having come into office with that party, he chose to retire with it, not having, as I can learn, any objection to remain with the Duke. And if the vote on the East Retford Bill had anything to do with these changes, he had no reason at all to retire, having voted in the majority, and against Husky. I am sorry he

---

[1] Lord Dudley.
[2] William Lamb, afterwards Viscount Melbourne.

has resigned; altho' a Whig, he is a very good one, a decided anti-reformer, and has, I believe, given great satisfaction in Ireland. Taken all in all, he is a good man, and very sound in his opinions.

The day after the division on the East Retford Bill, Paddy Holmes[1] met the Duke, and told him he had done his best to procure a good attendance of members, but that he was not prepared for some circumstances attending the division; and as that night a division was again expected, he wished to know whether he should advise gentlemen to vote with Mr. Secretary Huskisson or Mr. Secretary Peel. The Duke laughed and said, "By God, you're quite right, this won't do, it must be put a stop to." I only hope now we shall go on better in our House: things have not gone on at all well. It has been nothing less than the adoption of every measure of opposition, and weak concession on every point. Peel has disappointed the hopes of many people; he has not nerve enough, and wishes to have the idea of always acting what he calls a[2] . . . part; that, in fact, he gives way on everything, and, of course, the support he meets with is proportionally weakened. I only hope he will now take a decided line; any embarrassment he may have felt with the Canningites is now removed, and if he does not show fight when necessary, the party must fail. He wants political courage. What says that crocodile Hope to all this? Does he mean to follow Husky in his retirement? Or is resignation only a virtue he preaches, not practises?

I expect to sail for Corfu very shortly.

I am now going to celebrate the birth of Mr. Pitt at the City of London Tavern, Lord Skelmersdale in the chair.—Ever yours,
H. D.

ROBERT ADAM DUNDAS *to* ROBERT DUNDAS.

MIVART'S HOTEL, BROOK STREET,
June 3, 1828.

MY DEAR ROBERT,—You will see in the newspapers an account of last night's debate, in which the united efforts of the Whigs and Canningites to throw discredit on the Duke of Wellington were completely defeated. Huskisson's defence was lame and unsatisfactory to the House. Brougham could not defend it. The division of last night has established the Government, and the

---

[1] William Holmes, Esq., M.P. He filled the office of Clerk to the Ordnance, and acted for many years as Whip to the Tory party in the House of Commons, where his Irish wit and good humour made him a universal favourite.

[2] Word wanting, owing to the letter being torn.

second division, to which I particularly refer you, clearly shows the unpopularity of Huskisson's conduct, even in the House of Commons. After the first division the Whigs gave up all for lost, and left the House, with the exception of twenty-five, who retained their seats on the right hand of the chair, the side on which they divided. The other side of the House was brimfull of the friends of the Government to the number of 220, who to a man maintained their places behind Peel. The effect of this was more striking than anything I ever witnessed in the House of Commons, or anywhere else. Such decided and determined support I never saw given to any man, and the effect of the empty benches on the side on which the opposition divided was no less singular in its way. Peel's friends kept their places till he left the House, and followed him out.

The support which the Government received last night was beyond my most sanguine expectations, considering the influence Canning used in forming the Parliament. Now that the miscreants have been dragged through the mire by Huskisson, and left in *the slough of despond*, in which situation I trust they may long remain, we may again enjoy the happiness of seeing firmly established a united Tory Government, which, in my humble opinion, never was more required, considering the situation of public affairs at home and abroad, and considering the utter contempt in which foreign powers hold every individual of the Canning faction.

The Duke of Wellington, in spite of all the abuse lavished on him, has shown no want of energy in the late proceedings of the Government.—Yours sincerely, R. A. DUNDAS.

In February 1830 Sir S. Shepherd, on account of ill health, resigned the office of Chief Baron of Scotland. The event had been long anticipated, and it was considered in Scotland that on account of his position, long services, and fitness for the post, the vacant appointment should have been bestowed upon Sir William Rae. However, the policy of conciliating the Whigs which was then being pursued by the Duke of Wellington and Mr. Peel, induced them to pass over their own Lord Advocate in order to appoint Mr. James Abercromby Chief Baron, a man of whom it was felt by the Scottish Tories that his sole claim to the appointment lay in his being a Whig. Besides the respect felt for Sir William Rae on account of his long public services, he was personally popular. All this rendered stronger the irritation felt against the Government on account of the way in which they had behaved; and it is said that afterwards the Duke himself regretted the step, and acknowledged that he had behaved badly to Sir William Rae. At Arniston there are a variety of letters from John Hope, the Solicitor-General, to Robert Dundas, who was then in London, on the subject, expressive of the feeling in Scotland upon the treatment of Sir William Rae. "The treatment of the Advocate," he writes on the 10th of February, " is scandalous. I think it the very harshest and most unfeeling thing any Government ever did. I remember in history (that is, from 1689) nothing in political life more cruel, more infamous. . . . The cry against Lord Melville is louder and more general than any ever raised in my time as to any public and personal matter. I must fairly add that 9-10ths of people believe, and ever will, either that Lord M. desired to drive Rae to resign, or that Lord M. has as little to say as in July 1827. . . . I am too disgusted with the treatment of Rae to write more about it." On the following day he writes again : "Jeffrey said to me to-day that they all view this as a decided degradation to the Scotch bar, and are far from thanking Il Imperatore for it. . . . *What can they do for Rae?* The subject is to me full of disgust. There is not palliation or excuse."

Had Sir William Rae been appointed Chief Baron, John Hope would have succeeded Rae as Lord Advocate, and Robert Dundas expected to succeed Hope. But even if these arrangements had been carried out their duration would have been very brief, for the Scottish political régime was then tottering to its fall, and six months later the Tory Government had come to an end, and the old state of things with it.

The Catholic Emancipation Act had been unpopular among the Duke of Wellington's supporters in Scotland. "The Duke of Wellington," says the *New Scots Magazine* in February 1829, " before whom the fortunes and the genius of Napoleon were bowed down, has quailed beneath the gasconading rant of some Irish mountebanks and bog-trotters." From the day on which he rose in the House of Commons to declare his sudden conversion to Catholic Emancipation, Mr. Peel had been openly accused of the basest political apostasy by many of those who had been his warmest admirers. In the House of Commons, as well as in the country, the authority of the Government was seriously shaken; and their followers looked forward in many cases with grave apprehensions to the chances of a general election. In spite, however, of these untoward circumstances, William Dundas was again returned, at the election of 1830, for the city of Edinburgh, the seat he had occupied so long. Henry Dundas, Lord Melville's son, was returned for Winchelsea, and Robert Adam Dundas for Ipswich. This Parliament was dissolved on the 23d of April 1831, in the midst of the wildest political excitement which the country has probably ever known. The second reading of the English Reform Bill had been carried; but Ministers had been defeated in committee on General Gascoyne's motion that the number of members for England and Wales ought not to be diminished. Mr. William Dundas did not present himself for re-election; and the Tory candidate for Edinburgh was Mr. Robert Adam Dundas, son of Mr. Philip Dundas, fourth son of the second President.[1] Born in 1804, he was called to the Scottish bar in 1826, and married, two years later, Lady Mary, daughter of the seventh Earl of Elgin. From 1826 till the dissolution of 1831 he had been member for Ipswich. But he was now nominated for Edinburgh, which had been so long represented by some member of his family. The Whig candidate was Mr. Jeffrey, then Lord Advocate, who had consented to stand somewhat unwillingly, as he was well aware that, however strong the popular feeling in his favour might be, it was very improbable that the town-council would elect him. His opinion proved correct. The town-council still stood firm to their old colours, and, on the last occasion of exercising their ancient privilege of returning a member to Parliament, elected a Dundas. As their privilege was certain to be extinguished, to stand by their old political faith, and by the family with whom they had for so many years been politically connected, was perhaps the most

---

[1] Mr. Philip Dundas represented Gatton in Parliament from January 1803 till April 1805, when he was appointed Governor of Prince of Wales Island. He died, when on board ship on his way to India, in April 1807.

dignified mode of exercising it for the last time. There was, however, a division, and the numbers were 17 for Dundas, 14 for Jeffrey, and 2 for the Lord Provost, who had also been nominated.

Outside the Council Chambers, in the Royal Exchange, an immense crowd had collected, prepared to give a rough reception, not so much to the new member, against whom they had probably but little ill-will, as to the Provost, whose conduct in ignoring the wishes of the citizens was bitterly resented. The moment the Chief Magistrate appeared, the rioting began. "The Lord Advocate," said a paper of the day, "being a little man, and having to struggle only with the blessings of the people, got easily out of the throng. The Provost, who is, *ex officio*, a big man, did not escape so easily. We said last week, that an Edinburgh mob was no joke, and the Lord Provost's nose on Tuesday bore woful testimony to the truth of our assertion. What could tempt any man in his sober senses, the moment after he had braved the whole population of the town, to appear on foot in the midst of a numerous and exasperated band of them, we do not pretend to divine." It was with the utmost difficulty that the Provost was rescued; and at one time his life was actually in danger. He was caught up and held over the parapet of the North Bridge; but fortunately he had the presence of mind to seize one of his assailants and declare that he would not go down alone. Ultimately he reached his home in safety, but only under the protection of a guard of soldiers.

The city was for some hours in the hands of the mob, the useless civic guard having been easily overpowered. In the course of the night an attack was made on the Dundases' town house, No. 69 Queen Street. The family were at Arniston, and did not hear of what had taken place till next morning, when the terrified servants reported that the windows had been broken by stones, and that they had been compelled to take refuge in the back parts of the house.

It chanced that in the drawing-room there was a handsome mirror belonging to Lord Abercromby, which Mr. Dundas, before leaving for Arniston, had carefully covered up. Lord Abercromby had, early in the century, sat for Edinburgh as a Tory, but had afterwards joined the Whig party, to which most of his family belonged; and, on hearing of the damage done to the house, Mrs. Dundas laughingly said that it would have served their old friend right if his mirror had been left to the tender mercies of the Radical mob.

The result of the general election in Scotland was a majority of three in favour of the Ministry; while in England the supporters of the Reform Bill secured so many seats that, when Parliament met, the second reading was carried by a majority of 136.

After a year of turmoil the English Reform Bill passed on the 4th of June. As it was now certain that the Bill for Scotland must speedily become law, when a general election would at once take place, a serious question arose as to what seats should be contested in the Conservative interest. Midlothian and the city of Edinburgh were the seats in which most interest was felt at Arniston. As to whether Midlothian should be contested there was no doubt. There the issue was very uncertain. With occasional intervals the Dundases had possessed the seat for about one hundred and ten years, and it could not be relinquished without a struggle. The Arniston influence was given to Sir George Clerk, who, like his opponent, Sir John Dalrymple, was already in the field.

It was otherwise with regard to Edinburgh. There the Whigs, or rather the Radicals, were enormously strong; and it was felt to be almost a hopeless attempt. But the Dundases were naturally averse to giving up a seat which they had held for nearly forty years, and the following letters will suffice to describe the views which were entertained by Mr. Robert Adam Dundas and other practical politicians upon the subject:—

Mr. R. A. Dundas *to* Mr. Dundas.

LONDON, *June* 13, 1832.

DEAR ROBERT,—I had intended to have written to you yesterday with reference to the future representation of the city of Edinburgh, and it is necessary that you should lose no time in consulting our friends who meet at Blackwood's and so ably support the Conservative cause.

It is for them to determine what is to be done.

For my own part I see so little chance of success, or even of

Robert Adam Dundas
afterwards
Nisbet Hamilton

obtaining a reasonable minority in a constituency of at least 1200, that it may be a question whether we are prepared or not to hazard a contest. I am, however, willing to place myself in the hands of the party either to stand a contest *on certain conditions*, or at once to withdraw in favour of a more popular candidate. I cannot undertake a contest if the election is to be conducted in the manner in which elections generally are conducted. Were I to agree to this, I should inevitably *be ruined*. If however the party in Edinburgh are willing to conduct the contest, and professional men be ready to lend their gratuitous services so that I shall be liable only for my own personal expenses, then I am willing to place myself at the disposal of the party whether the struggle be successful or not. I have consulted Sir John Forbes on the subject, and suggested to him whether it were likely that the Radicals would let him come in with the Lord Advocate. If such an arrangement could be made, which I believe would be made more easily with another party than myself who am so objectionable to the Jacobins, and more especially to those in Edin^r, as having been elected by the Town Council, I believe it would be for the interest of the Conservative cause that I should withdraw and seek my fortune elsewhere. Sir John Forbes desires me to say that he is most unwilling to be a candidate, and that he must have time to make up his mind if he should be selected. He authorises me also to say that he will undertake no contest except on an understanding that it is to be the contest of the party and not for his own personal gratification. I beg that you will assure the gentlemen of the Committee at Mr Blackwood's that in coming to a decision on this question they will best consult my wishes in determining on what will be most advisable for the interest of the Conservative cause without reference to any views of ambition I may have in continuing to represent the city of Edinburgh. Let this, however, be distinctly understood, that neither Sir John Forbes nor I can acquiesce in any arrangement which will involve us in an engagement to be liable for more than our personal expenses. Pray lay this letter before the gentlemen of the Committee, and let me have their answer as soon as they have decided.—Y^{rs} very sincerely,   R. A. DUNDAS.

P.S.—Sir J. D.[1] swears till he is black in the face that there were no flags at the Radical meeting *such* as I described.

---

[1] Sir John Dalrymple. It was reported that flags of a disloyal character had been displayed at a reform meeting in the previous month.

Mr. Robert Adam Dundas *to* Mr. Dundas.

Private.

LONDON, *June* 15, 1832.

DEAR ROBERT,—I have received your letter this morning, and Sir John Forbes will explain in person his views and mine with respect to the representation of the city of Edinburgh. My opinion most decidedly is that if Aytoun split the Whig party, one Tory candidate will have a better chance than two, as I suppose no one dreams of the possibility of two Tory members for the city of Edinburgh. And if you can get in one you will be very fortunate. I must have it distinctly understood that I am to have *no agent* retained for me, nor will I hold myself responsible for the acts of any agent whatever.

The contest must be conducted by the party.

It is only at the solicitation of the party and in consequence of the complexion of the votes after they are registered that I shall allow myself to be an instrument in the hands of the Committee to carry their views into effect without rendering myself personally responsible for their actions.

There is no agent in Edinburgh whom I would trust with the unbounded use of my purse, and I believe that Sir John Forbes and I are of the same opinion on this point. I write this in confidence, in order that you may be prepared with my views as to the manner in which a contest is to be conducted in Edinburgh. Sir John Forbes will see you soon after his arrival in Edin^r, and will tell you more. In the meantime, till something is settled by the party, and I am informed of their plans, I shall remain here.

In haste.—Y^{rs} ever, R. A. D.

Mr. Robert Adam Dundas *to* Mr. Dundas.

Private.

CHARLES STREET, *June* 22, 1832.

DEAR ROBERT,—I received your letter this morning, and in answer beg to assure you that no man will be found in London to enter into a contest for Edinburgh on the expensive system which is likely to be created by the men of business in that place. I send you some suggestions which, if adhered to, will make people of Conservative principles come forward without compromising their character or ruining their fortunes. The suggestions which I enclose for the use of our friends in the north are founded on my own experience and on the principles on which all elections have lately been conducted in England and will be conducted under the

Reform Bill. On such principles contests for London and Westminster and the county of Dorset have cost the candidate nothing!!! Whereas on Mr. Fisher's principles of paid agents, drinking-houses, &c., I would not undertake a contest in Edin' if I had £30,000 given me to conduct it. Most heartily do I congratulate myself that I am out of the scrape. I expect an answer from Ipswich to-morrow. My last election there stood me less than eight hundred pounds. My first in £5000, thanks to the attorneys! and the freemen were better pleased with the last election than the first. If I am again invited, it will be still less, as there are no out-voters.

You should stir up the press against the system pursued in Berwickshire by Marjoribanks. Are the independent householders to be crammed into voting by dint of beef and pudding? And who canvasses on this plan? Why, those persons who railed against the expense and corruption of former elections. *Hit this point hard*, it will do good. The suggestions to which I alluded, and which are in a separate enclosure, are not to be made generally public, but you may safely show them to your confidential friends who are likely to take a share in the management of elections under the Reform Bill.—Very sincerely y^{rn}, R. A. DUNDAS.

P.S.—The Duke of B. is in communication with Irvine, but he will not place himself in the hands of the writers to be pigeoned.

Ultimately Mr. Forbes Blair was selected as the Conservative candidate, in opposition to Jeffrey and the Right Honourable James Abercromby, and the canvass of the city went on during the remainder of the summer. Mr. Aytoun, a Radical candidate, was also in the field, but he withdrew in favour of Mr. Jeffrey and Mr. Abercromby.

The county was also thoroughly canvassed during the summer; and there are some memoranda on the subject among the Arniston papers in the handwriting of Mr. Dundas which show that he did good work for his party at this exciting crisis.

The election for the City took place on the 18th and 19th of December, when, as was expected, Mr. Jeffrey and Mr. Abercromby were returned. The numbers were—

Jeffrey,	4035
Abercromby,	3850
Blair,	1519

On the same day as the result of the Edinburgh election was declared, Sir George Clerk and Sir John Dalrymple were nominated for Mid-Lothian. The voting took place on the 21st and 22d. There were three polling places, Edinburgh, Midcalder, and Dalkeith. At Edinburgh the numbers were very close. At Midcalder there was a large majority for the Whig candidate. But in the Dalkeith district, where the Arniston influence was strong, and where Mr. Dundas had canvassed so hard for his party, Sir George Clerk had a good majority. When the poll closed the numbers were—

    Sir John Dalrymple, . . . 601
    Sir George Clerk, . . . 536

Sir John Dalrymple, the new member for Mid-Lothian, well deserved his success as the reward of a life-long struggle against what had hitherto been hopeless odds. He was the active and unwearied leader of the Whig party in Mid-Lothian, and never missed a chance of forwarding their interests. Apart from political reasons, no one at Arniston grudged him the victory he had won. His second wife, Lady Adamina Duncan, was a niece of Chief Baron Dundas. Through all the trying years of political strife, both Sir John and his wife retained unaltered their friendship for their Tory relatives; and there are some letters in the collection at Arniston from Sir John to Mr. Dundas upon county matters, in which they had a common interest.[1]

When the first general election under the new system came to an end, the Scottish counties had returned twenty-one Whigs and nine Tories, and the burghs had returned twenty-two Whigs and one Tory. The single Tory burgh member was Colonel Baillie, who was elected by a majority of seven for the Inverness Burghs. There was thus a majority of forty-three votes to ten in favour of Lord Grey's Administration.

The highest hopes of the Whigs and the worst fears of the Tories had been realised; and with this election the long continued supremacy of the Tory party in Scotland came to an end. Few could have supposed, on the formation of the Duke of Wellington's Administration, that within the short space of

---

[1] In 1840 Sir John succeeded, as eighth Earl, to the Earldom of Stair. He died in 1853.

two years the whole of that elaborate structure of political power, which had been erected and maintained with such distinguished ability by the leaders of the ruling party, and above all, by the members of the house of Arniston, was to be shattered to pieces. But nothing less had taken place. The old system had completely disappeared, and its place had been taken by a new system, the results of which, then unforeseen, politicians are perhaps now only beginning to realise.

PLASTER WORK, HALL, ARNISTON.

CHAPTER XIV.

ROBERT DUNDAS OF ARNISTON—*continued*.

Conclusion of the Memoirs.

On the passing of the Reform Bill and the complete defeat of the Scottish Tory party, which implied the annihilation of the political influence which his family had for so many years enjoyed in Scotland, Mr. Dundas at once recognised that any hope he might have entertained of political advancement through the Scottish bar was at an end. He decided upon retiring to Arniston and settling there with the view of transferring his energies from political life to the management and improvement of the estate. This was no sudden change in his plans of life. So long before as February 1828, when the Duke of Wellington had returned to power, and the prospects of the party had brightened again, he opened his mind to Lord Melville upon the subject of his future career. His friend John Hope [1] had been advising him never to allow the thought of Parliament at any future period to enter his mind, that he ought to stick fast to the Courts, and if appointed Solicitor General to quit that office for the Bench as soon as he was able. In reply he said he never could agree to that doctrine. The object of his ambition was to represent Mid-Lothian in the House of Commons, and professional promotion was only the step whereby to attain it. Had he chosen a profession for pecuniary emolument, it would not have been at the bar, but in India that he would have sought a fortune. He could scarcely say, he concluded, with what difficulty he would resign the object of his ambition for the line pointed out by Hope.

---

[1] Afterwards Lord Justice-Clerk Hope.

Robert Dundas of Arniston.

But now the turn which public affairs had taken relieved Mr. Dundas from the necessity of choosing between the career which he had planned for himself and that which Mr. Hope recommended; and henceforth his life was that of a country gentleman. Fortunately, at this time, an opportunity presented itself not merely of developing the resources of his estate, but also of providing himself with an object of interest as a substitute for the occupation he had lost by leaving the bar. This was the fitting and working the coal of Stobhill by himself instead of leaving it in the hands of a tenant, as had of late years been done.

The advantages to be derived from railroads as a means of transport for minerals had become generally recognised, and endeavours were being made for their introduction into most of the mining districts. Some time before, a variety of plans had been set on foot for the construction of railways between the Mid-Lothian and East Lothian collieries, the city of Edinburgh, and the shipping port of Leith. Among the principal promoters of these plans were the Marquis of Lothian [1] and Mr. Dundas in Mid-Lothian, and Sir James Suttie [2] in East Lothian. Their collieries laboured under the disadvantage of a long cartage by road. Mr. George Suttie [3] advocated the construction of a line from the north side of Edinburgh near the Abbey Hill, with a branch diverging into East Lothian. Another line, however, starting from the south side of Edinburgh at St. Leonard's, was the one adopted at that time. But on the general introduction of the railway system, Mr. Suttie lived to see his scheme adopted by the North British Railway Company, as he had urged should be done twenty years before. Power had been got for the construction of a horse railroad from Edinburgh to Dalhousie; and the work was in progress when Mr. Dundas settled at Arniston. From Dalhousie it was being extended by the Marquis of Lothian to his colliery at Bryans. Through the kindness of Lord Lothian Mr. Dundas was enabled to extend the Newbattle branch as far as Arniston Colliery, thus bringing his coalfield into direct communication with Edinburgh. The

---

[1] The seventh Marquis of Lothian.

[2] Sir James Grant Suttie of Prestongrange and Balgone.

[3] Afterwards Sir George Grant Suttie. He worked his Colliery at Prestongrange for many years.

Arniston Colliery was at that time in the hands of an incompetent tenant possessed of neither capital nor energy. After much trouble Mr. Dundas succeeded in purchasing from him a renunciation of the lease; which was followed by his refitting the colliery on a scale suited to the enlarged trade which was expected. These operations gave him ample occupation, involving as they did a large outlay and the share of trouble and anxiety inseparable from mining adventure. However, he was spared to see the work on which he had embarked brought to a successful issue, and in full operation.

The period of nineteen years between 1819 and 1838, during which Mr. Dundas was possessor of Arniston, was not one of much progress in agriculture. The shock caused by the transition from the high prices of farm produce during the war to the stagnation which followed the peace pressed heavily upon the landed interests. Under the stimulus of high prices, improvements had been pushed forward at too rapid a pace. Landlords had incurred an expenditure in reclaiming waste land, and tenants had entered into corresponding engagements. This ended in bringing loss upon both, and it was long before the pressure ceased to be felt.

In 1823 a calculation was published by Mr. Scott of Airfield, near Dalkeith, showing the extent to which the price of farm produce had fallen since 1815. He took the instance of a farm of 240 acres, half clay, half sharp land, naturally dry, and suitable for turnip-growing. Supposing the clay land to be cropped on a six-years' rotation (fallow, wheat, hay, oats, beans, and wheat), and the turnip land to be cropped on a five-years' rotation (turnips, barley, pasture—two years—and oats), he found that the produce, deducting seed, was worth at war prices about £9, 9s. per acre, and at the prices current in 1823, about £5, 9s. per acre.[1]

It was not until shortly before the time of Mr. Dundas's death, in 1838, that the period of agricultural depression passed away. He lived to see the introduction of thorough drainage by Smith of Deanston, and a tile-work erected upon his estate for the purpose of carrying Smith's system into effect.

---

[1] The produce was reckoned at the following rates per acre: Wheat, 5 quarters; oats, 10 to 12 bolls; beans, 8 bolls; barley, 9 bolls; and hay 200 stones.

About the same time he had also seen the first threshing-machine upon the estate driven by steam power erected on his farm of Redheugh. But in 1838, tile-draining and the application of steam as a motive power for agricultural purposes had made so little way as to be rather indications of the direction of progress than improvements which had come into general use. On the whole, in the upper district of Mid-Lothian, little change had been effected upon agriculture in the nineteen years ending with 1838.

The first general election after the passing of the Reform Bill had found the Scottish Conservatives in a prostrate condition. The loss of the power which they had so long enjoyed was a source of deep mortification and regret. But feeling the revolution through which the political condition of the country had passed to be beyond recall, they set to work to do the best they could to retrieve their losses. To none of them was the change a greater blow than to Mr. Dundas. A keen partisan, as could not indeed well otherwise be the case, head of a family which had long borne the leading part in the administration of Scottish affairs, and endowed with abilities which qualified him for following in the steps of his ancestors, his keen temper chafed at the changes which had swept away the influence which it had taken so many years of strenuous exertion to build up. He and his friends, however, threw their whole energies, cheerfully and bravely, into the reorganisation of their defeated party on its new basis.

Not only had the constituencies of Scotland returned an overwhelming majority of Liberals; but when the first reformed Parliament met, the estimated strength of parties in the House of Commons was 486 Liberals to only 172 Conservatives. Yet the Government of Lord Grey, apparently so strong, and enjoying all the prestige of having carried the Reform Bill, grew weaker and weaker, and more and more unpopular, as each succeeding month passed by. In 1834, Lord Althorp resigned because of differences with his colleagues on the Irish question. Lord Grey, believing it to be impossible to carry on the Government without him, gave up the seals. Lord Melbourne was sent for and requested to attempt the formation of a Coalition Ministry with the Duke of Wellington and Mr. Peel. But he declined; and a purely Whig Ministry was formed.

In the new Ministry, Lord Althorp was Chancellor of the Exchequer and Leader of the House of Commons. So long as he remained in the Commons, the Administration retained the semblance, at all events, of vitality. But in the autumn he was called to the Upper House as Lord Spencer. This raised the delicate question of who should lead the House of Commons. The ministers decided that Lord John Russell was the man. The King objected. But the ministers were saved the embarrassment of a controversy with the sovereign; for on the 14th of November they were peremptorily dismissed from office. Sir Robert Peel was recalled from Rome, where he was spending the autumn; and a Tory Administration was once more in power. Parliament was dissolved; and Sir Robert Peel went to the country on the principles of reform announced in the famous Tamworth Manifesto.

In Mid-Lothian, Mr. Dundas and his friends had the satisfaction of regaining the lost county seat. There were now 1376 registered electors on the roll. Of these 1099 voted. The candidates were Sir George Clerk and Mr. William Gibson Craig,[1] younger of Riccarton. In the Midcalder district the latter had a large majority. But in Edinburgh and Dalkeith Sir George was far ahead. The result of the poll was:—

Sir George Clerk, . . .	565
Mr. Gibson Craig, . . .	534

When the new Parliament met on the 19th of February 1835, though the Conservatives had gained largely, there was a Liberal majority of about one hundred: and in a few months Lord Melbourne was again Prime Minister.

In the autumn of 1836 there was a contest for the Lord Rectorship of the University of Glasgow. Sir Robert Peel was nominated by the Conservatives. Sir John Campbell, afterwards Lord Chancellor, and at that time Attorney-General, was also put up. "But," he says, "I had a very powerful opponent—no less a person than Sir Robert Peel,—and Conservatism was making great progress among the professors, who exerted themselves to the utmost against me. When it came

---

[1] Afterwards Sir William Gibson Craig, Lord Clerk Register of Scotland.

to the election I had only one nation, and he had three." The election of Sir Robert Peel, a trivial matter in itself, gave an opportunity of uniting with his installation as Lord Rector a great political banquet, at which he might have an opportunity of addressing himself to the leading Conservatives of Scotland, who, it was hoped, would assemble from every part of the country.

The banquet was a great success, and was attended by more than three thousand persons. This crowded assemblage cheered the leader of the Opposition as he discussed three topics—the advantages of an Established Church, the necessity for preserving the House of Lords, and the dangers of a democracy. The speech was received with enthusiasm, and had a great effect upon the party at large. The banquet was held on Friday the 13th of January 1837, and the London *Morning Herald* performed the marvellous feat of giving a full report on the following night, Saturday the 14th; a man, for whom relays of horses were provided, having been sent with the report from Glasgow to London in the short space of twenty-two hours.

A large party had been invited to Blythswood, by Mr. Campbell, to meet Sir Robert; and Mr. Dundas was among the number. He returned home highly pleased with the results of the gathering in the west, and hopeful of its good effect upon the future prospects of the Tory party.

The short but memorable reign of William IV. was now drawing to a close. An Edinburgh newspaper of Thursday the 22d of June contained a bulletin which said, "When the last messenger left Windsor, His Majesty was still alive." But at that time news was longer in travelling from London to Scotland than it now is in travelling from London to Australia. The King had died early on the morning of Tuesday the 20th; and two days before the mail reached Edinburgh, the young Queen, whose good fortune it was to be to wear the British Crown during many years of unexampled prosperity, had, in the presence of her assembled councillors, accepted the "awful responsibility" of her new position.

Parliament was dissolved on the 17th of July. But long before that day preparations for the general election had been going on in Scotland. In Mid-Lothian the nomination day was the 31st of July, when a crowd of 10,000 people gathered at the town cross in Edinburgh. The candidates were Sir George Clerk, proposed by Captain Burn Callendar, and Mr. William Gibson Craig, younger of Riccarton, proposed by Lord Dalmeny. "The interest excited among all classes by this election is beyond all former example," says the *Courant*. There had been two elections since the Reform Act. The first had been won by the Liberals. The second had been won by the Conservatives. This, the third election, was therefore the cause of intense excitement in the country. The voting began at nine o'clock on the morning of the 1st of August; and when the poll closed at four o'clock on the 2d, the numbers were:—

Mr. W. Gibson Craig,	703
Sir George Clerk,	661

By the 12th of August the elections in Scotland were at an end. The Conservatives had gained seats in the counties of Caithness, East Lothian, Inverness, Lanark, Perth, Renfrew, Ross and Cromarty, Sutherland, and Wigtown. But they had lost Mid-Lothian, Banffshire, Orkney and Shetland, and Roxburghshire. The returns thus showed a clear gain of five county seats. In the burghs, however, the prospect was as dark as ever—the Kilmarnock district being the only burgh constituency in Scotland which returned a Conservative member.

The balance of parties in the Scottish constituencies was:—

Counties,	19 Conservatives, 11 Liberals.
Burghs,	1 Conservative, 22 Liberals.

When the new Parliament met the Scottish Conservatives had the satisfaction of seeing not only that their party had gained a substantial measure of success in the counties of Scotland, but also that in England the Liberal strength was considerably reduced.[1]

In past days the family at Arniston had been staunch supporters of the Church of Scotland, while in return the members of the Moderate party, so long dominant in the

---

[1] The estimated strength of parties in the first Parliament of Queen Victoria was 348 Liberals to 310 Conservatives.

Church, could generally be reckoned upon as safe and reliable Tory voters.

The owners of Arniston had also, for many generations, taken an active part in the deliberations of the General Assembly, as being inseparable from the secular politics of the country. But a change was now coming over the parties within the Church. The Moderate party was rapidly losing its ascendency; and its opponents, with their impatience of state control, were gaining the preponderance in the church courts. In 1837, the Presbytery of Dalkeith, as they had done for many years, appointed Mr. Dundas to be their lay representative in the General Assembly. But matters in the Presbytery looked so threatening that Mr. Goldie, the minister of Temple, felt himself bound to unburden his mind upon the subject.

REV. JAMES GOLDIE *to* ROBERT DUNDAS.

TEMPLE, 28*th March* 1837.

SIR,—By this time I suppose that you will have received a letter from the Presbytery of Dalkeith intimating that on Tuesday last they had elected you their Elder to represent them in the next General Assembly. Allow me to remind you to answer their letter, and also suggest some means to keep them in humour, for the majority of them next year will be *decidedly* on the wild side of the church. This, you will remark, is owing to the good sense or good taste of the Tory patrons. What appears to me might be done is that you should wait upon the Presbytery at Dalkeith at their first ordinary meeting, and thank them for electing you as their Elder, and invite them to dinner at Arniston.

Excuse the liberty I have taken, and believe me to be, &c.,

JAMES GOLDIE.

Mr. Dundas also attended the General Assembly of 1838, the Presbytery of Dalkeith having again elected him to represent it, and returned to Arniston disgusted with the proceedings which he had witnessed, and auguring evil consequences from the course on which the leaders of the majority seemed bent upon entering. But attendance at that Assembly proved to be the close of Mr. Dundas's public life—an attack of illness which proved fatal having seized him a few days after his return home. His active work upon his estate, in politics, and in the church, was thus brought suddenly to a close at an early period of life. He died at Arniston, on the 8th of June 1838, in his forty-second year, and was buried in the family burial place beneath the chancel of old Borthwick Church.

Mrs. Dundas survived her husband many years, continuing to live at Arniston during her eldest son's minority. But in 1845, by the death of her uncle, Sir Philip Durham,[1] the succession to the estates of her own family in Fife and in Mid-Lothian devolved upon her; and in compliance with the entail she assumed the name of Durham. She resided upon her family estate during many years, devoting herself to the good of the people upon it, until failing health compelled her to live abroad. She died in Italy in 1883 at the age of 84.

Mrs. Durham was the last of her race. And among the vicissitudes of families it is not often that a once tolerably numerous family disappears so completely as the Scottish Durhams have done. From Sir William Durham of Grange, who lived in the time of Robert Bruce, descended several families, who were settled upon estates in Forfarshire, Fife, and the Lothians. But one after another they have all died out, and so completely has this been the case that among the landowners, large farmers, and residents whose names appear in the County Directory of Scotland, the name of Durham is not to be found.

Mr. Dundas was survived by many of those who had started with him in life, some of whom have been mentioned in the later pages of these memoirs. His uncle, the Right

---

[1] Admiral Sir Philip Durham, G.C.B., of Largo and Polton, was both a fortunate and distinguished officer during the long French war. As a lieutenant he was one of the few of those who were saved when the *Royal George* sank at Spithead—and as a captain he was most fortunate in the number of prizes made by the ships under his command. Among these may be mentioned the French frigate *Loire*, captured after a severe action by his ship the *Anson*. He was one of Nelson's captains at Trafalgar, where he commanded the *Defiance*, 74; and was wounded. As Admiral his good fortune did not forsake him, for while on his way to the West Indies on board the *Venerable*, 74, he fell in with and captured the two French frigates *Iphigénie* and *Alcmène* of 44 guns each.

Sir Philip sat in two parliaments, first for Queenborough, and subsequently for Devizes; but attendance at the House of Commons was not to the old Admiral's taste.

By the deaths of his two older brothers and his two nephews, without male heirs, Sir Philip inherited the family estates. He died in 1845 at the advanced age of 83.

Hon. William Dundas, the Lord Clerk Register, so long member for Edinburgh, lived till 1845. Mr. Robert Adam Dundas was returned to Parliament for North Lincolnshire at the general election of 1837, and sat in the House of Commons till 1857. In 1852 he was Chancellor of the Duchy of Lancaster in Lord Derby's Administration. He assumed the name of Christopher instead of Dundas, in compliance with the will of Mr. George Manners of Bloxholm Hall, and afterwards took the name of Nisbet-Hamilton, when Lady Mary,[1] his wife, succeeded to the Belhaven and Dirleton estates in 1855. In East Lothian, Mr. Nisbet-Hamilton was very popular. He spent a great portion of each year in the county, and was a generous supporter of the good old sport of coursing. At one time he was asked to stand for the county, as a supporter of the Corn Laws ; but he preferred the seat for North Lincolnshire, and declined. He survived the repeal of the Corn Laws, the introduction of household suffrage in burghs, the introduction of the ballot, and many other changes which would have been thought impossible in his younger days. He died in London on the 9th of June 1877. One of Mr. Dundas's younger brothers, Mr. William Pitt Dundas (third son of the Chief Baron), who held the office of Deputy-Clerk Register for nearly forty years, was a well-known figure in the streets of Edinburgh until a short time ago. He had been called to the Bar in 1823, and at his death, in 1882, was one of the oldest members of the Faculty.

The second Viscount Melville's official life ended with the fall of the Duke of Wellington's Administration in 1830 ; but for twenty years after he continued to take an active and useful part in the public life of Scotland. In 1843 he was appointed Chairman of the Royal Commission of Inquiry into the Poor Law of Scotland. "The Commissioners," says Lord Cockburn, "have not been selected so wisely as they might ; but Lord Melville's being at the head of them is a sufficient guarantee for the whole. A more industrious, business-like, sensible, and candid chairman could not have been got, or indeed fancied." The Report of this Commission was presented to Parliament in May 1844. The valuable mass of

---

[1] Lady Mary Bruce, eldest daughter of the seventh Earl of Elgin.

evidence which it had collected bore ample testimony to the ability of Lord Melville; and in 1845 Lord Advocate M'Neill[1] carried through Parliament the Poor Law Act for Scotland, which was based on the recommendations of the Commission. Lord Melville died on the 10th of June 1851, in his eightieth year. "Robert, the second Viscount Melville, has gone," writes Lord Cockburn in his journal. "After holding high offices, and performing their duties well, he retired from public life about twenty years ago, and has ever since resided quietly at Melville Castle. But though withdrawing from London and its great functions, he did not renounce usefulness, but entered into every Edinburgh work in which it could be employed with respectability. He was at the head of the Scotch Prison Board, a very active member of the Board of Trustees, did the whole county business, and the friends of every useful measure deemed themselves safe if they could only get him to engage in it. He deserved this unanimous public trust by plain manners, great industry, excellent temper, sound sense, and singular fairness. There could not possibly be a better man of business." He was succeeded by his eldest son, Henry (the Henry Dundas, some of whose letters, written at the crisis caused by the resignation of Mr. Huskisson, are printed in these Memoirs), who, entering the army in 1819, commanded the 83d Regiment during the insurrection in Canada in 1837, and became Major-General in 1854. He received the thanks of Parliament, and was invested with the Order of the Bath for his services at the battle of Gujerat; and was appointed a General in 1868. He died in February 1876.

At his death in 1838, Mr. Dundas was succeeded by his eldest son, Robert, the present proprietor of Arniston.

But here this volume of family history must be closed. It ends where it began, among the old Temple lands on the banks of the South Esk in Lothian. The passing away of three centuries has brought about many changes in the appearance of the country, and in the habits of the people. But the whole of that fertile valley through which the North Esk and the South Esk flow, on their way to the Firth of Forth, is still full of the memories of the past. There is probably no other

---

[1] Afterwards Lord Colonsay.

part of Scotland where, within the circuit of a few miles, the student of history can find so many scenes of interest—the homes of men who have borne a distinguished part in the political, and legal, and literary history of Scotland—spots which have been sung of in our national poetry, Roslin's castled rock, Dryden's groves of oak, caverned Hawthornden; the battle-fields of Pinkie, Rullion Green, and Prestonpans; Craigmillar, Borthwick Castle, Crichton Castle, and Carberry, famous in the story of Mary Stuart; Dalkeith, the home of the Buccleuchs; Inveresk, where lived "Jupiter" Carlyle; Woodhouselee, Oxenfoord, Melville, Newbattle; all these places, and many others which have been mentioned in these Memoirs, are within a dozen miles of Arniston.

Much of Scottish history has been made by the men who, from one generation to another, lived and died within that narrow limit; and old George Dundas and Dame Katherine Oliphant little thought what an important part was to be played by the descendants of the younger son, for whom they thriftily saved money, and bought the Mains of Arniston.

ARTHUR'S SEAT FROM ARNISTON.

INDEX.

ABBEYHILL, where Lord Arniston died in 1753, aged 67, 109.
Abbotsford, 299.
Abercromby, George (Lord Abercromby), on Lord Melville's acquittal, 263.
—— Lord, writes to R. Dundas, Feb. 1827, 331: at one time M.P. for Edinburgh, 351.
—— Rt. Hon. Jas., is appointed Chief Baron, 348; elected for Edinburgh 1832, 355.
—— Sir Ralph, 263 *note*.
Adam, Sir Fred., 307.
—— R., architect of Arniston, 248.
—— Rt. Hon. Wm., of Blairadam, 277 **note**.
Adam Square, where President Dundas lived, pulled down in 1871, 189; house of second President Dundas in, 196.
'Adamant,' the, 249.
Addington, 219; ministry of, formed, 253; downfall of his ministry—created Lord Sidmouth, 259.
Advocats' Loyalty, a pamphlet so called, 55.
Airdrie, 312.
Aix-la-Chapelle, 206.
Aldan, xxv.
Alemore, Lord, votes in the Douglas Cause, 200 *note*.
Algitha, xxiii.
Alison, Archibald, author of *History of Europe*, 310.
Almack, Richard, of Melford, Suffolk, 31.
Alva, 38.
Althorp, Lord, proposed as chairman of finance committee, 1827, 334; resigns, 361; Chancellor of the Exchequer—created Lord Spencer, 362.
Amulrie, 95.
Andernach, 288.
Anderson, Adam (Lord), 334 *note*.
—— Adam, 328.
—— David, of Moredun, writes to Robert Dundas, July 1827, 334.
—— J., on the death of Admiral Duncan, 252.

Angus and Dudhope, estate of, 206.
Annexation Act, 161.
Anstruther, Lord, 90.
Antwerp, 286.
Apennines, 290.
Appin, 154.
Ardshiels, 154.
Argis, Monastery of, 309.
Argyll, Earl of, made a Marquis, 18; leads the Presbyterians in 1638, 21; sentenced to death, 39.
—— Duke of, his influence, 89; in the Cabinet, resigns, 97; suspected of Jacobitism, 98; writes to Lord Arniston, May 1748, 105.
Arniston, early history of, 1; tapestry at, 2; name of, substituted for that of Ballintrodo, 4; Mains of, rent, 9; limestone, 10; stock, 10; produce of, in crops, 15; entailed on heirs-male, 17; improvements at, old Manor-house of, oak-room of, 42; map of its woods and roads, 45; ash-tree of, described and sketched, 46; beech avenue of, 48; bowling green at—trees at, 49; plantations of—wilderness of, 73; plan of, 75; Gardener's Park at, 76; the Grotto, 76; plan of, in 1753, showing improvements of first President, 77; accident to Dundas at, 91; style of living at, a week's bill of fare in 1748, 107; consumption of wine and spirits at, 1740-49, 108; old clock in hall of, 110; additions made to, 189; expenses at, until 1780, 191; farm buildings on, 193; Mains, rotation of crops on, 1769-1778, 195; oak-room of, 211; north front of, 248; drains of, 295; garden gate of, built of stones from old Parliament House, 297; beech avenue, gate of, 298; bridge at, made of stones from old Parliament House, 300; colliery, 359.
—— Lord. *See* Dundas.
—— Lady (Anne Gordon), writes to Sol.-General Dundas, 1745, 132.
Arnolstoun, 18.

INDEX.

Arnot, author of a work on Criminal Law, 296.
—— Dr., his fee for embalming body of Sir James Dundas, 13.
Articles of Faith signed by Sir James Dundas, 5.
Artois, Comte d', 283.
Athens, 308.
Auchinleck, Lord, 182; votes in the Douglas Cause, 209 *note*.
Augustus, King of Poland, death of, 112.
Aviemore, 92.
Aytoun, the Radical, 354.

BADENOCH, 222; gentry of, 153; disaffection in, 155.
Bailey, Alex. (Capt. Bailey), suspected, 121.
Baillie, Elizabeth, daughter of second President, 186.
—— Henrietta (Mrs. Dundas), 95 *note*; letter from, dated Lawers, Oct. 1742, 117; her death, 152.
—— Dame Margaret (Lady Carmichael), mother-in-law of second President Dundas, 114.
Baird of Newbyth, 152.
Baker's Avenue, 191.
Ballintrodo, seat of Templars, 1; barony of, broken up, 2; name changed to Arniston, 4.
Balmerino, becomes a Lord of Session, 18.
Banffshire, Conservatives lose, in 1837, 364.
Bargany, Lord, 65 *note*; ward and nephew of Dundas, 81; letter of, to Robert Dundas (second President), 87; writes to his cousin, Dundas, in 1734, 112; letter from, to his cousin Dundas, dated Spa, June 1734—dies, 113.
Barjarg, votes in the Douglas Cause, 209 *note*.
Barham, Life of, 299.
Barnbougle, barony of, xxviii.
Bath, visited by Chief Baron, 257.
—— Earl of, succeeds Pelham, 142.
Bathurst, Lord (1735), at the Duke of Queensberry's, 84.
—— Lord (1827), retires, 330.
Bayll, John, innkeeper, Edinburgh, 247.
Beauclerk, Lord George, writes to Lord President Dundas, Oct. 1765, 178.
Beautiful Order, 228.
Bedford, Duke of, 172; presents a petition to the House of Lords, 84; resigns, Feb. 1746, 142.
Bedlay, Lord, 32, 33.

Beechwood, 38.
Beer, tax on, to be substituted for Malt Tax, 68.
Belhaven, Lord, supposed to be the author of *Countryman's Rudiments*, describes condition of East Lothian, 72.
Ben Alder, 222.
Bennet, Robert, Dean of Faculty, 52.
—— Dr., 296.
Bentinck, Lord George, 344 *note*.
Berlin, 286.
Bexley, Lord, in the Canning Ministry, 1827, 330.
Bills of Fare for a week at Arniston in 1748, 107.
Bingen, 288.
Birkenside, 10, 44; rotation of crops on, 1769-1778, 195.
Birmingham, 343.
Bishop's Land, where Lord Arniston resided in Edinburgh, 107.
Blair, 92.
—— Forbes, 355.
—— Jas. Hunter, member for the city, 218.
—— Robert, of Avontoun, Solicitor-General, 239, 254; death of, in May 1811, 267.
Blakehope, 10.
'Bloodie Mackenzie,' 39.
Blucher, 287.
Blythswood, 363.
Bogend, rotation of crops on, 1769-1778, 195.
Boig, Matthew, servand, 11.
Bolton, Duke of, at the Duke of Queensberry's, 84.
Bonar, John, 328.
Bonnington, 114.
Bonnymuir, 312.
Boroughbridge, 279.
Borthwick, John, of Crookston, 261 *note*; married Anne Dundas, 292.
—— Michael, of Glengelt, 2.
—— Sir William, builds Borthwick Castle, 7.
—— kirk, family burial-place in, 6; complaint by minister of, 6; vestry of, sold to Sir James Dundas, 7.
—— parish church of, burned down, 8.
—— parish, valuation of, 8.
—— where second President is interred, 1787, 198.
—— old church of, 299.
—— Castle, 369.
Bossy, 283.
Boswell, David, of Balmuto, xxvii., 2.
—— James, 218; his verses on Dundas, 219.
Bothkennar, xxvi.

INDEX. 373

Bovino, 309.
Boyd, Mistress Marion, marries James Dundas, 17; her issue, 38.
—— Robert, Lord, 17, 38.
—— Braxfield, Lord. *See* Macqueen.
Breteuil, 290.
Bride of Lammermoor, **characters** therein, 39.
Broad Bottom Administration of 1744, 124.
Broun, James, 329.
Browne, Robert, servant, **11.**
Bruce, General, of Kennet, xxxiv.
—— James, cuik, 11.
—— Lady Mary, 367 *note.*
Brussels, 286.
Bryans colliery, 359.
Buccleuch, Duke of, 303 **note, 221, 342**; fees Dundas, 217.
Buchan, George, of Kelloe, 252; **marries** Anne Dundas, 1773, 187.
Bukharest, 309.
Bulwer's *Life of Lord Palmerston,* 345 **note.**
Buonaparte, Jerome, 287.
Burgh Reform, 226.
Burke, Edmund, on **the** French Revolution, 1790, 229.
Burnett, Jas. (Lord Monboddo), succeeds Lord Milton, 1766, 179; is counsel for Mr. Douglas, 180; 'Attic Banquets,' 205; at Paris, **207**; on the Douglas Cause, 209.
Bute, Lord, advancement of, 169; ascendency of, 171.
Butler, Hon. Simon, **239.**
Burne, 10.
Buxton, 215.
Byng, Admiral, court-martial on, **119.**

CAITHNESS, Conservative victory for, 1827, **364.**
Calais, 289.
Calderwood, Lilias Durham, of Polton, 314.
Caledonian Mercury on Henry **Dundas's** re-election, 1783, 217.
Caledonian Chronicle, 233.
Callendar, Captain Burn, 364.
Cambaceres, 286.
Cambray, 289.
Camnethan, 152.
Campbell, Lord, his *Lives of the Chancellors,* 209.
—— John, M.P. for Dumbartonshire, 333.
—— Ilay, appointed Lord **President,** 1789, 221.
Camperdown, 249.
Canary Islands, 256.
Canning writes to Chief Baron Dundas, Feb. 1806, 264; on the one-pound notes, 315; requested to form a Ministry, 1827, 329; death of, Aug. 8, 1827, 334.
Canning, Lady, 337.
Carberry, 369.
Carleel, 33.
Carlisle, Lord, **adheres to** Canning, 330.
Carlyle, Dr. (Jupiter Carlyle), his description of the first President Dundas, 58; on the Tragedy of *Douglas,* 159; 'Jupiter,' 369.
Carmelite Friars, xxvi.
Carmichael, Sir James, of Bonnington, father-in-law of second President Dundas, 114.
—— Lady, 152. *See* Baillie.
Carnegie of Finhaven—murder of **the** Earl of Strathmore, 78.
Carrington, 3, 42, 91.
—— Water of, 43.
Carteret, Lord, 82; at Lord Cobham's, 83; opposes the Duke of Argyll on management of Scotland, 97; a royal favourite—his motto, 124; resigns Nov. 1744, 124; jealousy between, and Pelham, 136.
Cassiltoun, 5.
Castle Leod, **73**; **a resort of Lord** Arniston's, 93.
Castlereagh, Lord, **265.**
Castleton, 304, **3, 10.**
—— Burn, 76.
Catcune, 44.
Catholic Emancipation, 253.
—— Emancipation Act, 349.
Cato Street conspirators, 230.
Chantrey, his statue of Chief Baron Dundas, 292.
Chapman, 237.
Charles, Emperor, 112.
—— I., xxviii.; **mistaken policy of,** 16; in Scotland, **17.**
—— II., xxviii., 230; custom regarding verdict then established, 78.
—— Prince (Pretender), lands among Western Islands, Aug. 1745, 126; enters Derby, 136.
Chatsworth, 76.
Chesterfield, Lord, 102; opposes Walpole, Lord-Steward of the Household, dismissed, 79; his dismissal, 82; **at** Lord Cobham's meeting, 83.
Chevalier, his arrival in 1745, 126.
Chichester, Earl of, xxxii.
Chippenham election petition, 96.
Church, Established, advantages of, discussed by Sir Robert Peel, 363.
—— **of** Scotland supported by Arniston family, 364.

INDEX

Clackmannanshire represented by James Erskine of Grange, 83.
Clarence, Duke of, resigns office of Lord High Admiral, 339.
Clarendon, 21.
Clark, John, 328.
Clerk, Sir George, of Penicuik, 337 *note*; represents Midlothian, 281; M.P. for Midlothian, 313; defeated by Sir John Dalrymple 1832, 356; returned for Midlothian 1835, 362; defeated by Sir W. Gibson-Craig 1837, 364.
Clerkington, 304 *note*.
Coalition, 214, 216; unpopularity of, 274.
Coalston, Lord, 182; votes in Douglas Cause, 209 *note*.
Cobham, Viscount, 83, 84.
Coblentz, 288.
'Cobler of Messina,' 243.
Cochrane, Admiral, 256.
Cockburn, Baron, xxxi.
—— Lord, 88; on Henry Dundas, 214; bears no good-will to Robert Dundas, his cousin, 216; his *Memorials*, 221; describes Edinburgh Council Chamber, 228; on Chantrey's statue of Chief Baron Dundas, 292; on second Viscount Melville, 314.
—— Archibald, Sheriff of Midlothian, 88 *note*.
—— of Cockpen, 88.
—— Sir John, of Ormiston, 38.
—— Sir William, 88.
Cockpen, 17.
Cockpit, 69.
College of Justice, 32.
Collieries of the Lothians, 359.
Cologne, 287, 289.
Colonsay, Lord, 368 *note*.
Colquhar, 304.
Colt, Adam, of Auldhame, 189.
—— Oliver, 20.
Commissioners appointed to examine Borthwick Kirk, 7; sit at Dalkeith as Executive, 21; cease to act, 23.
Comrie, 222.
Constantinople, 308.
Cope, Sir John, sent to Scotland as Commander-in-Chief in 1744, 119; is consulted, 121; consults Lord Arniston, 122; starts for the North too late, 127; marches to Inverness, 128; is defeated at Prestonpans—his defeat, 131.
Corfu, 347.
Cornwallis, Lord, 174.
Corryburgh, 92.

Cotton, Sir John Hinde, fails to obtain a place, 97.
Couper, Rev. Robert, minister of Temple, 16; charged with tippling, 18 *et seq*.
Coursing in Scotland, 305 *et seq*.
Courant on the election of 1837, 364.
Court of Session from 1748 to 1787, 203; constitution of, 205.
Craig, Sir W. Gibson, defeated by Sir George Clerk, 1835, 362; returned for Midlothian, 1837, 364.
Craigie of Glendoick, a candidate for the President's chair, 99; Lord Advocate, 102, 117, 119; writes to Dundas, Jan. 1746, 138, 141; Lord President, dies, March 1760, 162.
Craigmillar, 369.
Cranston, William, 190.
Crawford, Lord, 24, 28.
Crebillon, 158.
Crichton Castle, 369.
Crieff, 96.
Croker replies to Malagrowther, 325.
Cromarty, Earl of, 23.
—— Countess of, 93.
Crombie, Thomas, servand, 11.
Cromwell, triumph of, 21.
Crops, rotation of, 1769-1778, 195.
Cruz, 256.
Cumberland, Duke of, 172.
Cummings, as a judge, 90.
Cunningham, David, 328.
Currie, 95.

DALHOUSIE, 91, 295, 359.
—— Lord, signs Covenant, 16.
Dalinagarry, 92.
Dalkeith, 295.
—— Presbytery of, 6, 16; questions Sir James Dundas regarding Solemn League, 21.
—— Small-pox at, 85.
—— Park, pheasants on, 303.
Dallas of Dawlish, 261.
Dalmeny, Lord, 364.
Dalnacardoch, 92.
Dalrymple, Daniel, 34.
—— Sir David, of Hailes, youngest son of first Lord Stair, 55; Lord Advocate (1709-14), displeases the Government, and is dismissed, 53, 60; retires, becomes Auditor of Exchequer, 64.
—— Sir David (Lord Hailes), 157; on the bench, 1766-1792, 204; attends Douglas Cause in Paris, 207; votes in Douglas Cause, 209 *note*, 225 *note*.
—— Sir Hew, President, death of, in

INDEX. 375

1737, 89; his opinion of first President Dundas, 109; old age, 204.
Dalrymple, James, Clerk of Court of Session, 39.
—— Sir James, of Stair, elevated to the bench, 23; letter of, to Sir James Dundas, dated Sept. 12, 1663, 25; letter of, to Sir James Dundas, of same date—letter of date Sept. 21, 26; letter from, to Sir James Dundas, Feb. 15, 1664, 33; his seat on bench declared vacant, 32; letters of, to Sir James Dundas of dates April 19 and May 26, 1664, 35; consenting **party** to son's marriage with Katherine **Dundas, 39**; driven into exile, 39.
—— Hon. Sir **J.**, of Borthwick, 38.
—— **John, writes to** Dundas, 1766, **182**.
—— **Sir John**, 305; opponent of Sir G. Clerk's, 352; elected for Midlothian, 1832, 356.
—— Colonel, 233.
Dalwhinnie, 92.
Dalzell, George, **Lord, sick of the** small-pox, 85.
Darlington, 144.
David, 287.
Davidson, John, 183.
—— Duncan, of Tulloch, M.P. for Cromarty and Nairn, 333.
Deadmanlees, 191.
Deanhead burn, 76.
Declaration to be taken by all persons in positions of public trust, 27.
'Defiance,' 254.
Delgado Bay, **257**.
Delphi, 308.
Dempster, George, of Skibo, 292.
Denison, Evelyn, **344** *note*.
Derby, 215.
Deskford, Lord, **comments on Sir** John Cope, 127.
Devonshire, Duke of, 172.
Dewar, 42.
De Winter, **250**.
Dick, Sir Alex., **of** Prestonfield, 149, **217**.
Dickson, John, 88.
Digges, West, 159.
'Douglas,' Tragedy of, 159.
—— Cause, 180; details of, **206**.
—— Duke of, 181, 206.
—— Lady Jane, 181.
—— Marquis of, 206.
—— Lord W. Keith, 337 *note*.
—— Katherine, wife of Sir **James** Dundas, 5.
—— of Torthorwald, 5.
—— old Baronage of Scotland, xxxv.
—— James, **of** Stanypeth, 17.

Dover, Duke of, his patent, 6 3.
Dresden, surrender of, 281.
Drummond, Eliza, 254.
—— Henry, banker, of Charing Cross, 220.
—— Henry, of Albury, 220.
—— Janet, servant, 11.
Drumore, garden of (East **Lothian**), 76.
Duddingston Loch, trout from, brought to Arniston, 189.
Dudhope. *See* Angus.
Dudley, Lord, Foreign **Secretary in** 1828, 335.
Dumbarton, 213.
Dunbar, Earl of, xxv.
—— David, of Baldoon, 'Bucklaw' of the *Bride of Lammermoor*, 39.
Dumbreck's Hotel, 239.
Duncan, Captain Adam (Viscount Duncan, Admiral Duncan), 189, 249; writes to Lord Advocate Dundas, 1797, 250; made Viscount Duncan of Camperdown, and Baron Duncan of Lundie, 252.
—— Alex., of Lundie, 251 *note*.
—— Lady Adamina, wife of Sir **John** Dalrymple, 356.
—— Lady Mary (Lady **Mary Tufton**), writes to Henry Dundas, **Oct. 1797**, **251**.
—— **Sir** William, M.D., 251 *note*.
Dundas of Beechwood, family of, xxxi., 38.
Dundases of **Duddingston and Manor**, **xi**.
—— of Dundas, 14.
Dundas, estate of, **sold, xxix**.
—— owners of, xxv.
—— Castle, xxviii., **2, 93**; modern, erected, xxix.
—— Alex., son of first **Lord, by Janet** Hepburn, 38.
—— Anne, marries **George Buchan of** Kelloe, 1773, 187.
—— Sir Archibald, xxvi.
—— Chas., son of first Lord, **by Janet** Hepburn, 38.
—— Christian, wife of **Sir Charles** Erskine of Alva, 38.
—— Sir David (Clerk **to the Signet**), born 1803, his **career, xxxi.; dies** 1877, xxxiii.
—— David, son **of** Robert, merchant in Edinburgh, born *circa* 1735, xxxii.
—— Elizabeth, daughter of George, 2; marries Sir Patrick Murray of Langschaw, 5.
—— Elizabeth (wife of first President), letter of, to her son, 1733, 85; death of, from small-pox, 1734, 86.

INDEX.

Dundas, Elizabeth (Chief Baron's wife), 219; on President Blair's death, 268.
—— General Francis, second son of second President, 223, 266 *note*, 284.
—— George, of Dundas, purchases Arniston—contract of excambion by, 10; consenting party to marriage of Dundas with Mistress Marion Boyd, 17.
—— George, served heir 1554, xxvii.
—— George, laird of Dundas *circa* 1700, xxviii.
—— George, son of James Dundas, sketch of, dies 1869, xxxiii.
—— Henrietta (second daughter of second President), marries Captain Adam Duncan (Viscount Duncan), 1777, 189, 249.
—— Grizzel, marries Adam Colt of Auldhame, 1778, 189.
—— Henry (*first Viscount Melville*), 45, 107; birth, in 1742, 94; appointed Solicitor-General, 1766, 181; writes to his brother the Lord President, Sept. 1770, 183; returned for Midlothian 1774, appointed Lord Advocate 1775, 184; correspondence with the Lord President, 1775-1783, 185; re-elected, 217; writes to his brother, second President, 1787, 220; returned for Edinburgh, 1790, 225; writes to Solicitor-General Blair, Nov. 1793, 238; writes to Lord Advocate, Nov. 1793, 239; to Lord Advocate, Dec. 1793, 240; writes to Mr. Smith, Dec. 1793, 240; writes to Lord Braxfield about Muir and Palmer, 241; retires with Pitt in 1801, 253; impeachment of, created Viscount Melville and Baron Dunira, 1802, 259; resigns 1806; his acquittal, 260; death of, 1811, aged 70, 269; his career, 269 *et seq.*; opposes Lord North in his first speech on America, 270; speaks for three hours on the Indian policy, 271; 'King of Scotland,' 272; his kindness, 273; as Treasurer of the Navy, 274; relation to the Act of Union—his character, 275.
—— Henry (Chief Baron's second son), Vice-Admiral, 292, 305.
—— Henry (Lord Melville's son), on Huskisson's secession, 1828, 346; returned for Winchelsea, 1830, 350.
—— Hugh de, xxxv.
—— James de, xxxvi.
—— Sir James, son of George, 2; succeeds George, 5; details about,

5; purchases land, 6; an agriculturist, 8; contract of excambion by, 10; death of, in 1628—his will—funeral expenses of—apothecary's bill for, 12; buys the vestry of Borthwick, 1606, 299.
Dundas, Sir James, *first Lord Arniston*, succeeds his father at age of eight, 14; attends St. Andrews University, 14; made an elder, 16; is knighted by Charles I.—a witness against Rev. R. Couper, 18; sits as judge, 19; returned to Parliament for Midlothian, 21; signs Solemn League in 1650, 21; his conduct at the Restoration, 22; applies to be made a Lord of Session, 23; letter of, to Lauderdale, Dec. 16, 1663, 31; letter of, to Lord Chancellor, Jan. 7, 1664, 32; refuses to sign the Declaration, 36; retires into private life—his marriages, 38; his death, 39; funeral expenses of, 40.
—— James (son of second Lord), his speech on the Jacobite medal in 1711, 52; issued a pamphlet in support of his conduct—is prosecuted for sedition, 53; at the bar of the High Court of Justiciary, 54; marries Mary Hope of Kerse, but predeceases his father without issue, 56; his Jacobite leanings, 59.
—— James, ancestor of Dundases of Beechwood, 38.
—— John of Dundas, xxxvi.
—— John, of Manor, his five sons and descendants, xxxiv. *note*.
—— Katherine, wife of Hon. Sir J. Dalrymple of Borthwick, 38; marries James Dalrymple, Clerk of Court of Session, 39.
—— Sir Lawrence, founder of the Zetland family, dies 1781, xxxiv.
—— Lawrence (Earl of Zetland), dies 1839, xxxv.
—— Professor Laurence, founder of Dundas Bursaries, 87 *note*.
—— Margaret, wife of George, 2.
—— Margaret (Miss Peggy), marries General John Scott of Balcomie, 1773, 187.
—— Mary, wife of Sir J. Home of Blackadder, 38.
—— Dame Marie, maintains the rights of her son, James, while a minor, 16.
—— Philip, 350.
—— Robert, son of George, 2.
—— Robert (*second Lord Arniston*), 38; succeeds his father, Sir James (1679), 40; lives abroad—supports Prince of Orange—appointed a

INDEX.   377

judge, Nov. 1, 1689, 41; marries
Margaret Sinclair of Stevenson, 56;
writes to his son, the Lord Advocate,
about retiring—his death in 1726,
57.

Dundas, Robert (*first President*)—son
of the preceding—born 1685, advocate 1709, 58; becomes Solicitor-
General in 1717, Lord Advocate
1720, and Dean of Faculty 1721, 57
—referred to in *Guy Mannering*—
marries, first, Elizabeth Watson of
Muirhouse, 1712, 59; appointed
Solicitor-General, 59; opposes the
Treason Law Assimilation Act,
60; obstructs the Commission of
Oyer and Terminer for trial of
rebels, 60; his opinion preferred
to that of Lord Advocate Dalrymple, 61; his illness in 1720,
63; appointed Lord Advocate, 64;
Assessor to the city of Edinburgh,
which he resigns in 1721, 65; letter
from, to Bailie Wightman, 65;
elected for Midlothian without opposition, 1722, 67; joins the malcontent Scottish members in Malt
Tax Riots—dismissed from office in
1725, 68; advises the Edinburgh
brewers — succeeds to the family
estates in 1726, 71; leader of the
Scottish opposition—builds modern
house of Arniston, 72; the condition
of his cattle in 1726, 73; vindicates
the rights of juries to return a
general verdict at the trial of
Carnegie of Finhaven, 78; letters
from, to his son at Utrecht,
in 1733, 80 *et seq.*; letter of, to
Lord Bargany in 1734, 81; letter
from, to his wife, 83; seconds
Lord Polwarth, 84; strange opinion
of, regarding the Lords, 84; as a
debater, 85; letters of, to his son
at Utrecht regarding smallpox, etc.,
1733-34, 85, 111; loses his first wife,
85 *et seq.*; marries, second, Anne
Gordon of Invergordon, 87; letter
to his wife, 1736, 88; takes his seat
on the bench as Lord Arniston,
June 10, 1737, 90; letter to his
son Robert, 1737—meets with an
accident, 91; letters from, to his
wife, dated Castle Leod, Rossdhu
and Shien, 1740-43, 93 *et seq.*; goes
to Rossdhu, 94; goes to Shien,
95; a candidate for the President's
chair—writes to Lord Chancellor,
Dec. 1747, 99; appointed President,
103; death of, in 1753—at the
Mansion House of Abbeyhill, 109.

Dundas, Robert (*second President*),
born in 1713, July 18th—his school
and college life, 111; studies at
Utrecht, 80; proposes visiting the
armies on the Rhine, 112; passes
advocate (1738)—in 1741 marries,
first, Henrietta Carmichael of Bonnington, 114; appointed Solicitor-General in 1742, **99, 115**;
accompanies Sir J. Cope from Dunbar to Prestonpans, 1745, **131**;
remains at Berwick, **134**; **letter**
from his father, Jan. 1746, 139;
resigns office of Solicitor-General,
140; suffers from gout—resolves to
retire, 144; declines to offer himself
for Lanarkshire in 1750, 145; writes
to the Hon. Charles Hope Weir,
March 1750, 146 *et seq.*; returned
for Midlothian, April 1754—Lord
Advocate in August — re-elected
Dec., 150; marries, second, Jean
Grant of Prestongrange (1756), 160;
appointed Lord President, March
1760, 162; autobiographical sketch
of, **166** *et seq.*; writes to Lord
George Beauclerk, 178; gives
his casting vote against claimant
in Douglas Cause, 181; his
children, 186; purchases Shank in
1753, 189; writes to the Royal
Dragoons, Dalkeith, 192; proposes
a rotation of crops at Arniston, 194;
dies Dec. 13th, 1787, 197; funeral
of, 198; remarks on, 199; his preeminence as a judge, 200; his final
judgment in Douglas Cause, 1767,
207.

—— Mrs. (Henrietta Bailie), writes
to her husband, May 1744, 123;
death of, 1755, 152.

—— Robert (Lord Chief Baron—son
of second President), born 1758,
214; visits England 1772—called
to the bar 1779, 215; appointed
Solicitor-General 1784, 216; his
fees—appointed Lord Advocate in
1790, 217; falls in love with his
cousin Elizabeth—his stature, **219**;
Lord Advocate, **1789, 221**; at **Loch**
Erich, 222; writes to Mrs. Dundas,
223; returned for Midlothian, June
1796, 246; attacked by **mob**, 1792,
231; election dinner, Oct. 1799,
247; on the victory at Camperdown,
1797, 249; becomes Lord Chief Baron
1804, 252; visits Lisbon and Madeira

1804-5, 254; returns from his voyage, 257; writes to his wife, June 1806, on Lord Melville's acquittal, 261; travels for health on the Continent, 1817,—his companions, 284; winters in Italy, 1817, 289; death of, June 17, 1819, 292; possessor of Arniston from 1787 to 1819, 294; improvements made by him at Arniston, 296; his account of the improvements, 74; his description of improvements made there from 1753 to 1776, 190.

Dundas, Robert (Chief Baron's eldest son), born in 1797—education, etc., 301; on the grouse shootings, 303; writes to his brother Henry, Feb. 1815, 305; writes to his mother from Greece, 1818, 306; in Constantinople in 1818, 307; at Vienna, 308; Captain of Dalkeith Yeomanry, 311; marries Lilias Durham Calderwood, 314; becomes Advocate-Depute 1822, 314; writes to Lord Melville, June 1826, 327; hesitates to stand for the county, 340; determines to retire, 358; death of, June 8th, 1838, 366.

—— Mrs., succeeds to estates of her family 1838—death of, in Italy 1883, 366.

—— Robert, succeeds his father Robert, 1838, 368.

—— Robert Adam, M.P., writes to Robert Dundas, May 1827, 332; on Sir George Clerk's return for Midlothian, 342; writes to Robert Dundas, June 1828, 347; returned for Ipswich, 350; writes to Robert Dundas, June 1832, 352; writes to Robert Dundas, June 1832, 354; returned for North Lincolnshire 1837—sketch of his career, 367.

—— Robert. *See* Melville (second Viscount).

—— Sir Robert, of Beechwood, xxxi.

—— Rev. Robert, of Humbie, xxxi.

—— Robert, Merchant, xxxii.

—— Sir Thos., born 1741—created Baron Dundas of Aske—dies, 1820, xxxv.

—— Thomas (son of second Lord), Sheriff of Galloway, writes to his grand-nephew 1781, 215.

—— Sir Thomas, 232.

—— Thomas, second Earl of Zetland, xxxv.

—— Sir Walter, xxviii.

—— Walter, son of George, 2.

—— Rt. Hon. William (third son of second President), member for Edinburgh, 248; his indiscretion, 280; again returned for Edinburgh, 1830, 350; Lord Clerk Register, 367.

Dundas, W. Pitt (third son of Chief Baron), his account of a journey from Arniston to England, 257; Deputy Clerk-Register of Scotland, 292; death of, 1882, 367.

Dundee, rioting in, 1792, 230.

Dundonald, Earl of, attends meeting at Lord Cobham's, 83; at the Duke of Queensberry's, 84.

Dunfermline, Abbot of, xxvi.

Dunira, 222; estate of, purchased by Sir R. Dundas of Beechwood, xxxi.

Dupplin, battle of, 1332, xxvi.

Durham, Admiral Sir Philip, of Largo and Polton, 254, 366.

—— Sir W., of Grange, *temp.* Robt. Bruce, 366.

EASTER HALKERSTON, value of, 8.

East Retford, 343.

Edgar Atheling, xxiii.

Edinburgh, Parliament in, 17; magistrates of, dine with Lord Arniston in 1747, 47; action by brewers of, 71; success of Tragedy of *Douglas* in, 159; influence of bar and bench in, 201; Town-Council of, chooses the Member, 213; riots of 1792 in, 230; Old Parliament House of, 297.

Edinburgh Advertiser on the elections of the Dundases in 1790, 225.

—— *Gazette*, 233; threat in, by the Dean of Faculty, 53.

—— *Gazetteer*, 247.

—— *Herald* on Dundas's election for Midlothian, June 1796, 246.

—— *Weekly Journal*, Malachi Malagrowther writes to, 315.

Eglinton, Lord, xxvi.

Elchies, Lord (Patrick Grant), 103.

Eldon, Lord, retires, 330.

Elgin, Earl of, 350, 367 *note.*

Eliot, Lord, 344 *note.*

Elliock, votes in the Douglas Cause, 209 *note.*

Elliot, Sir Gilbert, of Minto, his death, 60.

Elphinstone, Lord, attends meeting at Lord Cobham's, 83.

Elphinston, John, son of Nicol, 3.

—— Nicol, of the Shank, 3.

'Engagement' for relief of Charles I., 21.

England in 1795, 244.

Entail Act, 1685, 203.

Enzer, Joseph, 76.

Epithalamium on marriage of Robert

Dundas and Henrietta Carmichael of Bonnington, 115.
Ericht, Loch, 222.
Erskine, Sir Charles of Alva, **38, 105** *note*.
—— Charles, of Tinwald, a candidate for the President's Chair, 99; a friend of the Duke of Argyll's, 101; appointed Lord Justice-Clerk, 103; fails to secure the President's Chair, 162.
—— Henry (Dean of Faculty), writes to Robert Dundas on the death of the President, in 1787, 197; agitates for Burgh reform, 229; opposed by Dundas in the election of a Dean for 1796, 245.
—— James, of Grange, 82.
—— Thomas, Lord Chancellor, **229**.
Esk, 3.
Esperston, 5, 42; improvements on, 9; hill, 10; jointure of Mistress Marion Boyd, 17; **hamlet of, 43**.
Essonne, 290.
Ethelred, King, **xxiii**.
Excise Scheme, **withdrawal of, 79**.

FACULTY OF ADVOCATES presented with a Jacobite medal, 52.
Fairford, Alan, 205.
Falkirk, 96.
Falkland, **92**.
Ferguson of Pitfour, 204; member for Aberdeenshire, 219.
Fergusson, Colonel, his *Life of Henry Erskine*, 245 *note*.
Ferrol, 254.
Findlater, Earl of, relation to Dundas, 168; fees Dundas, 217.
Fitzharris, Lord, on Pitt's death, 260.
Fitzwilliam, Earl of, xxxv.
Fleming, Admiral The Hon. **Chas.** Elphinstone, 254, 255.
Flanders, Dundas and Lord Bargany tour through, 113.
Fletcher, Andrew (Lord Milton), 119, 149; Lord Justice-Clerk, thrust aside, 145; receives the Signet for life, 103; is narrowly watched, 156; supports Home, 159; dies Dec. 1766, 179.
—— Archibald, Advocate, **on Burgh Reform**, 1790, 227, *note*.
—— Henry, of Saltoun, **105** *note*.
Florence, 310.
Forbes, Duncan, of Culloden, succeeds Dundas as Lord Advocate, 70; appointed President, 1737, 90; dies Dec. 10th, 1747, 99; compared with Dundas, his successor, 109; writes to Dundas, Solicitor-General, in 1742, 116; writes to Dundas on his resignation of Solicitor-General in Jan. 1746, **141**; his relation to Dundas, 168.
—— Sir John, 353.
—— Peter, 328.
Forfeited Estates Act, 67.
Fort-Augustus, Governor **of, 153**.
Fountainhall, Lord, 170.
Fox, Charles, 229; plagued by Henry Dundas, 215; on Muir and Palmer's trials, 244; suspicion of, aroused against Dundas, 274.
France, war with, 123; Douglas Cause in, 207; termination of war with, 1815, 283.
Frankfort, 287.
Frasers attack Culloden House, **135**.
Frederick the Great, 118.
Freeman, quoted, xxiii.
—— **Rev. Dr. W., of Hammels,** Herts, 161 *note*.
French war, 117.
Fullarton Burn, 303.
Funchal Bay, 255.
Fushie Bridge, 304.

GALLOWAY, ALEXANDER, servand, 11.
Garden, **Francis (Lord Gardenstoune), opposes Wedderburn before the Parliament of Paris, 204**; votes in Douglas Cause, 209 *note*.
Garlies, **Lord, death of his son from** small-pox, **85**.
Garrick, 159.
Gatton, 350 *note*.
Genappes, **287**.
General Assembly attended by Dundas in 1837 and 1838, 365.
George II. dies Oct. 25, 1760, 169.
—— III., birthday 1792, 230; mobbed and insulted, 245.
Gerard, xxv.
Gerrald, Joseph, **241**.
Ghent, 286.
Gibbon, David **M., 328**.
Gibson, Jas., 340.
Gilchrist, W., 328.
Gilmour, Sir Alex., 172.
—— Sir Charles, of Craigmillar, M.P. for Midlothian, writes to Lord Arniston, Dec. 1747, 101.
—— Sir John, of Craigmillar, Lord President, 23.
Glasgow, 312 *note*; Malt Tax riot in, 71; only partially represented, 213; potatoes taxed in, 227; University of, **362**.

Glencairn, William, Earl of, becomes Lord High Chancellor, 23.
Glengarry men, 94; insolence of, 153.
'Glory,' 254.
Goat-Whey cure, 93.
Goderich, Lord, succeeds Canning as Premier, 334.
Goldie, Rev. Jas., writes to Robert Dundas, March 1837, 365.
Goolburn, Chancellor of the Exchequer, 1828, 335.
Gordon, George, first Duke of, 52.
—— Duke of, fees Dundas, 417.
—— Duchess of, offers a Jacobite medal to Faculty of Advocates, 52; in the *Heart of Midlothian*, 56.
—— Capt., 291.
—— Sir John, 102.
—— Lewis, 135.
—— Sir William, of Invergordon, Bart., 87, 93 *note*; father-in-law of first President Dundas, 83 *note*.
Gore, 3.
Gospatric, son of Maldred, xxiii.
Gouda, 286.
Gower, Lord, at the Duke of Queensberry's, 84; resigns the Privy Seal, 142.
Graeme, Robert, 305.
Grafton, Duke of, 174, 270.
Grammont, Duc de, 263 *note*; writes to Mrs. Dundas, 1813, 282.
Granby, Lord, 174.
Grant, Chas., 344 *note*; President of the Board of Trade, 1828, 335.
—— Patrick, of Elchies, dies July 1754, 150.
—— William (Lord Adv.), of Prestongrange, a candidate for President's Chair, 99; succeeds Craigie as Lord Advocate, 143; succeeds Patrick Grant of Elchies on the bench, 1754, as Lord Prestongrange, 150, 160; descendants of, 163 *note*.
Granville, Lord. *See* Carteret.
Greendale Oak, in Welbeck Park, Notts, 48, 258.
Greenock not represented, 213.
Grenville dismissed, 1765, 176.
Grey, Earl, 229; government of, 361.
Grotto, the, at Arniston, 44.
Guerin, Marie, 207.
Guthrie, John, 328.

HADDEN, KATHARENE, servant, 11.
Haddington, Earl of, xxviii.
Hagley, 258.
Haig, Katharene, servant, 11.

Hailes, Lord. *See* Dalrymple.
Haldane, Patrick, succeeds Dundas as Solicitor-General in 1746, 143.
—— Professor Robert, visits Waterloo, 283; travels with Dundas, 284; 289.
Halkerston, 5, 17.
Hall, Robert, town-councillor, 328.
Hamilton, first Duke of, leads Presbyterians, 1646, 21.
—— fifth Duke of, at Lord Cobham's, 1735, 83; at the Duke of Queensberry's, 84.
—— seventh Duke of, 181.
—— Duchess of, 180.
—— of Aikenhead, 148.
—— Capt. Sir Charles, 254.
—— Dame Christian, Lady Boyd, 17.
—— Sir J., death of, 145.
—— John, apothecary, 13.
—— Sir Patrick, of Prestoun, 17.
—— Col., of Pencaitland, 261 *note*.
Hampton Court, 24.
Handasyd, General, at Haddington, 136.
Hanwell, 301.
Harcourt, Duc de, writes to Chief Baron Dundas, 1813, 282.
Hardwicke, Lord (Lord Chancellor), 99 *note*; writes to Dundas, 1747, 100; writes to congratulate Lord Arniston on the Presidentship, 1748, 106; writes to Dundas, June 1755, 156; letters of, to Lord Advocate, 161; congratulates Lord President Dundas, June 1760, 163; on the Militia, 165; on king's death in 1760, 169; correspondence with Dundas, June 1763, 174 *et seq.*; his measure for abolishing Heritable Jurisdictions, 202.
Harrington, Earl of, succeeds Lord Granville (Carteret), Nov. 1744, 124; resigns the Seals, 142.
Harrowby, Lord, in the Canning Ministry, 1827, 330.
Hart of Glasgow, a president of the Convention, 242.
Harvieston, 44.
Haughead, 44.
Hay, Sir Adam, M.P. for Selkirk, 339.
—— Dr. D., 328.
—— John, 34.
—— Thomas, of Huntington, Keeper of the Signet, entertains Dundas and Craigie, 131.
Helias, son of Huctred, xxiv., xxv.
Henderson, Alexander, 328.
Hepburn, Sir Adam, of Humbie, 38.

Hepburn of Clerkington, 221, 304.
—— Janet, second wife of first Lord Arniston, 38.
—— John, servand, 11.
Heriot Water, 42.
Heritable Jurisdiction abolished, 201.
Hermanstadt, 309.
Herries, Col., 291.
—— Chancellor of the Exchequer resigns, 334.
Hewit, Helen, 206.
High Court of Justiciary, James Dundas brought to bar of, 54; Provost of Glasgow arraigned before, 71.
Highland Railway, 225.
Highlanders, Acts for disarming, 203.
Hinde's *History of Northumberland*, xxiii. *note*.
Holland visited by second Lord Arniston in 1688, 45; Chief-Baron Dundas's tour in 1817, 285.
Holmes, W., M.P., 347 *note*.
Holyrood Palace, regiment stationed at, 82; royal forces at, 84; where the Comte d'Artois resided, 283.
Home, Alexander, succeeds Dundas as Solicitor-General in 1746, 143.
—— Sir David, of Wedderburn, 5; consenting party to marriage of Dundas with Marion Boyd, 17.
—— George, of Wedderburn, 14.
—— John, of Blacadder, 14, 17.
—— Rev. John, 159.
—— Mary, wife of Sir James Dundas, 5; her jointure and fortune, 5.
—— Marie, daughter of George Home of Wedderburn, manages estate of Arniston, 14.
—— Dame Mary (Lady Arniston), 17; her death in 1661, 22.
Hope, Sir Alexander, of Kerse, 56.
—— Sir Archibald, 192.
—— Right Hon. Charles, 277 *note*.
—— Sir John, 305, 342.
—— John, Solicitor-General, 314, 327, 337 *note*.
—— of Craigiehall on the rising of 1745, 127.
—— Sir Thomas, of Kerse, Lord Advocate in time of Charles I., 314; appointed Justice-General, 18.
Hopetoun, xxix.
Hopetoun, Earl of, 146, 177, 342; advises Dundas to marry again, 160; writes to Chief Baron, June 1806, 262.
—— House, where Mrs. Dundas visits, 123 *note*.
Horn of Westhall represents the Faculty, 53.

Hospitallers obtain Ballintrodo, 1.
House of Commons, attendance of Scottish members, 67.
—— of Lords, proposal by, that the Scottish Peers be chosen by ballot, 82; reverse decision of Court of Session in Douglas cause, 181; preservation of, advocated by Sir Robert Peel, 363.
Houston, 262.
Howburn, 10.
—— balance-sheet for crop of 1699, 50, 51 *note*.
Hughes, Dr., 299.
Hugomont, 283.
Hume, Sir Alex., helps his cousin, Sir James Dundas, 23 *note*; letter to Sir James Dundas, dated 17th May 1662, 24; letter, dated Nov. 4th, 1662, 25; letter of, to Sir James Dundas bearing date Nov. 3d, 1663, 27 *et seq.*; letter of, to Sir James Dundas, Dec. 8th, 1663, 29; letter of, to Sir James Dundas, April 18, 1664, 34; letter of, to ditto, June 23, 1664, also Aug. 9, 36; letter to Sir James Dundas, July 4, 1665, 38.
—— Baron, on Sir Thomas Miller of Glenlee, 204.
—— David, appointed keeper of Advocates' Library, 1752, 156; letter of, to Dundas, Nov. 1754, 157 *et seq.*; 213.
Hunter's Park, 190.
Huntly Castle, 135.
Huskisson, 266, 334; in the Canning Ministry, 1827, 330; on the East Retford Election, 344.
Hyndford, Lord, friendship with Dundas, 168.

ILAY, LORD, letter of, to Secretary of State, 53; manages the affairs of Scotland, 79; his administration condemned—adviser to the Scottish Peers, 80; impeached, 84; his influence, 89; letter from, to Dundas, 1737, 90.
'Illustrious,' voyage in the, 254.
Inchgarvie, xxiii., xxix.
India Board, acceptance of, by Lord Melville, 338.
Inglis, Sir John, of Cramond, Bart., 246.
Innerleithen, 42.
Inver, 92.
Inveresk, 369.
Invergordon, 92, 93.
Inverness, Lord Arniston's journey to,

INDEX

92; Sir John Cope at, 128; Conservatives victorious, 1837, 364.

JACKSON, JAMES, smith, 11.
Jacobins, 353.
Jacobite attempt, fear of, 117.
Jacobite Medal, 52 *et seq.*
James II., xxvi., 230.
—— III., xxvi.
—— IV., xxvii.
—— VI., xxviii; knights James Dundas, 5.
—— VIII., Medal of, 52.
Jeffrey, Lord Advocate, 350; elected for Edinburgh, 1832, 355.
Jenner's discovery, 85.
John of Gragin, xxv.
Johnston of Warriston, 21; knighted, 18.
Judges prevented from becoming members of Parliament, 83.

KAMES, LORD, his *Sketches of the History of Man*, 49; character of, 204; votes in Douglas Cause, 209 *note*.
Keith, 215.
Kennet, Lord, votes in the Douglas Cause, 209 *note*.
Kent, Duke of, his intimacy with the Earl of Zetland, xxxv.
Kepock, 92.
Ker, Thomas, drinks with a minister, 18.
Kerr, Lord R., 304.
Killin, 223.
Kilmarnock Burghs return a Conservative in 1837, 364.
Kincardine, Earl of, attends Lord Cobham's meeting, 83.
'King's List,' 63.
King's list of peers, 82.
Kinghorn, 92.
Kinnoull, Earl of, 45; his patent, 63; fees Dundas, 217.
Knights Templars in Scotland, 1.
—— of St. John obtain Ballintrodo, 1.
Knock of Kincardine, 121.
Knox, W., 18.

LA FONTAINE, 157.
Laggan, Loch, hunting match on, 153.
Lanarkshire, Dundas's connection with, in 1750, 145.
Lansdowne, Lord, adheres to Mr. Canning, 330.
Lamb, William (afterwards Lord Melbourne), 249; goes out of office, 344.
Lamington, 114.

Lanark, Conservative victory, 1837, 364.
Largschaw, teinds of, 6.
Lauderdale, Earl of, leads Presbyterians, 21; 23, 24, 28; letter from, to Sir Jas. Dundas, Dec. 8, 1663, 30; 31 *note*; of service to Dundas, 38.
—— Lord, in 1792, 229.
Le Brun, Madame, 206.
Legate, Robert, 328.
Leighton. *See* Lichton.
Leipzig, battle of, 281.
Leishman, James, councillor, 328.
Leith, 92.
Lewis Frankland, 344 *note*.
Leyden, 285.
Lichton, Robert (Archbishop Leighton), 20, 27.
Linlithgow, 96.
Lintz, 288.
Lisbon, visited by Chief Baron Dundas, 255.
Lismore, 154.
Little Johnsschott, 5, 10.
Livadia, 308.
Liverpool, Lord, seized with apoplexy 1827, 329.
Loanhead, 295.
Lockhart, Sir C., 312.
—— of Covington, 204.
—— George, of Carnwath, 55; refrains from opposing Dundas as member for Midlothian, 67.
—— Sir John, of Castlehill, 94 *note*.
—— John, of Castlehill, 147; writes about the health of Mrs. Baillie (wife of second President). 1755. 151.
—— Capt. John, engaged to Elizabeth Baillie, their descendants, 187 *note*.
—— Martha (Mrs. Sinclair of Woodhall), 94.
London, fatigue of journey to, in 1722, 67.
—— roads between, and Scotland, in 1739, 92.
Londonderry, Lord, retires, 330.
Loretto, 290.
Lorimer, James, servand, 11.
Lothian, Earl of, 10; signs covenant, 16.
—— Marquis of, 305; promotes railway construction, 359.
Loughborough, Lord, 274.
Lovat, Simon Lord, 92; his trial, 145.
Lowthiane, Isabel, servand, 11.
—— W., 11.
Luffness, 261.
Lugton, Midlothian, 295.
Luke, Adam, 328.
Lumsden's gate, 191.

INDEX. 383

Luss, **a resort of Lord** Arniston's, 93.
Lyndhurst, **Lord, Lord** Chancellor, 1828, 335.
Lyndsay, Lord John, 17.
Lyttelton, Lord, writes **to** Dundas, Aug. 1761, 186.
—— Lord (Sir George), death of, **in** 1773, 187.

M'DONEL of Aberarder, 153.
—— of Keppoch, 153.
—— of Tullacrombie, 153.
Mackay, 320.
Mackenzie, Sir George, of Rosehaugh, Lord Advocate, 'Bloody Mackenzie,' **39, 189.**
—— Sir George, of Tarbet (Earl of Cromarty), **obtains a seat on the** bench, 23.
Mackenzie, Prof. **Kenneth, 156;** writes to Pulteney 1793, 234.
M'Kinlay, Archibald, 328.
Mackintosh, Sir Jas., 229.
Mackintosh, Robert, his journal, 134.
M'Lellan, Robert, his account for larch-trees, **73.**
Macleod, Col., **M.P., 239.**
M'Neill, Lord **Advocate, carries the** Poor Law Act **through Parliament,** 1845, 368.
Macpherson of Cluny escapes **to** France, dies at Dunkirk, 1755-6, 155; 222.
Macpherson of Strathmashie, 153.
Macqueen, Robert (Justice-Clerk Braxfield), 204, 236.
Madeira, visited by Chief Baron Dundas, 255.
Mahon, Lord, on the ministerial revolution of Feb. 1746, 142.
Maitland, Sir Thomas, 307.
Malagrowther, Malachi, letters **of,** 315.
Malcolm, King, xxiii.
Malt-tax Riots of 1725, proposal to substitute **a** beer-tax, 68.
Mamhead, 254.
Mamhead Cottage, 257.
Manners, Geo., of Bloxholm **Hall,** 367.
Mansfield, Lord, on Henry **Dundas,** 1766, 182; congratulates **Lord** President on his brother's **success,** May **1775,** 185; on the **Douglas** Cause, **210.**
Marchmont, Hugh, third Earl of, **dismissed** in 1733, 79, 82; **attends meeting at** Lord Cobham's, 83; at **the Duke** of Queensberry's, 84; his diary, 101; visits the Duke of Newcastle, 102.
Marchmont, Earl of (fourth), congratulates Lord Advocate Dundas, 1754, 151.
—— Papers, 83, 101.
Margaret, Queen, xxiii.
Margarot, 241; **sentenced, 244.**
Marjoribanks, 355.
Mary, Queen, 1.
Maxtone, Mrs., of Cultoquhey, **305.**
Mayence, 287.
Meame, 250.
Medmenham Abbey, 210.
Meggit, Thos., Laird of Cockpen, 17.
Melbourne, Lord, declines to form a Ministry, 361; Prime Minister, 1835, 362. *See* Lamb.
Melville, Lord (*second Viscount*), President of Board of Control, appointed First Lord of Admiralty, 281; **on** the Chief Baron's refusal to become President, 277; **on the representation** of Midlothian, 314; **Scottish Manager,** 314; anger **of,** at **Malachi** Malagrowther, 315; **on** Paper Currency, 316 *et seq.*; on the election of the Provost for Edinburgh, 329; retires, 330; President of Board of Control, 1828, 335; his position in 1828, 337; accepts the India Board, **338; at the** Admiralty once more, **339; writes** to Robert Dundas, Feb. **1828, 341;** Chairman of Committee on the Poor Law, 1843. **367; death of,** June 10, 1851, 368.
—— Lady, on Sir Geo. Clerk, **342; writes to Robert** Dundas, Jan. **1828** 335.
—— Henry (first Lord). *See* Dundas.
—— Henry (third Lord), 338 *note.*
—— John White, of Mount Melville, xxxi.
—— Castle, 273, 368.
Memorial presented by **Sir D.** Dalrymple for **release of Jacobite** prisoners, 60.
Menzies, John, **328.**
—— of Ferntower, **263** *note.*
Middleton, Lord, **23.**
—— Inn, 221.
Midlothian, first purchase of land in, made by George Dundas of Dundas in 1571, 1; Turnpike Act for, 51; farms of, 193; agricultural improvements in, **194;** electors **of, 213;** Heritors of, **form an association for** preserving **game, 302; Coursing** Club, 304; **Yeomanry Cavalry of,** 311.
Mignon, Nicolas, 207.

Militia, for Scotland, 165.
Miller, Thos. (Lord Glenlee), 157; becomes Lord Advocate 1660, 162, 328.
Miller, Sir Thos., of Glenlee, 204; votes in the Douglas Cause, 209 *note*; dies 1789, 221.
Milne, James, councillor, 328.
Milroy, Deacon, 47.
Milton, Lord, 103. *See* Fletcher.
Minto, Lord, 260.
Mitchell, Sir Andrew, ambassador at Berlin, 89 *note*; a friend of Lord Arniston's, 101; writes to Robert Dundas, younger, May 1748, 105; writes to second President Dundas in Aug. 1742, 115; ambassador to Brussels and Berlin, Under Secretary for Scotland, intimacy with Dundas, 118; his readiness in reply to Frederick the Great, 119; writes to Solicitor-General Dundas, March 1744, 122; writes to Solicitor-General Dundas, Nov. 1744, 124 *et seq.*; writes to Dundas, Sept. 1745, 128 *et seq.*; writes to Dundas, Jan. 1745-6, 137 *et seq.*
—— Robert, town-councillor, 328.
—— Rev. W., of High Church, Edinburgh, 118.
Mitchelson, 298.
Moderate Party, 159, 364.
Monboddo, Lord. *See* Burnett.
Moncrieffe, Lady, 95.
Moncrieffe, Sir David, on the rising of 1745, 127.
—— Sir T., of Rapness, 127 *note*.
Montgomery Entail Act, 1770, 203.
Montgomery, Sir James, of Stanhope, 232; becomes Solicitor-General, 1760, 162; Lord Chief Baron, 253.
Montrose, trial of, 1641, xxviii.
—— Duke of, 139; dismissed in 1733, 79, 82; at Lord Cobham's, 83; at the Duke of Queensberry's, 84.
Moray, Lady, 264.
Moresone, Alex., of Prestongrange, 17.
Morning Chronicle, 335.
—— *Herald* on Henry Dundas, 274; reports Sir Robert Peel's address at Glasgow, Jan. 13, 1837, 363.
Morpeth, 144.
Morton, Earl, draws Arniston Ash-tree, 46.
Mountmorris, Earl of (Viscount Valentia), 187.
Muir, Thomas, of Huntershill, 235, 239; trial of, 241; discussion on trial of, 244.
Murehouse, 80.
Murray, Alex., councillor, 329.

Murray, Sir George, succeeds Huskisson, 346.
—— Sir Gideon, of Elibank, Treasurer-Depute, 5.
—— John, 135.
—— Sir Patrick, of Elibank, 14.
—— Sir Patrick, of Langshaw, marries Elizabeth Dundas, 5.
—— Sir Robert, of Craigie, the friend of Lauderdale, obtains a seat on the bench, 23.
Mutiny in British fleet of 1797, 249.

'NAIAD,' voyage in the, 254.
Napier, Captain, 304.
Nasmyth, James, 328.
National Covenant, 21; signed by James Dundas, 16; declared an unlawful oath, 27.
Nepean, Sir Evan, 233 *note*, 240.
Newbattle, 6, 295, 369.
Newbigging, James, 220, 246.
Newbyres, 18; jointure of Mistress Marion Boyd, 17; tower of, 19; rent of, settled on Lord Arniston's son, 114; terms of lease of, 194; Mains, 10.
Newcastle, 19; gibbet at, 215.
—— Duke of, visited by the Earl of Marchmont, 102; writes to Lord Arniston, May 1748, 103; in a strait, 124; resigns the seals, 142; becomes Prime Minister, 150; assures Dundas of his friendship, 1763, 172; Lord Privy Seal in the Rockingham Ministry of 1765, 177; on Douglas Cause, 210.
New Scots Magazine on the Duke of Wellington's position in 1830, 349.
Nisbet-Hamilton, 367.
Nisbett, James, servand, 11.
North, Lord, 214; his Administration of 1775, 184; moves a reconciliation with America, 270; fall of, 271.
Northumberland, Earl of, xxv.
Nottingham, 215.

OLIPHANT, LORD, xxvii., 2.
—— Alexander, of Kelly, 2.
—— Dame Katherine, wife of George Dundas, 2, 369; litigation of, 3.
Orford, Earl of. *See* Walpole.
Orkney lost by Conservatives, 1837, 364.
Orm, xxv.
Ormiston Hall, 133.
Orr, Mr., 243.
Oswald, 262.
Outerston Moss, 42.

INDEX.

Outerston, plan of, 44; hamlet of, 43.
Owsteane, James, servand, 11.
Oxenfoord, 369; Record Office, 82.
Oyer and Terminer, Commission of, in 1794, 244.

PAGE as a judge, 90.
Paine, T., 235.
Paisley, 312; unrepresented, 213.
Palmer, Rev. Thomas Fyshe, **sentenced** at Perth, 237; 239, **241**; discussion on trial of, 244.
Palmerston, Secretary-at-War, 1828, 335; on the Cabinet of, 1828, 343; votes on the East Retford transfer, 344.
Paris, 290.
Park of Halkerston, 10.
Parliament in Edinburgh, 17.
—— Act of, regarding Covenant, 1663, 25; meeting of, in 1720, 64.
Parliamentary Reform (1790), 226.
Paterson, W., 329.
Patison, W., 328.
Peel retires, 330; Home Secretary under the Duke of Wellington, 335; his vote on the East Retford transfer, 343; converted to Catholic Emancipation, 349; recall from Rome, 362; elected Lord Rector of Glasgow University, 363.
Peers, election of, 61; twenty-five **to** be named by the king, 62.
—— Scottish, to be chosen by **ballot**, 82.
Pelham, 102; writes **to** Lord Arniston, May 1748, 103 *et seq.*; becomes Prime Minister, 123; is estranged **from** Carteret, 124; his ministry of 1744, 125 *note*; resigns the Chancellorship, **142**; death of, in March 1754, 150.
Pembroke, Earl **of, resigns in Feb.** 1746, 142.
Penston, 114, **187**.
Perceval, 277; assassination of, **281**.
Perth, Duke of, 135.
—— 92; Highlanders approach, 127; Conservative victory, 1837, 364.
Piebald Administration, 330.
Pinkie, 369.
Pirnhall, 191.
Pitfour, Lord, votes in **Douglas Cause,** 209 *note*.
Pitt, his Administration comes to an end, 1801, 253; death of, in 1806, 259; supports Lord Melville, 260; on Parliamentary Reform in 1782, 271; Prime Minister in 1783, 214.
Planta, Jos., M.P. for Hastings, 344 *n*.
Plate of wedding service, 114.

Polwarth, Lord, speaks on the Scottish Peers question, 84.
Portal, John, of Laverstoke, Hants, 254 *note*.
Portland, Duke of, 48; his Ministry, 265; on Mr. Canning's investments, 266, 344 *note*.
Portsmouth, where Queen Catherine lands in 1662, 24.
Potsdam, xxxii.
Powis House, 100.
Prestongrange, Lord, congratulates Lord President Dundas, March 1760, 160.
Prestonpans, 369.
Pretender. *See* Charles (Prince).
Primrose, Sir Archibald, of Carrington, author of *Act Rescissory*, obtains a seat on the bench, **23**.
Prince Regent, 276.
Prince of Wales Island, 350 *note*.
Pringle of Alemore, 204.
—— Alex., of Yair, M.P. for Selkirkshire, 310; writes to R. Dundas, 1820, 311.
—— David, chirurgeon, **13**.
—— Sir John, 305.
—— Sir Walter, of Newhall, nominated for a judgeship, 60; his death in 1737, 90.
—— Col., 238.
Privy Council, **32**.
Protestant Succession, Faculty declare their loyalty to, 53.
Pulteney, meeting at his house, 84; his system of managing Scotland, 97.
—— Wm., 234.
Purvis, W., 328.

QUATRE-BRAS, 283.
Queensberry, Duke of, his patent, 63; at Lord Cobham's, 83; meeting at his house, 84; 139; on the Douglas Cause, 180.

RAE, David (Lord Eskgrove), at Paris in Douglas Cause, 207.
—— Sir William, 284; Lord Advocate, 337 *note*; **on** the Retford question, 344.
Raeburn's picture of Lord Braxfield, 236; portrait of Chief-Baron Dundas by, 292; receipt by, 293.
Railroads, construction of, 359.
Rannie, Captain, of Melville, 217 *note*.
—— Janet, 217 *note*.
Ramsay, Robert Balfour, 148.
—— of Whitehill, M.P. for Midlothian, 149 *note*.
Rannoch, Loch, and Barracks, 222.
Rebellion of 1745, 123-145.

Reform Bill, effect of, on Scottish constituencies, 341; passed June 4th, 1832, 352.
Regency Bill, 176.
Register House, Edinburgh, **Arniston papers** in, 3.
Renfrew, Conservative victory, **1837,** 364.
Renwick, James, xxviii.
Richmond, Duchess of, 289.
Ridie, Robert, 329.
Robert the Bruce, xxviii.
Robert of Saint Michael, xxv.
Robertson, Principal, 213.
—— David, of Loretto, 267 *note.*
Robinson, F., in the Canning Ministry, 1827, 330.
Roslin, 295.
Rothes, 28.
—— Earl of, 139.
Rowan, Hamilton, 237, 238.
Rockingham, Marquess of, 172; forms a ministry 1765, 177; ministry of 1765, Dundas's services wanted for, 201; succeeds Lord North, **214;** death of, 271.
Ross, Lord, signs Covenant, **16.**
—— General, of Balnagowan, **187.**
—— Master James, 34.
—— Admiral, Sir John Lockhart. *See* Lockhart.
—— Lady Lockhart, **of Balnagowan,** 95 *note.*
—— Dame Margaret, 39.
—— William, Writer to the Signet, 34.
—— Conservative victory, 1837, 364.
Rossdhu, a resort of Lord Arniston's, 93.
Roxburghe, Duke of, letter to Dundas, June 14, 1717, regarding his appointment as Solicitor-General, 59; letter to Dundas regarding the **representative** Peers, 61 *et seq*; encourages opposition to Malt Tax, **68;** letter from, to Dundas, June 4, **1725, 69;** letter regarding Dundas's dismissal in 1725, June 10, **70;** deprived of seals of office, 71.
Roxburghshire lost **by Conservatives** in 1837, 364.
Roy, General, his map **of Midlothian,** 295.
Royal Bank, St. Andrew Square, the house of Sir Lawrence Dundas, xxxv.
Ruddiman, keeper of Advocates' Library, 156.
Rullion Green, 369.
Russell, Lord John, 229.
Russia, operations against, **118.**
Ruthen, 92.

Rutherglen, 213.
Ryder, Home Secretary, 279.
Rylawknowe, 5.

ST. ANDREWS, Sir James Dunda studies at St. Leonard's College, 5.
Sandilands, Sir James (Lord Torphichen), obtains a grant of estates belonging to Knights of St. John, 1; sells lands of Ballintrodo, 2.
Sandys, moves the impeachment of the Earl of Ilay, 84.
Sandwich, Lord, **on Douglas Cause,** 210.
Sawyers, T., 329.
Scotland, Executive of, consists of eight commissioners, 21; proprietary improvements of, 41; improvements in Lowlands of, 50; coarse wool, manufacture of, 67; home-spun, manufactures of, 72; opposition to Walpole gains strength in, 79; roads between, and London, 92; Secretaryship for, revived in 1742, 96; administration, 98; heritable jurisdictions in, **101** *note*; Marquis of Tweeddale, Secretary for, 118; legislation, 1748-1787, 203; burghs, 227; effect of French Revolution on, **229**; state, in 1795, 244; drainage, 295; greyhound owners, 305; Tory party in 1832, 361; Poor Law, 367.
Scott of Airfield on farm produce, 360.
—— Henry Francis, M.P., for Roxburghshire (Lord Polwarth), 333.
—— Gen. John, of Balconie, 263; marries Margaret Dundas (Miss Peggy), **188.**
—— Sir Walter, 299; his 'Lady Ashton' identified, 39; on Arniston, **211; member** of the Yeomanry Cavalry, **311;** on Scotch banking, **315; writes** to Sir Robert Dundas on banking, 322 *et seq.*
Scots Magazine on Dundas, second President, **111**; on President Dundas's funeral in 1787, 198.
Scotch Militia Bill, 163.
Secretary of State for Scotland, office of, abolished in 1725, 71; revived in 1742, 96; finally abolished in 1746, 143.
Sedan, 208.
Selkirk, Earl of, **206.**
Session, Court of, abolished, 21; reestablished, **23.**
Seven years' war, **118.**
Shank, tenants, 4; plan, 3; rent, 10; barony, purchased by Dundas in 1753 for £3000, 189.

INDEX.   387

Sharpe, Archbp. James, murder of, 230.
—— William, 29.
Shelburne succeeds Rockingham, 214.
Shepherd, Sir S., resigns office of Chief Baron, 348.
Sheridan supports Henry Erskine, 229; on Muir and Palmer's trials, 244.
Sheriff Courts, present system of, begun, 202.
Sibbald, Patrik, 19.
Sidmouth, Lord, Home Secretary, 292.
Sidney, Lord, 216.
Sinclair, George, of Woodhall, 89, 94 *note*.
—— Sir John, of Stevenson, **17, 89.**
—— John, 17.
—— Margaret, **wife of second Lord** Arniston, 58; **letter from, to Mrs. Dundas,** 64.
—— **Sir** Robert, of Stevenson, 56, 58.
Sinking Fund, Walpole's proposal to encroach upon, 78.
Skene, Helen, third wife of Sir James Dundas, 38.
—— General, 320.
—— Sir James, President of Court of Session, 38.
Skelmersdale, Lord, 347.
Sketches of the History of **Man**, by Lord Kames, 49.
Skirving sentenced, 244.
Small-pox at Arniston, 85.
Smith of Deanston, drainage **by, 360.**
—— John, 328.
—— Robert, 328.
Smythe, David, of Methven, 127 *note*.
'Society of Friends of the People,' 229.
' —— of Improvers in Agriculture,' **72.**
Solemn League and Covenant, **20**; an unlawful oath, 27.
Solicitor-General, position of, in Scotland, 60.
Stair, Lord, 109; establishes a manufacture of fine linen, 72; dismissed in 1733, 79; dismissed, 82; attends meeting at Lord Cobham's, 83; **at the Duke of Queensberry's,** 84.
'Standard,' 335.
Stanhope, Lady Hester, **258.**
Steuart, Archibald, **181.**
—— Sir John, of Grandtully, **181, 206.**
Stewart, Donald, suspected, **121.**
—— Sir James, of Goodtrees, succeeds Sir D. Dalrymple as Lord Advocate, Dec. 26, 1711, 53, 314; letter of, to Secretary of State, March **11, 1712,** 54 *et seq.*; dismissal of, **59.**
—— James, Lord Garlies' son, **death** of, from smallpox, 85.
Stirling of Keir, 262.
Stirling, Sir Samuel, 312.

Stirlingshire Yeomanry, 312.
Stobhill coal, 359.
Stonefield, Lord, votes in the Douglas Cause, 209 *note*.
Strathmore, Earl of, murder of, 78.
Strichen, Lord, votes in the Douglas Cause, 209 *note*.
Struan, a resort of Lord Arniston's, 93.
Stuart, Patrick, of Torrance, 148.
Sutherland, Conservative victory, 1837, 364.
Survey of Midlothian, 1793, **294.**
Suttie, George, 304.
—— Sir George, 359.
—— Sir James Grant, **of** Prestongrange and Balgone, 255, 304 *note*; promotes railway construction, 359.
Sweden, operations against, 118.

TAILORS PENDICLE, **10.**
Tamworth Manifesto, **362.**
Tandy, Napper, 238.
Tarbett makes the **renunciation, 33.**
Templars in Scotland, 1.
'Temple,' parish of, 1.
—— Mill, pheasantry at, 303.
Tennyson, M.P. for Blechingley, 343.
Test Act, 39.
Thanet, Earl of, 251 *note*.
The Flying Post, its account of the Jacobite medal proceedings, **52;** editor of, threatened, 53.
The Heart of Midlothian, **Arniston** figures in, 56.
Thomson's Braes, 190.
Titchfield, Lord (Duke of Portland), 263.
Tierney with Mr. **Canning, 330.**
Tone, Wolfe, 238.
Torphichen, Lord, 2. *See* Sandilands.
Torthorwald, Douglas of, 5.
Town-Council (1826), list of, 328.
Townshend, Lord, his interpretation of Sir D. Dalrymple's conduct, 60.
Traquair, Lord, Chancellor of Scotland, 43.
Traquair's Bridge, 43, 91 *note*.
Treason Law of Scotland abolished, 1709, 244 *note*.
Trotter and Co., 247
—— Provost, 327.
Turnbull, Rev. Mr., 91.
Turnpike Act for Midlothian, 51.
Tweeddale, Marquis of, appointed Scottish Secretary in 1742, 96; on the Duke of Argyll's resignation, 97; his influence, 118; suspects a rising in the Highlands—writes to Solicitor-General Dundas, 1744, 120; resigns, 136; congratulates Lord Advocate Dundas, Aug. 1654, 150.

UNION threatened by the manner of electing the Peers, 61.
United Irishmen, 237.

VALCIMARA, 290.
Valenciennes, 289.
Vaudreuil, Comte, congratulates Chief Baron on Lord Melville's acquittal, 262.
Victoria, Queen, first Parliament of, 364 *note*.

WADE, GENERAL, his system of Highland roads, 92.
—— on Canning, 329.
Wages paid at Arniston, 11.
Waldevus, xxiv.
Wales, Princess Dowager of, 166.
—— Princess of, writes to Chief Baron, 258.
Wallace, Sir W., xxv.
Walpole, Horace, on Carteret, 124; on Charles Yorke, 209.
—— Sir Robert, writes to Lord Advocate Dundas regarding his attendance on Parliament, 68; letter to Dundas, June 19, 1725, 71; star begins to sink in 1733—his measure regarding the Sinking Fund, 78; does not re-introduce his Excise Scheme, 79; movement against, 85; request from Dundas, 90; resigns, and retires to House of Lords as Earl of Orford, 96; fall of, 115; opposed by Dundas, 212.
Watson, General David, xxii., 154.
—— Robert, of Muirhouse, xxii., 59, 85 *note*.
—— Elizabeth, of Muirhouse, 59.
Watt, Robert, a spy, 233; trial of, 244.
Wauchope, John, 267.
Waugh, John, 328.
Wedderburn opposed by Garden of Gardenstoune, 204.
Weir, Hon. Charles Hope, writes to Lord Hopetoun, March 1750, 146.
Welbeck Park, Notts, 48, 258.
Wellington, Duke of, 287; invites Chief Baron to dine with him, 289; retires, 330; forms a Cabinet, 1828, 335.
—— Duchess of, 289.
Wemyss, 262.

Wentworth, Lady Charlotte, xxxv.
Wester Halkerstoun, 5; value of, 8.
Westmoreland, Lord, retires, 330.
Wharncliffe, Lord, 337.
Whitbread, 229; accuses Lord Melville, 260; in effigy, 261.
Whitefriars, Church of, at Queensferry, xxx.
Whitehall, Scottish Department at, 119.
Whitehouse, 6; farm of, 10.
Whitelaw, Lord, 90.
Whitney, Mrs., 187.
Wightman, Bailie, letter from, to Dundas, Aug. 2, 1721, 65 *et seq.*
Wigtown, Conservative victory, 1837, 364.
Wilkes, 175.
William, the Conqueror, xxiii.
—— IV., death of, 363.
—— of Copland, xxv.
—— of Hellebet, xxv.
Williamson, Alexander, 247.
Wilmington, Lord, Prime Minister, 96; dies July 1743, 123.
—— Ministry, 115.
Wilson, Simeon, 18.
Wine, consumption of, at Arniston between 1740 and 1749, 108.
'Winterton' Indiaman, xxix.
Witches' Knowe, 190.
Wodrow, quoted, xxix.
Wood, Dr., 327, 328.
Woodhall, Lord (George Sinclair), 89.
Woodhouselee, 369.
—— Lord, on Dundas's last illness in 1787, 197; his Life of Lord Kames, 204.
Wraxall, on H. Dundas's eloquence, 275.
Wright, Robert, 328.
Wylie, merchant in Perth, 233.
Wynn, in the Canning Ministry of 1827, 330.
Wynyard, General, 304.

YESTER, 150; plantations at, 49.
York, Duke of, 278.
Yorke, Hon. Chas. (Lord Morden), 152 *note*; Horace Walpole on, 209.
—— Mrs., death of, 161.

ZETLAND, Earl of, his character, xxxv.

www.ingramcontent.com/pod-product-compliance
Lightning Source LLC
Chambersburg PA
CBHW031957300426
44117CB00008B/806